D1713777

Public Law, Private Practice

HARVARD EAST ASIAN MONOGRAPHS 348

Public Law, Private Practice

Politics, Profit, and the Legal Profession in Nineteenth-Century Japan

Darryl E. Flaherty

Published by the Harvard University Asia Center
and distributed by Harvard University Press
Cambridge (Massachusetts) and London, 2013

The Harvard University Asia Center publishes a monograph series and, in coordination with the Fairbank Center for Chinese Studies, the Korea Institute, the Reischauer Institute of Japanese Studies, and other faculties and institutes, administers research projects designed to further scholarly understanding of China, Japan, Vietnam, Korea, and other Asian countries. The Center also sponsors projects addressing multidisciplinary and regional issues in Asia.

Library of Congress Cataloging-in-Publication Data

Flaherty, Darryl E., 1967–
    Public law, private practice : politics, profit, and the legal profession in nineteenth-century japan / Darryl E. Flaherty.
        pages cm.— (Harvard East Asian monographs ; 348)
    Includes bibliographical references and index.
    Summary: "Traces the transition of law regimes from Edo to Meiji, showing how the legal profession emerged as a force for change in modern Japan and highlights its lasting contributions in founding private universities, political parties, and a national association of lawyers that contributed to legal reform during the twentieth century"—Provided by publisher.
    ISBN 978-0-674-06677-9 (hardcover : alk. paper)   1. Practice of law—Japan—History—19th century.   I. Title.
    KNX1629.F53 2013
    340.023'52—dc23

                                                                                    2012050269

Index by June Sawyers

∞ Printed on acid-free paper

Last figure below indicates year of this printing

23 22 21 20 19 18 17 16 15 14 13

In memory of Ari Norman, 1937–2005

Contents

Acknowledgments

Over the course of conceptualizing, researching, and writing this book, I have benefited from the advice and encouragement of many. Carol Gluck gave support selflessly, from the proposal onward. Henry Smith, Gregory Pflugfelder, Frank Upham, Eiko Ikegami, and Louise Young commented on early proposals, chapters, ideas, and arguments. From Tokyo to New York (and places north, south, and in between), Patricia Steinhoff, Hamano Ryo, Nomura Akio, Yoshida Shin'ichi, Verena Blechinger-Talcott, Fujiwara Kiichi, Miyazawa Setsuo, Andrew Gordon, Iwatani Jurō, Iida Taizō, Asako Hiroshi, Awaya Kentarō, Nojima (Katō) Yōko, Murakami Kazuhiro, Sugita Atsushi, Shimotomai Nobuo, Daniel Botsman, Richard Rabinowitz, and countless others opened doors intellectual and institutional. The seminar participants at the Jackson School of International Studies (University of Washington), particularly Kōno Kensuke, Ted Mack, Robert Pekkanen, and Veronica Taylor, offered insight and advice on chapter 1. In Delaware, Jim Brophy has given invaluable support. David Lurie, Laura Neitzel, Mark Jones, Leila Wice, Takashi Yoshida, and many other colleagues at Columbia University and at the University of Delaware have offered fellowship and more in the trenches.

A number of organizations provided access to the sources for this study, including the Tokyo University libraries, the Waseda University libraries, the Boissonade Institute of Modern Law and Politics, the Hōsei University libraries, the Yokohama Bar Association, the Japan Federation of Bar Associations Library, the Tokyo Second Bar Association Library, the Ministry of Justice Library, the National Diet Library Kensei Shiryōshitsu, the Library of Congress, the Morris Library at the University of Delaware, the Harvard University libraries, and Columbia University's C. V. Starr East Asian Library. Although the staff at every institution was extraordinarily helpful, Eiichi Itoh at the Library of Congress and the staff of what was at the time an unindexed and unshelved collection at the Boissonade Institute require special mention.

Research for this project was made possible with the financial and institutional support of the Japan Foundation, the Institute of Social Science at the University of Tokyo, the Foreign Scholars Fellowship Program of the Hōsei International Fund, the Hōsei University Law Faculty, the Japan Studies Dissertation Workshop of the Social Science Research Council, a postdoctoral fellowship from the Reischauer Institute of Japanese Studies at Harvard University, and a Heyman Center postdoctoral fellowship in the humanities. The manuscript benefited from a close reading by Mara Naselli and James Huffman. Elena Norman, Jordyn and Arielle Flaherty, and the rest of my family have been indefatigable. The personal and professional generosity and wisdom of the above and many more have buoyed this project; I cannot thank you all enough.

Tables

Introduction

Until relatively recently, the legal and political past remained a largely unquestioned bastion of the modernization paradigm in Japanese history. The absence of an indigenous tradition of rights discourses and protections marked Japan as a laggard. As the story went, individuals of the West enjoyed expanding political participation and increased protection from the power of the state while persons in Japan did not. Particularly in U.S. history, lawyers put themselves at the center of a triumphalist narrative in which rights protections became the cornerstone of both private legal practice and social and political change. In East-West comparisons, the East fell short of Europe and the United States. One of the key Eastern shortcomings was the absence of a distinction between public and private law that would countenance litigated solutions to private disputes; thus, private complaints and disputes required public intervention. A 1981 history of early modern lawsuits and litigants on the Iberian Peninsula stated that, by way of comparison:

In the Orient, private law scarcely existed, and its absence implied that all disputes, no matter how trivial, automatically lay within the public realm . . . every dispute among humans simultaneously disrupted the natural order and harmony of the universe and, consequently, called for punishment by public authorities. Recourse to law, therefore, necessarily ended in the assignation of guilt and punishment to one of the parties involved. . . . Eastern potentates . . . relied principally upon military and other nonlegal institutions to enforce their power.[1]

---

1. Kagan, *Lawsuits and Litigants in Castile*, xvii–xviii.

From the vantage of Japan's emperors and shoguns sitting in Kyoto, Kamakura, or Edo-Tokyo, the above description was accurate. Rulers in Japan saw law as a tool for social ordering since the adoption of Chinese legal models in the seventh century.[2] Their worldview did not accommodate private disputes; they believed that their subjects should live in state-mandated harmony. Shoguns in Edo found inconceivable the idea of a robust public sphere from which people might question or criticize officialdom. Even as elites held to state centrism through the late nineteenth century, the conditions for its unraveling had emerged during the Edo (or Tokugawa, 1600–1868) era.

At the same time, the modernization paradigm as applied to the world's political past requires reconsideration. Europe and the United States did not craft legal modernity and export it to Japan. Recent scholarship on Japan's legal past has widened its lens to include social history and practice; this broader view recognizes that state aims did not constitute the whole of people's lived experiences. As this exploration of private legal practice reveals, there already existed in early-nineteenth-century Edo society a vibrant legal culture that produced politically engaged and even wealthy private practitioners, a culture captured in poetry and popular tales that laid the foundation for an epistemology of law in the late nineteenth century. As for "Oriental despots," Asia did not have a monopoly on oppression.[3] Political leaders East and West demonstrated considerable ambivalence toward the nineteenth-century changes that opened law and politics to broader publics. Government officials from Paris to Tokyo drove hard bargains with emergent opposition movements and politically active legal practitioners over the course of the 1800s.

Revisiting Japan's nineteenth century with a focus on private legal practitioners challenges conventional readings of Japanese law, legal practice, and politics across the Meiji transition.[4] From the 1700s, legal practitio-

---

2. Steenstrup, *A History of Law in Japan until 1868.*
3. Wittfogel, *Oriental Despotism.*
4. A word on terminology: I use the term "legal practitioner" rather than "lawyer" by design. In contemporary U.S. usage, "lawyer" is capacious, yet the term neither illuminates change in legal practice over time nor does it accommodate difference across early modern geography. The social and political meaning of the American and Japanese lawyer, the British barrister, the French *avocat*, and the German *Rechtsanwält* differ in the present and differed even more before the nineteenth century. There were

ners expanded the realm of private litigation and opened the way for two changes that occurred after 1868: the codification of both public and private law, and a change in the social meaning of law. From the 1870s onward, private legal practice delineated public morality and wove it together with rights and responsibilities. This innovation opened the way for the Japanese nation-state to advance its aims in the world beyond its borders. At the same time, private practitioners and government policy makers grappled with treaties that the shogunate had signed that limited Japanese sovereignty. With law as the measure, foreign powers applied a moral metric to Japanese society; they used barbarism as the justification for unequal treaties.

After 1868, the Meiji government sought to overturn these treaties by refashioning society and government through law. Thus, the Meiji state's legal reforms were externally oriented. Yet even as officials emphasized the merits of foreign systems to the detriment of domestic tradition, legal practitioners benefited from an indigenous past while navigating a globalizing future. This was a future of tumult, rife with contradictions. Judges in the United States invoked Christianity in a supposedly rational, post-Austinian age of distinct legal and moral spheres.[5] Meanwhile, Meiji judges invoked French law while asserting the sovereignty of a new Japan. Private legal practitioners operated within and upon this welter of change. By the end of the 1870s, former samurai in particular had embraced legal practice as an occupation from which to promote the emergence of a public sphere and the dissemination of legal thought as a way of understanding society. At times the efforts of legal practitioners corresponded to state aims, and at other times they contested them.

During the centuries before 1872, a form of private legal practice had emerged under the Tokugawa, despite prohibitions. The reigning orthodoxy had repudiated litigation but could not suppress it. By the end of

lawyers in Japan only after 1893, when the national Diet passed the Lawyers Law. For comparative works, see Bouwsma, "Lawyers and Early Modern Culture"; Burrage, "Revolution"; Karpik, "Lawyers and Politics in France"; and Rueschemeyer, "Comparing Legal Professions Cross-Nationally."

5. The influential legal thinker John Austin conceptualized analytical jurisprudence and was a proponent of positive law as opposed to law that emerged from the mores or spirit of a people. At the root of his thought was a distinction between law and morality. Austin, *The Province of Jurisprudence Determined*.

the eighteenth century, there were two main categories of Edo-era legal practice. In towns and cities, the proprietors and employees of state-sanctioned establishments known as "suit inns" (*kujiyado* or *gōyado*) provided housing for parties to disputes, drafted documents, escorted litigants to the offices of magistrates and commissions, and provided services to the state in return for state sanction and guild recognition. In the shadows of law and propriety, a parallel, unsanctioned practice also existed, that of the suit solicitor, who operated under such different names as *kujishi* (公事師), *deirishi* (出入師), or *deirinin* (出入人). These freelance suit solicitors, who practiced everywhere—in towns, cities, and the countryside—also drafted documents and advised clients. Although there existed parallel official and unofficial systems of legal practice, at times these overlapped and interconnected. When the employees of suit inns quit to become start-up competitors and when the government-sanctioned inns flouted shogunal laws to bribe officials, solicit clients, and instruct litigants in legal practice, legal practitioners blurred the lines between official and unofficial practice. Shogunal and local authorities constrained litigation while accommodating the emergence of private legal practitioners. These two seemingly contradictory impulses gave rise to some confusion among historians—confusion that can be cleared up by thinking comparatively about early modern legal practice and by peeling back layers of historical misunderstanding.

Legal historian Dietrich Rueschmeyer offered a formulation of early modern private legal practice that in its breadth opened the possibility for meaningful comparison. Rueschmeyer defined legal practice as "all specialized work that require[d] knowledge of the 'language of the state.'"[6] Both proprietors of suit inns and suit solicitors in Edo-era Japan spoke this language, interpreted it for their clients, translated the concerns of their clients into this language, and charged fees for their efforts. Rueschmeyer's broad definition of legal work points to a reconsideration of the transformations that legal practitioners drove in Japanese society. His definition opens the Edo period to cross-national comparison at the level of private practice. The comparison between Japan and Europe need not extend to the famous jurists of early modern England and

---

6. Rueschemeyer, "Comparing Legal Professions Cross-Nationally," 429.

the Italian states—the Francis Bacons and Paolo Sarpis.[7] For the period before the mid-nineteenth century, the more appropriate object of comparison would be the anonymous scrivener and others in Japan and Europe who, like the Japanese suit inn proprietor and the early modern French *huissier,* mediated among disputants and between litigants and the state.[8] Legal practitioners working in the gray area between state and society connected litigants to new economic, political, and social systems in an urbanizing, commercializing, and industrializing world.

Dramatic changes in Japanese legal practice occurred after the overthrow of the Tokugawa shoguns in 1868. From 1872, the Ministry of Justice displaced suit inns and suit solicitors with three new occupational categories defined by law and based on French models: the legal advocate (*daigennin*), the legal scrivener (*daishonin*), and the notary (*shōshonin*). Many legal practitioners from the old regime took up work under these new categories; others continued legal work unregulated and uncounted. During the turbulent 1870s, past and present mingled in extraordinary ways. Even as Meiji officials denied the relevance of domestic tradition as a means of fitting into an international order governed by European and American legal and moral norms, domestic ideas remained relevant in legal practice. New personalities entered the arena, too, as women and former-samurai legal advocates navigated judicial interpretation of European-inflected codes.

By the end of the 1870s, local associations of legal advocates (*daigensha*) had laid the foundation for national political parties, and they used the language of law and rights to identify an emergent public that could challenge the state's dominance of the policy agenda and public discourse. Individuals and groups of legal advocates operated as part of the political opposition throughout the 1880s, and then as part of a constitutional polity with the promulgation of a constitution and the establishment of the Diet after 1890. By the 1880s, these associations also served as the foundation for many of Japan's private universities; in short order,

---

7. It is important to note that Bacon's social eminence stemmed from association with the royal court and Sarpi's from the church. Bouwsma, "Lawyers and Early Modern Culture," 308.

8. Jones, *A History of the French Bar,* 16.

the associations morphed into law schools that then added other academic disciplines. Indeed, by 1893, legal advocates led the way in passing a law replacing themselves with lawyers (*bengoshi*). By the turn of the twentieth century, Japan's legal landscape extended from nameless unlicensed practitioners to cosmopolitan jurists such as Hozumi Yatsuka, who gave a lecture on law at the 1904 Louisana Purchase Exposition (the St. Louis World's Fair).

Escaping from Edo: Law, Morality, and the Rule-of-Law State

Legal histories of Japan have long paralleled the dominant modernization narratives of Japan's past. In these narratives, an enlightened and more advanced nineteenth-century West launched a country mired in timeless tradition on the path toward progress. Repudiation of the Edo era (1600–1868) began immediately after its end.[9] Not only did the Charter Oath of 1868 issued in the name of the Meiji Emperor call for the wide convocation of "deliberative assemblies," it also declared that there would be a break with "evil customs of the past." Edo became a repository for all that was retrograde—Japan's dark ages. This narrative of a regressive, feudal society overturned by an enlightened West dominated for at least a century. Yet with Japan's mid-twentieth-century economic rise, historians revisited the Edo era en masse. On subjects ranging from samurai feces to Tokugawa forestry, historians discovered a highly ordered and even sophisticated population in the city and countryside.[10] Whether the subject of research was environmental conservation or play, analysts found deep roots of Japanese success, portents of modernity, and even signs of a precocious postmodernity that predated the putative transition to modernity in 1868.[11]

Despite the emergence of a more nuanced history of early modern Japan, the social history of law and legal practice remains largely unrevised. Until recently, legal histories and studies of legal practice deni-

---

9. Gluck, "The Invention of Edo."

10. On feces, or "nightsoil," see Walthall, "Village Networks." On village politics as an antecedent to democracy, see Ōishi and Nakane, *Tokugawa Japan*.

11. On forest conservation, see Totman, *The Green Archipelago*. On the culture of play during the Edo era, see Harootunian, "Late Tokugawa Culture and Thought."

grated Edo. The persistence of the modernization narrative as related to Edo-era legal history rested on three main assumptions about the period: there was no broad social knowledge of law; there was no meaningful private legal practice; and tradition favored harmony over conflict. As the modernization narrative would have it, only the Meiji reception and embrace of foreign legal thought and practice overturned these conditions. Generally speaking, these three assumptions reflected scholarly analysis of the elite orthodoxy; they were also the norms and ideals of the state.

As I show in this study, empirical analysis of private legal practitioners reveals a different history. Chapter 1 draws on recent (and some not-so-recent) Japanese and English-language scholarship on the Edo era to call this state-centered narrative into question. First, this scholarship challenges the assumption that social knowledge of law and legal ideas was not widespread. Neo-Confucian principles as interpreted by the Tokugawa held that knowing law would foster litigiousness; thus, the Tokugawa state prohibited the dissemination of legal texts. Parts of Shogun Tokugawa Yoshimune's early-eighteenth-century project of legal codification, the *Kujikata osadamegaki*, were drafted for high officials only. Yet the idea that Tokugawa society was unfamiliar with shogunal or domainal law is untenable.

In a range of forms and venues, law as it related to adversarial and inquisitorial matters was widely known. From an administrative perspective, higher laws required that the compacts of each village, the rules governing affairs at the local level, comply with domainal and shogunal statutes. Village headmen took the lead in drafting local regulations in compliance with higher authority. This meant wide dissemination of legal literacy on the village level, at least at the level of the headman. In the realm of inquisitorial matters, Daniel Botsman has noted that the Tokugawa posted rules and prohibitions publicly, a practice adopted by domainal lords throughout the archipelago. The consequences of criminality also played out in the streets when convicts were forced to march on parade.[12] From the early eighteenth century, when litigants brought suits in Edo, they copied out sections of laws related to their cases and brought those transcriptions

---

12. Botsman, *Punishment and Power.*

back to the village. Furthermore, law and legal practice were central themes in Edo-era fiction, which provided vernacular illustrations of the law. This was evident in accounts of the revered and celebrated eighteenth-century magistrate of Edo, Ōoka Tadasuke (Echizen-no-kami), who served as the shogun's town magistrate for 20 years and financial magistrate for 12 years. It was also clear in oral tales of peasant martyrs who used legal petitions to demand that authorities provide debt or tax relief during times of drought and famine.

Legal practitioners were instrumental in disseminating knowledge about law and legal solutions to public and private problems. Under Neo-Confucian orthodoxy, however, profiting from the conflicts of others was seen as injurious to social harmony; thus, legal representation was prohibited from the level of the village to the shogunate. The Tokugawa state and the domains were at best uninterested in and at worst hostile toward litigation. Even so, their attempts to eliminate legal conflict by edict failed. Despite prohibitions, individual legal practitioners sold legal services that went beyond document preparation to include advice. State-sanctioned suit inns interpreted increasingly complex relations of production and commerce. At times, their activities shaded over into representation for their clients.

In early modern Europe, commercialization and capitalization generated a need for legal procedures to resolve disputes. Rueschmeyer described how regimes of private property and market economies required "reliable guarantees of contractual claims . . . [which called forth] law work in other, related ways. Disputes about property multiplied, and demands for its protection increased."[13] Under Weber's analysis of the relationship between capitalism and the legal-rational society, legal practitioners in particular contributed to the process of industrialization by interpreting law both for the state and for the public.[14] As histories of the domestic origins of Japanese capital have demonstrated, early modern Japan underwent its own processes of capitalist development.[15] As in Europe, Tokugawa rulers recognized the importance of property—in particular, real estate—and gave precedence to property disputes in

13. Rueschmeyer, "Comparing Legal Professions Cross-Nationally," 431.
14. Weber, *Max Weber on Law in Economy and Society*, 267–68.
15. Howell, *Capitalism from Within*.

deciding what kinds of matters would come before its magistrates and commissions. And as in Europe, Edo-era merchants demanded legal protection for property and enforcement of contracts. Tokugawa policy on litigation hewed closely to Weber's analytical focus on property, yet differed as a result of its antagonism toward litigation. The Tokugawa response was to suppress suits over money while more readily adjudicating transactions secured by property, such as defaults on loans backed by real collateral. Suit inns and suit solicitors exploited opportunities created by state reluctance and even intransigence. It was out of the ongoing processes of state centralization and the emergence of a capitalist economy that a form of state-sanctioned legal practice emerged.

The suggestion that Japanese culture has a peculiar predilection for harmony over legal conflict reflects a reading of history through the lens of orthodoxy and state aims, not actual practice. Those on all rungs of the Edo-era economic ladder used law strategically to resolve disputes. Codes of merchant houses called on their members to order law-related behavior in two primary ways. First, they were to abide by shogunal injunctions. At the same time, codes stated that litigation was a key to the commercial success of the merchant household. On the lowest rung of the economic ladder, peasants brought lawsuits to local overlords and shogunal magistrates, including intervillage litigation over common areas and interpersonal contests over matters from unpaid loans to failed business ventures.

In their relations with the state, peasants and townspeople did not simply submit to arbitrary rule. The extensive literature on peasant uprisings (*ikki*) shows how villages and even regions rose up and challenged local authorities.[16] These activities combined legal processes and appeals with folk traditions. The histories of *ikki* reveal that before their leaders turned to violence, village heads usually pursued redress through legal channels, including forcing legal petitions upon the authorities. When the leaders of a peasant uprising ignored the proper channels for pushing a claim, the authorities deemed this a "forced petition"—a criminalized act. Yet over time, the shogunate established an elaborate categorization of acceptable and unacceptable forms of forced petition.

---

16. For a thorough English- and Japanese-language historiography, see White, *Ikki*.

Thus, despite blanket prohibitions on unauthorized appeals to state authority, the continued resort to forced petitions stretched the definition of the legally and politically acceptable. When petitions failed, peasants rose up. The process of petitioning, pursuing legal channels, and then protesting foreshadowed similar practices by early-twentieth-century Japanese labor activists who turned to violence when legal appeals foundered.[17]

Even though legal practitioners spread knowledge about the law and helped clients resolve conflicts through mediation or informal representation vis-à-vis the authorities, litigants did not enjoy a right to legal representation. There was no independent judiciary during the Edo era, and private disputes could be punished as disruptions of public harmony. With the state identifying itself as the sole arbiter of law and public morality, it engaged in what Dan Fenno Henderson called "didactic conciliation," a somewhat coercive process through which the authorities pushed parties toward a mediated solution to their conflict.[18] Yet alongside "didactic conciliation" an elaborate system of private dispute resolution emerged. This system came into existence despite the official line that lawsuits undermined social and political harmony. As John Haley notes, "By the mid-nineteenth century Japan had perfected the official forms, processes, and procedures of an intricate web of bureaucratic controls within which . . . the adjudicatory institutions of an incipient private law order were also prominent."[19] Both suit inns and suit solicitors drove the legal groundwork for the resolution of private disputes under the Tokugawa shogunate. This process intensified throughout the nineteenth century.

Weber notes that the bureaucratization of law and the state included "separating sharply and conceptually an 'objective legal order' from the 'subjective rights' of the individual which it guarantees; [and] separating 'public' law from 'private' law."[20] In part, Edo society reflected Weber's theory. It bureaucratized both law and the state. At the same time, however, it made no sharp distinction between an objective legal order and subjective rights. A number of factors drove the shift—from law as a tool

---

17. Gordon, A., *Labor and Imperial Democracy in Prewar Japan.*
18. Henderson, *Conciliation and Japanese Law*, 4–5.
19. Haley, *Authority without Power*, 64.
20. Weber, *From Max Weber*, 239.

for rule to a social and moral order emergent out of law—that began to take root during the early 1870s. While it is true that the speed and depth of Meiji legal reforms responded to externally imposed treaties, the reforms also emerged out of Edo-era processes driven by market demand and internal conflict. The early 1870s shift in the framing of the social meaning of law opened up the possibility for the separation of public and private spheres in society.

Following the events of 1868, legal practitioners continued to work in the interstices of state and society, sustaining the conditions for what Haley described as the incipient private law of the Edo era. Legal practitioners during the 1870s navigated the fluid conditions of a legal system in flux. From the 1880s, legal practitioners drove debates and influenced policy that animated distinctions between an "objective legal order" and "subjective rights." The fluidity experienced in Japan during the 1870s and 1880s was typical of conditions in nineteenth-century Europe and the United States. These decades included years of learning and adaption to changing theories and practices of law in Japan and worldwide. Distinctions that now seem clear in retrospect were formulated and debated at the time. For example, what was the distinction between law and morality? What were public and private spheres in law?

Chapter 2 looks at the lived experience of morality and law during the 1870s through the careers of two legal advocates, Sono Tel [also Teruko] and Kodama Jun'ichirō. Both grappled with ways that past expectations about law and morality collided with contemporary conditions in private legal practice. For contemporaries, Sono was "the first woman lawyer in Japan."[21] During the early 1870s, she practiced law-as-folk-justice (or law-as-morality) alongside others who still practiced law in the mode of the Edo era. In 1874, she left her children and parents to become a legal advocate in Tokyo. Sono's legal practice reimagined the Meiji-era private legal advocate as a substitute for Edo-era lawgivers like Ōoka Echizen, interpreters of moral dicta for the wayward in society. In her autobiography, Sono depicted herself as a private arbiter of social morality who borrowed from Confucian conventions. She repackaged these conventions with European legal inflection. While the turmoil of the early 1870s first

---

21. *Japan Daily Mail*, V. 18, (1892): 440.

tolerated a woman legal advocate, she faced increasingly constrained possibilities for legal practice in the early 1880s. Thus, she took her Confucian Puritanism global and joined the international Christian temperance movement. Sono's story reveals an early Meiji reinterpretation of domestic public morality folded into a revised form of legal practice. When Sono found this hybrid form of legal practice no longer tenable in a rapidly masculinizing judiciary, she launched a career of international activism.

Former low-level samurai Kodama took a different tack, yet he, too, blended the law and public morality that was then being negotiated between early Meiji legal practitioners and Meiji society more broadly. Maruyama Masao and others have identified the conflation of law and morality as an obstacle to the completion of Japan's project of modernity. However, a similar conflation was evident in the United States and Europe where the Meiji state sent its subjects to learn "civilization and enlightenment." Kodama studied law in the United States during an internship in a court in Washington, D.C. While there, he converted to Christianity before returning to Tokyo in 1874 to become a legal advocate. Where Kodama accepted legal education and Christian conversion as part of a comprehensive civilizing process, a more discerning Oliver Wendell Holmes critiqued the intermingling of law and morals prevalent in U.S. legal circles. In an 1897 dedication of a hall at the Boston University School of Law, Holmes urged fellow legal practitioners to make a greater distinction between the two, lamenting the "evil effects of the confusion between legal and moral ideas" prevalent across the U.S. legal landscape.[22] Holmes's cautionary tone at Boston University stood in contrast to Japanese reformers' almost unconditional enthusiasm for foreign legal practice as a model of rationality free of moral taint.

At the time and in retrospect, the idea of the West as a paragon of secular, legal rationality served as a grail for Japanese practitioners and observers alike. That idea has obscured the history of Japan's indigenous private legal practice. The conventional narrative of the history of Japan's private legal practice strips away the powerful moral conversion that ac-

---

22. Holmes, "The Path of Law," 458.

companied Kodama's legal apprenticeship. In its place, it adopts the triumphal story of secular and rational Euro-American progress to identify him as "Japan's first lawyer." Meanwhile, it placed the woman, Sono, outside of the story completely; her continuity with law as public morality and then her activities as a female legal advocate removed her from qualifying as part of a narrative of the advance of private law that came to focus on former-samurai men. Sono, Kodama, and much of 1870s Meiji officialdom accepted North American and European legal practices as models of progress and rationality, worthy of enthusiastic veneration. Yet within this idealized West, the conflation of law and morality persisted, as it did in Japan. Sono and Kodama served as unwitting connectors between the domestic tradition of legal practice and foreign models. Their approach to law foregrounded public morality while also partaking of the legal cosmopolitanism of the late nineteenth century. In the background, nameless and unheralded, former practitioners from the Edo era continued to litigate cases before judges who themselves grappled with the ebbs and flows of the old and new.

A scholarly focus on architects of Meiji legal reform—such as Minister of Justice Etō Shinpei—explains, in part, the persistence of a narrative of modernization centered on officialdom and state orthodoxy, a narrative that writes out both women and actual practice. The narrative follows such reformers as Etō and Mitsukuri Rinshō, who believed that something called "Western law" would be the key to opening participation in "the comity of nations." All the while, Etō and others dismissed domestic legal practice as underdeveloped and insignificant. Yet Etō was wrong. The domestic legal tradition was robust and the incipient private legal practice within it connected the people to the state, translating popular concerns into the language of law and translating the language of law into the popular vernacular. The vexed question of the relationship between public morality and litigation as a means of dispute resolution blinded Etō and others to domestic traditions.

By the end of the Edo era, an odd juxtaposition had formed between a Neo-Confucian orthodoxy that abhorred conflict on one side and, on the other, an everyday practice of litigated dispute resolution that called forth systems of formal and informal legal practice. The unequal treaties highlighted this disjuncture between orthodoxy and practice and opened a critique of Japanese society grounded in its supposed barbarism.

The conventional narrative replaces complexity with Japanese receipt of Western legal and political enlightenment. Yet the end of the nineteenth century was not a moment in which a monolithic West created a rational, progressive, enlightened modernity that was then received and emulated by the world. In Europe and the United States, both regressive and progressive elements of law and public morality operated in tandem, justifying imperialism, unequal treaties with Japan, and racial and class inequalities at home and abroad while also opening up opportunities for social change grounded in rights claims.

The bridges between Japan and the world at the level of legal practice in the early 1870s were not simply the high ideals imported by state reformers in the name of the Meiji slogan of "civilization and enlightenment." Sono was a heterodox figure in that she imagined and then created a world in which a woman could be a legal practitioner. When domestic constraints confounded her vision, she left Japan for the larger stage of international temperance activism. Kodama went abroad to learn the foreign approaches to law that at the time were so coveted at home. He embraced Christianity as the moral frame then ordaining law in the United States, where he studied. Both Sono and Kodama inform our understanding of the early 1870s in world history. This was a moment when public morality was a prominent feature of law and legal practice, East and West.

Toward a World History of Professions: Legal Practitioners into Legal Professionals

If we define "profession" as an occupational group that creates and controls expert knowledge, enjoys a (de jure) monopoly on control over market entry, and expresses its interests through a national voluntary association, then professions emerged in Europe and the United States, as well as Japan, during the nineteenth century—early or late, depending on the country.[23] It was only by the end of the late nineteenth century that the work now identified as the province of barristers in England, *avocats* in France, *avvocatti* in Italy, *Rechtsanwälte* in Germany, and lawyers in the

---

23. Krause, *Death of the Guilds*; Larson, *The Rise of Professionalism*; and Abbott, *The System of Professions*.

United States became fully formalized.[24] In Japan, the emergence of the lawyer in 1893 and the Japan Lawyers' Association in 1897 was consistent with this timing. The goal of securing a de jure monopoly on courtroom representation united lawyers the world over as they competed with all manner of legal entrepreneurs.

The global emergence of legal professions during the nineteenth century responded to competition among service providers; local context dictated regional and national differences. Recent comparative scholarship on early modern legal practice highlights how market, state regulation, and legal thought varied from country to country. At the same time, a broad formulation of "legal work" as the interpretation of the language of the state allows for broader comparative scope. Bailiffs, notaries, conveyancers, legal scriveners, and persons the nineteenth-century British labeled "pettyfoggers and vipers" translated the "language of the state" for their clients. Eric Ives wrote that, in early modern England, there were legal "services graded for every need and pocket."[25] In England and elsewhere, the quest for jurisdictional control by legal practitioners characterized the nineteenth-century transition to legal professionalism. In Japan before 1872, practitioners called *kujishi*, *deirishi*, and *kujiyado bantō* all sold legal services. Suit inns of the Edo era sought a state-sanctioned monopoly on the production of documents and other services they provided to clients. The partial monopoly the suit inns won was a state grant that was inheritable by each establishment. Yet competing enterprises such as teahouses and upstart inns episodically challenged the suit inns' dominance.

The environment changed dramatically during the 1870s. Legal advocates established associations that foreshadowed self-governing professional associations. These associations enjoyed considerable control over

---

24. For example, legal historians of Germany have written that "the concept of a 'legal profession' was misleading in the German states." "Legal professional" generally referred to judges and procurators, not private practitioners; private practitioners being highly regulated, they did not merit identification as a "profession." Blankenburg and Schultz, "German Advocates," 124.

25. Ives, "The Common Lawyers in Pre-Reformation England," 147. Ives also discusses the contest over practice area and the diversity of practitioners in *The Common Lawyers of Pre-Reformation England*, 146–49. In "Lawyers and Early Modern Culture," Bouwsma notes that "in England, scriveners also provided some legal services," 306.

the activities of their members. In their earliest incarnations, the associations combined the functions of what today would be called law firms, political action committees, and private law schools. They selected from among their members the legal advocates who would go before the courts, what policies members backed, and what laws they would study. Part of their influence arose from affiliation with local powerbrokers, newspapers, other associations, and political parties. One such organization was the Legal Research Institute, affiliated with the Risshisha political association in Kōchi. The institute sought to control legal practice in Kōchi and suppress unaffiliated legal advocates or advocates affiliated with competing groups.

Professionalization in Japan correlated to the processes of industrialization. The earliest sociological study of the professions in Europe—a 1933 work by Carr-Saunders and Wilson—pointed to industrialization as a shared starting point for the emergence of professions, as the guild gave way to the factory. *The Professions* was the first study to theorize the professions as a whole and show how hereditary occupations of an earlier age gave way to certifying associations.[26] As Magali Larson demonstrated in *The Rise of Professionalism*, "modern industrial society" was the seedbed for all kinds of professional activities.[27] In England, traditions of heredity or status as qualification for work began to disappear in the early 1800s, consistent with the process of capital formation and industrialization. In Japan, too, formal certification for participation in an occupation marked the rise of industrialization and the beginning of the end to guild and status society. Yet in Japan, unlike in Europe, it was the state that initiated the certification process for legal practitioners (1876). Within four years, however, bar associations began electing their own leadership, enforcing ethical practices, and calling for control of entry into the practice of legal advocacy.

Another marker of the move toward professionalization in Japan was the rise of the legal advocate as an expert on law. Chapter 1 shows how,

---

26. Carr-Saunders and Wilson, *The Professions*.

27. Larson, *The Rise of Professionalism*. On collegial autonomy in a comparative light, see Burrage, "Revolution"; on improvement of social status, see Karpik, *French Lawyers*.

even though the shogun prohibited the Edo-era legal practitioner from writing or publishing legal commentaries (a prohibition the Tokugawa state could and did enforce among commercial publishers), suit inn proprietors circumvented this provision in numerous ways. For example, they disseminated legal knowledge by allowing clients to copy laws related to ongoing cases. Chapter 3 demonstrates how, from the 1870s onward, legal practitioners became interpreters and producers of expert knowledge. They took on students and apprentices in schools and associations. By the mid-1880s, private law schools in Japan trained both government officials and members in institutions that became the predecessors of some of Japan's leading private universities, such as Meiji University. They published journals that debated the legal questions of the day. They took to the stump, lecturing people on legal issues. They wrote for and at times funded newspapers, while also writing and publishing popular and specialist works on law.

Though the term "lawyer" began to have some shared resonance across national histories at the turn of the twentieth century, it still meant different things in different places. The authority of legal practitioners in Italy, for example, did not necessarily derive from expertise and knowledge. Rather, group affiliation determined professional status before the court. In early-nineteenth-century Italy, legal practitioners embraced "the order" (*ordini*), self-governing bodies that maintained their own membership rolls. Advancement had little to do with expertise. By the twentieth century, political parties and then fascism replaced *ordini* and again ensured that group affiliation, not merit, determined how and whether one practiced law.[28] Though we can identify differences in the legal practice traditions that have emerged from distinct historical contexts, the similarities are also instructive. A modernization narrative that falsely identifies Europe and the United States as the source of modern, private legal practice oversimplifies an influencing West and a receiving East. Like other industrializing countries during the same period, nineteenth-century Japan grappled with the broad implications of social, legal, and political change. The world historical emergence of

28. Krause, *Death of the Guilds*, 187–88.

professions in the late nineteenth century proceeded with domestic and international dimensions, as did the emergence of a politicized legal practitioner.

Legal Practitioners and the Making of a Public Sphere

During the Edo era, shogunal officials identified themselves as the interpreters and spokespersons for the public (*ōyake* or *kō*). Yet early in the Meiji period the term "public" took on multiple meanings.[29] For some, it referred to a community as a whole, as in the "general public" or "general interest." For others, it referred to society as a counter to the process of defining a public. It also signaled transparency and openness, as in 1874, when Itagaki Taisuke used the term as part of the name for Japan's first political party, the Public Party of Patriots (Aikoku kōtō). "Public" in the name of the party forestalled any reading of the group as a "private party" or faction.[30] When legal advocates used the term in public speeches during the 1880s, they imagined the public as a counter to the power of the state. In Euro-American political theory, too, the nature of the public reflected competing understandings of social and political orders. Rousseau's assertion that public interest found reflection in an ethereal "general will" collided with Madisonian worries about the dangers of faction— debates that translators later made available to avid Japanese readers. For many former-samurai political activists, the public was a space of activity free of government intervention. It was out of the vibrant exchange among these various meanings of "public" and enactments of these ideas that a public sphere emerged toward the end of the nineteenth century. Legal practitioners joined newspapers and political party activists in driving the process of defining a public.

It might seem that these efforts grew from barren ground. By grouping society into hierarchical status groups and regulating everyday life through sumptuary laws, the Tokugawa state sought total political and social control. Yet Tokugawa control was not as total as its rulers hoped. Philip Brown has argued that the Tokugawa regime did not have the capacity to exercise the power it claimed. Its pose as the arbiter of public

---

29. Kim, *The Age of Visions and Arguments*. See also Huffman, *Creating a Public*.
30. "Wagakuni kenseishi no yurai," cited in Osatake, *Nihon kensei shi ronshū*, 446.

morality was just that, the presumption of a "flamboyant state."[31] Even so, the state brooked few direct challenges. Although episodes of local conflict between villages and local lords occurred with some regularity, open challenges to the shogunate, such as the 1837 uprising by samurai Ōshio Heihachirō, were rare. There is little evidence that suit inn proprietors were inclined to transform the system that had granted them monopoly status. If contemporary accounts are to be believed, profit was their primary aim. Even so, the Edo-era emergence of private legal practitioners was in itself a challenge to the status quo.

Through their activities, legal practitioners revealed the incomplete achievement of the totalizing vision of the Tokugawa orthodoxy. As *The Analects* put it, when the moral authority of the ruler blew over society like wind over grass, "surely it would bend."[32] Yet legal practitioners did not bend to exhortations to live harmoniously. They sold their skills and helped people bring lawsuits before the authorities. While early modern legal practitioners did not directly challenge the shogunate's political authority and its grounding in public morality, their very existence belied claims of shogunal-enforced harmony or the idea that government officials created social order by fiat.

The ideal of officialdom as moral and harmonic polestar persisted past the regime change of 1868. Intellectuals and oligarchs such as Katō Hiroyuki and Itō Hirobumi claimed the legacy of Tokugawa moral superiority and nurtured it. Bernard Silberman, in *Cages of Reason*, has described how Meiji leaders regularized their authority after 1868. They attempted to "establish the publicness of their positions and roles by appeal[ing] to a higher transcendent moral order and . . . deny[ing] any notion of private interest."[33] In other words, they justified their authority by conflating law and morality. Maruyama Masao's critique of Japanese modernity hinged on its failure to separate law and morality: "[T]he Japanese state, being a moral entity, monopolized the right to determine values."[34] Maruyama singled out proponents of freedom and popular rights for failing to distinguish between "national rights" (sovereignty) and individual

---

31. Brown, *Central Authority and Local Autonomy*, 232.
32. Confucius, *The Analects of Confucius*, 83.
33. Silberman, *Cages of Reason*, 191.
34. Maruyama M., *Thought and Behavior in Modern Japanese Politics*, 5.

freedoms. While this was an apt description of Meiji-state elites and their backers, such as Katō and Itō, it did not apply to legal advocates who were also activists in the late-nineteenth-century movement for freedom and popular rights. Many former samurai worked as private legal practitioners while promoting individual freedoms as the foundation for national sovereignty. To this end, they campaigned for a range of reforms including the establishment of a constitutional polity, the rights of the criminally accused, and rights of assembly and expression.

By the 1870s, the Meiji state recognized a distinction between public and private spheres in law, a distinction that provided an opening for the legal careers of Sono and Kodama. In 1872, the Ministry of Justice defined the terms of private legal practice. In succeeding years, former samurai increasingly joined the ranks of private legal practitioners. From the mid- to late 1870s, former samurai worked as legal advocates as they defied officialdom and worked against the vision of the state as a totalizing and transcendent moral order. In the late nineteenth century, the legal practitioner working against an all-encompassing state was not a phenomenon unique to Japan. The long-standing question of the relationship between the individual and the state remained a subject of activism, debate, and theorization worldwide. Theorists of individual rights framed their question in international as well as domestic terms. In 1872, Rudolph Gneist gave a lecture before the German parliament on the rule-of-law state, "Der Rechtsstaat," published as a book in the same year. At the time of his talk, Germany's various principalities had just united and ensured their "national rights" vis-à-vis France. Just four years earlier, the Restoration coup precipitating political centralization in Japan also signaled a shift toward an assertion of national rights, or state sovereignty, in the international arena. This conceptual framing influenced activists who linked the defense of individual rights with the outward expression of national sovereignty. In Japan, legal advocates, Meiji officials, public intellectuals, and political activists read *Der Rechtsstaat* as a commentary on the relationship between the power of the state controlled by law on one side and the duties and interests of the individual protected by civil rights on the other. From the 1870s, opposition activists joined their calls for individual rights to the national quest to ensure Japan's national rights, or sovereignty, vis-à-vis the foreign powers that had subjected Japan to treaties with unequal terms. Legal-advocate samurai claimed that broader political participation at home would lead to greater national strength, thus linking domestic concerns about a rule-of-law state with international affairs.

In Japanese, *Rechtsstaat* became *hōchikoku*, "a state established under the ideology of law, where the principle of liberty reigns . . . a rule-of-law state."[35] Gneist's works found their way into the private collection of legal advocate Hoshi Tōru, a figure at the center of chapters 3 and 4. Hoshi worked to make Gneist's thinking on the distinction between state and society a reality in Japan. The stories of legal advocates such as Shimamoto Nakamichi, Hoshi, and associations of legal advocates reveal how Japanese thinkers and practitioners joined their European counterparts in engaging with ideas of law, public and private spheres, and state-individual relations to transform law and politics before the turn of the twentieth century.

A culture of cosmopolitanism and the wide availability within Japan of foreign legal commentary during the 1870s and 1880s connected former samurai working as legal practitioners to a global conversation. The framing of opposition to the Meiji regime in legal terms created fertile ground for reflection on contemporary writing in the fields of law and politics. Former samurai such as Ōi Kentarō and Shimamoto Nakamichi began to conceptualize a society of checks and balances. Ōi's idea of a legal society derived from his reading of French legal thought, particularly Montesquieu's ideas of separation of powers, from which he argued for a separation of the legislative and executive branches where each should not intrude "into the other's sphere of influence."[36] Upon reading J. S. Mill's *On Liberty*, former samurai Kōno Hironaka reflected, "Neo-Confucianism and nativism, all of the thought up to that time excepting loyalty and filial piety . . . was scattered like the leaves of trees. At the same time I knew the importance of a person's liberty and a person's rights."[37] This was Kōno coming to a position on the social order grounded in law, a position foreshadowed by the

---

35. "Rudolf Gneist, *Der Rechtsstaat*, Berlin: J. Springer, 1872" appeared in a list of books in Hoshi Tōru's collection. The translation of *Rechsstaat* is from Wagatsuma, *Shin hōritsugaku jiten,* 879.

36. Kim, *The Age of Visions and Arguments,* 111.

37. Cited in Osatake, *Nihon kenseishi taikō,* 2:505. See also Maruyama M., *Thought and Behavior in Modern Japanese Politics,* 5.

work of Edo-era legal practitioners but anathema to the Neo-Confucian training of the samurai. By the end of the 1870s, the former samurai's embrace of legal practice linked global discussions in political theory with domestic political concerns. This connected a tradition of legal recourse to dispute resolution with political thought that moved toward the emergence of a new kind of public space. On the ground, former samurai began to assemble in major cities, establishing associations selling legal services that matched their reading of legal theory with practice. These associations issued a direct challenge to state hegemony, speaking of "curing the ills of the nation," "extending rights to the people," and "eliminating inappropriate violence" from the courtroom.

By identifying themselves as intermediaries between society and the state, legal practitioners joined the process of carving out a public sphere. From the 1870s, legal advocates operated in figurative and literal public spaces, including newspapers and public speeches and debates. Their activities intensified during the 1880s when they turned the courts into a stage from which to criticize and demand change in government. This was the case in high-profile trials, such as the 1883 trial in the Fukushima Incident, in which a prefectural governor's attempt to suppress political party activism led legal advocate Hoshi Tōru to stand alongside Ōi Kentarō in championing the rights of political party activists such as Kōno Hironaka. Associations of legal advocates were also the foundation for private law faculties that, until the mid-1880s, cultivated an alternative to the state-sanctioned educational path.

In their activism, legal advocates identified themselves as spokespersons for "the public" even as they imagined themselves to be the primary beneficiaries of the policies for which they campaigned. The writings of legal advocates, charters of associations, resolutions of association meetings, legal cases, and appeals to the government revealed a change over time in the "public" invoked by legal practitioners. The potential beneficiaries of activism by legal advocates transformed in response to changes in society and as a result of legal-advocate activism itself. The boundaries of this "public"—who was included and who was excluded—corresponded closely to changes in those who claimed such political rights as free expression and free assembly. Calls for the establishment of a nationally elected assembly in 1874 limited participation to former samurai. By the 1880s, the boundaries of this "public" had expanded to include educated farmers and merchants in the notion of "public debate and public opinion" (*kōgi kōron*).

Establishment of the Diet transformed considerations of the public during the 1890s by creating an institution charged with representing the general interest. Yet electoral participation was limited to little more than 1 percent of the population. In this new environment, national groups such as the national voluntary association of the legal profession increasingly competed with the state in its function as the arbiter of the "public interest" (*kōeki*).

The contest over the emergent distinction between public and private spheres was not as one-sided as those might believe who look at Japanese history from the other side of 1930s and 1940s totalitarianism. On the basis of their legal expertise, legal advocates opened up spaces from which to question, critique, and shape politics. Late-nineteenth-century legal advocates opened the door for the democratic activism of the early twentieth century. Increasingly, others stepped through. From the turn of the twentieth century, new publics streamed into the public space, including the socialist "masses" (*taishū*) and the democratic "people" (*minshū*).

Laws, Customs, and Codes

By the end of the Meiji period, law had become more than the sum of written law, precedent, and custom. It had also become a society-wide framework for understanding and organizing the world. Some in the Meiji government thought that they could create a new legal order simply by translating foreign legal codes into the Japanese language as a tactic for reversing the unequal treaties. Yet the powerful tradition of domestic law coupled with the former samurai's embrace of legal practice turned law into something more—an increasingly universal way of thinking about society and its governance.

The activities of private legal practitioners evolved in relation to the state's legal reform project, in particular the translation of the French civil code that began from the first years of Meiji rule. This project gained urgency from the disadvantageous treaty regime imposed on Japan by foreign powers. In Goethe's *Faust*, Mephistopheles bemoaned,

> Customs and laws in every place,
> Like a disease, an heir-loom dread,
> Still trail their curse from race to race,
> And furtively abroad they spread."[38]

---

38. Cahn, "Goethe's View of Law," 907.

Goethe published *Faust* during the age of Napoleon's imperial predations and the crafting of his civil code. In Japan as in Europe, foreign soldiers and diplomats led "custom and law's" furtive spread. In the Japanese context, Napoleon's heirloom collided with multiple layers of shogunal, domainal, and village authority and, later, their vestiges. Throughout the treaty negotiations of the 1850s and 1860s, foreign powers held up two self-serving principles disadvantageous to the Japanese government. First, the laws of the home country should govern foreign nationals in Japan; second, the barbarism of Tokugawa law justified this arrangement. These principles operated in tandem to reinforce the foreign understanding that Japanese legal and political practices were inferior to those of Europe and the United States. This understanding found a mirror in Meiji-era calls for civilization and enlightenment, along European and American lines.

After 1868, Meiji legal reformers sought, by reforming domestic law, to break the curse of international power politics as it was visited upon Japan in the treaties. With the Napoleonic Code viewed internationally as a set of best practices, legal reformers in the Meiji government saw legal codification along French lines as the answer. Etō Shinpei, the first minister of justice in the new government, stated that "short of drafting the [French] legal code in haste, there is nothing better we can do—even if the work is incomplete—in order to achieve the goal of revising the treaties."[39] In focusing on French law, Japanese government officials joined a global engagement with that country's code. In the century after its promulgation in 1804, the code had won the admiration of governments throughout Europe and the world. There were even legal reformers in the United States who promoted the adoption of a national civil code. This was in the United States, a country firmly in the camp of the Anglo-American legal system based on stare decisis—deciding cases based on legal precedent. In Japan, legal reforms instituted during the decades after 1868 rewrote the rules governing everything from national politics to

---

39. Cited in Kikuyama, "Etō Shinpei no shihō kaikaku," 94. See also Robert Epp on civil code translation, including his dissertation, "Threat to Tradition: The Reaction to Japan's 1890 Civil Code," Harvard University, Departments of History and Far Eastern Languages (Cambridge, MA), 1964, and also his resultant journal article, "The Challenge from Tradition."

hairstyles.[40] In this increasingly codified sphere, new actors and institutions emerged, adding their voices to the process. Both the codification project and the new agents of it, including legal advocates, law journals, and (later) law schools, sparked a reformed politics of dispute resolution that opened the courts to everyone from farmers to former samurai.

In retrospect, the legal codes drafted under the supervision of the Ministry of Justice may look like an inexorable march toward an externally defined modernity.[41] Yet the Meiji codification project would have remained little more than a façade if the laws had not come alive in the hands of private legal practitioners and the public, who, during the Edo era, had embraced litigation and legal processes. Practitioners joined government officials in translating works from Locke to Rousseau into Japanese. Private legal practitioners also disseminated and interpreted legal reforms then being instituted by the Meiji government. And government programs employed legal translators, sponsored overseas study for legal scholars and practitioners, contracted foreign legal advisers such as Frenchman Gustave Emile Boissonade de Fontarabie to consult on law, and established government programs for legal training to achieve legal reform goals.

Yet state and society differed on the way forward. Revision of the unequal treaties and the completion of the codification project were both in sight in 1890, but neither goal was a reality. So commenced a

---

40. O'Brien, "Splitting Hairs."

41. The ministry first codified criminal law in the Chinese-influenced Principles of the New [Criminal] Statutes (1870), which was revised in 1873 and then replaced by a French-influenced criminal code and a code of criminal instruction (both promulgated in 1880 and implemented in 1882). A code of criminal procedure replaced the code of criminal instruction in 1890. In the meantime, the Meiji constitution was promulgated in 1899 and with it a national assembly, the Diet, was established in 1890. In 1907, the Diet passed a revised criminal code that was heavily influenced by German legal thought. As for laws governing disputes between private individuals, other civil matters, and administrative affairs, 1890 saw the establishment of laws governing the courts, a code of civil procedure, and the promulgation of a civil code and a commercial code. The last two were postponed following a debate between legal-advocate and legal-scholar partisans of French and English approaches. The compromise position was the adoption of German principles on some civil matters. After undergoing revision, a "new" civil code came into force in 1898. The commercial code was implemented piecemeal between 1893 and 1899. On codification, see Takayanagi, "A Century of Innovation."

season of social events, including balls and banquets, intended to convince diplomats that Japanese elites had mastered the form as well as the content of foreign law and society. An association of Tokyo legal advocates censured the Meiji regime for avoiding hard choices on legal reform in favor of "danc[ing] its way into the hearts of foreigners with fancy balls."[42] Meiji reformers had focused on the Napoleonic Code as a vessel through which to import the West. As a goal of transformation, codification of Meiji laws along French lines had opened up a world of new ideas and practices. It had not opened up the West, however, in the sense of transforming Japan's position in world affairs. State officials discovered that their belief in a fully formed, universal legal model was ill founded when the British blocked treaty revision through the end of the decade. The British ambassador believed that Meiji legal reforms were too French.

New actors and new institutions had made the legal transition less a march through history and more a dance, but a dance even more complicated than the fancy state balls hosted at the Rokumeikan. New actors, including legal advocates, their associations, and their clients—the litigating public—took advantage of new possibilities under legal reform to press professional, private, and political claims. By the 1880s, it was clear to all of these actors that law mattered in new ways. Meiji legal reform was not just the adoption of foreign codes in the interest of treaty revision. Legal practitioners operating on new legal terrain had made law a leading framework for understanding and ordering a person's world—a new epistemic.

A curious notion has influenced perceptions about Japan's legal and political past: that, relative to other developed nations, law and legal practice in Japan was somehow insignificant. History reveals just how inaccurate this perception is. Interactions outside of the black–and-white politics that appears in the narratives of "state versus society" or "bureaucrats versus politicians" must be puzzled out. It was in the gray areas that legal practitioners connected the market to the state and negotiated questions of power and social justice. What follows is a social and political history of legal practice in Japan from the late seventeenth to the turn of the

---

42. Matsuo S., "Shihō shiryō," 50–51.

twentieth century. It focuses on legal practitioners who have often been overlooked in narratives of shogunal and imperial Japan, narratives that tell of bureaucrats prevailing over politicians, the state suppressing the people, and social movements protesting against the state. Despite their small numbers, during this period legal practitioners in Japan exercised disproportionate influence through their work within the courts and before the public.

CHAPTER I

Early Modern Legal Practice: Overcoming Antagonism and Decorticating Tokugawa Law, 1615–1868

The relative invisibility of Japan's early modern legal practice stems from the antagonism suit inns and suit solicitors faced during their day, and their subsequent encasement in and concealment under layers of history told through the lens of the modern state and nation. A return to the beginnings of the Tokugawa shogunate and its grounding in law reveals the possibilities out of which private legal practitioners crafted their practice, despite official animosity.

In 1615, the Tokugawa shogunate grounded its claim to authority in the Laws Governing Military Households. Article 3 illustrated law's scope, stating, "Law is the foundation of ceremonial decorum. Law prevails over reason and reason yields to law."[1] The establishment of the Laws Governing Military Households came fifteen years after the Tokugawa's defeat of its enemies on the battlefield, twelve years after its receipt of an endorsement from the emperor, and two years before the apotheosis of Tokugawa Ieyasu in the shrine at Nikkō. Edicts governed the relations between the new political center that was the Tokugawa shogunate and those in its orbit, including the emperor and samurai families, and marked the end of decades of warfare. They prefigured a totalizing vision of state and society under law. In other words, rules articulated by the shogunate would order society alongside the quest for civility in ceremony, as prescribed

---

1. Haley, *Authority without Power,* 54–55; Hall, "The Tokugawa Legislation, Part II," 288.

by interpreters of the Confucian tradition. In fact, morality, law, and justice were bound up in Tokugawa authority and reached not just the emperor and samurai but everyday life at the village level. Dan Fenno Henderson has written of how the Tokugawa and its officials wove together "individual behavior, social practice, positive law, and justice (basic, moral, or political values)."[2] Thinkers such as Yamaga Sokō suggested that samurai were the physical embodiment of just such an amalgamated vision of law and morality, and the martial enforcers of its principles in practice. By the end of the Tokugawa period in 1868, the theoretical underpinning of state orthodoxy had changed very little, but practice had transformed. In the areas of both public and private law, legal practitioners were a driving force in the transformation of the practical dimension of official orthodoxy. Private legal practitioners had gone a considerable way toward overcoming official antagonism or subverting the layers of official authority that aimed to suppress litigated resolution of conflict. Private legal practitioners included the operators of suit inns who moved from the margins to a state-sanctioned place within the justice process and suit solicitors who practiced in the shadows throughout the Edo period. Both advised clients how to navigate judicial processes, from mitigating charges of criminal behavior to translating disputes arising from everyday life into a lexicon that would gain a hearing in officialdom.

The process of binding state legitimacy to law has a long tradition in Japan, dating from the emulation of Chinese codes in the seventh century.[3] Centuries later, the shogunate's seventeenth-century version of a legal society built on the work of earlier architects of a centralized state. Social and political reforms concentrated samurai in castle towns in more than 200 domains. Beginning in 1635, an alternate attendance system required daimyo to maintain households in the Edo capital. These changes, which buttressed the center at the expense of local control, contributed to a concentration of authority in the hands of the Tokugawa shogunate and to the promulgation of new rules for relations between lord, vassal, and subject. Legal scholar John Haley has noted that "on a national scale law and lawmaking [changed] from simply an expression

---

2. Henderson, *Conciliation and Japanese Law*, 1:48.
3. Steenstrup, *A History of Law in Japan until 1868*, 28–40.

of legislated regulation, custom, and precedent into a manifestation if not source of legitimacy as well."[4] The Tokugawa shogunate used law to override the competing prerogatives of local lords and the supranational authority of the emperor. At the same time, the shogunate aimed to create and maintain a status quo.

With the shogunate and the various domains having arrogated to themselves the authority to rule, to them also fell the authority to resolve disputes among parties. In short order, the shogunate became the final arbiter of private conflict. In 1633, it stated that farmers and townspeople could submit disputes to the local authorities; in cases of unclear jurisdiction or "where there was good reason," disputes would ultimately be resolved in Edo.[5] Although the Edo-era authorities formally espoused the position that litigation was to the detriment of social harmony, they made themselves arbiters of the last resort. This vision of society from the top down was later met with action from the bottom up in the form of lawsuits wending their way to the shogun's officers. Legal frameworks for control had opened up unintended possibilities for change, particularly in the area of legal practice.

While Tokugawa and domainal lords ruled from above through samurai officials, commoner legal practitioners increasingly connected townspeople and agricultural communities to systems of social order and dispute resolution from below. Though the state forbade formal legal representation, the legal practitioner interpreted the language of the state for disputes and conflicts that arose in day-to-day social and economic activity. As early as the 1630s, the record suggests that those who came before the state seeking redress of local wrongs had recourse to expert advice on the drafting of their petitions. For example, when local headmen appealed the fairness of a Shōnai domain tax increase to top shogunal officials, mastery of the legal formalities of petitioning and the framing of their complaint, along with the context of the conflict, enabled them to overcome the usually fatal flaw of pursuing the matter outside of prescribed channels.[6]

---

4. Haley, *Authority without Power*, 55.

5. "Buke genseiroku," cited in Aoki, "Kinsei minshū no seikatsu to teikō," 174.

6. Kelly, *Deference and Defiance in Nineteenth Century Japan*, 54–55.

Historian Takikawa Masajirō has drawn on proscriptive edicts and other evidence to show that suit solicitors and later suit inns pursued a whole range of activities in the legal sphere from the earliest decades through the end of the Edo era. In the interest of suppressing private practice, from the 1640s the shogunate began prohibiting the activities of private legal practitioners through edicts such as those included in the *Shōhō jiroku* that forbade teaching about law, disseminating legal texts, speaking before a magistrate on behalf of parties in adversarial disputes, and representing the criminally accused. Hereditary samurai administrators such as the Taruya family, town councilors in Edo, directed ward heads in the capital to watch out for suit solicitors. They singled out as particularly egregious acts "instructing others in the ways of having pleadings [*meyasu*] recognized" and being paid for this service.[7] Despite suppression and prohibition, the act of framing a complaint in the prescribed manner and gaining a hearing became a particular skill of the Edo-era suit solicitor and suit inn.

Though the Tokugawa shogunate had developed a complex administrative apparatus, it sought to limit the number and kinds of suits it heard. It grounded its approach to dispute resolution in an idiosyncratic interpretation of Neo-Confucian rationales. In addition to Confucian concerns, Hiramatsu Yoshirō summarized other reasons successive shoguns favored mediated over litigated resolution of disputes: (1) they preferred a focus on the particulars of a case (facts over broad principles of law); (2) they favored community norms over law; (3) the theoretical basis for private law was underdeveloped; (4) the government lacked the capacity to hear cases; and (5) shoguns had a policy of "noninterference" within the domains.[8] Despite the creation of systems to adjudicate private conflict, the regime embraced the dictum in *The Analects*, "What we need is for there to be no lawsuits."[9] The shogunate singled out suits arising from conflict over money (as opposed to conflicts over property) as targets of control and even elimination. This reflected its view that such suits arose from society's most craven inclinations. Episodically, as in edicts of 1622, 1661, and six other times through the mid-nineteenth

7. Takikawa M., "Edo shoki ni okeru kujishi kin'atsu," 19–20, 32.
8. Hiramatsu, "Tokugawa Law," 37–38.
9. Confucius, *The Analects*, 83.

century, the shogunate refused to hear suits arising from transactions unsecured by property.[10]

Yet despite the regime's continued attempts to suppress litigation as an example of social conflict and its efforts to displace private disputes from formal sites of legal resolution, two parallel tracks of legal practice emerged in early modern Japan. A state-sanctioned track of suit inns, their proprietors, and their employees came to dominate private legal practice in Edo and other sites of shogunal and domainal authority, while unaffiliated suit solicitors guided people through legal processes from the shadows, both rural and urban. From the establishment of guilds of inns beginning in 1699, suit inns were permitted to draft documents for parties in adversarial matters and provide lodging for litigants. Over the course of the eighteenth century, they increasingly inserted themselves into the adjudication process. By the end of the eighteenth century, the state had approved four guilds of suit inns to organize room, board, and legal drafting services for litigants. Originally focused on just these services, the suit inns began to operate in other areas as well over the course of the eighteenth century, including the dissemination of legal information and all kinds of advocacy for clients—even in the presence of magistrates and commissioners. State-sanctioned legal practice became more sophisticated and diverse until a range of new legal practitioners replaced suit solicitors and suit inns in 1872.

Paralleling the state-sanctioned regime of legal practice, an informal set of practices emerged in both the cities and the countryside, with suit solicitors competing with their sanctioned counterparts in drafting documents and selling advice on how to navigate the legal system. There were various names for private legal practitioners, such as *kujishi, deirishi,* and *deirinin.* Initially, these terms referred to those who provided assistance in drafting legal documents or in reaching an arbitrated resolution of a dispute, including holding money in escrow for parties to disputes. Freelance sole practitioners operated unattached to any kind of corporate or guild body. These sole practitioners, perhaps itinerant, faced repeated and emphatic prohibition in village compacts and shogunal

---

10. The 1661 prohibition can be found in Takayanagi and Ishii, eds., *Ofuregaki kanpō shūsei,* 1194. On prohibitions generally, see Henderson, *Conciliation and Japanese Law,* 1:107.

regulations.[11] The ongoing presence of this unsanctioned realm can be discerned in regular efforts at its suppression over the two and a half centuries of Tokugawa rule.

Meanwhile, state-sanctioned guilds moved closer and closer to the legal apparatus of the shogunate, enjoying increased support from shogunal officials of their monopoly on selling legal services vis-à-vis upstart competitors, such as tea houses and suit solicitors. During the 1790s, litigants were allowed to appear before magistrates without village representatives, at times accompanied by suit inn proprietors instead. By the nineteenth century, suit inn proprietors and their staff had carved out a space for themselves in the judicial process. Thus, the shogunate's exercise of judicial authority opened a process of legal change in which suit inn employees and freelance suit solicitors emerged as agents who shaped how people experienced and understood law. These private legal practitioners promoted the lawsuit as a form of dispute resolution and, in so doing, disseminated legal knowledge that the state had held close.

Edo-era authorities exercised broad influence over the movement of their subjects through control of the major roads and by establishing a system of registration and designated lodging for all travelers. In particular, officials recognized the desirability of regulating disputes by controlling where litigants stayed while pursuing their claims. In Edo and other urban centers, litigants found their way to officially designated inns. In response, a subset of these designated inns began to specialize in legal matters, giving rise to suit inns that conducted business near the emergent legal apparatus of the Tokugawa state across the archipelago, wherever it existed. When farmers and merchants dissatisfied with the resolution of their problems at the local level traveled to a castle town in their domain and then to the capital to seek hearings with higher authorities, they registered their location with the authorities from their domain. A party summoned to Edo, either in an adversarial proceeding (*deirisuji*) or an inquisitorial proceeding (*ginmisuji*), faced a requirement that they lodge at a specific inn designated by the summoning commission or magistrate.

How these lodgings appeared in the sources varied from place to place and changed over time. Suit inns were most broadly a subset of "designated

---

11. Takikawa M., "Edo shoki ni okeru kujishi kin'atsu," 19–20.

lodgings" (*gōyado*) in the sites of Tokugawa authority, including the three major shogunal cities of Edo, Osaka, and Kyoto. There were also designated lodgings in the castle towns of the domains. Suit inns were at times called *kujiyado* in Edo and *shitayado* in Osaka. Even though the state prohibited legal representation, suit inns accommodating people with business before judicial bodies formed a guild by 1699. Officials focused on monitoring the litigation process had opened up the possibility that, by the end of the Edo period, the suit inns and their guilds would further inject themselves into the processes of private dispute resolution.

Histories of Edo-era practices published since the turn of the twentieth century have generally denied the importance of private legal practitioners. Early accounts identified employees of suit inns and suit solicitors as insignificant charlatans whose craft was to "circumvent the other side by trickery, by falsehood, by forgery, or by treachery."[12] The venerable 1914 *Nihon bengoshishi* (History of Lawyers in Japan), by Okudaira Masahiro, stated unequivocally that the shogunate forbade legal practice.[13] Drawing on Okudaira, the history of the Tokyo Bar Association published in 1935 stated there was no pre-Meiji history of lawyering in Japan. Suit solicitors "were absolutely not like today's lawyer."[14] Herman Ooms has written, "Tokugawa Japan did not have an independent judiciary and was a society without lawyers."[15] This was more or less true. The judiciary was an extension of the administrative bureaucracy, and there were no lawyers in early modern Japan in the contemporary sense of the term.

Yet the absence of a right to representation does not mean that representation did not exist. Suit solicitors evaded Tokugawa prohibitions, as did others in a wide range of pursuits. Prohibitions on women performers, for example, failed to de-eroticize Kabuki theater.[16] Prohibitions on samurai commercial activity failed to keep some warriors

---

12. Brinkley, *Japan and China*, 73.
13. Okudaira, *Nihon bengoshishi*, 13. See also Rabinowitz, "The Historical Development of the Japanese Bar," and Matsui Yasuhiro, *Nihon bengoshiron*.
14. Adachi G., ed., *Tokyo bengoshikaishi*, 1.
15. Ooms, *Tokugawa Village Practice*, 7.
16. Mezur, *Beautiful Boys/Outlaw Bodies*, 65–68.

out of the markets.[17] Similarly, the prohibition on legal representation foundered.

Moreover, one would be hard-pressed to find the equivalent of the contemporary lawyer in any other part of the early modern world. Private legal practitioners in early modern Europe offer a more apt comparison to legal practice in early modern Japan. As in Europe, legal practitioners in Japan worked in the interstices of state and society; the *kujiyado*, or suit inn, occupied a gray zone between the two. In Europe, private legal practitioners did not overlap with providers of lodging as they did in Japan, but in both places, private legal practitioners often overlapped with officialdom. In France, the early modern notary enjoyed a grant from the state and served as a legal practitioner in the interest of property owners. In England, manorial stewards were "more ambiguous than local attorneys"—sometimes serving the interests of clients and sometimes acting in the interest of the local lord.[18] Even though the specific traditions out of which legal practice emerged differed in Europe and Japan, legal practitioners served similar functions. As William Bouwsma has put it, across the early modern world, legal practitioners shared in common their provision of assistance to clients "who were in trouble, feared trouble, sought the clarification of some ambiguous situation, or aimed to twist the social system in some novel and advantageous way."[19] They supported the commercial and financial transformations unfolding over the seventeenth and eighteenth centuries in London, Paris, Berlin, and Edo.

From the 1950s, the pioneering work of historian Takikawa Masajirō has suggested the transformative importance of the Edo-period legal practitioners on the juridical landscape.[20] His research describes an increasingly stable position for suit inns, particularly from the late eighteenth into the early nineteenth centuries. Other scholars have expanded on Takikawa's initial inquiry and revealed how Edo-era legal practitioners

---

17. Ravina, *Land and Lordship in Early Modern Japan*; discusses how Yonezawa domain cultivated samurai commercial activity.
18. Brooks, *Pettyfoggers and Vipers of the Commonwealth*, 45.
19. Bouwsma, "Lawyers and Early Modern Culture," 311.
20. Takikawa M., "Nihon bengoshishi zenshi kujiyado no kenkyū."

contributed to three processes that connected society and the state through legal resolutions of disputes. First, legal practitioners regularized commerce and created a demand for their services, both from clients and, later, from the shogunate. Over time, inns focusing on legal advice created a niche for themselves in castle towns and cities, as they addressed needs that the state would not.[21] Second, lobbying by the guilds for protection of their monopoly made the guilds themselves agents of political change. The suit inns won recognition from the state for their work on authorities' behalf.[22] Advocacy by the suit inns changed their occupation from a pursuit prohibited by the all levels of Edo-era government to one that performed key functions for judicial administrators. Finally, as argued here, legal practitioners schooled disgruntled village agriculturalists in the language of the state apparatus so that they might advance their concerns by legal means.

As legal practitioners established themselves, every level of society increasingly had access to the litigated resolution of private disputes. Though the Tokugawa regime frowned upon litigation of any kind, the growth of suit inns in urban centers expanded the authorities' capacity for mediating conflicts it neither wanted to resolve nor acknowledge. Official efforts to suppress threats to social harmony drove the emergence of the parallel tracks of legal practice: state-sanctioned suit inns (with their proprietors and employees) and nonsanctioned legal practitioners (such as *kujishi* and *deirishi*). Whereas the former served the shogunal domains and castle towns, receiving cases referred by magistrates, the latter practiced everywhere, in the shadows. As a result, the dissemination of legal knowledge was broader than the Tokugawa regime would have wanted to admit.

The emergence of legal practice that promoted the interests of villagers did not mean "evolution" or "development" toward the protection of legal rights, particularly a right to legal representation along European lines. Throughout the Edo period there was no such right. Shogunal edicts on lawsuits made no provision for legal representation.[23] In the aspirational ethic of Tokugawa Neo-Confucianism, disputes between individuals be-

---

21. Kukita, "Naisai to kujiyado," 322.

22. Minami, *Bakumatsu toshi shakai no kenkyū.*

23. Hall, "The Tokugawa Legislation, Part IV," 691–92 and Takayanaga and Ishii, eds., *Ofuregaki kanpō shūsei*, 1195, for prohibition of suit solicitors.

came public matters when they disturbed harmony, and the disruption of harmony made officials parties to the conflict. This meant that the authorities could physically punish parties (by caning, in particular) in ostensibly private, adversarial proceedings; as a consequence, there was always the potential for the arbitrary imposition of a penalty when a petitioner appeared before an Edo magistrate. Although suit solicitors, suit inns, and the related guilds did not create a right to legal representation, they did meliorate legal proceedings and, in the process, created a space of stability and continuity that persisted after the decline of Tokugawa rule.

In tandem with the refinement of the authorities' approach to litigation and the proliferation of commerce, suit inns had made litigation commonplace. Emerging in the mid-1600s, suit inns consolidated their position in the national capital from the first decade of the 1700s through the Kyōhō Reforms of the 1730s. While doing so, they successfully circumvented the authorities' predisposition against litigation and deflected pressure to resolve disputes through conciliation. They also undermined efforts to shroud the litigation process in secrecy. At the same time, suit inns capitalized on a proclivity among merchants to seek external resolution to such conflicts as those arising from defaulted payments or disputes over sales of rice futures.

The ready resort to litigation, even as the state encouraged conciliation, increased the prominence and presence of suit inns. In Edo, suit inns formed into guilds; by the end of the eighteenth century, four guilds coordinated with judicial bodies within the shogunate to issue summonses, supervise and hold litigants and the criminally accused, and provide fire protection. Guilds of suit inns used their proximity to political power to suppress competitors that arose at mid-eighteenth century, with partial success. In the meantime, both suit inns and their unsanctioned counterparts, suit solicitors, cultivated an awareness of the legal means for the resolution of private and public conflicts that arose in everyday life. As described below, this awareness was honed and amplified by a proliferating range of print matter, from poems to celebrations of samurai heraldry. At the heart of judicial administration of adversarial proceedings, samurai interpreted legal codes and applied these, at times arbitrarily, to disputes among their commoner inferiors. In the meantime, merchants and farmers understood that legal processes could be interpreted and applied to serve their interests as well.

Recognition of Legal Practice: Suit Inns and the Shogunate

The two main categories of legal matters during the Edo era, *deirisuji* and *ginmisuji*, suggest a rough equivalence to categories within the Anglo-European legal world: private disputes (adversarial or civil matters) and matters of public concern (criminal or inquisitorial matters). The category of *deirisuji* encompassed what would now be called a civil dispute, and *ginmisuji* covered what the modern state would call a criminal case. Yet Edo categories of *deiri-* and *ginmisuji* do not match contemporary methods of classification. The porous boundary between the two categories meant that the samurai administrators of justice during the Edo era could arbitrarily assign a matter to one category or the other. Magistrates and the recording officers who often stood in for them pressured parties to resolve conflicts through conciliation and not litigation by threatening to redefine an adversarial proceeding as an inquisitorial proceeding. Judicial administrators found statutes that could be used to criminalize a particularly nettlesome proceeding as leverage for forcing conciliation.

Samurai officials did this, for example, in an adversarial proceeding where one party in the case brought a claim against another party for defaulting on a loan. It turned out that the defaulter had forged a document in the dispute. Article 62 of the 100 edicts of the *Kujikata osadamegaki*, the comprehensive legal code enacted in 1742, stated: "Anyone who forges a document or a seal is to be led around for exposure, decapitated, and his head gibbeted."[24] In what was ultimately an unrealized threat, the magistrate in the case cautioned both parties to reconcile or face punishment.[25] The parties resolved their differences. As this example makes clear, Tokugawa statutes were notoriously severe. However, such severe punishments were not meted out as frequently as they might have been, not least because legal practitioners helped parties navigate their way to negotiated settlements or resolutions within the bounds of a system that encouraged mediation.

---

24. Hall, "The Tokugawa Legislation, Part IV," 759.

25. For the threat of decapitation, see Henderson, *Conciliation and Japanese Law*, vol. 1:149–50. On recording officers (*tomeyaku*) standing in for commissioners, see Henderson and also see "Shihō no koto (Hyōjōsho)" cited in Yoshimoto, ed., *Kyūji shimonroku*, 105–58.

Evidence shows that over the course of the eighteenth century, private legal practitioners operating out of suit inns became increasingly important to the resolution of commercial disputes. In this capacity, they achieved a measure of acceptability to the shogunate. Historians who have focused on the shogunate and domainal lords as the primary axes of power during the Edo era have explained the gradual move from suppression to recognition of suit inns as evidence of the diminishing ability of the authorities to enforce their aims. However, one need not focus on the power of the central state, a perpetual question in Edo history, to explain the gradual accommodation of private legal practice. Takikawa has convincingly demonstrated that it was not the rise and fall of Tokugawa authority but change outside of the state that drove the rise of private legal practice. "It became difficult for parties to lawsuits to represent themselves as society became increasingly complex. . . . by necessity this called forth experts in lawsuits."[26] The trend toward the increasing presence of private legal practitioners in judicial processes became all the more pronounced with an increase in lawsuits from the beginning of the eighteenth century. The story of the emergence of the state-sanctioned suit inn is one in which these inns overcame prohibitions on their practice to participate in the increasingly complex worlds of law and commerce. In the process, they carved out a space for political involvement and sought to edge out competitors—further evidence of a growing market for legal services.

The sale of legal services to parties in conflict was not new to the Edo era. Since the Kamakura period, a whole range of people—including itinerant monks and mountain ascetics—provided advice to those involved in private disputes. Before 1600, private manors and also religious sects occupied spheres of autonomy outside of central control, making them logical sites for the mediation of local conflict.[27] The consolidation and legalization of authority that marked the beginning of the Tokugawa regime meant an end to many forms of ecclesiastical and secular autonomy. This served the centralizing state in two ways: it dismantled the bases of power that had threatened earlier regimes in the form of combative

---

26. Takikawa M., "Edo shoki ni okeru kujishi kin'atsu," 20.
27. Kukita, "Naisai to kujiyado," 319–20.

monks, ecstatic prayer movements, and sites of support for warrior in-
surgents; it also limited religious roles and other avenues for intervention
in the settlement of disputes.

As part of its larger project of political centralization, officials in the
early-seventeenth-century Tokugawa shogunate prohibited the involvement of religious persons in commercial disputes and forbade monks
from leading chants invoking the benevolent intervention of the Amida
Buddha. Controlling compassionate Kannon did not eliminate conflict,
however, and other forms of legal practice that had emerged under the
Kamakura and Muromachi shogunates, including practitioners that
served within the manor system (*shōen*), continued. To meet the needs
previously met by itinerant monks, ascetics, and manor-system factotums,
some legal practitioners from earlier times recast themselves as suit solicitors or opened suit inns. The Kyoto inn Nijōjin'ya, which had previously
provided legal services as the Kasuga-sha in Nara, opened in the early
1600s.[28]

In other cities and castle towns, mercantile activity intensified over the
course of the seventeenth century. Social and economic complexity precipitated increasingly tangled legal cases, including various claims against
lost wages, money held in escrow, losses from currency speculation, and
disputes among villages such as contests over access to water—some disputes lasting decades and more. At the intersection of the private economy and shogunal authority, parties to disputes found lodging in state-
designated inns in the shogun's capital in the Bakurōchō and Kodenmachō
neighborhoods.[29] In the vernacular, Edo-ites called the inns "farmer
inns" (*hyakushō shuku*) while farmers identified them as "Edo inns" (*Edo
shuku*).[30] State-sanctioned legal practice had emerged. As part of the increasingly commercial Edo-era economy, private legal practitioners positioned themselves to profit, both as mediators of disputes and as merchants themselves.

---

28. Takikawa M., "Nihon bengoshishi sobyō," 20.

29. Aoki, "Kinsei minshū no seikatsu to teikō," 196.

30. The literature varies widely on terminology for Edo-era lodging. In discussing
inns in the capital, Minami Kazuo makes a distinction between inns for travelers in
general (litigants, pilgrims, tourists, and others) and inns for farmers. Minami, *Bakumatsu toshi shakai no kenkyū*.

Markets grew in sophistication and reach. During the eighteenth and nineteenth centuries, farmers increasingly supplemented their income with such by-employments as rope weaving and cash crops, and commercial networks connected cities and villages. As private enterprise expanded, it increasingly transcended the boundaries of geography and status and challenged an economic orthodoxy that denigrated merchants and their pursuits.[31] In the process, commercial activity confronted a multilayered administrative system that was, at times, indisposed and ill equipped to accommodate the challenges of increasing commerce. By the middle of the eighteenth century, the shogunate as arbiter of harmony faced increasingly complex social and economic relations. Even poets had something to say about the proliferation of legal conflict and legal practitioners in it. The *senryū* collection *Haifū yanagidaru* included an ode to litigiousness suggesting that Edo legal practitioners would "build a storehouse from the disputes of the denizens of Bakurōchō."[32] And, in fact, the inns' proprietors did become so wealthy that they built storehouses to hold their earnings. At the other end of the Tokaido, it was the storehouse of one of Kansai's leading private practitioners that yielded the records Takikawa would later mine to write a history of early modern litigation. And in Osaka, suit inns that served parties coming before the Osaka Castle Deputy built storehouses as a matter of course.[33] In addition to drafting documents and offering legal advice, Osaka suit inn operators brokered the sale of rice and dabbled in the commodities market. Analyst of Tokugawa law John Wigmore noted that by the nineteenth century the Tokugawa commercial system was "on a par with that of then contemporary Europe. . . . [It had developed b]ills of exchange and banks, the clearing house and the produce-exchange, the promissory note and the check, the insurance policy and the bill of lading, the chain-store and the trade-guild . . . the clearing-house check, and 'future' sales on the

---

31. See Hauser, *Economic Institutional Change in Tokugawa Japan*; Howell, *Capitalism from Within;* Toby, "Both a Borrower and a Lender Be"; Wigen, *The Making of a Japanese Periphery*;

32. Lawyer and Edo-era legal history enthusiast Haruhara Gentarō compiled a collection of law-related poems in *Senryū to hōritsu.*

33. Henderson, *Conciliation and Japanese Law,*1:168. See also Haruhara, *Osaka no machibugyōsho to saiban.*

rice exchange."[34] By the end of the eighteenth century, guilds of suit inns aided the shogun's judicial apparatus as it grappled with a sophisticated and increasingly complex economy.

Although suit inns were not of Tokugawa design, they shared the growing burden of legal administrative work borne by the regime. The authorities designated some 200 inns in Edo as lodging for visitors to the capital on all manner of official business. During the eighteenth and early nineteenth centuries roughly 100 inns among these operated in relationship to the shogunate's legal apparatus, the various offices of magistrates and commissions. The incorporation of suit inns in official processes reflected the increasing caseload of Tokugawa administrative bodies—the Temple and Shrine Commission (jisha bugyō), the Metropolitan Commission (machi bugyō), and the Finance Commission (kanjō bugyō). These three commissions were joined by the Conference Chamber (hyōjosho).[35] Councilors (rōju) and commissioners chosen from among the direct vassals of the shogun (hatamoto) and daimyo variously served on these bodies. The Temple and Shrine Commission was chaired by four daimyo. Responsibilities of the Metropolitan Commission included the administrative, judicial, police, and firefighting functions of the shogun's domain. Consistent with the reinvention of the samurai fighter as samurai administrator, high-level samurai and direct vassals of the shogun occupied the top positions in this Commission and the Finance Commission. Officials hearing legal cases were magistrates drawn from the upper ranks of direct shogunal vassals (those receiving an annual stipend of rice between

---

34. Wigmore, *A Panorama of the World's Legal Systems*, 481.

35. Less studied, other sites for the sale of legal services included the local castles and the Edo lodgings of the daimyo and the various offices of intendants and other officials that combined judicial and administrative functions. The Conference Chamber, the highest adjudicative body during the Edo period, heard disputes involving different domains, matters that transcended the jurisdiction of one of the three commissions, suits from daimyo, suits from the shogun's direct vassals, and any case that was important enough to necessitate its intervention. The chamber staff, which included eight commissioners, a member of the senior council, a senior inspector (ōmetsuke), and a regular inspector (metsuke), also responded to legal queries from the shogun and his councilors. Importantly, the chamber could, of its own accord, make, revise, interpret, or eliminate laws and took part in the major legal codification project of the Edo period—the compilation of the *Kujikata osadamegaki* legal codes, launched by Shogun Tokugawa Yoshimune as a part of the Kyōhō Reforms and completed in 1742.

3,000 to 10,000 *koku*).[36] The Finance Commission handled suits related to finance and tax matters within the Tokugawa domain.

Outside of the capital, suit inns served all of the judicial bodies of the shogunate. They opened in proximity to offices that combined administrative and judicial functions: the Kanto district deputy, the deputy governor of Kyoto, the deputy governor of Osaka Castle, the highway commission, and commissions in Fushimi, Kyoto, Nara, Osaka, Sakai, and the distant provinces (such as Nagasaki, Sado, and Hakodate). These were all offices and entities that adjudicated cases and issued legal rulings, at times in consultation with the three Commissions of Edo, the Conference Chamber, or the Senior Council.[37] Suit inns also opened in the vicinity of the shogun's mausoleum complex at Nikkō.[38] A growing body of scholarship on suit inns that practiced at many sites of shogunal authority has begun filling out the picture of numbers of suit inns and their activities, including the six inns at Nikkō, yet this work has only begun to sketch the full scope of Edo-era private legal practice, let alone the scope of suit inns connected to the shogunate.[39]

Consistent with what it identified as a Confucian understanding of lawsuits as a sign of insufficient social harmony, the shogunate discouraged litigated resolution of private conflict. First, the state mandated that parties attempt to resolve their differences among themselves at the local level. Article 1 of the *Kujikata* stated, "Let the village headmen (*nanushi*) and the house-heads (*ienushi*) and the . . . five-family group (*goningumi*) of both parties come together and settle the matter in dispute."[40] For some parties, this encounter was little more than a first step toward litigation.

---

36. After 1721, the shogunate severed the finance and tax functions from dispute resolution in this office, alternating commissioners annually between each function. The number of commissioners varied over time, never exceeding three, with commissioners alternating between a northern and a southern office. Wigmore, *Law and Justice in Tokugawa Japan*, 57.

37. Henderson, *Conciliation and Japanese Law*, 1:81.

38. Takesue, *Nikkō no shihō*.

39. Beyond the 100 or so inns in Edo, there is not yet a comprehensive picture of the numbers of suit inns and suit solicitors throughout the domains and in all of the shogunal offices. For an example of recent scholarship on the suit inns outside of the three major cities, see Takesue, *Nikkō no shihō*.

40. Hall, "The Tokugawa Legislation, Part IV," 692.

When mediation failed, farmers, artisans, and merchants traveled to castle towns and if that failed, on to the great cities of Edo, Osaka, and Kyoto to petition domainal or shogunal officials. To have a case heard, parties to a dispute submitted multiple copies of petitions to a commission.[41] This was not merely the filing of papers. Hearing a matter was a privilege granted by the authorities; thus, submissions required the provision of a rationale for why the state should take up a matter.[42] There were multiple means of petitioning, ranging from the legitimate to the illegal. The proper method was to submit paperwork through the village headman, who then dealt with the matter or forwarded it to higher officials. Before a body heard a suit, the recording officer evaluated the petition: Was it submitted to the correct authority? Did the local authorities confirm that the parties had attempted conciliation? If the case crossed the boundaries of different fiefs, had the relevant bannermen and lords applied their seals?[43] There were conflicts that, in principle, the magistrates preferred not to review, such as disputes from within families, among "non-persons," or from commercial guilds.[44] These required particularly persuasive justification to be heard. A suit solicitor or suit inn was instrumental in the proper drafting of documents at this stage; if a petition for a hearing was not in order, it faced summary rejection.

Though the government began to accommodate petitions, the shogunate feared that knowledge of the law by common people would encourage litigiousness and therefore undermine the harmony on which the shogunate predicated its existence. Thus, it made the litigation process as difficult as possible. Having cleared the hurdle of petitioning, a non-samurai entered a world that drove home one's modest place within the

---

41. For an account of Edo-period procedure for adversarial matters, see Henderson, *Conciliation and Japanese Law*; Kobayakawa, "Kinsei minji saiban tetsuzuki ni okeru 'kuji.'" See also Sonoo, *Minji soshō, shikkō, hasan no kin-gendaishi*.

42. Ōhira, "Kinsei Nihon no sojō."

43. Henderson, "'Contracts' in Tokugawa Villages," 69.

44. On resolution of disputes among *hinin*, see Tsukada, "Danzaemon shihai to shinchō yado." In principle, the state would not adjudicate conflicts within a guild or mutual enterprise (*nakamagoto*); involving theater operators, brothels, and disputes between daimyo and samurai; or between parent and child—although, at times, it did entertain such disputes by request or of its own choosing. Kobayakawa, *Kinsei minji soshō seido no kenkyū*, 20–21.

Tokugawa status hierarchy. Litigating an adversarial matter meant an encounter with extreme formality. When appearing before a magistrate, commoners and townspeople—farmers, artisans, and merchants—kneeled in an enclosed courtyard. The samurai authorities occupied vantage points above the commoner on platforms that reflected official rank.[45] On hierarchically arrayed platforms, they rustled about like birds of prey in the high-shouldered, formal garb of *haori* and *hakama*. At the center of the walled courtyard was a field of white gravel (*shirasu*). In the minds of the architects of this particular site of adjudication, the white gravel symbolized the "strength and fairness" of the judicial administrators.[46] This was a place that was not to be sullied. One widespread story recounted how a father who accused his pregnant daughter of being unfilial received his comeuppance. He petitioned the magistrates to interrogate his daughter, despite the Tokugawa disavowal of involvement in family matters. While being questioned, his daughter gave birth, turning the white *shirasu* red. The magistrate required the father to replace the gravel at great cost.[47] This story revealed the awesomeness of state power; an appearance before an adjudicative body of the Tokugawa needed to be undertaken with great foreboding.

In this environment, the Tokugawa encouraged mediation and set limits on the filing of suits as a response to persistent demands for adjudication of private conflicts. To render litigation difficult, the Tokugawa shrouded its legal processes behind figurative as well as literal walls. In addition to general prohibitions on the discussion of shogunal statecraft, commentary on and interpretation of law were prohibited.

Yet the story of the sullied *shirasu* had another lesson: with insistence, the intrepid could have their cases heard. There remained those who

---

45. "On the first and second platforms sat the *gokenin* or lower samurai; according [to] whether their office was for life only or was inheritable; on the third, the . . . *hatamoto* [bannermen]. This rule obtained when these persons appeared as witnesses or otherwise. Where higher nobles were involved, the trial was conducted" on the highest platform behind sliding doors. Wigmore, *Law and Justice in Tokugawa Japan*, 1:54–56. As for masterless samurai (*rōnin*), they were required to kneel in the gravel. Haruhara, *Osaka no machibugyōsho to saiban*, 35.

46. Haruhara, *Osaka no machibugyōsho to saiban*, 35–36.

47. This is an oft-repeated story from the *Enseki jisshū*, recounted in ibid., 36–37. See also Kobayakawa, *Kinsei minji soshō seido no kenkyū*, 20–21.

insisted on a hearing and who pressed for a litigated solution even in the face of shogunal commands that they resolve conflict among themselves through mutual settlement (*aitai sumashi*). Episodically, since the mid-seventeenth century, the shogun had suspended hearings of unsecured money suits (*kanekuji*), requiring parties to resolve them without official involvement. In 1719, with the number of money suits exploding, Shogun Tokugawa Yoshimune commanded mediated resolutions for all such disputes. Although the order stood for a decade, enforcement was uneven. Litigants continued to reject the conciliatory process that was encouraged and at times commanded by the authorities. When they did so, they faced the possibility of being "instructed" by the state that their disputes had overstepped the bounds of what was conscionable and had thus threatened social stability.[48] For example, magistrates might threaten parties in disputes over loans unsecured by property with capital punishment or less severe punishments, such as caning.[49] Henderson described the goal of setting limits on lawsuits as an exercise in "didactic conciliation," in which officials encouraged mediated (*naisai*) rather than litigated outcomes. The preference for didactic conciliation reflected both the shogunal disinclination to hear suits on ideological grounds and, along with it, a limited systemic capacity to hear and resolve litigated conflict. The key point was that the "didact" was the state. The subject received instruction in social propriety, not law. Thus, didactic conciliation was an act of the ruler disciplining the subject.

From the perspective of the shogunate, subjects needed to know only enough of the law to follow it. Yet what was to be known shifted over time, and by the turn of the eighteenth century was not apparent to the shogunate himself. Various branches of the shogun's justice administration seldom communicated with one another and seldom spoke in one voice, with magistrates at each site of justice administration collecting rulings into multiple and sometimes competing bodies of precedent. By the end of the 1600s, the individual records of various magistrates required internal harmonization. A drive to synthesize the rulings by magistrates shaped

---

48. Henderson, "'Contracts' in Tokugawa Villages."

49. Takikawa M., "Nihon bengoshishi zenshi kujiyado no kenkyū." See also Henderson, *Conciliation and Japanese Law*, and Upham, "Weak Legal Consciousness as Invented Tradition." On caning (or "flogging"), see Botsman, *Punishment and Power*.

the project of legal codification launched by Yoshimune.[50] Once consolidated, the *Kujikata osadamegaki*, rules written by and for Tokugawa magistrates, transformed the law into a kind of state secret. Although the *Kujikata* offered a comprehensive vision of law and legal procedure, its circulation was limited; the document itself included a colophon that read "For Magistrates Only."[51] Even though the second volume of the *Kujikata* may have ultimately been circulated more widely than originally conceived, the aim of secrecy emerged out of a tradition in which each individual magistrate's rulings were kept under seal.[52] In addition to substantive legal text, process was also concealed from potential litigants. Magistrates adjudicated matters behind large gates and the long walls of government buildings. Proceedings were closed. Rulings were not publicized. Regulations forbade "instruction in law."[53] Reproduction of shogunal laws without permission was a crime. As late as 1841, the shogunate banned the sale of two books for inclusion of legal texts.[54] The regime promulgated rules; the people should follow them.

Even with punishment for those who produced law-related texts, concealment of legal ideas and exegesis was more an ideal than practice. Legal practitioners made the interpretation of legal principles and texts their métier, and as legal historian Dietrich Rueschmeyer has noted, legal practice constituted "all specialized work that require[d] knowledge of the 'language of the state' as John Austin called the law."[55] Lay people listened to this language as well. If law was the language of the state, the shogunate communicated to its subjects regularly. As early as 1642, the shogunate dictated the legal terms of everyday life through postings on notice boards, called tall signs (*kōsatsu*).[56] These boards were omnipresent. More kiosk than simple sign, their physical structure telegraphed the authority of officialdom. The most prominent examples, constructed in places at the symbolic center of shogunal authority such as the Nihonbashi

50. Henderson, "Promulgation of Tokugawa Statutes," 10–12.
51. Takahashi S., *Edo no soshō*, 75.
52. Hiramatsu, "Tokugawa Law," 15.
53. Takayanagi and Ishii, eds., *Ofuregaki kanpō shūsei*, 1196.
54. Kornicki, *The Book in Japan*, 345.
55. Rueschmeyer, "Comparing Legal Professions Cross-Nationally," 426.
56. Dore, *Education in Tokugawa Japan*, 231.

bridge, rose from elaborate stone pedestals worthy of a castle foundation, with large notice boards hovering beneath a tiled roof. In the capital alone, there were 6 major signs and 35 lesser signs. Notice boards also appeared in castle towns and at post stations along major highways; they announced edicts, regulations, domainal transfers, and appointments of officials. Edo-era poets satirized the signs, jesting, "The notice boards are read by eyes and alongside read by ears as well" (*Kōsatsu wa me de miru soba de, mimi de miru*). The joke here arises from the existence of two kinds of readers: Henderson suggests that there were those who feigned literacy by reading with their eyes, while others flaunted literacy by reading aloud.[57]

The awesome exercise of shogunal authority also intruded on everyday life, providing the nonliterate many opportunities to bear witness to the criminal justice system. Public parades humiliated and shamed convicts for their crimes; severed heads on poles reminded subjects of the dangers of lawlessness.[58] More prosaically, authorities communicated through boards or sheets of paper (*kabegaki*) posted outside of the office of the village headman. At the local level, villages constituted themselves through compacts that established basic, written rules of conduct and social order.[59] And subjects took it upon themselves to read what they could about the law and legal processes. As noted below, while litigants lodged at a suit inn, the inn served as something of a legal reading room, with village headmen who were parties to disputes reading all kinds of texts, including purloined copies of laws, stories of petitioner-martyrs, and accounts of magistrates.

Systems of legal control and order, in part, created the conditions for economic growth that belied the Neo-Confucian rationale for Tokugawa claims to authority. The legal orthodoxy of an absence of conflict did not take into account the possibilities of a vibrant commercial economy and the disputes that would accompany it, particularly in urban centers. Merchants had their own approach to law. Edo merchant houses commonly inscribed their social visions in house codes (sets of injunctions for employees and heirs). As early as 1627, decades before the emergence of state-

---

57. Henderson, "Promulgation of Tokugawa Statutes," 19–23.
58. Botsman, *Punishment and Power*.
59. Henderson, " 'Contracts' in Tokugawa Villages."

sanctioned suit inns, an early instructional text for townsmen reflected a sensibility grounded in litigiousness. The Chōjakyō listed proclivities that would lead to commercial success; the first on a list of ten instructed merchants to "be inclined toward lawsuits."[60] By the late seventeenth and early eighteenth centuries, a Neo-Confucian tradition scornful of profit applied even less. Perhaps protesting too much, merchant codes also encouraged obedience to laws. "Respect the various laws," enjoined the first article of the 1670 code of the Shiragiya dry-goods house.[61] A Genroku-period (1688–1703) code from a branch of the Mitsui house called for "strict adherence to laws."[62] Following the dictates of their martial betters, merchants pledged to be law abiding even as they increasingly engaged in litigation.

Commerce not only increased, it also became more multiform. The emergence of a futures market in rice at Dōjima in Osaka meant the appearance of financial transactions that had little historical precedent.[63] This market tied regional economies to a national commercial center. It also shaped the sale of rice, a commodity so central to Tokugawa authority that it was the measure of domainal power and the basis for calculating the stipends of samurai. The Conference Chamber and other adjudicative bodies weighed in on the changing commercial environment, refining their definition of main suits (*honkuji*) during the middle of the eighteenth century; these were the suits secured by property that the state was more inclined to hear. Suits arising from land pledges, sharecropping agreements, the sale of rice futures, and nonpayment of money held in escrow topped the revised list of main suits. The state was less inclined to hear money suits (*kanekuji*), but gave precedent to money suits that included claims for "money due on goods sold, return of dowry, [and] return of earnest money."[64] Commercial complexity and the gradual refinement of the legal conflicts that the state would entertain opened up

---

60. "Chōjakyō" cited in Nakamura Y., ed., *Kinsei chōnin shisō*, 14.

61. Yoshida, ed., *Shōka no kakun*, 148.

62. Undated code, ibid., 90.

63. On Osaka as a commercial center, see Hauser, *Economic Institutional Change in Tokugawa Japan*; McClain and Wakita, ed., *Osaka*; Schaede, "Forwards and Futures in Tokugawa-period Japan"; and Haruhara, "Kinsei Ōsaka no senso, koso, dōjitsunegai."

64. Henderson, "'Contracts' in Tokugawa Villages," 73–75.

opportunities for suit inns to read the system in ways advantageous to their clients. The suit inn could aid in classifying a matter so that it would pass muster with the recording officers (*tomeyaku*) and be heard.

From the perspective of the shogunate, the suit inns addressed a distasteful but undeniable need. Even though the shogunate abhorred conflicts engendered by commerce, suit inns responded to the inevitable financial disputes that arose. In Edo, lodgings for litigants sprang up in Bakurōchō, an area that had historically been dominated by horse traders and Buddhist temples. As early as the 1640s, a small group of around thirteen inns had formed to serve the needs of litigants in the capital.[65] Around the time of the 1657 Meireki fire, the office of the Kanto district deputy (*daikan*) moved to this area; the deputy was charged with administering Tokugawa lands. As a result, the number of petitioners visiting Bakurōchō increased.[66] Inns also opened in areas previously populated by horse traders, such as Kodenmachō.

Suit inns flourished in the three major cities in particular. In Osaka, the suit inns were less expensive than inns for pilgrims or other travelers.[67] In contrast, the Edo inns parlayed their proximity to the three commissions and the Conference Chamber into monopolies that guaranteed high prices. By 1699, inns for travelers (*tabininshuku*) formed a guild in order to room petitioners to the town commissioners. Inns in the areas of Bakurōchō and Kodenmachō joined to form the Travelers Inn Guild.

Literacy was the core skill of the suit inns, with proprietors feeding a document-hungry officialdom. Suit inns drafted multiple documents for petitioners—including the petition itself, receipts, notices to the adjudicating body (e.g., regarding efforts at conciliation), reports of failure of conciliation, final conciliation agreements, and corrected documents—as required by the magistrate or commission. The deputy required two copies of a petition, and charges for these documents ranged from 200 to 300 *mon,* depending on the complexity of the matter in the filing.[68] Inquisitorial proceedings also required documents from those summoned.

---

65. Minami, *Bakumatsu toshi shakai no kenkyū*, 176–77.
66. The above draws on Kukita, "Naisai to kujiyado."
67. Haruhara, *Osaka no machibugyōōsho to saiban*, 46.
68. Minami, *Bakumatsu toshi shakai no kenkyū*, 180.

These included notifications to daimyo and the relevant magistrate of arrival in the capital, reports on matters at hand, requests for extensions of a proceeding, and requests for members of a party to return to a village. Producing the documents necessary for a case could be expensive, even with fees for documents fixed by the authorities. Suit inns charged other fees, including ink surcharges, honoraria, board, and, of course, lodging. At times proceedings lasted for months, sometimes prolonged by the proprietors of the suit inns themselves who were dilatory in processing and submitting documents or issuing summonses. Prolonging the resolution of a suit was one way that suit inns profited despite set fees on documents. Even as contemporary observers disparaged suit inns for prolonging proceedings for profit, the overburdened commissions also contributed by making lawsuits protracted affairs.

With its legal apparatus choking on forms and filings, and a century after his forebears articulated the legal relationship between the state and society, Tokugawa Yoshimune launched the Kyōhō Reforms of 1716–1744. The reforms marked a reexamination of governance in part called into question by a rising tide of litigation. In 1720, Yoshimune personally observed fifteen matters adjudicated by the three commissions of Edo. Built on Yoshimune's empirical observations of the legal process, legal reforms began with the establishment of a petition box through which the aggrieved might anonymously seek redress of wrongs (1721). The petition box opened a channel for direct communication between merchants or farmers and their samurai betters, but at best, it promised to increase, not diminish, petitions finding their way to shogunal authorities. Likewise, the compilation of a comprehensive code, the *Kujikata osadamegaki*, which has dominated accounts of the Kyōhō Reforms, really had little to say about reducing the causes of legal conflict. With its emphasis on procedure and punishment, the *Kujikata* focused more on public matters than burgeoning private disputes.

Thus, the reforms did little to stem the tide of litigation. Despite regulations encouraging conciliation or resolution of disputes, the number of petitions to shogunal administrative and judicial bodies mounted.[69] Buyō Inshi noted that during the tranquility of the early 1600s Itakura

---

69. Sone, "Kyōhōki no soshō saibanken to uttae."

Katsushige, Kyoto's first deputy governor, prepared tea while listening to lawsuits. That era was long gone.[70] The early 1700s brought a backlog of cases involving defaulted loans due to shogunal orders that conflict be resolved mutually (*aitai sumashirei*). Yet coerced conciliation flagged as petitioners pursued litigated solutions to their claims. In 1754, the Kyoto magistrates heard disputes nine days a month, at times hearing 60 cases a day.[71] An increasing number of cases met an ill-equipped bureaucracy. In 1808, parties arriving for a review of their petition by the Finance Commission encountered such a large crowd that there was no space in the waiting room. The many people driven outside "suffered in the cold and rain."[72] In 1828, on a day when the Conference Chamber heard cases, a crowd of petitioners pressed up against the gates. "There were many litigants in the waiting area [*koshikake*], many outside . . . from early morning [around 7 A.M.] nearly 300 had gathered."[73] Officials found this spectacle troubling in light of exhortations of Confucian harmony. Third parties—including commercial guilds, conferences of village elders, and informal conciliators—eased the burden, but parties to disputes still sought state-sanctioned resolution to their conflicts.

In part, the communitarian nature of shogunal legal processes invited a crowd. When petitioners finally came before the Edo judicial apparatus, they did not necessarily do so alone. Depending on the situation, a range of others from family members to village headmen might also speak to the authorities in one's stead. During the earliest years of Edo-era conflict resolution, magistrates permitted and at times required that a head of house be present during a proceeding. Alternately, a commission might summon a village headman or another august person from the community to speak for the disputant. This member of the village elite came before the commission in a range of capacities identified as *sashizoenin*, *tsukizoe*, or *kaizoe*. This auxiliary party might answer whether or not the disputants had first endeavored to resolve the dispute at the local level. The *sashizoenin* might also speak to the veracity of the petitioner's account

---

70. Buyō, "Seji Kenmonroku," 695.
71. Usami, "Kinsei Kyoto no aitai sumashirei," 178–79.
72. Nakada, *Hōseishi ronshū*, 760.
73. Ibid., 814.

and the petitioner's character.[74] Even though heads of house and community members at times spoke for petitioners, they did not necessarily serve as advocates. In contrast to a legal advocate, who would have focused on the applicable rules in a case or interpreted facts to a party's benefit, the testimony of the *sashizoenin* or *kaizoenin* served a kind of oral notarial function. Even so, it was possible for the testimony of a *sashizoenin* or *kaizoenin* to shade into advocacy for a petitioner.

As petitioners sought dedicated advocates, suit inn proprietors, senior clerks, and even freelance suit solicitors insinuated themselves into the litigation process over the course of the eighteenth century by exploiting the ambiguous roles of parties in a Tokugawa proceeding.[75] In addition to the *sashizoenin* or *kaizoenin*, who was known to the petitioner, impersonal representation became an increasing possibility. Such representation was significant when the interest of an injured party contradicted community aims, as in the case of Ken who took on village authorities, below. In part, suit inns and suit solicitors made representation possible by exploiting loopholes. For petitioners who were in suit inns in the capital, the proprietors of those inns had shogunal approval to identify themselves as the litigant's "head of house." This meant that the suit inn proprietor could appear before magistrates and vouch for the litigant.[76] For a time, suit inn solicitors and even freelance suit solicitors exploited the authorities' lax regulation of representation, posing as close relatives or village officials. However, magistrates episodically quashed this brazen move by suit solicitors.[77] Suit solicitors were ingenious, also resorting to another loophole that allowed ill litigants to send a representative in their stead.[78] Yet the commissions clamped down on this in the early nineteenth century, requiring ill persons to be brought before the magistrate in a palanquin.[79] In short, justice was not so blind that it could not see the legal advice parties received both from suit inns and suit solicitors. In

---

74. Minami, *Bakumatsu toshi shakai no kenkyū*, 183. See also Wigmore, *Law and Justice in Tokugawa Japan*, 1:56.

75. Minami, *Bakumatsu toshi shakai no kenkyū*, 188.

76. Takikawa M., *Kuijishi, kujiyado no kenkyū*, 110. See also Henderson, *Conciliation and Japanese Law*, 1:167.

77. Henderson, *Conciliation and Japanese Law*, 1:145.

78. Takikawa M., *Kuijishi, kujiyado no kenkyū*, 113.

79. Henderson, *Conciliation and Japanese Law*, 1:145.

fact, magistrates enforced distinctions between suit solicitors and their state-sanctioned counterparts—the proprietors of suit inns—by suppressing upstart competitors ranging from teahouses to inns. By the final decades of the Tokugawa era, the proprietors of state-sanctioned suit inns were allowed to come before magistrates; freelance suit solicitors were not.[80] To control and monitor trends in legal representation, the guilds of suit inns brought lawsuits that drove the authorities to make the freelance legal practitioner beyond the pale.

The gradual easing that allowed suit inn proprietors and staff members to come before magistrates was more than an oversight. Social and economic conditions had eroded an orientation ill disposed to the litigated resolution of conflict. The suit inn's translation of the complexities of a commercial or real estate dispute into an accepted legal vernacular benefited the authorities. Gradually it dawned on officials that private legal practitioners could serve the state in a number of capacities, a realization expressed in allowances for suit inn representation of clients. From 1790, the town magistrate of Edo permitted the proprietors of suit inns and their assistants to stand beside parties during proceedings.[81] At the same time, the Tokugawa officially removed the requirement that a party to a matter be accompanied by a local village leader or the head of the local five-family group (*goningumi*), the collectivity that policed family affairs, assured tax payments, and resolved low-level conflicts.[82] This marked a turning point in the handling of disputes. From the perspective of the state, the local community was the first site in which disputes were to be resolved. By removing the requirement that a local official accompany a party to a private dispute, the authorities allowed the petitioner to take a step away from the early modern collectivity. This was a step toward social individualization, a step abetted by the suit inn. It was also a step that the judicial administration increasingly condoned as it allowed the presence of suit inn staff to appear before magistrates.[83] The

---

80. Ushiomi, ed., *Nihon no bengoshi*, 2.

81. Minami, *Bakumatsu toshi shakai no kenkyū*, 180–81.

82. Ibid. As for the *goningumi*, the initial aim of the five-family group was to control Christians and enforce collective responsibility in matters of tax collection and maintenance of order.

83. Ibid., 183.

oral history of one of the last town magistrates of Edo, Yamaguchi Na-oki, revealed an overworked and understaffed bureaucrat seeking all measures and methods that would lighten his load. Yamaguchi remi-nisced how as a town magistrate he would hand off complex and seem-ingly intractable litigation, the "great many suits that would pile up on a rectangular tray," to his most accomplished underlings.[84] Such an envi-ronment opened the door for legal practitioners who clarified complex matters for officials. Minami Kazuo has found that "[i]n the case of the various government offices such as the Finance Commission, the Temple and Shrine Commission, and the Metropolitan Commission, the propri-etor of the suit inns or a representative would invariably accompany the party."[85] Then the proprietor of a suit inn might sit behind a client during a proceeding and ask, during a particularly heated exchange, for a contin-uance if things were not going the client's way.[86] In effect, the representa-tive from the *kujiyado* increasingly displaced the old, *gemein* relations that valued hereditary authority and status.

The spread of suit inns beyond Bakurōchō and Kodenmachō paral-leled reorganization of the offices of the Tokugawa judicial administra-tion. Beginning in the mid-eighteenth century, suit inns spread to other administrative offices beyond the commissions and the Conference Chamber. By the end of the eighteenth century, the southern office of the Finance Commission had settled in Sukiyabashi and the northern office was located in Gofukubashi, with each counting more than 100 samurai officials on its staff. (It is important to note that no evidence suggests that samurai provided paid legal advice to litigants.) Newer inns opened in Kōjimachi, Yotsuya, and Asakusa. By the 1760s and 1770s, like the travelers inns before them, they began to form guilds. The largest among them was the 82-Inn Group, which received recognition as a guild in 1770 and operated in the area of the Finance Commission and the Con-ference Chamber. (Its total membership numbered around 80 through the middle of the nineteenth century; inns specializing in lawsuits con-stituted a subset of the total.)[87] Inns formed into guilds in order to control

---

84. Beerens, "Interview with a Bakumatsu Official," 177.
85. Ibid., 181.
86. Henderson, *Conciliation and Japanese Law*, 1:152.
87. Minami, *Bakumatsu toshi shakai no kenkyū*, 172–73.

competition in the face of increasing demand. The number of suits heard at the contentious turn of the nineteenth century was "ten times more than during the Genroku (1688-1704) and Kyōhō (1716-1736) eras."[88] By 1800, the suit inn was a prominent and accepted feature on the Tokugawa juridical landscape.

In part, the import of the suit inns in history rests on what came later—capitalism and the legal state. Though Edo processes of capitalization did not directly track various European experiences, if one generalizes about the Edo-era economy at the national level, then innovation characterized the seventeenth century. The situation had changed by the mid-eighteenth century, when established interests sought to defend their economic advantage from upstarts, whether they were carters and haulers in the Iida Valley, rice brokers in Osaka, or guilds of suit inns in Edo. Strategies for defense included many measures; among them, litigation. Stability and consolidation became the hallmarks of the eighteenth century. Stability was not stasis. Economic transformation continued into the nineteenth century, on the foundation of the processes begun during the eighteenth. In his study of protest and politics in Shōnai, *Deference and Defiance in Nineteenth Century Japan*, William Kelly has highlighted how "the 19th century in Japan marked the transition from a mercantile economy and tributary polity to a capitalist economy and constitutional polity."[89] The legal work of the suit solicitor and his legal-advocate successor were at the core of both processes.

In 1965, Henderson noted that "historians have failed to distinguish between [state-sanctioned legal practice] and *kujishi* [suit solicitors], and therefore they have tended to overlook this legitimate element of the modern lawyer's forebears in Japan."[90] At the same time, caution is necessary in highlighting Henderson's comment and Weber's earlier observation that, by interpreting law both for the state and for the public, private legal practice drove the process of capital formation. This history of the suit inn was not a prolegomenon to a narrative of the triumphal ascent of Japanese legal practice. At the same time, a reading of

---

88. Buyō, "Seji kenmonroku," 695.
89. Kelly, *Deference and Defiance in Nineteenth Century Japan*, 8.
90. Henderson, *Conciliation and Japanese Law*, 1:169.

Japanese legal tradition as being in some ways inferior to European tradition also requires reconsideration. Private legal practitioners across the early modern world negotiated positions of ambiguity with the state, clients, and competitors. As the next section shows, suit inns used their place at the intersection of commerce and bureaucracy to promote their and their clients' interests. There is no record of suit inns promoting a vision of the greater good. Even so, their mere presence in the face of state antipathy toward private legal practice points to myriad possibilities. In the first instance, suit inns used their position at the intersection of market and state to establish their own legal practice and to suppress competition.

Guilds: The Protection of Monopolies and the Practice of Politics

That inns lodging parties to disputes formed guilds is not remarkable. Tokugawa officials condoned and even promoted all manner of guilds across a variety of sectors for "controlling trade" or "policing purposes."[91] Membership in a guild amounted to a license to produce a product or service in a field. Responding to officialdom's disinclination to adjudicate disputes among members of guilds, the guilds also arrogated to themselves the responsibility for resolving business disputes among members. Okazaki Tetsuji argues that the centrality of guilds in early modern Japanese dispute resolution explains, in part, a shift away from the shogunate as the font of justice in certain kinds of private matters.[92] Thus, many disputes between merchants found resolution in spheres outside of shogunal control. Nevertheless, other disputants remained focused on officialdom as the final arbiter of conflict, including the guilds of suit inns themselves.[93] To control the market while responding to demand, suit inns organized guilds while moving closer and closer to the shogunate in the quest for protection of their monopolies. In return, they provided the state with various services. In 1699, the suit inns among the inns of travelers emerged to lobby for their own political and market interests; by 1770 they were joined by three other guilds of suit inns that competed with

---

91. Maeda M., "Japanese Popular Association Law."
92. Okazaki, *Edo no shijō keizai.*
93. See Minami, *Bakumatsu toshi shakai no kenkyū.*

one another for market share and influence. Later, guilds of suit inns competed with the teahouses that threatened their monopolies on lodging and legal advice. In competing, the guilds emphasized their support of the shogunate's judicial structures including the firefighting services they provided to the commissions, the holding of parties in custody, and the service of summonses for the magistrates. At the same time, their members translated increasingly complex commercial disputes into officialdom's language of law. Tokugawa-era guilds and associations in general had a history of defining their legitimate scope of activities quite broadly. The guilds in Edo were no exception; in addition to attending to the needs of their clients, they fought for protection of their lucrative monopoly in Edo. As providers of lodging, they profited from a litigant's presence whether the party's legal claim was a success or a failure.[94] In the highly regulated lodging market in Edo, the inns sought to monopolize the rooming of parties to disputes in the capital.

The context in which inns operated changed over time. Suit inns were a subset of lodgings in urban centers that catered to litigants, pilgrims, and the general traveler. In Edo, suit inns constituted nearly half of all licensed inns (about 100 out of 200). By 1699, a group of suit inns in the capital had formed the Travelers Inn Guild. From the 1770s, this guild competed with three other guilds—the 30-Inn Group, the 82-Inn Group, and the 13-Inn Group—for clients. Meanwhile, unsanctioned, upstart inns and also teahouses that offered legal advice entered the legal lodging business themselves. In response, the guilds made their services indispensable to the commissions and magistrates with which they worked. As collectives, the guilds promoted their members' interests and by the nineteenth century had become agents of political change. Advocacy by suit inns on behalf of themselves was an antecedent of the opening up of space for political action that proceeded in the late nineteenth century.

Like many Edo-era institutions, suit inns were fundamentally conservative. Yet inadvertently, as they promoted member interests, they contributed to processes of gradual change that altered the conditions in which they operated and created possibilities for the future. The position

---

94. Minami, "Edo no kujiyado," 68–79.

of head of household in a suit inn was inherited. Once suit inns and their proprietors had established profitable practices, they sought to protect their hereditary prerogatives. With government-set fees for lodging at a suit inn, the suit inn business initially proved highly remunerative.[95] Yet currency fluctuations and vagaries of the economy meant that these fixed fees did not hold their value over time. In particular, suit inn proprietors faced changing conditions in the arena of legal practice—namely, encroachments on their cartel—which proved inimical to their accumulation of profit. As a consequence, the guilds themselves began to negotiate and advocate on their own behalf, using increasingly established connections with the judicial apparatus of the shogunate.[96] These negotiations focused on the guilds' relationship to legal officialdom, resolving conflict around matters of competition among the guilds and among newly emergent competitors such as teahouses and unofficial inns.

Competition arose from a process of petitioning and pleading that produced new markets for client services. In addition to room and board at a suit inn, parties to disputes found that there were other points in the litigation process in which they might benefit from assistance or even diversion. A person summoned to appear before a commission waited to be called in an exterior courtyard, a small outbuilding, or an anteroom (*tamari* or *koshikake*).[97] Parties to a dispute or petitioners would arrive and submit their names and their cases to a bailiff at the gate or door. Then they would wait. Even if the body with which they had business required them to appear early in the morning, it was common for parties to wait hours, if not days. When the case came up, a bailiff would call the names of the persons or village(s) involved. As early as the seventeenth century, enterprising merchants responded by opening stands outside the offices selling tea, food, stationery, and even sake to waiting petitioners and litigants.

The fluid environment around the magistracies encouraged the growth of unofficial legal practice that then competed with the suit inns. Gradually, eating and drinking establishments added the drafting of documents and the selling of advice to their offerings of food and drink. By

---

95. Ibid., 326.
96. Minami, *Bakumatsu toshi shakai no kenkyū*, 171–72.
97. Kukita, "Naisai to kujiyado," 327.

the turn of the eighteenth century, ten or so sweets shops and other stores converted to lodgings for plaintiffs. Former suit inn assistants were also drawn to the prospect of establishing teahouses selling legal advice, as was the case with the opening of the Kakegakeai Teahouse (懸懸合茶屋) in a backstreet of Bakurōchō.[98] Teahouses and other establishments entertained parties to conflicts and offered to aid in the resolution of their disputes. In response to this and other entrepreneurial ventures, suit inn proprietors joined state officials in lamenting the unregulated servicing of petitioners. In 1735, the Travelers Inn Guild appealed to the Metropolitan Commissioner Ōoka Echizen to prohibit neighborhood teahouses and noodle shops in Asakusa, Ueno, and Kanda from providing overnight accommodations to parties to lawsuits in Edo.[99] In response, Ōoka issued an injunction on teahouses as lodgings, setting fines for those who broke the injunction. When the guild or its members discovered other enterprises selling legal services or establishments lodging litigants, they would inform the authorities, and the authorities would then punish the offenders.[100] If recurrent objections were any indication, the measure was ineffective; the guilds continued calls for suppression in 1740.

Despite the occasional crackdowns, the demand for cheaper lodgings by petitioners prompted teahouses and other establishments to serve as inns. Yet teahouses did not only compete in the provision of lodging; they, too, became part of the dispute resolution process in other ways. Parties to disputes might meet at a teahouse in advance of their scheduled appearance before the authorities. The teahouse proprietor would then serve as a neutral mediator. There is no record of how many parties settled their differences in a teahouse or an eatery outside the Conference Chamber or in the area of the three commissions; yet, over the course of the eighteenth century, teahouses outside of the offices of the Edo commissions began to play a semiofficial and intermediary role in the judicial system. The magistrates used them to relay calls to parties scheduled to appear before the commissions and also to deliver correspondence to suit inns.

---

98. Minami, *Bakumatsu toshi shakai no kenkyū*, 188–90.
99. Ibid., 170.
100. Kukita, "Naisai to kujiyado," 325–29.

Not surprisingly, suit inn operators desired a share of the market that teahouses had carved out for themselves. When state suppression efforts in the early 1700s failed to contain competition from teahouses, the suit inns and their guilds changed their approaches to both potential clients and the state. They entered the teahouse business and competed with teahouses on their merits and through marketing.[101] Proprietors of suit inns found the teahouse a fruitful ground on which to meet villagers involved in disputes who, during their wait outside of the offices of the commissions, tried to negotiate a resolution of their conflict. From the mid-1700s, suit inns went further, advertising the expertise that made them superior to teahouses and other unofficial sites of dispute resolution. They hung out shingles (*kanban*) promoting their services and distributed name cards and pamphlets that indicated knowledge in "official matters, suits, and petitions."[102] In doing so, the suit inns flouted shogunal edicts that governed their practice. Promotional activities were contrary to the state's general opposition to litigation and specific prohibitions against encouraging litigation. Episodically, Edo's civic administrators summoned proprietors of the suit inns to chastise them for contravening prohibitions on soliciting clients. Shogunal officials also confiscated name cards and promotional materials. The metropolitan magistrate ruled that soliciting business, bribing officials, and obstructing attempts by the state to investigate such practices would lead to the termination of guild privileges.

In response to this castigation, suit inns convinced the shogunate of their indispensability. They did so by making themselves even more useful to official judicial and administrative processes. Even as the suit inns attempted to evade state controls on fees and soliciting clients, they cultivated their relationships with the offices of the commissions, daimyo, or shogunal official that they served. From the 1770s, a series of disputes among the guilds over jurisdiction led to a clear enumeration of which guilds provided which services to the various magistrates, government agencies, and commissions, including:

---

101. Kukita, "Naisai to kujiyado," 328–29.
102. Haruhara, "Kujiyado no senden bira," 39–40.

1) the holding, supervision, and provisioning of the accused in inquisitorial proceedings,

2) the delivery of summonses, and

3) aid in fighting fires and other relief actions around the offices to which the guilds of the suit inns were tied.[103]

The suit inns' services to the state eased the burden of administering adversarial proceedings for an overtaxed judicial apparatus. At the same time, suit inns continued to straddle the official and unofficial realms of legal practice under Tokugawa rule.

The services the inns performed for commissions and magistrates included confining the accused before trials. The earliest record of a suit inn holding a person coming before the Conference Chamber and the Metropolitan Commission dates to the 1690s; over time, such action became increasingly formalized and regular.[104] The nature of "holding" (*yado azuke*) varied. In some instances, particularly those involving disputes among parties (*deirisuji*), the suit inn simply monitored people, documenting their movements so that the suit inn operator could bring them before the magistrate if they were unexpectedly called to appear. In other cases, suit inns had, in a sense, a police function: they physically restrained persons awaiting appearance before a magistrate in an inquisitorial proceeding.

Various issues arose out of holding parties in inquisitorial proceedings; for the suit inn, the greatest concern was the cost. These concerns were allayed somewhat with the requirement that those found guilty pay the costs of confinement. Article 24 of the *Kujikata osadamegaki* required that in a case where a party "be sentenced to punishment by the [magistrate] he alone must defray the amercement."[105] Competing guilds in Edo brought a suit in 1770 contesting which guild might lodge whom and other issues, including the jurisdictions served by the various guilds. The judgment in the suit determined that the uncompensated food cost for holding parties ordered to appear before the Kanto district deputy

103. Kukita, "Naisai to kujiyado," 324–25; Minami, *Bakumatsu toshi shakai no kenkyū*, 170; and Takikawa M., "Nihon bengoshishi zenshi kujiyado no kenkyū."
104. Minami, *Bakumatsu toshi shakai no kenkyū*, 181.
105. Hall, "The Tokugawa Legislation, Part IV," 710.

would be borne by the Travelers Inn Guild. The terms for detention in an inn stated that up to three people could be held at each inn within the guild. If the person held was seriously ill, the inn need only lodge that one person.[106] Each inn lodged a person for 100 days before the person was sent to another inn. Every 10 days, the inns lodging persons for the state settled their accounts with the guild. In compensation for this finding, the ruling also designated the Travelers Inn Guild as the monopoly lodging for parties called before the Metropolitan Commission and also prohibited teahouses and other unlicensed establishments from lodging pilgrims to Edo.

Providing a custodial role had social and political implications. Socially, it rendered the relationship between the suit inn and the shogunate ambiguous in the eyes of the petitioner or lodger. In the subsequent development of legal practice, this slowed efforts by legal advocates to assert their independence of the state. At the same time, the provision of this kind of service made the suit inns and their guilds all the more integral to official processes of justice administration and dispute resolution. Politically, it created opportunities for inns to seek preferential treatment from the authorities.

Such an opportunity arose around the delivery of summonses. Magistrates faced a challenge in tracking the summons delivery process. As Minami Kazuo notes, "from earliest times, the suit inns of Edo engaged in the delivery of summonses to the parties [to a dispute] or related persons."[107] From the perspective of the magistrate, this was more desirable than the alternative, in which parties to a dispute themselves would, at times, summon other parties in the name of an official. As an edict of 1787 indicated, there were instances in which parties served each other false summons.[108] To control such infractions, the commissions made the suit inn the legitimate server of papers, thus shifting the burden of authenticating documents onto the guilds.[109] The various guilds also arranged fire protection, as noted in the same 1770 ruling. The 82-Inn Group provided fire protection services to the Finance Commission. The 30-Inn

---

106. Minami, *Bakumatsu toshi shakai no kenkyū*, 181–82.
107. Ibid., 178.
108. Takikawa M., "Nihon bengoshishi zenshi kujiyado no kenkyū," 124.
109. Aoki, "Kinsei minshū no seikatsu to teikō," 196.

Group performed fire protection duties for the Edo offices of daimyo in Bakurōchō and also assisted with flood relief. As it had in other areas through other actors, the shogunate compensated for a lack of resources by co-opting seemingly private entities and engaging them in matters that might otherwise fall under the aegis of the state.

In return for handling these matters, the authorities awarded guilds further monopolies on services related to the adjudication of disputes. As part of the Kansei Reforms of 1790, the shogunate put the burgeoning trade in legal services emerging at the gates of its offices under the control of three of the guilds.[110] It allowed the guilds to open their own teahouses and agreed to continue prohibition on lodging of litigants by unaffiliated enterprises. The affirmation of ties came with a warning. As had been the case in the recognition of the Travelers Inn Guild at the turn of the eighteenth century, the state condemned gouging clients and exploiting the suit inn monopoly in the capital. In 1791, the Finance Commission summoned suit inn proprietors and apprentices to reprimand them for charging fees (for drafting petitions) in excess of officially set prices.[111] Even so, the guilds were given broad prerogatives in the teahouse trade. Around the northern and southern offices of the Finance Commission, the shogunate allowed the guilds of the suit inns to maintain six teahouses each. These teahouses, consistent with the reciprocal relationships with the state, provided bailiffs to the commissions. Suit inn–operated teahouses established during the 1790s may have driven out nonsanctioned operators; complaints do not appear as frequently in the early-nineteenth-century record as they did during the latter half of the eighteenth century.

Yet suit inns had ignored the other part of the shogunate's accommodation of organized private legal practice in the closing decades of the 1700s: they made little effort to control the cost of litigation, further exploiting their domination of the private legal service market in the capital and, at the same time, working ever more closely with officials. By 1800, the relationship between the guilds and the commissions they served was so close that the guilds managed the summoning of parties among

---

110. Kukita, "Naisai to kujiyado," 328.
111. Minami, *Bakumatsu toshi shakai no kenkyū*, 180.

themselves. The 30-Inn Group had a special relationship with daimyo residences, delivering summonses to the provinces by messenger (*hikyaku*). When it issued a summons, the state presumed that, while a case was pending, the parties to the dispute would lodge at the suit inn that delivered it.[112] If the parties summoned wished to lodge elsewhere, they could do so by making a written request to the summoning official. In 1801, the Travelers Inn Guild sought to translate its monopoly on the delivery of summonses for the Metropolitan Commission into an ironclad monopoly on the lodging of all persons whom the commission had called to the capital.[113] Although that request was denied, the Temple and Shrine Commission identified eleven inns from among the various inns and used these as official agents.

By the 1830s, suit inns in the vicinity of both the Temple and Shrine Commission and the Finance Commission used their close relationship with the shogunate to charge prices for legal services at double or triple government-set rates. Through their guilds, suit inns had displaced teahouse competitors offering lodging and legal advice, worked even more closely with the state, and then raised prices above those set by government fiat with either willful, or negligent, acquiescence by the authorities.

Formal service to officialdom lasted through the dissolution of guild monopolies under the Tempō Reforms begun in 1841.[114] As one part of the reforms, the shogunate sought to restore the moral imperative it had launched more than two centuries earlier. This included removing official approval for guilds. Yet the reforms did not achieve their goals. In the case of the suit inns, guilds remained constituted as informal associations. Two years after the edict eliminating state-sanctioned guild monopolies, the suit inns continued to provide services to the various commissions; many suit inns continued delivering summonses on behalf of the authorities. Yet the lodges longed for a return to monopoly status. Guilds of inns folded their interests into the wave of opposition to the Tempō Reforms that began in the late 1840s. Eventually, the guilds shepherded a successful petition through the shogunate. The shogun reestablished privileges for the guilds of suit inns in 1851.

---

112. Aoki, "Kinsei minshū no seikatsu to teikō," 193.
113. Minami, *Bakumatsu toshi shakai no kenkyū,* 183.
114. Aoki, "Kinsei minshū no seikatsu to teikō," 198–99.

Guilds of suit inns had achieved state sanction while incrementally becoming part of the judicial order. Initially operating on the margins, they ultimately caused a radical shift: a reversal by the shogunate of its general suppression of legal representation. As they did so, suit inns opened up legal processes not just to merchants or themselves, but also to others who included farmers (aggrieved over taxes and overbearing village authorities) and those charged with crimes. The regularization of legal practice itself was part of a process of popularizing legal knowledge, driven by suit inns at sites of official authority and by suit solicitors throughout society.

The Popularization of Legal Knowledge

Suit inns and suit solicitors worked between state and society and, in doing so, provided opportunities for people to better navigate the everyday processes that constituted samurai and shogunal authority. Doing so, legal practitioners accumulated knowledge of the complex terrain of inquisitorial and adversarial matters during the Edo era. In the absence of published interpretive resources outlining legal processes, litigants in private disputes and criminal defendants pieced together a vernacular understanding of the ways and places their lives intersected with officialdom. Overlapping with the world of private practice, this vernacular understanding was powerfully colored by an approach to the shogunate as a just ruler and font of legal morality. By contrast, in popular accounts most local lords emerged as petty tyrants. Suit inns were caught in the middle—their service and proximity to officialdom rendered them suspect. In the meantime, villages, domains, and the shogun had at best vilified and at worst criminalized the work of the individual suit solicitor. Suit solicitors did not appear as heroes in what have become the representative examples of vernacular accounts of legal processes. Analyses of popular understanding of Edo-era law have focused either on samurai as interpreters and enforcers of justice or martyred petitioners as victims of injustice, ignoring the critical contribution of suit inns and suit solicitors as they aided litigants and expanded access to legal process as a form of dispute resolution.

Dominating accounts of Tokugawa juridical virtuosity was a real-life hero, a metropolitan magistrate in Edo (*machi bugyō*) and the leading jurist of the Edo era, Ōoka Tadasuke (Echizen no Kami, 1677–1751). He achieved celebrity during his lifetime and mythic stature in death. In his day, printed accounts of Ōoka's rulings circulated as *Ōoka seidan* (Ōoka's virtuous rulings). Even these celebrations of Ōoka's wisdom were subject to suppression; they were disseminated surreptitiously because they dealt explicitly with legal matters. By the end of the nineteenth century he had also become a regular in the repertoire of comedic folk tales (*rakugo*), stories that spared little sympathy for the opportunistic petitioners who came before him.[115] Folk accounts of Ōoka popularized him as an exemplar of the just expression of the power of the shogunate, celebrating his perspicacity and heralding him as a lawgiver and fair arbiter of conflict in daily life.[116] Tales elevated Ōoka above the greedy, arrogant, and misguided fools who sought to resolve their disputes with the shogunate's help.

Common sense marked Ōoka's jurisprudence. The father who lorded over his pregnant daughter, mentioned earlier in this chapter, suffered at the hands of Ōoka when he required the father to replace the bloodstained white gravel in the courtyard. When two women made competing claims for a child, each potentially benefiting from custody, Ōoka adopted a Solomonic ploy. To identify the pretender, Ōoka told each woman to take a hand of the girl and pull as hard as possible; the one who pulled the child to her would be declared the mother. The birth mother yielded, fearing for her daughter's safety; the pretender declared victory. Ōoka honored the birth mother's claim and punished the pretender. Parties to disputes rooming at a suit inn in the shogun's capital could borrow a 30-fascicle set of Ōoka tales from their inn.[117] The popularity of Ōoka in vernacular storytelling was an appreciation for a wise magistrate

---

115. Sasaki and Morioka, "Rakugo," 439. Ōoka (as "Tadasuke" and, more often, "Echizen no Kami") figured prominently in stories, including "Sanbō ichiryō zon," "Jitsubo yōbo no arasoi," and "Sasaki seidan." Tokugawa Yoshimune elevated Ōoka to the rank of daimyo, allowing him to serve on the Temples and Shrine Commission. See also Ōishi and Hayashi, eds., *Ōoka Echizen no Kami Tadasuke no nikki.*

116. Ihara Saikaku, drawing on Chinese motifs, was a popularizer of the moral tale. Along with Ōoka, Hasegawa Heizō (1745–1795) was another figure associated with the Tokugawa shogunate who achieved mytho-historical dimensions. Takikawa M., *Hasegawa Heizō.*

117. Takahashi S., *Edo no soshō,* 70.

at society's political center who discerned and corrected the foibles of the common people. A collection of Ōoka stories printed in the late-nineteenth-century ended with the following phrase, "The people looked on and said, 'The judgment is indeed founded on a knowledge of human nature.' "[118] However, jurisdictional rules meant that only a small percentage of parties to disputes would ever come before an official like Ōoka. Nearly 80 percent of the Edo-era population lived in farming villages, many of these outside of the direct jurisdiction of the shogun. In retrospect, Ōoka stood in for shogunal justice, yet few had access to his rulings. Here again, the state projected an ideal; the practice was something else entirely.

The incongruity between ideal and actual practice expanded over the course of the eighteenth century. Suit solicitors served as a bridge between the nearly unattainable ideal of shogunal justice dispensed by someone like Ōoka and daily life under a petty tyrant on the periphery. Concretely, this meant that suit solicitors drafted the documents that won villagers a hearing and helped them advance their claims beyond grumbling. Rules required that a villager first turn to local authorities as defined by village compacts and charters of five-family groups. When these steps failed, and the conflict was not contained within the community, a person then turned to daimyo and regional magistrates. Where public memory distilled Ōoka into a paragon of the distant yet benevolent Tokugawa state, the actions of local officials fermented into a bitter brew in public memory. High taxes became a frequent source of conflict. Tales of martyrs (*gimin*), first and foremost among them the story of Sakura Sōgorō, moralized on the just and unjust administration of law.[119] By the 1800s, the tale of Sakura Sōgorō and similar stories of peasant martyrs pointed to the chasm between shogunal ideals and everyday experiences, revealing the incongruities of state orthodoxy.

---

118. In Wigmore, *A Panorama of the World's Legal Systems*, 489. There were at least four collections entitled *Ōoka meiyō seidan* extant during the time Wigmore was in Japan, three published in the late 1880s and one published in 1893. The story of the false mother likely derives not from Ōoka's own experiences but from a collection of Chinese decisions dating from the early fifteenth century, popularized in Japan by Ihara Saikaku at the turn of the eighteenth century. Ibid., 528.

119. Walthall, "Japanese Gimin."

Increasingly popular in the nineteenth century, oral accounts of peasant martyrs incorporated information about legal processes for the discerning listener. One of the most prominent accounts described how the mid-seventeenth-century farmer Sakura Sōgorō suffered an increasing tax burden and then joined with other village headmen to appeal a new tax increase. With his first appeal falling on the deaf ears of daimyo Hotta Masanobu, Sakura Sōgorō ignored jurisdictional rules and forced an appeal outside of permitted channels. The action he pursued as the leader of a group demanding redress challenged legal and social norms. Ultimately, he "inserted his petition in the tip of a six-foot long bamboo pole that he had readied beforehand and . . . tried to thrust his petition into the palanquin" of the Shogun.[120] This thrust violated the ruler's sanctified space, a transgression punishable by crucifixion. According to one version of the tale, Sakura witnessed the decapitation of his children before his own execution. Ultimately, the shogunate intervened on behalf of the villagers while vengeful ghosts from Sakura's family hounded the evil daimyo Hotta to his demise. As a martyr in an oral tradition, the suffering that Sakura Sōgorō experienced lived on long after his death. Yet what was the message of his story? While it mourned the heroism of Sakura Sōgorō, at the same time, it revealed the dangers of direct challenges to the state apparatus. Part cautionary tale, the story was also a reflection on the possibilities and pitfalls of forced petitions and challenges to defined legal procedure.

Oral recitation of tales like the Sakura Sōgorō story were part of a popular culture that caricatured greedy local officials while groping for relief from distant authorities. Beyond entertainment, the Sakura Sōgorō stories, much like the Ōoka tales, provided other information. They offered oblique interpretations of legal norms and procedures, revealing the kinds of matters the state might hear, how one should frame a complaint, and how forceful one could be in pressing a petition. In the absence of expository texts elucidating legal processes, fiction provided a vernacular guide to petitioning, with details that both engaged and informed readers. The "Sakura Sōgorō Story" told of how Sakura met other village headmen in Edo to have their petitions approved by domainal and

---

120. "The Sakura Sōgorō Story," in Walthall, *Peasant Uprisings in Japan,* 57.

shogunal officials.[121] They lodged at inns in Bakurōchō and met in the teahouses of Asakusa. Fictionalized accounts of encounters with official-dom introduced villagers to the basic elements of legal processes that were deliberately obscured by the authorities. For the historian, these narratives contain trace references to Edo-era private legal practice from outside of the Edo center.

Shogunal beneficence and evil local lords became popular motifs of Edo-era justice, homogenized by the veils of myth and lore. Beneath this veneer lay differences across more than 250 years and 250 domains. Pop-ular accounts of justice may have shaped a national popular culture in the late nineteenth century, but the context of domain and village grounded local experiences of law before 1868. Each domain developed its own terms for resolution of adversarial disputes and inquisitorial proceedings, with terms consistent with Tokugawa principles.[122] In contrast to the im-age expressed in popular accounts, statutes of some domains professed sympathy to petitioners. Yonezawa domain regulations stated that "if there is a petition then the town commissioner should be solicitous toward the people."[123] Below the level of the domain, villages and guilds enjoyed considerable autonomy within what Herman Ooms has called—after Foucault—the Tokugawa "juridical field," drafting their own rules, guid-ing resolution of disputes, and, at times, meting out punishments. Thus, many disputes were worked out in spaces free of oversight from shogu-nal and even domainal authorities.

Yet when the measures or personalities in these spaces fell short, then a party might pursue an appeal.[124] How to proceed? A basic challenge for the person pressing a suit was finding the proper receiving authority. The Tokugawa had deliberately rendered much of its administrative ap-paratus indecipherable. Further, prohibitions on the practice of the free-lance suit solicitor, beginning in the mid-seventeenth century and then repeated through the nineteenth century, made it difficult for the lay

---

121. Redesdale, *Tales of Old Japan*, 199–200.
122. Ravina, *Land and Lordship in Early Modern Japan*.
123. Aoki, "Kinsei minshū no seikatsu to teikō," 176. Early didactic texts tied to-gether farmers and their samurai superiors. Ooms, *Tokugawa Ideology*, 150.
124. Aoki, "Kinsei minshū no seikatsu to teikō," 176.

person to find help reading and drafting the necessary documents.[125] Even so, it was in a range of printed material and in the person of the suit solicitor, acting illicitly, that the petitioner found a guide on the journey toward justice.

An exploding print culture aided the litigant and the suit solicitor in deciphering and disseminating access to the authorities. In addition to orally communicated tales of martyrdom, celebrations of official wisdom, and other accounts, keys to the legal processes and petitioning appeared in various forms.[126] Commentaries on laws and reproductions of legal texts were out of the question, yet legal processes, practitioners, and suit inns emerged as figures in literature, the travel diary, and even *senryū*. Ihara Saikaku's *Honchō ōin hiji* (Trials in the shade of a cherry tree) circulated widely.[127] The *Morisada mankō* travelogue offered highly detailed accounts of justice processes. One poem in an anthology described how Bakurōchō concentrated and "lodged the logic of every domain."[128] The verse satirized the centrality of suit inns and suit solicitors to the dispute resolution process. Tokugawa prohibitions meant that commentaries or essays could not point out how legal practitioners linked local communities to the central state, on a terrain shaped by legal ties. Satirical verse could point out that they did.

Village unrest in the early nineteenth century and the unfulfilled promise of state benevolence increasingly meant that conflicts overflowed prescribed channels. Beyond officially designated approaches to resolving conflict, a gray area of prohibited yet tolerated forms of direct petition appeared, such as thrusting papers into the hands of a councilor of state or other authority or into the palanquin of an official on the way to or from his office, or throwing a petition over the wall of a commission office. Plaintiffs brought their concerns to another level when they engaged in a "forced suit," in which a group of people pressed on the door

---

125. There were repeated local, domainal, and shogunal prohibitions on legal practice, as ubiquitous as suit solicitors themselves; see, for example, the Shogunal prohibition of 1702 in Minami, *Bakumatsu toshi shakai no kenkyū*, 187.

126. On lending libraries and Edo-era print culture generally, see, for example, Kornicki, *The Book in Japan*.

127. Silver, *Purloined Letters*, 24–29.

128. Aoki, "Kinsei minshū no seikatsu to teikō," 174–77.

or the gate of a government office en masse. For the party who wished to bring such actions, suit inns and suit solicitors turned all manner of material, including material designed to affirm state authority, into resources that revealed the structures of authority to the people.[129] Pursuing a suit outside of official channels could be hazardous, yet for those such as Sakura Sōgorō who persisted, finding the relevant official was key. To whom should the petition, drafted "in fear and trembling," be addressed? Where was the office located? In an account of guides to military households (*bukan*), Mary Elizabeth Berry pondered their readership and suggested that these books served as guides for the 250-odd daimyo to their own ranks or castoffs for commoners to mull over. The guides to military households celebrated the might of the shogun and daimyo and illustrated the ceremonial elements of authority: crests, banners, and the like. Their large print runs suggest that they may have been drafted from the beginning to serve audiences beyond members of the samurai status group and their admirers. The guides to heraldry included information useful to potential litigants and petitioners. With his coconspirators sitting around him, Sakura Sōgorō recounted how, "on the twentieth day of the present month, the Shogun will go in state to worship at the shrine of his ancestors in [Ueno]."[130] How did he know? The information the guides provided to the potential petitioner, alongside heraldry, included locations of offices of Tokugawa magistrates, descriptions of daimyo processions to Edo, dates of daimyo attendance in Edo, and schedules of daimyo presence in castle towns.[131] Berry has noted how the guides to military households constituted "synoptic texts . . . which listed with copious formulaic notes every single daimyo of the nation as well as every significant officeholder in the Tokugawa bureaucracy."[132] At the time of the Sakura episode, private publishers began making these compendia on military households widely available. From the late seventeenth century, "[s]uccessive editions [included] expanding information on schedules and conduct."[133] Such information would have been helpful to a

---

129. Berry, *Japan in Print*.
130. Hayashi T., *For His People, Being the True Story of Sogoro's Sacrifice*, 68–69.
131. Berry, *Japan in Print*, 43.
132. Ibid., 22.
133. Berry, "Conventional Knowledge in Early Modern Japan," 46.

range of litigants and petitioners, from a creditor faced with a default on a loan to a peasant farmer determined to toss an appeal for benevolence into a passing palanquin.

Suit inn proprietors themselves disseminated other kinds of information directly to potential litigants. When the management of an inn changed hands, the new proprietor might send an announcement to the clients of the previous proprietor.[134] An 1817 announcement circulated by suit inn owner Tanbaya Shirobei identified officeholders in the local and shogunal juridical apparatus by name and function. Although these kinds of resources were helpful to all legal practitioners, they were likely more helpful to the freelance suit solicitor than to the suit inn operator who was already closely connected to the office of a magistrate or daimyo.

As seen, the urban-based suit inns institutionalized into guilds whose interests became intertwined with the commissions and magistrates over the course of the Edo period. At the same time, in rural and urban settings, a different kind of practitioner—the suit solicitor—served the lower and less mobile orders of society. Herman Ooms analyzed a legal case involving a farming woman named Ken that reveals how the legal process and official ideals collided in rural areas, outside the purview of state-sanctioned suit inns. In Ooms's account, Ken faced off against her entire village and, later, the authorities, with guile and courage.[135] In this mid-eighteenth-century case, the village authorities commanded Ken to establish a (male) heir in order to continue her family line and fulfill tax obligations to the village and the five-family group. Ken had already weathered failed marriages and had also survived the killing of her brother, a wayward horse trader, by members of her extended family and other villagers by order of the local headman. When Ken did not establish a male heir through marriage or adoption, as she was pressured to do by her family, the local leaders perniciously blocked her departure from the village. This led her to take legal action against the local headman, local administrative authorities, and members of her family.[136] She submitted a petition to the local magistrate regarding the murder of her

---

134. Haruhara, "Kujiyado no senden bira," 39–40.
135. Ooms, *Tokugawa Village Practice.*
136. Ibid., 16–18.

brother, Shinzō. She won a hearing in part because she was able to document her claims in the correct form. To her misfortune, the petition was not correct enough. As Ooms noted, "it gave too much vent to her resentment and hatred and was devoid of the obligatory deferential formulae."[137] What unfolded was a duel of legal documents, with the village furnishing material showing that Shinzō had been disinherited. The village also countered Ken's call for an investigation of her brother's death with its own account, arguing that villagers had killed Shinzō in self-defense. When Ken sued the local authorities, she entered a world in which "[c]onflicts and disputes revolved around, and were ultimately resolved by, the creation of legally recognized documents."[138] Such legal documentation was beyond the daily life experience of even the most literate farmer. Successfully challenging the status quo required mastery of esoteric forms. Ooms described how, in Ken's case,

> the crucial role of documentation come[s] to mind: the ability to write petitions in proper form; the manipulation of population records; the importance of written and certified disinheritance documents that were forwarded beyond the village; a petition for a memorial service that could not be suppressed because it contained a charge of murder; the many occasions where written promises were exacted (to not drink sake, to establish an heir, to move in with a new husband in another village, to live in harmony, to work the fields, etc.).[139]

Ooms suggests that the village's exculpatory appeal to self-defense might have come from communication with the authorities; it—and Ken's petition—might also have been derived from communication with a suit solicitor or suit inn.

When Ken submitted her petition to the magistrate, he demanded that she reveal the name of the party who had penned the document. She refused. Ken's village compact, the rules that governed her hamlet, identified suit solicitors—those who had mastered the form and content of filing a grievance—as persona non grata in the village: "People who are not engaged in cultivation, trade, or any other occupation, or with-

---

137. Ibid., 41.
138. Ibid., 69.
139. Ibid., 70.

draw from consultation with the village, or like quarrels and lawsuits, or do all kinds of bad things should not be hidden [but reported]."[140] Village compacts prohibited harboring those who practiced litigation as an occupation, which suggests that the suit solicitor may have been itinerant. In any case, the suit solicitor enabled the aggrieved or injured parties to confront structures of power on their own terms. It was the suit solicitor who helped the illiterate farmer translate a grievance into a legal case. Yet the fact that the suit solicitor practiced under shogunal and local prohibitions means that there is no data on this elusive figure.

Though the shogunate had come to recognize suit inns as legitimate, the practice of suit solicitors remained illegal through the nineteenth century. Suit solicitors occupied a realm more precarious than that of the suit inns; there were penalties for those who disturbed social harmony by assisting parties challenging local authority or pursuing tax or debt relief by legal means. Accounts tell of the self-styled "great law experts" of Osaka facing arrest.[141] In an addendum to the shogunate's 1702 reversal of its earlier repudiation of money suits, it warned of penalties for those harboring persons who solicited suits to excess and those who taught the art of the lawsuit.[142] In the capital, the Travelers Inn Guild complained to the Finance Commission of the ubiquity of suit solicitors in 1788.[143] The shogunate repeatedly issued edicts seeking to control the actions of suit solicitors.[144] Its frequent attempts to stamp out their activities acknowledged them as fixtures of Edo-era life.

The processes and principles of dispute resolution established by the shogunate and the domains meant that, in the words of Aoki Michio, "the lawsuit, as a means for asserting one's self-interest, gradually took hold among the people."[145] Having a case heard was a grant, not a right, so farmers framed their appeals in language that noted that they were beseeching their betters "in fear and trembling."[146] Such petitions will be

---

140. Ibid., 33.
141. Haruhara, *Osaka no machibugyōsho to saiban*, 47.
142. "Shōhō jiroku," cited in Aoki, "Kinsei minshū no seikatsu to teikō."
143. Minami, *Bakumatsu toshi shakai no kenkyū*, 187.
144. Takikawa M., "Nihon bengoshishi zenshi kujiyado no kenkyū," 116–19.
145. Aoki, "Kinsei minshū no seikatsu to teikō," 176.
146. Walthall, *Peasant Uprisings in Japan*, 58.

familiar to readers of histories of peasant uprisings (*ikki*) that have focused on these accounts for what they reveal about the political consciousness of the Tokugawa peasant.[147] As historians have noted, petitioning often figured in the early stages of an uprising, marking the first steps of an uprising as a legal process as well. Petitions preceding direct action by farmers occupied a gray area of the Tokugawa legal process because they emerged out of group complaints to the authorities. Edo records reveal an elaborate categorization of illegal methods of petitioning. In the categorization process, the state opened up the possibility for petitions to proceed, becoming in some cases a condoned occurrence.[148] A suit solicitor or suit inn's assistance could be critical in identifying the line between the acceptable and unacceptable "illegal petition." Petitions that were sufficiently self-effacing, at times even those that proceeded without approval of a local headman and daimyo could receive a hearing. Yet when a petition was insurrectionary—when it directly criticized an official or reflected a group grievance—it crossed a line. Forced petitions—those that reflected the demands of a group and were thrust upon an official, as in the case of Sakura Sōgorō's petition—met the severest rebuke. Yet when the petition combined the proper degree of deference and a clear call for state benevolence, it might be heard.

The histories of uprisings show that the protagonists focused on the specific grievances they faced, to the exclusion of broader critiques of society and politics. In this, village headmen and other protest leaders revealed a clear awareness of the narrow passage through which a grievance could receive redress under extant laws. The narrow grounds on which peasants made their claims, including claims that may have ultimately led to armed attacks on the local authorities or the wealthy in their midst, were not evidence of a limited political consciousness. Rather, this approach revealed a sensitivity to, and awareness of, the

---

147. See Bowen, *Rebellion and Democracy in Meiji Japan* and Vlastos, "Opposition Movements in Early Meiji."

148. There were cases when petitions received outside of the usual channels did win consideration, a development that was institutionalized with Yoshimune's establishment of a petition box. Roberts, "The Petition Box in Eighteenth-Century Tosa." There was also a range of private disputes in which the shogun would not intervene. See Takeuchi, "Festivals and Fights."

legal problems and limited possibilities of pursuing petitions that reflected group concerns. While calling on benevolence, petitioners also
framed their demands in the language of law. This was the fertile ground
that nurtured the post-1868 seeds of local engagement with legal processes and legal forms of political activism, including calls for representative government.

By the final decades of the Edo period, a "deep relationship had developed between village officials and the suit inns, with the suit inn
serving as a source of various kinds of information."[149] The connection
between the metropole and the periphery was not just one between
government officials and individuals; individuals acting in the private
interest had begun mediating the encounter. Legal processes bound together group identities, including the tax and administrative collectivity
of the five-family group and the village as a whole. Such connections
come to light in an inquisitorial matter, the state-initiated proceedings
against a village just east of Mount Fuji, in which a suit inn played a central role in the resolution of the charges. The story reveals that private
legal practitioners were central not just in adversarial matters, but in
criminal matters as well.

The murder case, grippingly chronicled by Takahashi Satoshi, tells of
how, in August 1849, a group of marauders slipped into the village of
Mishuku in the early morning. The band swarmed into the house of one
Gen'emon and killed a person there. Gen'emon had not registered the
person with village officials. He buried the body of his fallen guest on
the grounds of an abandoned temple nearby. This turn of events included
a number of criminal acts. In addition to the murderers, Gen'emon, his
family, and, by association, his entire village were at fault. Hosting an
unregistered person overnight contravened the rules of Gen'emon's five-
family group.[150] This was similarly forbidden by Article 25 of the *Kujikata osadamegaki*: "When an outsider, without being entered in the local
register of inhabitants, is allowed to stay in a place, both the person himself and the inhabitant who keeps him, are to be sentenced to expulsion:
The mayor (*nanushi*) of the village is to be heavily fined; and the head of

149. Aoki, "Kinsei minshū no seikatsu to teikō," 200.
150. Goningumi chō zensho, art. 27, cited in Takahashi S., *Edo no soshō*.

the [five-family group] is to be fined."[151] Furthermore, Gen'emon was wrong to bury the body in an abandoned temple. There were penalties for improperly disposing of a corpse; these included fines for the perpetrator, fines for the village association, fines for the village headman, and an ouster from office for the village headman.

The village banished Gen'emon in its first effort to protect itself. This foreclosed an inquiry by domainal authorities into Gen'emon's relationship (and, by extension, the relationship of the village) with the marauding vagrants. Yet this did not end questions from the shogun's investigators. The band that had swarmed into Gen'emon's home had committed other crimes across multiple domains. Through the Sanoya Inn, the shogunate summoned Gen'emon's father and village officials to Edo by messenger. Those summoned lodged at the Yamashiroya Inn in Bakurōchō. The case reveals the range of services an inn provided to a party, even those involved in an inquisitorial matter; it also provides rare details of the experience of those who lodged at inns.

Arriving in Edo, the Mishuku villagers entered the world of the suit inn and Tokugawa magistrates. As in the case of adversarial matters, inquisitorial matters proceeded at a slow pace; the villagers spent 189 days in Edo, with only 21 of those days involving any contact with the authorities.[152] Initially, the villagers made a circuit of tourist sites, presumably under the watchful eye of the suit inn proprietor. Money for this kind of activity soon ran low, so the suit inn staff drafted and submitted a petition to allow some of the villagers to return home. This was successful. All told, the village spent hundreds of *ryō* in its defense of actions related to the murder. The greatest share of the burden fell on the village headman, Gin'emon. As in other kinds of litigation, including disputes over common areas, the proceeding in the Incident at Mishuku Village placed in high relief both the collective burdens and the individual costs related to the common interest.

Even though it was costly to be summoned to Edo, there was an educational and even strategic benefit. With the passage of days, parties to disputes could learn about the laws related to their cases under the in-

---

151. Hall, "The Tokugawa Legislation, Part IV," 711.
152. Takahashi S., *Edo no soshō*, 63.

struction of the suit inn staff or perhaps from a suit solicitor working the crowds outside one of the commissions. Suit inns had access to the *Kujikata osadamegaki* and made it available to their patrons.[153] The headman from Mishuku village spent some of his time in the capital copying sections from the laws available at the Yamashiroya suit inn. Having made his own bootleg copy, he brought it back to the village. Takahashi notes that "copies of the *Kujikata osadamegaki* definitely circulated down to, and were maintained by, the village-headman class."[154] Even as the esoteric knowledge contained within the *Kujikata* became exoteric, it did so under the sign of secrecy. The title page of the Mishuku village headman's 1850 copy of the *Kujikata* read "Secret Record."[155] All the while, village representatives drew on what they had learned at the suit inn to shape the course of the inquisitorial proceedings opened against them. Ultimately, they escaped punishment through a combination of bribery and family connections, revealing a certain amount of irony in the Tokugawa juridical processes. Although the state reviled private legal practitioners for profiting from the resolution of disputes as an occupation, some of their samurai betters had slipped from their prescribed social function as moral exemplars of benevolence into avarice. They sold influence tied to their position as administrators of the law and accepted bribes. It was only the extraordinary figure, such as Ōshio Heihachirō, who emerged to question systemic corruption including bribery.

With the backdrop of a corrupt and inefficient state ill equipped to address the erosion of its worldview, suit inn proprietors escorted parties to court, assisted litigants in the preparation of documents, brokered negotiations between parties, forwarded bribes to officials, and generally instructed litigants in the realities of the legal process. All the while, the suit inn collaborated with the authorities. Meanwhile, suit solicitors outside of the official system sold legal services under a cloud of criminality. Thus, both the suit solicitor and the suit inn proprietor occupied ambiguous positions in relationship to their clients. It is no surprise that, in the social imagination, the legal practitioner was the target of both resentment and appreciation. In particular, the public resented legal practitioners for

153. Ibid., 72–73.
154. Ibid., 77.
155. Ibid., 73.

exploiting their position in the gray area between the state and clients for material gain.[156] According to Okudaira Masahiro, townspeople despised suit solicitors and considered them "snakes and scorpions" for taking on clients from opposing sides of the same suit.[157] Once, an angry crowd ran suit solicitors out of Edo —even so, "this did not reduce their numbers."[158] Even though the custodial role that the suit inns performed signaled to petitioners the suit inn's alignment with the state, the suit inn also served as an advocate for the petitioner, giving rise to monetary reward. Clients appreciated suit solicitors and suit inns as guides to the legal process; as such, when they were of assistance, they were worthy of generous gratuities.[159] It was not cultural disinclination toward litigated resolution of disputes or faith in official justice that hindered the demand for representation in adversarial and inquisitorial matters. Even as suit inns received grudging state sanction, prohibitions on suit solicitors and the general disfavor in which the state held litigation rendered access to legal representation difficult.

At the same time, private legal practitioners disrupted the state's ideal of social harmony by familiarizing themselves and others with the laws and using them for their own and clients' purposes. Suit solicitors and suit inns promoted litigation as a means of resolving disputes, a means of dispute resolution that people came to expect and seek out. Application of a comparative definition of law as the language of the state reveals an expanded terrain of Edo-era private practice. Further, the use of petitions in uprisings reflected an awareness of legal processes among the aggrieved, in turn revealing an expanded cast of characters moving on that terrain. It was on this ground that suit inns and suit solicitors spread knowledge of legal procedures, despite efforts by the officials of local, regional, and shogunal governments to discourage them.

---

156. Efforts to suppress suit solicitors as independent operators meant that they increasingly came to be associated with criminality. Takikawa M., *Kujishi, kujiyado no kenkyū*, 112. Kukita, "Naisai to kujiyado," 326.

157. Okudaira, *Nihon bengoshishi*, 14.

158. Ibid., 14. Ōno Masao later drew on Okudaira to make the same claims about the treatment of *kujishi*, in Ōno, "Shokugyōshi toshite no bengoshi oyobi bengoshi dantai no rekishi."

159. Takahashi S., *Edo no soshō*.

History and the Legacies of Early Modern Legal Practice

The elimination of designated lodging for litigants with the dissolution of guilds during the Tempō Reforms had little impact on suit inns. Their specialist knowledge and long service to the state insulated them from reforms.[160] In the meantime, increasing contact with the rest of the world made legal practice a subject of mutual interest to the Japanese and their foreign observers. These cross-cultural observations took place at a world-historical moment when private legal practice had not yet fully formed into the legal profession. Public intellectuals from Adam Smith to Fukuzawa Yukichi grappled with the meaning and place of the legal practitioner in (pre)industrializing society. More often than not, the conclusions drawn by such thinkers reflected their predispositions, not close analysis of underlying practices. Japanese "discoverers" of Europe idealized European legal practitioners while criticizing legal practice at home.[161] Fukuzawa, writing of his 1861 travels to Europe, was struck by the prominence of legal advocates and European systems of representation for criminal defendants.[162] Others focused on the integrity of foreign legal practitioners in private practice. In 1867, Kurimoto Jo'un, the first Japanese ambassador to France, wrote about the French *avocat* in the record of his travels, *Gyōsō tsuroku*:

There is a person who mediates legal suits, this person resembles Japan's suit solicitors somewhat but differs greatly. These people have memorized the laws and their personality is characterized by honesty. . . . They receive a larger salary than officials. . . . When there is reason to bring a legal suit they do so, when there is no reason to file, they endeavor to put a stop to the suit.[163]

Kurimoto's description, so common to international comparison designed to prompt reform at home, vilified the failings of his compatriot legal practitioners and idealized the French.[164]

---

160. Minami, *Bakumatsu toshi shakai no kenkyū*, 198–99.

161. Or they misunderstood. In 1811 Shiba Kōkan, known for, among other things, his study of perspective in painting, mistakenly described legal advocates (*adobokaato*) as physical scientists. Shiba, "Shuparo hikki," cited in Osatake, *Meiji keisatsu saiban shi*, 185.

162. Ibid., 186–87.

163. Kurimoto Jo'un, "Gyōsō tsuroku," cited in Osatake, *Meiji keisatsu saiban shi*, 187–89. See also Kurimoto Jo'un, "Gyōsō tsuroku," in Nihon shiseki kyōkai, ed., *Hōan ikō*.

164. Akin to Alexis de Tocqueville on American democracy.

Kurimoto's complaint was that the Japanese petitioner received very little value for the expense of a suit inn's services. High cost was one source of broad animosity toward legal practitioners in the eighteenth and nineteenth centuries. Low qualifications and the ambiguous status of the private legal practitioner in relation to the state was another. Suit inns were notorious in nineteenth-century accounts of Edo culture, including the 1816 social commentary "Seji kenmonroku" (Record of things seen and heard) and Kitagawa Morisada's 1853 miscellany. Both texts provide a sense of the low regard for the high cost of litigation in Edo society.[165] Buyō Inshi's "Seji kenmonroku" discussed litigation and suit inns at length leading to conjecture that the pseudonymous Buyō "may have been a suit solicitor . . . with a life supported by a good income."[166] Writing on Edo-era customs and manners four decades later, Kitagawa described the substandard accommodations offered by the Edo inns: "The lodgings designated for travelers to Edo who have business with the government . . . are not as commodious as the lodgings in Kyoto and Osaka. The [lodgings in Edo] are inferior in the extreme."[167] Kitagawa scored them poorly on food service, too. "In contrast to inns in Kyoto and Osaka they gather guests in the kitchen to feed them rather than serving each person individually."[168] And trying to cut through the array of fees and surcharges was hopeless. "If one asks for a set price for lodging, one will not receive one."[169] Expensive and low-quality amenities earned suit inns notoriety. Edo's suit solicitors brought suits in order to profit from the prolonged trials and absconded with monies left to them in escrow.[170] In the 1790s, the poorer petitioners of Osaka and Kyoto who could not pay the prices at officially designated inns slept on the thresh-

---

165. On state efforts to control costs, see Takayanagi and Ishii, eds., *Ofuregaki kanpō shūsei*, 1197.

166. According to Harada Tomohiko, Takikawa Masajirō concluded that the author, pen-named Buyō Inshi, was likely either of the *gosanke* class or a suit solicitor who was a masterless samurai from a *shinpan* family. Introduction to Buyō Inshi's "Seji Kenmonroku" in Miyamoto et al., comp., *Nihon shomin seikatsu shiryō shūsei*, 641.

167. Morisada Mankō in Haruhara, *Ōsaka no machibugyōsho to saiban*, 43.

168. Ibid.

169. Ibid.

170. Henderson, *Conciliation and Japanese Law*, 1:169. See also Minami, *Bakumatsu toshi shakai no kenkyū*, 186–87.

old of government offices or, "in good weather, by the side of the road."[171] These comments reflected the criticisms of Edo-era legal practitioners in what was ostensibly a moral economy. Observers complained that they cheated clients and society.

As for low status and ambiguous standing, Edo-era suit solicitors and suit inns were not alone. The social image of the *kujishi* as a pettifogger, or "rascally attorney," resonated with negative depictions of the venality of early modern legal practitioners elsewhere.[172] Even though Japanese observers asserted that suit solicitors were unique in bringing matters without any basis in law just to collect fees, they often failed to recognize a similar ambiguity or even contempt in Europe and the United States, where private legal practitioners also came under criticism. At the same time that Japanese observers celebrated the *avocat*, their French counterparts complained of the excesses of their own domestic profession. In France, "one of the objectives of the [French] Revolution was to make [advocates] unnecessary."[173] This objective failed, and in the French social imagination the legal advocate became identified with elitism and privilege.[174] Manorial stewards in England of the late sixteenth and early seventeenth centuries who provided legal services were persons "on the borderline between the lawyers and the man of affairs."[175] Lawrence Friedman in his *History of American Law* notes the low regard in which colonial Americans held practitioners of law. During the eighteenth century, "lawyers, like shopkeepers, moneylenders, and lower bureaucrats, [were] social middlemen . . . lightning rods that [drew] rage during storms in the polity."[176] In New Jersey and other places, mobs rioted against legal practitioners. In England, there were also complaints about the high cost and low qualifications of legal practitioners. Despite this, economies in the midst of market and industrial transformation witnessed high demand for expert assistance in dispute resolution.

---

171. Ibid., 46.

172. A definition for a pettifogger is "a legal practitioner of inferior status, who gets up or conducts petty cases; *esp.* in an opprobrious sense, one who employs mean, sharp, cavilling practices; a 'rascally attorney,'" Murray, et al., eds. *Oxford English Dictionary*, 755.

173. Merryman, *The Civil Law Tradition*, 28.

174. Bell, *Lawyers and Citizens*.

175. Brooks, *Pettyfoggers and Vipers of the Commonwealth*, 45.

176. Friedman, *A History of American Law*, 96.

One justification for the high pay of legal practitioners can be found in Adam Smith's comment that this was a person to whom one trusted one's "fortune and sometimes [one's] life and reputation."[177] Even as a burgeoning market economy called forth the legal practitioner, this person's place in society and politics remained in question. During the Edo era, the uncertain place of suit inns and suit solicitors complicated the processes of private law. In contrast to the state-approved position legal practitioners occupied in the Euro-American judiciary, the Tokugawa suppressed legal representation and private legal practice. Even though magistrates at times ignored the presence of legal practitioners, there were no grounds on which a client could demand to have legal representation in an appearance before a judicial official. In 1881, a little more than a decade after the fall of the Tokugawa, legal advocate (*daigennin*) Machida Iwajirō put it this way: a party going before a Tokugawa magistrate faced an atmosphere of "inappropriate violence" (*fushō bōkō*).[178] In other words, the party could be punished, simply for engaging in a private dispute. Moreover, the party called before a magistrate languished in the "darkness of the law."[179] In an inquisitorial matter, the accused might not know the charges she faced or the statutes by which she would be tried. Machida imagined a system in which law would constrain the actions of even the highest political authorities while a legal advocate identified and defended the interest of the lowest litigant. Although Edo legal proceedings were not always as inimical to a party's interest as Machida described, no Edo-era proceeding approached his ideal. The recording officers of the magistrates arbitrarily determined how one entered the *shirasu*, the arena of the state's juridical power. If the recording officer wished, a defendant might kneel on the uneven surface of the white gravel, isolated and alone. In other instances, parties were permitted to employ a representative who might translate their case into a language that would soften or even neutralize the power of the judicial authorities.

In the late nineteenth century, an increasingly powerful centralized state and an increasingly organized field of legal advocates associated the shortcomings of the Meiji legal system with Edo practices. A backward,

---

177. Smith, *The Wealth of Nations*, 173.
178. Machida, ed., *Tokyo daigennin retsuden*, 3.
179. Ibid.

feudal Japan could not have yielded legal representation, they concluded; this could only come from abroad. The self-Orientalism of the 1880s and 1890s buried the domestic history of private legal practice. It also rendered invisible the broader international changes in legal practice typical of late-nineteenth-century industrialization and the possibility that Japan and Europe might have similar historical experiences. In this vein, a 1935 history of Japanese legal practice by the Tokyo Bar Association argued that the legal profession in Japan was a foreign transplant. The association claimed that there were no legal representatives during the Edo period because proprietors of suit inns (*kujiyado*) and their employees prepared documents for clients in the manner of notaries and law copyists. Suit inns and suit solicitors transcribed accounts of events and drafted petitions and pleadings; thus, they fell short of Anglo-American systems that emphasized oral pleading. Echoing the British distinction between solicitor and barrister, the early-twentieth-century Japanese bar focused on courtroom representation as a sign of modernity. If one did not argue cases before judges, then one was not a modern lawyer.[180] Here the Tokyo bar marked itself off from the perceived dark ages of the Edo era by pointing to a modernity imported from the outside.

Yet the collapse of the Tokugawa invited multiple perspectives on its approach to law and legal practice. Where Japanese observers saw mostly domestic darkness, John Henry Wigmore, a law professor from the United States teaching in Japan, took a brighter view. An 1889 letter to Wigmore from Herbert Baxter Adams, then president of The Johns Hopkins University, urged a sympathetic reading of Japanese history. "I believe you could render a substantial service to New Japan by Historical investigations into the social and legal History of Old Japan."[181] Wigmore did just that in *A Panorama of World Legal Systems*: "[D]eveloped by native genius, [the Tokugawa legal system] might in the local course of events have produced more distinctive fruits."[182] By this he meant that there were clearly dramatic shifts before 1868. A comprehensive system of laws governing disputes among individuals broke with patterns of conflict

---

180. Adachi G., ed., *Tokyo bengoshikaishi*, 1.

181. Letter from H. B. Adams to John H. Wigmore, cited in Riles, ed., *Rethinking the Masters of Comparative Law*, 101.

182. Wigmore, *A Panorama of the World's Legal Systems*, 519–20.

resolution based on personal loyalty and vendettas.[183] In Europe, this, along with the break between property and sovereignty, yielded a system of civil law and protection of political rights for former warrior estates. In the tradition of John Locke, Blandine Kriegel tied the rise of human rights to protection of property. "[K]ings and states became sovereign over subjects residing in a given place but no longer belonging to a domain."[184] Separation of aristocrats from their fiefs as physical spaces that they inhabited generated demands for guarantees that protected aristocratic privilege. In the Tokugawa system, although samurai were removed from the land and relocated to castle towns, they still retained a tenuous connection to the lands that produced their stipends; the income of both domainal lords and samurai remained nominally tied to specific places. By the early nineteenth century, this system yielded the farce of a samurai in hard times returning to the fief of his overlord and extorting a loan from villagers with a threat that he would commit suicide in their midst if they did not cooperate.[185] In Europe, protection of aristocratic privilege separate from land evolved into rights protections. In Japan, the maintenance of ties to geography, as tenuous as they were, supported fictions of connection and hierarchy. The early 1870s erased the formal dimensions of these hierarchies, yet their residue continued to shape understandings of private legal practice. The ambiguous history of the suit solicitor, in particular, drove former samurai in the 1870s and 1880s to recast their past in ways that would open up possibilities for recharacterizing the relationship between state and subject along legally defined lines.

It was not until the early twentieth century in Japan that the suit solicitor and suit inn began to emerge from the obscurity of historical amnesia and ill-fated happenstance to catch the attention of discerning observers of domestic legal traditions. In 1919, suit solicitor-turned-beer-magnate Makoshi Kyōhei offered to donate the materials from his Edo-era legal practice in Osaka to the Reading Room of the First Tokyo Bar Association. At the time, lawyer-politician Hara Yoshimichi noted the

---

183. Ikegami, *The Taming of the Samurai.*
184. Kriegel, *The State and the Rule of Law,* 59.
185. Katsu, *Musui's Story.*

paucity of primary source material preserved by Edo-era private practitioners. Sitting alongside Makoshi at a roundtable he observed, "[T]here exists a considerable record on the side of the state about the activities of both the magistrates and the constables [*yoriki*], yet for the private side—the suit solicitors [*kuijishi*], in other words—I have seen nothing."[186] In an unfortunate turn for historians, Tokyo-resident Makoshi tarried in fulfilling his promise; his records from his days as a private legal practitioner at the Harimaya suit inn in Osaka turned to ashes in the widespread fire following the Great Kanto Earthquake of 1923, leaving only a slender sheaf of papers.

As Hara Yoshimichi noted, beyond the narrative of the bureaucratization of law and the state, early twentieth-century analysts of the indigenous legal tradition had paltry grounds on which to puzzle together an indigenous history of an Edo-era legal transformation in private practice. Only recently, as historians have again turned their attentions to suit solicitors and suit inns, can one begin to discern Edo-era shifts that contributed to economic and political changes of the nineteenth century, including capital formation and the emergence of the individual as a political subject. Since early modernity—in Europe and the United States, as in Japan—the private legal practitioner has been an object of simultaneous adulation and scorn. In more recent history, the American lawyer has become a figure upon whom rests societywide hopes and fears of dramatic social and political change. Although the Edo-era suit solicitors and suit inns occupied a different place in the social imagery, their ubiquity and influence opened the way for the dramatic legal changes of the last quarter of the nineteenth century.

Three legal actors—the suit solicitors, suit inns, and guilds of inns lodging parties to disputes—helped petitioners tell the stories of their disputes. By crafting accounts of petitioners' cases that conformed to the expectations of the shogun, they shored up legal processes in daily life while also expanding the capacity of the authorities to serve as the legal arbiters of disputes among nearly all members of society. Even as

---

186. Hara, *Bengoshi seikatsu no kaikō*, cited in Takikawa M., "Kujishi Makoshi Kyōhei Okina no kotodomo," 49–52.

they translated the vernacular of an increasingly commercialized everyday life into the language of the official orthodoxy, suit solicitors, suit inns, and their guilds undermined Tokugawa efforts to enforce ideals of social harmony. In the end, this made authority vulnerable to influence; at its narrowest, this influence included the processes through which the suit inns and their guilds created space for legal and political activity.

CHAPTER 2

Processes and Practitioners: The Fluid Morality of Early Meiji Legal Practice

Legacies of domestic legal practice and social engagement with law shaped the new legal processes that emerged during the first years of the Meiji era. Early Meiji private legal practitioners harbored ideas of justice reminiscent of the Edo era, sustaining them even within new legal reforms. In addition to former suit solicitors and suit inn proprietors, there emerged private practitioners unconnected to the Edo past. As the state adopted reforms to reorder relations with foreign powers, it accepted the notion that private legal practice could be available to all people, even as it sought to regulate and mold it. Two individuals—one a woman who wove together indigenous moral and legal ideals, the other a man who embraced foreign moral and legal traditions—illustrated the complexity of the transitional moment from 1868 through the end of the 1870s. Female legal advocate Sono Tel practiced a hybrid form of law that sought to achieve the Edo-era goals of justice and harmony on a new legal landscape. For Sono, Meiji legal reforms created an opportunity to extend even further the moral ideals characteristic of Tokugawa Neo-Confucianism. Sono, who practiced from 1874 to the early 1880s, was mentioned only briefly in late-nineteenth-century accounts as a prototype of Japan's female lawyer. In contrast, historians of legal practice in Japan have long identified former samurai Kodama Jun'ichirō, who also began his practice in 1874, as a harbinger of the modern lawyer in Japan.

Even as Meiji reforms made Sono's and Kodama's practices of law possible, their practices did not entirely embody the regime's ideals. Their careers were not unambiguous symbols of an approach to law that was "enlightened" or "Western"—terms that many contemporaries read as synonymous. Rather, the way in which Sono and Kodama approached the practice of law embodied the historical fluidity and possibility of the early 1870s. Their careers manifested, in different ways, the originating influences on Meiji legal reforms: the intersection of domestic and international legal thought, domestic attempts to incorporate and overcome Edo-era traditions, and the tacit moral trappings of Japanese, American, and European legal cultures. Whereas Meiji legal reformers rejected the Tokugawa vision of law and society that put morality in the foreground, Sono's and Kodama's practices remained enthralled with a moral legal vision. While working in Tokyo, Sono wove together Confucian piety and law in her life and legal practice. Kodama's embrace of Christianity, which included ordination as a minister, occupied a more ambiguous place in a career ultimately focused on achieving success through service to the state.

Much as Tokugawa legal reforms had unexpected consequences, so too did Meiji legal reforms. Laws aimed at shoring up the power of the central state created opportunities for new personalities to try their hands at new forms of legal practice. The changes were dramatic, and they altered the landscape upon which private legal advocates operated. Sono and Kodama followed different paths toward the future that emerged out of the early 1870s. Sono brought a folk understanding of law as morality to her practice as a legal advocate. As one of the first female legal practitioners in Japanese history, her gender may have signaled change, but her approach to legal conflict drew on vernacular ideas about justice from before 1868. From the turn of the twentieth century, historians regarded legal advocate Kodama's appearance as a turning point. Meanwhile, Edo-era practitioners, including suit solicitors (*kujishi*), remained mainstays in the legal field.

Sono, Kodama, and former suit solicitors and suit inn operators joined together in an extraordinary historical moment to integrate the old and the new into a hybrid legal practice. While revealing the domestic legal and social fluidity of Japan during the early 1870s, their careers also unfolded in a larger international framework of contention over the relationship between morality and law. Even as the work of Sono and Kodama reflected these debates, both advocates addressed these issues not at the level of theory but at the level of practice. Theirs was the story of the legal advocate (*daigennin*) now free to operate on the judicial landscape, but a landscape in transition, a landscape of shifting moral, legal, and political grounds.[1] In the context of early Meiji discourses on civilization, legal reform meant encoding Euro-American practices as the new universal. As for the old universal, a Neo-Confucian–inflected legal moralism, its elements were recoded or discarded by practitioners such as Sono, Kodama, and former suit solicitors who served as legal representatives during the early 1870s.

Meiji Legal Reform: Bridging Regimes of Legal Practice

The final years of the shogunate and the first years of the Meiji era brought an explosion of peasant uprisings in agricultural villages, the evisceration of Tokugawa legitimacy by leading samurai intellectuals, and the ultimate collapse of the shogunate-domainal system; judicial processes, however, experienced working and reworking from the inside, with many of the personnel, including legal practitioners and magistrates (turned "judges"), remaining after 1868. After the reforms of the 1870s, law began to shift from a tool for ruling to a totalizing, epistemological framework that called forth a national state and set the terms for political, social, and economic relations within society.

Characterizing this shift was a synthesis of earlier practice traditions including the public's ready resort to litigation, reformulated through encounters with legal theories from Europe and the United States. The numerous private disputes that the shogunate failed to keep outside of its ambit had created a vernacular understanding of the law. Meiji legal reforms of the 1870s and 1880s encountered a populace ready to navigate a system in which the Meiji authorities finally came to condone what had long been actual practice.

As a new regime that came to power through the overthrow of the prevailing orthodoxy, the Meiji government gained at home and abroad by repudiating the legal practices of its predecessor as hidebound. The quest to restore national sovereignty called forth reforms rejecting Edo norms and practices while catering to Euro-American sensibilities. Reformers believed that the Japanese government could undo unfair treaties

---

1. Reitan, *Making a Moral Society*.

and convey to observers at home and abroad that Japan was, in the terms of the day, civilized and enlightened. An enlightened judiciary rejected torture as a means of extracting confessions, did not use brutal punishments, and did not threaten to punish parties for bringing private disputes. In response to foreign pressure, the state made clear the inchoate distinction between public and private law, already emergent during the Edo era.[2] Yet Meiji reforms were not simply foreign imports; the complex unfolding of state reforms was not a march toward a single outcome where Japan received modern law from Europe and the United States. Rather, the project of reconciling earlier legal practices to late-nineteenth-century ideals of rational progress occurred nearly concurrently on Japanese and international stages.

As is so often the case, the story of Meiji change begins with the state and its reforms. Yet the state was not the motive force but rather a bridge between the practices established by legal practitioners during the Edo era and an emergent global legal order of the last decades of the nineteenth century. As the Ministry of Justice focused its energies on translating foreign laws into the Japanese context, legal practice and the litigating public were enlivened by, and enlivened, legal reforms through dissemination of laws in print, resolution of disputes through litigation, normalization of legal practice in 1872, the redesign of the courtroom, and the opening of the courtroom to the press and public.

For the Meiji government, unequal treaties provided the impetus for sweeping reforms designed to protect state sovereignty and answer foreign condemnation of earlier forms of punishment as barbaric. As William Elliot Griffis noted in *The Mikado's Empire*, "[W]hile Japan maintained the institutions of barbarism, [signatories to the unequal treaties] refused to recognize her as a peer in the comity of nations."[3] Since the 1850s, the so-called unequal treaties signed by countries including Britain, France, the United States, Germany, and the Kingdom of Hawai'i had removed first shogunate and then Meiji control over tariffs and duties and imposed a system of extraterritoriality. This meant that for foreign sailors and merchants, the laws of one's home country governed a person's actions in

---

2. For a description of the evolution of distinctions between criminal and civil procedure, see Maki and Fujiwara, eds., *Nihon hōseishi*, 306–12.

3. Griffis, *The Mikado's Empire*, 572.

Japan. Initially, the unequal treaties rested on the logic of force; over time, their maintenance was based on claims about shortcomings in the Japanese justice system. In 1871, Minister of Justice Etō Shinpei responded by initiating a sweeping transformation of Japanese laws that he hoped would cause "every foreign country to recognize the fact of our independent nation."[4] The reform of Japanese law hinged on a civilizational critique by foreign treaty powers focused on public morality. To escape the inequities of the unequal treaties, early Meiji legal reformers called for a complete overhaul of Tokugawa practices. They began with the eighteenth-century *Kujikata osadamegaki,* with its harsh punishments (including decapitation for adultery). Revised codes limited crucifixion to cases of regicide or parricide. Public exposure of the decapitated head replaced burning at the stake. Imprisonment replaced expatriation.[5] Meiji oligarchs also ordered the eradication of a host of social and cultural practices foreigners deemed abhorrent, such as public urination and nudity.[6] Shortly after the Restoration, the Meiji government established new national legal codes based on Chinese models (codes of the Tang and Qing dynasties) including a provisional criminal code (1868, *Kari keiritsu*), a revised outline of the criminal code called the Principles of the New Statutes (1870, *Shinritsu kōryō,* instituted in 1871), and the 1873 Amended (Criminal) Code (*Kaitei ritsurei*).[7] According to Tokugawa practice, when the *Kujikata* offered no guidance in complex cases, magistrates substituted reason (*dōri*) derived from earlier rulings to make their decisions. New codes departed from the shogunate's commitment to domestic precedent as articulated in the *Kujikata osadamegaki.* In another departure from Edo practice, the government printed copies of the

---

4. Kikuyama, "Etō Shinpei no shihō kaikaku," 94.

5. Fujii J., *Outline of Japanese History in the Meiji Era,* 7:35.

6. Reitan, *Making a Moral Society,* 12–13.

7. For a discussion of early Meiji criminal law, including a discussion of the provisional [criminal] code (*Kari keiritsu*), the Principles of the New Statutes (*Shinritsu kōryō*), and a translation of the *Shinritsu kōryō,* see Ch'en, *The Formation of the Early Meiji Legal Order.* With gradual revision, first in the *Kaitei ritsurei* of 1873 and then by decree, the criminal codes of the 1870s began to depart from the Chinese model, abandoning caning and favoring confinement and hard labor as forms of punishment. Also, revisions in the Chinese-influenced codes increasingly gave judges leeway in sentencing, 22–27. Also, see Umemori, "Spatial Configuration and Subject Formation."

Principles of the New Statutes and distributed them widely. Codes, the reasoning went, would create certainty and transparency.

Early codification efforts did not placate foreign critics: there remained powerful continuities with the Edo era too numerous to overlook. Although codification met one demand of continental Europeans, the ready resort to corporal punishment and an emphasis on the family as a unit of responsibility, among other factors, rendered early reforms unacceptable. Also, foreign critics cited the practice of torture as a means of extracting confessions and the brutality and publicity of punishment as persistent signs of Japanese backwardness. As Griffis noted, foreign powers could not overlook that Japan "slandered Christianity . . . imprisoned men for their belief, knew nothing of trial by jury, of the habeas corpus writ, or of modern jurisprudence."[8]

Even if the codes had met foreign expectations, the ability of the political center to enforce a national vision was limited. Throughout the 1870s, the national judiciary's grasp was tenuous at best. Through 1876, regional differences dominated courtroom approaches to both criminal prosecutions and civil disputes.[9] In some regional courts, it took even longer for national legal reforms to take hold.

Reformers soon realized that overturning the unequal treaties required a rooting out of the underlying assumptions of the Tokugawa Neo-Confucian orthodoxy supported by local and regional practices. The Meiji regime turned to French legal codes as a solution. Codification along French lines promised to concentrate power in a process that would work in two directions: outward vis-à-vis foreign powers and inward toward local governments. Etō Shinpei and his successors took a comprehensive approach to reform. To understand and create a system of jurisprudence that would meet foreign standards and reflect not just the ideals but also the practice of law, the Meiji state hired foreign advisers and established a translation bureau for European laws, focusing initially on French law. Foreign scholars of law included Frenchmen Georges Bousquet (in Japan from 1872 to 1876) and Gustave Emile Boissonade de Fontarabie (in Japan from 1873 to 1893). Later, others including the American John

---

8. Griffis, *The Mikado's Empire*, 572.
9. Kasumi, "Criminal Trials in the Early Meiji Era."

Wigmore consulted the Ministry of Justice on legal reform and penned draft laws. In 1869, Mitsukuri Rinshō, in consultation with Boissonade, translated the French penal code, which formed the basis for replacing the Provisional Code and New Statutes. The penal code (or old criminal law) was established in 1880. Boissonade also contributed to early drafts of civil and commercial codes translated by Mitsukuri. For court personnel, including procurators and judges, the government established a training institute. The Meihōryo, established in September 1871, trained justice bureaucrats primarily in French law, with instruction from government-employed foreign legal specialists.[10] The student body consisted mainly of former samurai.

Among government officials worldwide, Meiji reformers were not alone in their embrace of the French civil law model. An 1861 report to the British Parliament enthused, "[I]t is its rational form . . . [it is] its rational spirit, that the [Napoleonic] Code has to thank for a popularity that makes half the nations of Europe desirous to adopt it."[11] Legal reformers across continents viewed the French legal system and its Napoleonic Code as a paragon of comprehensiveness and rationality. In such places as Italy and Germany that underwent parallel processes of unification during the latter part of the nineteenth century, the code provided guidance. During the 1870s, even the United States, with its tradition of legal precedent (stare decisis), witnessed a movement to introduce legal science in ways that would mirror civil law along French lines.[12] Bousquet observed how some Meiji legal reformers thought that because the Napoleonic Code was "the greatest law among the civilized nations . . . they need do little more than translate this and promulgate it as quickly as possible."[13] Napoleon had a similar easy optimism about his codification project. Although in his day an elaborate judiciary and multiple layers of legal practice marked the French legal system, he imagined that the code would speak to every possibility and foreclose independent legal thought and interpretation.

---

10. Iwatani, "Kindai Nihon hōseishi kenkyū ni okeru 'gakushiki' hanji to no sōgū," 2.
11. Arnold, "Report on the Systems of Popular Education," 99.
12. Merryman, *The Civil Law Tradition*, 79.
13. Bousquet, *Le Japon de nos jours*, 283–84.

A comprehensive, rationalizing vision was part of the code's appeal. In contrast to the Anglo-American tradition of celebrating leading lawyers and barristers as important figures in legal interpretation, the French tradition that Japanese officials emulated was one of "mythologizing law" rather than "mythologiz[ing] the work of courtroom advocates."[14] In Napoleon's conception of the code, both bench and bar were mere functionaries. Judge and private legal advocate alike existed solely to process legal cases according to statute. Moreover, legal advocates, particularly associations of legal advocates in Paris, had contributed to the fall of France's old regime. Because of this revolutionary legacy and in a move reminiscent of Tokugawa attempts to enforce social cohesion through control on legal commentary, Napoleon's government required legal advocates to swear that they would not "say or publish anything contrary to laws, to rulings, to morals, to the security of the State or to public tranquility."[15] Despite his optimism, Napoleon's code did not eliminate the need for interpretation nor did it limit the political power of private legal practitioners in France. When Napoleon heard that a commentary had been written on the civil code, he is reported to have said, "My code is lost."[16] In France, judges and legal advocates alike engaged with the code and interpreted it. By the 1870s, legal advocacy in Paris had become a powerful force in politics.

Similarly, the Meiji reforms of the 1870s did not miraculously remove all of the vestiges of Japan's past practices. In 1877, foreign legal adviser Georges Bousquet observed, "The ministers of Japan are relying on the illuminating knowledge of foreign countries, yet I think that they have little understanding of how large and difficult this job is, and how long it will take."[17] From the outside, the reform of the Japanese judiciary may have looked like a headlong rush toward the adoption of foreign practices, but what was unfolding was an internal negotiation over the locus of power and authority. Although the complaint of later generations was

---

14. Provine, "Courts in the Political Process in France," 202.

15. Bell, *Lawyers and Citizens*, 210–15.

16. Merryman, *The Civil Law Tradition*, 28, 58–59: "My code is lost because the lawyers and commentators have already clarified what I meant when I adopted it." In Dawson, *Oracles of the Law*, 387.

17. Bousquet, *Le Japon de nos jours*, 283–84.

that the central state was too powerful, the extension of its reach into people's daily lives was tenuous during the first half of the 1870s. Thus, early Meiji legal reforms of that decade not only looked toward shoring up the outward strength of the national state, they also projected state power inward.

The extension of national control into historically semiautonomous or self-governing spaces of local communities, guilds, and domains was a central feature of early Meiji legal reform. Acts of national political consolidation between 1868 and 1871 included the establishment of a national currency; the termination of the barrier system on highways; a revision of the tax system, directing revenue to the central government; and central political control over the archipelago including the establishment of an administrative system for prefectures and cities. Yet the terms defining the balance of power between the political center and the localities, now prefectures and not domains, remained unresolved. In 1872, the Ministry of Justice unsuccessfully demanded for the national courts the power of calling out troops to put down local uprisings, a power previously held by local governors. Echoing an earlier understanding of the state as Confucian moral exemplar, the ministry argued that riots and uprisings stemmed from the failure of prefectural governments to educate the people. Still in the grip of Confucian didacticism, the ministry augmented its claims with an emphasis on private property. The ministry argued that it was the prerogative of the courts to protect "civil and property rights" when regional government failed. The executive rejected these claims, leaving local government the victor.[18] Yet, central government officials won a separate victory the same year. In the Ono-gumi Relocation Incident, a dispute over whether a financial group could move its operations from Kansai to Tokyo, the courts called on the governor of Kyoto to testify. He refused, and was later found in contempt of court, fined, and sentenced to 100 days of confinement.[19] During the 1870s, the balance of power continued to shift toward Tokyo, yet successful centralization was

---

18. *Kōmonroku*, "Shihōshō no bu" (Jan. 1873), as cited in Kikuyama, "Etō Shinpei no shihō kaikaku," 110.

19. Legal scholars mark this incident as a turning point in early Meiji state formation and an example of the separation of powers in action; see Koizumi, *Meiji reimeiki no hanzai to keibatsu*, 22–25.

not yet certain. Whether or not a dominant regime would emerge and rule out of Tokyo remained in question at least through the end of the decade.

Even as the early Meiji state embraced codification of law along European lines, ambiguities of Edo-era history, including the lack of a distinction between civil and criminal matters, use of torture to elicit confessions, and uncertainty about the source of law, lingered well into the mid-1870s (and beyond). In a move toward a distinction between adversarial and inquisitorial matters, an August 1872 edict reduced the instances in which a judge might threaten caning to induce an arbitrated settlement between private parties.[20] Even so, adherence to old practices remained. In criminal matters, procurators continued to use torture as a means for extracting confessions. Accounts credit foreign legal adviser Boissonade with the abolition of the use of torture to extract confessions in criminal cases. However, prohibition of torture did not mean an end to the practice in imperial Japan. Through the 1940s, the national associations of lawyers—the Japan Lawyers' and the Imperial Lawyers' Associations—led campaigns to end the torture of those accused of crimes.

In the absence of universally accepted legal codes, hybrid interpretations and competing ways of thinking about law, custom, and reason wrestled before judges in the courtroom. In part, civil litigation reflected old practices and included personages from the old regime, including former magistrates-turned-judges and former suit solicitors-turned-legal advocates. In part, it emulated the most progressive European, American, and Japanese ideals of the day.

In 1867, the Ministry of Commerce had abolished guilds and monopolies and in April 1872, the Ministry of Justice under Etō Shinpei issued the Judicial Staff Regulations and Operating Rules (*Shokumu teisei*), which laid out the first steps toward a complete overhaul of the justice system. These measures marked decisive shifts away from the structures in which legal practitioners operated before 1868. The Operating Rules established new categories of legal representation and removed vestiges of the old Tokugawa framework.[21] Ōno Masao has written, "[I]n terms

---

20. Takikawa E., "Meiji shoki no hikiainin," 32–33, 38–39.

21. Judicial Staff Regulations and Operating Rules of 1872, or Shihō shokusei narabi ni jimu shōtei, often abbreviated as *Shokumu teisei*. This was an unnumbered Dajōkan

of its form, this new system was 'revolutionary,' completely removed from the previous, traditional system."[22] Gone was a state policy that suppressed legal practice and sanctioned private monopolies for suit inns and their guilds. Individual legal practitioners could now represent parties to private disputes, in contrast to the informal and tenuous practices of the suit solicitors (*kujishi*) before 1872. The rules, based on French regulations, articulated the role and function of the various participants in the judicial process, on the side of state and society. Judges and public procurators (who would serve as investigators and prosecutors in the Ministry of Justice) filled the courts. As for private practitioners, there would be legal advocates, notaries, and legal scriveners, corresponding to the French *avocat, notaire,* and *avoué.*[23] One of the earliest iterations of the Japanese translation of the French term *avocat* (*daigennin*) appeared in Iwakura Tomomi's 1872 accounts of his travels. This was the term that the Meiji regime adopted for those who took up legal representation in court, "one who speaks on behalf of others."[24] The Staff Regulations and Operating Rules charged the legal advocate with "bring[ing] a suit on behalf of one who does not do so on his or her own . . ."[25] Former suit

---

decree, issued on Apr. 27. The regulations on legal practice were modeled on French laws regarding legal practice. See Inoue, *Fukkoku shihō sanshoku kō.*

22. Ōno, "Shokugyōshi toshite no bengoshi oyobi bengoshi dantai no rekishi," 8–9.

23. Osatake, *Meiji keisatsu saiban shi,* 187–89. A foreshadowing of the successor term for the legal advocate, the "lawyer," or *bengoshi,* appeared as *bengonin* in the text of the 1880 Code of Criminal Instruction.

24. See also translations of the term *daigennin* in an English-Japanese dictionary from 1862. *Daigennin* was defined as a "talesman," which in mid-nineteenth-century usage referred to both a juror in a legal trial and a teller of tales. Hori Tatsunosuke and Horikoshi Kamenosuke, *Wa-ei taishaku shūchin jisho,* as cited in Sōgō and Hida, eds., *Meiji no kotoba,* 344.

25. 1872 Aug. 24, Ministry of Justice Unnumbered Circular, chap. 10, Duties of Conveyancers, Copyists, Advocates, arts. 41–43, in Tokyo bengoshikai hyakunenshi hensan kankō tokubetsu iinkai, ed., *Tokyo bengoshikai hyakunenshi.* For articles in the *Shokumu teisei* relevant to legal practice, see Nihon bengoshi rengōkai, ed., *Nihon bengoshi enkakushi,* 5–10. In addition to the *Shokumu teisei,* other regulations governed legal practice, including the "Sotō bunrei narabi furoku," effective 1 Sept. 1873. From 1 Jul., Dajōkan Circular No. 247, on *daigennin:* vol. 1, sect. 10, arts. 30–32; vol. 2, sect. 3, arts. 35–37, apps. 11–12; on *daishonin:* vol. 1, sect. 2, arts. 3–5; vol. 2, sect. 2, art. 34. See also Okudaira, *Nihon bengoshishi,* 39–42, and Murakami K., "Kindaiteki daigennin no tōjō," 44.

solicitors and others flocked to the new occupations created by legal reform. Before, the licensing of legal advocates in 1876, these people went
uncounted. With increasing documentation and regulation of legal
practice there were more than 900 licensed legal advocates throughout
Japan by 1880. Additionally, there were many more unlicensed legal advocates who appeared before judges, particularly in jurisdictions under-
served by licensees.[26] For example, in 1880 the court at Shizuoka counted
only 29 licensed legal advocates on its register; yet the *Tokyo-Yokohama
mainichi* newspaper cited sources showing 40 legal advocates practicing in the city.[27] The article stated that this was not just a Shizouka
phenomenon but a national trend. Legal advocates practiced without
making any pretence whatsoever of having a license. Among these
were many of the leading former-samurai proponents of legal advocacy
during the 1870s and 1880s, including Numa Morikazu and Shimamoto
Nakamichi.

Beyond the legal advocate, the Regulations and Operating Rules created two other categories of private legal practitioner. The first was the
"notary or conveyancer" (*shōshonin*), the forerunner of the notary public
(*kōshōnin*), who "certified contracts in matters of buying and selling
[property], lending [money], and the holding of rice land, fields, dwellings,
and stores."[28] Following the dissolution of the land tenure system that
obtained during the Edo period, work by notaries was particularly important. As specified in the Staff Regulations and Operating Rules, every municipality required a notary to certify titles and deeds.[29] In many
cases, the ward head of the community worked as a notary, thus maintaining an overlap between public and private roles that had marked
the Edo period—where legal practitioners also operated as functionaries
of the state when they summoned parties to court, held parties in in-

---

26. Hattori, "The Legal Profession in Japan," 119.

27. *Tōkyō-Yokohama mainichi shinbun* (16 Jan. 1880), cited in Yokohama bengoshikai
kaishi hensan iinkai, ed., *Yokohama bengoshikaishi*, 1:23–24.

28. For the text of the *Shokumu teisei*, see the appendices of the Tokyo bengoshikai
hyakunenshi hensan kankō tokubetsu iinkai, ed., *Tokyo bengoshikai hyakunenshi*, 1–21.

29. Chap. 10, art. 41, sect. 1 of the *Shokumu teisei*. See Nihon shihōshoshikai
rengōkai, ed., *Nihon shihōshoshishi*, 99–100.

quisitorial proceedings, and performed other work for the judicial bureaucracy.[30]

Legal scrivener was the other category of legal practice created by the rules. In terms of function, the legal scrivener was something of a replacement for the *sashizoenin*. During the Edo period, the *sashizoenin*, and other parties with ambiguous standing in the court, spoke on behalf of defendants or parties to disputes and vouched for the veracity of their statement(s) and the documentary evidence that they provided.[31] The 1872 regulations eliminated this party from the courtroom and replaced their authenticating power with documents certified by the legal scrivener. After 1873, document preparation services were mandated for parties to civil disputes. In that year a regulation stated that "in a trial, one must cite materials that had been prepared by a scrivener (*daishonin*)."[32] This marked a shift favoring documentary evidence over the oral testimony of a village head. Although the legal advocate was imagined as the appropriate representative for the parties appearing before the court, the range of new occupations raised questions about which practitioner might best serve the litigant. In practice, parties might enter the courtroom in the company of a legal advocate and scrivener, who was retained for on-the-spot drafting of supporting documents.

The indeterminacy of how French categories might work in a Japanese context, and how Japanese practices would change in response to a host of political, economic, and social shifts was typical of the late 1860s and early 1870s. In a 1904 lecture, Hozumi Nobushige reflected on the study and application of the law during the first years of the Meiji legal transition. Many of the era's early judges were Tokugawa holdovers. They adjudicated out of their experience in domainal or shogunal tribunals while "consult[ing] the translations of the French and other European codes

---

30. The Ministry of Justice rejected an element under criticism in France at the time—venality of office—in which notaries bought and sold their positions, with a share of their income going to the state. For a discussion of the function of the *notaire* in France, see Suleiman, *Private Power and Centralization in France.*

31. Osatake, "Daishonin to iu koto." In this article, Osatake outlines the vagaries of demands for the services of the copyists as related to changes in the laws of civil procedure. See also Osatake, "Shihōshoshi-hō kaisei jicchi, sanshū-nen kinengō," in Nihon shihōshoshikai rengōkai, ed., *Nihon shihōshoshishi*, 367–388.

32. Okudaira, *Nihon bengoshishi*, 43.

and textbooks."³³ In 1867, the government ordered that deliberations follow the "good laws" of the "Tokugawa system."³⁴ The first steps toward reform were incremental, with great continuity in personnel. In the cases where parties hired legal representation, the judges usually faced a former suit solicitor from the Edo era.³⁵ Things changed quickly after 1875, when a Great Council of State (Dajōkan) decree strengthened the trend toward the adoption of foreign practices that "flung wide open the door for the ingress of foreign law."³⁶ Historically, magistrates had drawn on precedent to decide cases for which there was no written law; until 1875, the application of reason (*dōri*) in a legal proceeding referred to domestic precedent. The 1875 decree stated, "In civil trials, those matters for which there is no written law are governed by custom, and those matters for which there is no custom shall be adjudicated by inference from reason (*dōri*)."³⁷ In its new sense, "reason" referred to standard practices abroad, particularly France. With this decree, the Great Council reframed the meaning of reason, while reducing the degree to which domestic custom might shape how a judge adjudicated a dispute. Less and less did "reason" mean an inquiry into Japan's past. More and more it meant an outward examination of foreign law.

In response to the order of 1872 and the decree of 1875, the 1870s witnessed an explosion of publicly and privately published legal material. The decree prompted the state to translate European legal and political thought, and French publications in particular.³⁸ By 1881, Ministry of Justice officials interested in the French legal tradition could read nearly 20 translations of French law and political theory from among 44 foreign law titles listed in the ministry's library. These included texts on French politics, commercial law, civil law, criminal law, contracts, civil procedure,

33. Hozumi, *The New Japanese Civil Code*, 18–19. See also Spaulding, *Imperial Japan's Higher Civil Service Examinations*, 38.

34. Sonoo, *Minji soshō, shikkō, hasan no kin-gendaishi*, 65.

35. Ōno, "Shokugyōshi toshite no bengoshi oyobi bengoshi dantai no rekishi," 8–9.

36. Hozumi, *The New Japanese Civil Code*, 18–19.

37. Art. 3 of Dajōkan Decree No. 103 of 1875, cited in Takayanagi, "A Century of Innovation," 25. See also "Zappō," *Hōgaku kyōkai zasshi* 50, no. 6 (1932): 186–87.

38. Hōsei daigaku daigakushi shiryōka iinkai, ed., *Hōritsugaku no yoake to Hōsei daigaku*, 85.

finance, and local and prefectural government.[39] Yet law in translation and domestic statutes were not the exclusive provinces of the authorities. In a dramatic departure from the Edo period, when laws were putatively secret and publishers faced punishment for producing legal materials, private practitioners and litigants now read legal texts in the open where before they did so through subterfuge. Many of these new publications specifically targeted the private legal practitioner.

In a reversal, the state now made information about laws and procedures available to private legal practitioners and their clients (see appendix). From 1867, before the drafting of comprehensive civil and criminal legal codes, the Ministry of Justice published serials, including the *Dajōkan nisshi* (Great Council of State digest, published February 1867 to January 1877) and the *Shihōshō nisshi* (Ministry of Justice digest, January 1873 to October 1876). These publications and others recorded courtroom proceedings and rulings and served as early guides to dispute resolution. Another early journal transcribed laws into the more easily read Japanese syllabary (*Kanatsuke ofuregaki*, 1873 to 1875).[40] Law-related publications, along with the clarification between civil and criminal matters and the erasure of status distinctions, made the courts increasingly accessible. Moreover, litigant and legal advocate alike enjoyed greater access to the texts of applicable laws, the diminishing legal power of status hierarchies, and greater transparency for legal proceedings.

Private legal practitioners seized upon newly available texts, including an innovative genre of manuals for legal advocates, to prepare themselves for court. Under the previous regime, suit inns served as private repositories of knowledge about law. Suit inn proprietors trained successors within their families and took on apprentices. This was an esoteric model of knowledge, in which mastery of legal forms required affiliation with a suit inn and its proprietor. Meiji legal reforms made legal knowledge exoteric. With the shift in state policy, the vibrant commercial publishing world turned to legal publications. Much as

---

39. In addition to a few titles on international law and legal theory, there were also texts on the specific laws of other countries, including English financial law and Italian commercial law. Ministry of Justice Library Archive, *Shihōshō futatsu*, Memorandum to the Courts, Ministry of Justice Circular No. 6, art. 17, 1881, 1468.

40. For sources documenting Meiji laws, see "Zappō," 186–88, app. A.

Diderot's *Encyclopedia* had categorized and revealed the esoteric knowledge of the various guilded occupations of eighteenth-century France, the publication of law and legal manuals in mid-nineteenth-century Japan opened up access to knowledge necessary for private legal practice and began overturning any advantage that the suit inns and suit solicitors may have enjoyed.

Private practitioners still faced challenges in learning their métier. Law in the early 1870s remained a moving target, and practitioners who "read law" did so informally. There were no public or private law schools in the contemporary sense during the early 1870s. For private practitioners, apprenticeship—which was also typical in much of the United States through the end of the nineteenth century—remained the norm in Japan through the end of the 1870s.[41] In turn, manuals explaining civil procedure proliferated. They described legal practice in layman's terms, focusing on court procedure, including the introduction of evidence as well as matters of debt, lending, and borrowing. One of the earliest was the *Soshō hikkei* (Lawsuit handbook), published in 1874 by Negishi Kinjū. It laid out the terms of practice for legal advocates and discussed topics that included the basis for bringing a lawsuit, the statute of limitations, loans and interest, the forms and procedures for the transfer of property, and legal appeals.[42] Other titles included the 1876 *Minji soshō meyasu gaihyō* (Overview of standards for civil suits) and the 1878 *Daigennin dainin teiyō* (Compendium for the advocate and representative). The *Minji soshō meyasu gaihyō*, edited by Yamanouchi Katsurō, had 30 accordion-folding pages that measured 2.5 by 6 inches.[43] It was the perfect size for folding into the sleeve of one's kimono. It offered "to the person conducting a legal suit" an outline of "official promulgations and matters in the *Shihōshō nisshi* [Ministry of Justice digest] related to civil suits since the Restoration."[44] Sections of the *Minji soshō meyasu gaihyō* offered excerpts from court rulings and government orders on such matters as authentication of documents, interest rates, lending, statutes of limitation, allowable evidence, and forms for the preparation of legal

------

41. Stevens, *Law School*, 21–22.
42. Negishi, *Soshō hikkei*.
43. Yamanouchi, ed., *Minji soshō meyasu gaihyō*, 1.
44. Ibid.

documents. Much like the fold-out *Minji soshō meyasu gaihyō*, the *Daigennin dainin teiyō*, edited by Ōmori Takayuki, was sleeve pocket–sized, 3.75 by 5 inches, and 108 pages.[45] The *Daigennin dainin teiyō* focused on the details of private legal practice. It cited the rules governing where legal advocates could practice, described the preparation of legal documents, and included cautionary tales of advocates who committed crimes either on or off the job. The topics covered in these materials reveal the primary concerns for civil litigators during the early 1870s. Echoing earlier types of litigation, legal advocates wanted to know how to contest "land matters," which largely arose out of disputes over title and seized collateral, and "financial matters," which largely consisted of efforts to collect unsecured loans—loans not backed by collateral.

As had been the case during the Edo era, most litigants were farmers, as might be expected in an overwhelmingly agrarian economy. Yet the farmer was no longer fixed within a prescribed status group. And the commoner no longer had to beseech the state to hear a matter or pressure the state to provide justice in disputes between farmers and their status superiors. Government delineation of a revised social hierarchy included a new aristocracy (*kazoku*) consisting of the old royalty and former daimyo. Beneath the aristocracy were former samurai (*shizoku*), with common people (*heimin*) on the bottom (including the "new commoners" [*shinheimin*]). The revision opened the way for commoners to sue former samurai in private disputes. Status differences may have affected the terms of loans, as indicated in the guides for civil suits cited above, but the civil court was not to favor one party or another based on its status in the resolution of a dispute. Litigants responded to this promise of equality before the law by going to great lengths to have their disputes heard in the high court in Tokyo. For example, in an age before transnational rail, a farmer traveled half the length of Japan, from Nagasaki to Tokyo, to plead a case.[46]

As a result of reforms that dramatically reduced status distinctions and made litigated solutions even more accessible than they had been

---

45. Ōmori, ed., *Daigennin dainin teiyō*, opening pages. For another introduction to legal suits, see Tsuchiya Tetsu's *Soshō binran* (1885), cited in Nakamura F., *Meiji gentō*, 108.

46. Iwatani, "Meiji shoki minshū no soshō seikatsu," 8.

during the Edo era, the number of court cases increased. With the unfolding of national legal reforms, parties to private disputes turned to
courts knowing that the physical and statutory environment in which
court cases played out was new, even if litigation itself was not new to
the Meiji period.[47] Iwatani Jūrō's study of civil appeals in the records of
the Court of the Ministry of Justice shows one effect of this change: increasing numbers of cases heard on appeal during the first years that the
state permitted legal advocacy (1872–1875). The court, established in
1872, was mandated by the Judicial Staff Regulations and Operating
Rules in 1872 and was replaced in 1875 by the Great Court of Cassation
(Daishinin). The Court of the Ministry of Justice was the only appeals
court in Japan and the "de facto high court."[48] From 1873 to 1874, new
civil matters heard in regional courts of the first instance nearly tripled,
from 47,850 cases to 140,993 cases. In 1875, the number reached 305,527
cases.[49] Two years later, the number of cases had increased to 850,000. Parties employed an advocate in more than half of the cases.[50] As had been
the case under the Tokugawa, litigants disputing financial conflicts hired
legal representation in numbers disproportionate to parties in other
kinds of cases. For example, nearly 70 percent of appellants in financial
matters relied on representation by legal advocates.

Who represented these and other litigants during the early 1870s?
Ōno Masao has noted that the reforms of 1872 may have revolutionized
legal practice, "yet from the perspective of the people of which it consisted, it had not excluded the *kujishi*. Instead, it had incorporated them
completely."[51] There were few limits on who could work as a legal
advocate—the rules only excluded minors, the deaf, and the blind.[52]
Legal historians agree that the suit solicitors and suit inn operators who
had practiced law during the Edo era numbered first in the ranks of legal
advocates during the early 1870s, yet the general absence of regulation

47. Upham, "Weak Legal Consciousness as Invented Tradition."
48. Iwatani, "Meiji shoki minshū no soshō seikatsu," 8. The Court of the Ministry of
Justice was the forerunner of the Tokyo Appeals Court, later succeeded by the Tokyo
High Court.
49. Murakami K., *Meiji rikon saiban shiron*, 64.
50. Iwatani, "Meiji shoki minshū no soshō seikatsu," 9–12.
51. Ōno, "Shokugyōshi toshite no bengoshi oyobi bengoshi dantai no rekishi," 8–9.
52. Ibid., 7.

and licensing makes it difficult to identify the numbers and backgrounds of these earliest advocates.[53] In lower courts, one finds that parties in civil disputes often continued the Tokugawa practice of having relatives speak for them well after the laws of 1872 allowed them to hire a trained legal advocate.[54] Having renamed themselves *daigennin,* or legal advocates, former suit solicitors focused on their historical strengths: soliciting clients and selling services such as the drafting of legal documents.

The practices that were familiar for suit inns and solicitors gradually gave way to a new legal advocacy and a litigation process that was increasingly open to the public. The end of the Tokugawa status system also meant a reconfiguration of sites of adjudication. From finding a legal representative to the courtroom appearance itself, the 1870s meant a transformation of the relationship between the litigant and the state. In addition to the emergence of legal advocates—and, later, associations of legal advocates—newly constructed court buildings appeared on the urban landscape. In Tokyo and other major cities, advocates worked within a new idiom of public architecture, an idiom celebrated in wood-block prints that featured post offices and national banks as signs of modernity. Hiroshige III included the Tokyo Court House in his print collection of the various government ministries of Tokyo, completed in 1876.[55] No longer did proceedings unfold in the anonymity of an administrative office; no longer would commoner parties to a dispute kneel before their samurai betters on a gravel courtyard. The layout of the Meiji civil court leveled litigants and their legal representatives, having eliminated the hierarchically arrayed platforms that had highlighted status during the Edo period. At the same time, the Meiji courtroom elevated the

---

53. Until the late 1990s, the low regard in which judicial archivists held records of early Meiji rulings and proceedings and the inchoate nature of the court system rendered the study of court proceedings from 1868 through the mid-1870s difficult. See Hayashiya, Ishii, Aoyama, et al., *Zusetsu hanketsu genpon no isan.* Even so, Murakami Kazuhiro did considerable research identifying the transition from *kujishi* to legal advocates in the early 1870s. Records of court proceedings have since been digitized and are database searchable through the International Research Center for Japanese Studies (Nichibunken) website.

54. Murakami K., "Kindaiteki daigennin no tōjō," 45–46.

55. Hiroshige III *Tokyo shokanshō meishoshū* cited in Nakamura F., *Meiji gentō,* 111–12.

representatives of the state (the judge and the clerk of the court), who sat on a dais. No longer did private parties face the possibility that they would have limited access to appeals or might even be liable for criminal punishment on the basis of their involvement in a civil dispute.[56] From 1872, newspaper reporters could observe legal trials, and from February 1875, "ordinary people" were permitted to watch adversarial proceedings.[57] It was likely a shock for observers to see these new structures open to the general public. The courthouse joined the legal advocate's proliferating signboard or "shingle" (*kanban*) as a harbinger of Japan's shift away from the cloistered legal processes of Edo-era practice. As a result of early Meiji legal reforms, parties to private disputes could confront each other in these new public spaces and seek resolution.

Even as the state made its transformation of the legal terrain concrete, the structures it created both revealed and obscured elements of the legal reform story. In particular, the statist narrative excluded many of the ways that private legal practitioners and society more broadly made Meiji legal reforms work. If reform had just been new laws and new buildings, it would have been an empty endeavor. Society brought legal reform to life. For those litigating a dispute in the early years of the 1870s, private publishers disseminated texts of applicable laws and legal advocates interpreted them. Commoner legal advocates stood before their former-samurai betters, challenging them in court. Poets, journalists, and woodblock print artists all bore witness to the transparency of legal proceedings. In short, the state may have regulated legal practice into being, but it was the population of suit solicitors and others from the Edo era and the new practitioners who brought the courts to life. And figures such as Sono mixed in a measure of celebrity (or notoriety) to legal practice while bringing clients to court.

The history of how private legal practice bridged the events of 1868 is largely absent in the current narrative of the transition from Edo to Meiji. In the widely used university textbook *Nihon hōseishi* (Japanese legal history), Edo practices appear only as an obstacle to changes that came after

---

56. Takikawa Eiichi describes how even people with unclear standing in civil suits (*hikiainin*)—the question being, were they parties or not?—may have been susceptible to criminal penalties into the first years of the Meiji period; "Meiji shoki no hikiainin."

57. Okudaira, *Nihon bengoshishi*, 58.

1868. Consistent with the general treatment of the nineteenth century, the textbook account places the state at the center while obscuring the concerns that animated private legal practitioners. Sono, Kodama, and the many anonymous former suit solicitors who filled the courts were agents of modernity who connected clients to the broader project of state centralization and the construction of a national subject. The rapidity and scope of the social and political transformation during the early Meiji years derived from action by society as well as the state. The stories of two legal practitioners reveal how individuals inhabited this moment of possibility.

Sono Tel: A Woman's Translation of Edo Justice

For many in Japan, the years after 1868 turned into an emancipatory moment, with people slipping the bonds of gender, geography, family, and status to embrace opportunities to (re)invent themselves. The occupational opportunities that emerged out of the reformed legal system meant that law was practiced in the open. Social and occupational fluidity made it possible for a woman to turn to the work of private legal practice. The story of Sono Tel demonstrates how a legal practitioner of the 1870s integrated a Confucian-grounded, Edo-influenced practice of law with new approaches. During the 1870s, Sono cast herself as an emergent legal professional, bringing morality to clients through a revised form of legal practice. A decade later, she left Japan and again recast herself, this time as a Christian cosmopolitan. Yet aside from her 1892 autobiography, some mentions in the temperance literature, and a few recent explorations of transnational feminism, her story has largely been lost and had not made a ripple in the historiography of legal practice. This is the case for two reasons. First, over the course of the 1870s, licensing and bureaucratization increasingly closed entry to the field of legal practice to women, particularly after the regulations of 1880. Second, Sono's focus on morality as the heart of her legal practice (and her subsequent Christian conversion) did not fit the masculinized and hyper-rational narrative of Meiji modernization. Radical as a woman, yet conservative in her worldview, her legal work confounded those wishing to draw a straight line from the Edo dark ages to civilization and enlightenment. It was legal practice that launched Sono on a path away from her parochial upbringing, allowing her to transcend a national narrative and join other cosmopolitan woman of the late nineteenth century. She is an allegory for an alternate course in Japanese history. She creatively mixed tradition and novelty in ways that, for a time, allowed her to escape the categories and classifications that narrowed opportunities to women. Confronted with the closure of such opportunities at home, she launched a quest for moral universalism and professionalism during the 1880s that found answers in the Christian temperance movement then appearing worldwide. Yet before she embarked on her extended *wanderjahre*, Sono joined other legal practitioners in the early 1870s who drew on elements from the Edo past and translated them into the hybrid legal lexicon of their 1870s present.

Sono's autobiography may be full of the conventions of late-nineteenth-century Christian spiritual texts, yet she infused the genre with Confucian cultural and Buddhist religious pieties as well. In typically filial fashion, Sono identified her grandfather and father as life models and the sources of her moral fiber. She began with her grandfather from Nagoya. "Moan Waka Sono . . . was a philosopher. . . . [H]e would sit down . . . engaged in prayer for hours, not moving nor taking any nourishment."[58] Sono's father also "never worshipped idols."[59] She added to this a suggestion of professionalism. Although professions in the sense that sociologist Andrew Abbott has described them did not become a feature of Meiji society until the 1890s, in Sono's description, her forebears were professionals ahead of their time.[60] Her father "studied medicine" before he moved to Tokyo, where he began medical practice. Sono's brother also became a doctor, and her sister "was a teacher in a public school for women."[61] Until the age of 19, when she married, Sono lived happily with her siblings and parents, exemplars for the moral values of an earlier age and scions of the emerging professional middle classes characteristic of industrializing societies the world over.

Marriage to a samurai bureaucrat working in the finance commission of a local daimyo connected Sono's life to national political upheaval,

---

58. Sono, *The Japanese Reformer*, 9. The autobiography was serialized in *The Parents Review* 4 (1893/94).

59. Ibid.

60. Abbott, *The System of Professions*.

61. Sono, *The Japanese Reformer*, 9–11.

opening up possibilities different from those expected of an obedient wife of a samurai during the earlier, Tokugawa age. Mirroring the tumultuous connection between her daily life and national events, a tension between self-effacement and self-aggrandizement animated her autobiography, *The Japanese Reformer: An Autobiography*. Sono opened her book with the statement, "I am a little Japanese woman."[62] Yet she soon transcended the bounds of her physical stature and late-nineteenth-century Japanese womanhood by treading far beyond the obediences to father, husband, and child assigned to the samurai daughter, wife, and mother.[63] In 1865, betrothal and the birth of a daughter transformed Sono's life. Her husband, a Tokugawa loyalist, moved to Edo for a year; in her estimation, the experience turned him into an alcoholic. As the Tokugawa regime crumbled and then collapsed, the turmoil of the Restoration moment unsettled the nation. At Sono's home, her husband's rice wine consumption led to physical abuse and demands for a "wine feast."[64] Fearing that her husband's depravity would drain family finances, Sono fled with her daughter. She returned to her natal home in May 1871. This move opened the way toward independence more typical of patterns of familial dissolution in Edo-era farming villages, yet atypical for wives of samurai.[65] As the ties binding Sono's new family unraveled, so too did the ties that had bound together the Tokugawa state. In 1871, the domains "returned" their land to the emperor, the Ministry of Justice was established, and Iwakura Tomomi led a mission to Europe and the United States to examine institutions of law, politics, and industry.

Leaving her husband had released Sono from spousal bonds but presented her with the challenge of supporting herself and her daughter. It was in the context of the promulgation of the 1872 Staff Regulations and the opening of legal practice to (nearly) all that Sono wondered what "a woman could do to earn money sufficient [to support her child]." She and her father began to "study together, and in addition to other

---

62. Ibid.
63. Rumi Yasutake offers Sono Tel as a new kind of activist in *Transnational Women's Activism*.
64. Sono, *The Japanese Reformer*, 22.
65. Fuess, *Divorce in Japan*.

studies . . . read books of law."⁶⁶ As in her description of her father's work as a "doctor," Sono wrote as if in 1871 "law" existed as a coherent field of knowledge; it did not. Nevertheless, in 1874, consistent with the easy entry to legal practice and thinking of her daughter's future, Sono at "last decided to be a lawyer." In other words, she became a legal advocate. She left her daughter with her mother and departed for Tokyo, where her final preparation for legal work was a three-month stint as a "secretary of judgment."⁶⁷

Sono's description of her legal practice reproduced the folk justice understanding of law that had prevailed before 1868, with its focus on morality tales about human foibles stemming from greed, infidelity, trickery, vengeance, and general depravity. She updated it with new language and new orientations. By "reading law," she became conversant in an internationalizing language of legal norms and translated these into accepted ideas of Japanese morality. In 1879, a shop employee delivered expensive clothes to a customer, leaving them with the customer overnight. The customer appeared well off, "an officer of the law"—a state official, perhaps. When the employee went to collect payment (or the clothing) the following morning, the goods were gone. In leaving the goods, he had "broken the law of [his] store." The customer had used the clothes to pay off a debt. Sono visited the wayward customer and heard a story of failing eyesight and a failed business. He cried out in front of his daughter, "[T]his lady can send [your father] to prison . . . if I go to prison . . . [y]ou will die of hunger. . . . Ask this lady to forgive my sin for the sake of our family." Moved, Sono recovered the clothes, paid off the man's debt, and returned the clothes to the shop. She restored the shopworker to good graces with his employer. The failed businessman promised to repay Sono but never did. In a bizarre twist, Sono encountered him some time later in even more reduced circumstances. "The children were crying of hunger, all were like skeletons, and the mother was almost crazy with grief," Sono wrote. "I forgave him, but he could not escape the justice of God."⁶⁸ An early death from sickness was his penalty.

---

66. Sono, *The Japanese Reformer*, 23–24.
67. Ibid.
68. Ibid., 29–33.

The story reveals two things about hybrid legal practice during the first years of the Meiji period, as recounted by Sono. First, law was infused with morality. Second, law permeated social interactions and was everywhere. As for law as morality, Sono's authority as a mediator in the conflict between the shop employee and the wayward customer derived from her presumed righteousness and the threat of punishment. Sono mediated conflict in ways reminiscent of Saikaku's *Tales of Japanese Justice,* in which the commoner's pathetic attempts at treachery or demonstrations of greed withered in the face of moral superiority.[69] In a sense, Sono trafficked in the memory of Edo magistrate Ōoka Echizen no Kami and other such revered justice officials as Kyoto magistrate Itakura Katsushige. Rather than interpreting written law and parsing the boundaries of the acceptable on a legally codified landscape, Sono's legal practice emerged out of a notion of justice embodied in the stories of great Tokugawa magistrates that remained popular through her time and beyond. In this old orthodox notion, private disputes had a moral dimension and the punishment of a party—and sometimes both parties—to a dispute signaled justice.

As for the ubiquity of law, again her account extended a legacy of the Edo era, even as it also foreshadowed the primacy of law as a lens for the social and political understanding that took hold during the course of the Meiji period. In Sono's story, there were "officers of law" and merchant houses still had "laws." Sono's account of the theft of the clothing reveals how the thief, who was posing as an official, could pull "law" on like a mantle of unquestionable authority to pursue dubious aims. Or, as in the case of the shop clerk, one could fall afoul of law-as-rules. Sono cut through all of these conflicting "laws," intervening on the shopworker's behalf, to arrive at justice. Sono pointed the customer toward the proper path but did not compel compliance (repayment of her loan), although, as he said, she could have sent him to prison. Although she did not compel the clothing thief to fulfill his obligations, he nevertheless faced the ultimate punishment—early death.

Despite many connections to and continuities with the old regime, 1868 had brought a shift. Yes, Sono framed her practice within

---

69. Ihara, *Honchō ōin hiji,* trans. as *Tales of Japanese Justice* by Kondo and Marks.

state-sanctioned moral traditions of justice. And yes, her practice was profoundly conservative. At the same time, the very existence of her practice marked the beginning of a different age. What was radical was that she presumed to be the interpreter of what Mark Silver has called the "benevolent, infallible wisdom" claimed by the Tokugawa authorities.[70] At the level of practice, folk justice was transformed when the protagonist was a woman and a private legal practitioner working in the open.

Early Meiji Japan was an extraordinary time and place; in the context of global trends, it would have been even more extraordinary if the licensing and credentialing of legal advocates had not led to the narrowing of legal practice to men.[71] Sono's notoriety may have been part of her downfall. Her contemporaries found her legal practice of great interest. In 1875, "two poets [Ōhashi Nao and Keta Shin'itsu] who lived in the city of Tokio . . . wrote one hundred poems about the wonderful things Japan now possessed. One poem was about the woman lawyer. . . . [Sono's] name became known throughout Japan."[72] Although apparently rare, Sono was not the only female legal advocate practicing in Tokyo during the 1870s. An October 20, 1876, newspaper article in *Tokyo akebono* newspaper described sisters who worked as legal advocates out of Asakusa in Tokyo.[73] Yet from 1876, when licensing was first instituted, judges in both local and national courts could, and did, prohibit women from arguing cases before them. In 1876, the Hyōgo regional courts clarified the minimum age for legal advocates (21 years) and stated that legal advocates must be male. Such prohibitions in the regions suggest that female legal advocates had appeared outside of the capital, too. In the same year, the Tokyo High Court prohibited female advocacy in its chambers.[74] Yet, generally, the courts left it to the practitioners to refuse to argue a case across from an unlicensed practitioner or to identify such a party. Unlicensed legal representatives practiced at the pleasure of the

---

70. Silver, *Purloined Letters*, 27.

71. On sexism and professions, see Witz, *Professions and Patriarchy*.

72. Ōhashi Nao and Keta Shin'itsu, *Tōkei shinshi,* as cited in Sono, *The Japanese Reformer,* 24.

73. Cited in Nakamura F., *Meiji gentō,* 108.

74. Hyōgo Prefecture, Edict of Mar. 19, 1876, art. 19; and "Tokyo Court" [no specification], Edict of Mar. 13, 1876. See Ōmori, ed., *Daigennin dainin teiyō,* 94–96.

court, with judges enforcing licensing requirements loosely.[75] One cause for weak enforcement on the part of judges was the small number of licensed advocates in some jurisdictions; for example, in 1876 there was only one licensed legal advocate in Kanagawa. There were four in Kyoto. Until the end of the 1870s, a person who primarily worked as a scrivener or notary might also argue before the court.[76] Here, too, the past pressed in on the present. The absence of clear and uniform enforcement of who might enter the courts created an open field for those who identified themselves as legal advocates. This created opportunities for unlicensed advocates to informally insert themselves into the dispute resolution process—more continuity with earlier times.

Gender bias was not the primary force driving the licensing process that appeared in 1876. The justice bureaucracy grappled with ways to regulate and mold a legal practice that had few hurdles to entry. The ubiquity of suit solicitor holdovers from the Edo era and the ease with which anyone could stand on behalf of another in court had become an issue. The target of reform was all manner of private legal practice reminiscent of the backwardness of the Edo era. First, local jurisdictions issued orders, including Kōchi prefecture's rules on the number of matters a person could represent at any given time. The aim was suppression of the common practices of one advocate working for both sides of the same case or handing cases off to unqualified assistants. The measure became an order of the Ministry of Justice in March 1875.[77] With the French bar in mind, the Ministry of Justice introduced a licensing procedure in 1876 in which local jurisdictions certified those who called themselves legal advocates (*daigennin*).[78] It created three paths to becoming a licensed legal advocate. One could receive a license through government training; one could become a legal advocate by earning a law degree abroad; or one could have an evaluation of one's abilities at the local level—a test.

---

75. Tokyo bengoshikai hyakunenshi hensan kankō tokubetsu iinkai, ed., *Tokyo bengoshikai hyakunenshi*, 22–29.

76. Osatake, "Daishonin to iu koto." In this article, Osatake outlines the vagaries of demand for copyists' services, as related to changes in the laws of civil procedure. See also Nihon shihōshoshikai rengōkai, ed., *Nihon shihōshoshishi*.

77. "Kōchi-ken ukagai" (20 Oct. 1874) and "Shihōshō shirei" (24 Mar. 1875), in Okudaira, *Nihon bengoshishi*, 50.

78. Okudaira, *Nihon bengoshishi*, 176.

This third avenue was the most common course—written evaluation by a local official in which licensees passed a background check and demonstrated familiarity with current law, including edicts and regulations, criminal laws, and rules of procedure.[79] The first licensing test on October 1876, a four hour exam, reflected the idiosyncratic concerns of the examiner. Legal advocate Matsuo Seijirō recounted how a friend was asked, "What was the content of order number 300, issued in 1870, by the Ministry of Justice?"[80] Another question asked for the candidate's understanding of the regulation of the "three trades." Matsuo protested that the "three trades"—police parlance for prostitution, procurer tea houses (*hikite chaya*), and brothels—were unknown to the examinee. In a statement that reflected the gendered definition of human rights at the time, he proclaimed that candidates for legal advocacy were earnest and "knew nothing about the regulation of brothels; we were drawn to the practice of law in order to extend people's rights."[81] In Matsuo's circle, enthusiasm for a narrowly politicized legal advocacy was at the fore. Candidates for the license to practice as legal advocates resented the imperiousness of the examiners and the lack of a clear standard for measuring their legal mettle.

The absence of a uniform test meant that legal advocates entered practice with a range of qualifications. Table 1 lists the number of licensed advocates by year from 1876 (445 advocates nationwide) to 1884 (1,029). Graduates of the law programs administered by the Ministry of Education and the Ministry of Justice Law School were exempt from the licensing examination, as were those who had earned law degrees in programs abroad. So, too, were students who took the Ministry of Justice short course for becoming judges, but failed to pass the qualifying exams to become a judge.[82] As one can imagine, this last provision opened private

---

79. The regulations excluded anyone who had served a criminal sentence of a year or more, civil servants, and those who did not live in "the region" (later revised to limit the license to practice in a court within three *ri* of one's residence). *Daigennin kisoku* (22 Feb. 1876), Ministry of Justice Circular, no. 1.

80. Okudaira, *Nihon bengoshishi*, 21–22.

81. Ibid., 22.

82. After 1884, graduates of the Meihōryō and the Shihōshō gakkō of the Ministry of Justice were allowed to become advocates without passing an examination. Murakami K., "Kindai Nihon no zaiya hōsō to sono hyōden," 47–48.

Table 1: National Pass Rate for the Legal Advocacy Exam, 1876–1892

Year	Applicants	Licensees	Pass Rate (%)
1876	439	193	44
1877	447	328	73
1878	244	198	81
1879	163	149	91
1880	1,111	181	16
1881	1,644	137	8
1882	1,584	115	7
1883	2,091	72	3
1884	2,311	62	3
1885	1,468	51	3
1886	939	30	3
1887	606	35	6
1888	1,132	41	4
1889	1,803	50	3
1890	2,113	132	6
1891	1,984	208	10
1892	1,906	108	6

SOURCE: Based on data for number of applicants and licensees in Okudaira, *Nihon bengoshishi*, 1371–72.

practitioners to criticism for being inferior to judges. At the same time, certain private practitioners, including those who had completed courses of study abroad, were often better prepared than homegrown, local judges to understand and interpret the evolving legal landscape of the early 1870s.

The fact that the courts permitted Sono to practice, even after the institution of a licensing system that excluded women, demonstrates the courts' inconsistent application of licensing requirements. Sono had no license, yet she claimed that her practice continued into the early 1880s, well after the institution of licensing. Even with the licensing system in effect, licensed legal practitioners competed with lay advocates for clients.

As Sono herself noted, her career "was recognised by all as most successful." This observation was echoed by contemporary foreign observers who saw her as a harbinger of gender equality in Japan. Yet Sono's historical presence dimmed for two reasons. First, she was a woman. Second, her story did not fit into the tidy narrative of an impersonal form of legal practice learned from abroad and imported to Japan. The regulation of advocacy began in 1876 and intensified with national licensing and mandatory membership in local bar associations after 1880. Sono described how, from the early 1880s, "the low position of woman was brought more clearly than ever before my mind."[83] The realization dawned on Sono that, as a woman, she could not sustain her position as a moral arbiter in the Confucian tradition. (Little did she know that former-samurai males would soon lay claim to that position.) By the early 1880s, she had hit a low within an occupation that was grappling with its own status vis-à-vis government officials.

The terms defining legal advocacy rendered advocates subordinate to the bureaucratic administrators of justice: procurators and judges. Legal advocates complained that they were treated like their Edo-era forebears— suit solicitors and suit inn proprietors (and their employees). Judges had summary power to discipline legal advocates, including immediate removal from a case.[84] Obstreperous advocates could be suspended for up to three months without appeal.[85] Courts left advocates little room, procedural or otherwise, to shape the legal process in the interest of their clients. Judges did not coordinate the trial calendar with advocates. Instead, echoing Edo-era practices, the bailiff shouted for parties from a gate or sent a runner to a teahouse to summon parties to the court. Legal advocates could only leave the courthouse if they had a seal on their name cards confirming dismissal by the judge or procurator.[86] This was officialdom mythologizing government lawgivers—not private legal practitioners.

Officialdom was not alone in its disparagement of legal advocacy. Sono herself never shook the folk understanding of legal practice as a suspect or disreputable pursuit. Before she left for the United States, she forgave her clients' outstanding fees and loans, worth more than 1,000

---

83. Sono, *The Japanese Reformer*, 23–25.

84. "Saibansho torishimaru kisoku" (12 Jul. 1874), art. 5, in Okudaira, *Nihon bengoshishi*, 56.

85. Ibid., art. 7.

86. On an incident in which a bailiff restrained a legal advocate, see Matsuo S., "Shihō shiryō," 50–51.

dollars. She concluded, "[I]t would not have been right for me to use this money, which had been obtained in the business of law, because in making one person happy I had made another sad, in making one love me I had made another hate me, and that surely could not be right."[87] Her focus had shifted from legal practice to "God's law." That said, even after she forgave her debtors, Sono's legal career made it possible for her to save enough money to leave Japan for the United States.

If Sono had quit legal practice and simply returned to her natal home, her story would likely have ended there, but instead she mounted the international stage. Her entry into the international Christian temperance movement revealed the compatibility of Tokugawa moralism and late-nineteenth-century Christian temperance activism. One could argue that Sono did not convert to Christianity, but rather she converted Christianity to her own moral vision. Her husband's alcoholism was a turning point in Sono's life, authorizing her departure from her household and later her home country. In December 1885, she "set sail for America, arriving in San Francisco the 7th of January, 1886."[88] There, after a stint as a household domestic, she became a Christian temperance activist and social reformer. In 1891, Sono received considerable attention and caché as the kimono-clad, sole Japanese participant at the Eighteenth Annual Meeting of the National Woman's Christian Temperance Union in Boston.[89] As a marker of the internationalism of the movement, Sono was in great demand. At home, Sono's gender had come to exclude her from the work of legal advocacy; yet abroad, her femininity (and Japaneseness) gave her access to a politically active Christian sisterhood. Sono had seemingly escaped the gender inequalities that were being institutionalized under the banner of "civilization and enlightenment" in Japan.

Sono had turned to a larger stage. Her life story highlights relationships between law, morality, and political change that are often buried beneath narratives of the nation that have dominated accounts of the

---

87. Sono, *The Japanese Reformer*, 38.

88. Ibid., 37.

89. "National Woman's Christian Temperance Union: Eighteenth Annual Meeting from Our Own Correspondent," *Christian Union* 28 (Nov. 1891): 1047.

1870s and 1880s. When she was a child, her father had told her to "minister to the needs of the destitute whenever an opportunity presented itself, resting assured that a pure life and kind deeds would be rewarded."[90] With this philanthropic mission as her goal, Sono came of age during the collapse of the Tokugawa regime. Its collapse, and the collapse of her marriage along with it, freed her to turn first to a career as a private legal practitioner. In her account, that position enabled her to guide others to justice. In her work, she integrated vernacular ideas of Edo-era justice into a revamped Meiji legal system. Confounded by gender discrimination and with her interpretation of law and justice increasingly out of step with the times, she moved on, her mobility created out of the possibilities inherent in the fluidity of her time.

Kodama Jun'ichirō: Tacit Moralities and the Samurai Legal Advocate

The accumulation of past and present, along with threads of cosmopolitan Christianity and legal practice, also converged in another figure, one dubiously identified as Japan's first modern lawyer—Kodama Jun'ichirō.[91] Kodama is an odd figure to identify as the harbinger of modern private legal practice because his true goal was a position in the Meiji bureaucracy, not the elevation or advance of private legal advocacy. From the late 1860s, the Meiji government sent trainees and officials on short-term study missions abroad. Many of these focused on law and courtroom observation in the United States, France, England, and later Germany.[92] Charged with learning firsthand the elements of foreign society that would enable Japan to overturn the unequal treaties, they studied the theoretical

---

90. Sono, *The Japanese Reformer*, 11.

91. Tezuka, *Meijishi kenkyū zassan*, 81. See also Murakami K., "Kindaiteki daigennin no tōjō."

92. Kikuyama, *Meiji kokka no keisei to shihōseido*. See also Spaulding, *Imperial Japan's Higher Civil Service Examinations*, and Murakami K., ed., *Nihon hōsōkai jinbutsu jiten*. In addition to those who took government positions, 100 people became advocates after studying law abroad or receiving degrees in law offered by predominantly foreign instructors at what was originally the law school attached to the Ministry of Justice but became the law faculty of the University of Tokyo. Okudaira, *Nihon bengoshishi*, 1363.

distinctions between positive law and custom and between public and private law. In the classroom, these students encountered firsthand the claim made by early-nineteenth-century legal positivist John Austin that "law is absolutely independent of morality."[93] Yet what they were taught and what they lived often differed. Law was not independent of morality in Europe and the United States; however, few called attention to the fact that theory and practice often diverged overseas, as they did in Japan. When Kodama Jun'ichirō arrived in the United States, he encountered law bound up in the morality of Christian religiosity. Even as legal scholars in Europe and the United States preached the desirability of law sculpted out of rationalism, the conflation of law and religion prevailed. In the United States, Christianity, not Confucianism, provided the moral frame. An 1855 Pennsylvania court ruling put it clearly: "Christianity is part of the law of the land . . . even those among us who reject Christianity, cannot possibly get clear of its influence."[94] Ironically, these were the words of a court in the land that had criticized Tokugawa and Meiji justice for grounding punishments in a punitive legal morality; that irony was lost on many who navigated the early encounter between Japan and the world.

While observing courtroom practice in Washington, D.C., government-sponsored student Kodama Jun'ichirō could not "get clear" of Christianity, either. He became immersed in the religion, converting to Christianity in 1872. Here was a representative of the Meiji state sent to study law abroad—law putatively absent of all moral taint. Kodama, however, learned both law and Christianity during his U.S. sojourn. At the same time, he inhabited an America in the grips of its own version of punitive moralism and barbarism. Claims of civilizational and moral superiority that international powers used in support of unequal treaties the world over served as justifications for inequality within the United States, as well, where violent racism, vigilante justice in the form of the lynch mob, and ethnic cleansing of native peoples typified post–Civil War America. Despite the inescapable aftereffects of American slavery and the brutality of the Indian Wars, the punitive moralism that

---

93. Taylor, "On the Conception of Morality in Jurisprudence," 36.
94. *Mohney v. Cook,* cited in Zollman, "Religion in Public Education," 242.

Kodama likely encountered in the United States of the 1870s went unremarked.[95]

Some elements of his biography suggest that Kodama was capable of deeper self-reflection. Born the third son of a Hagi domain samurai in 1846, Kodama studied Confucian classics at the domainal academy. "Dissatisfied" with Chinese studies as inappropriate to the times, he went to Nagasaki with domainal support to study English with Guido Verbeck, the Dutch-American missionary from the Reformed Dutch Church of the United States.[96] From 1859 to 1868, Verbeck taught foreign languages, history, and politics, first in his own private school and then in government schools. His students included such future Meiji luminaries as Ōkuma Shigenobu, the founder of Waseda University; Minister of Justice Etō Shinpei; Minister of Justice Ōki Takatō; Itō Hirobumi, the drafter of the Meiji constitution; and Katō Hiroyuki, a theorist of human rights.[97] After the Restoration, the Yamaguchi domain sent Kodama to the United States in June 1869 to observe legal courts, hoping to develop his language and legal skills. A little more than a year later, Kodama returned to Japan, only to be ordered back in December 1870 by the Great Council of State to study U.S. criminal law; this time, the national government sponsored him.

Kodama's activities in the mid-Atlantic, including his time in Washington, D.C., suggest a social and political climber who was attentive to those around him, particularly those who had achieved success. Kodama was eager to mirror their values. While in the States, Kodama converted to Christianity and later argued against Meiji religious intolerance, suggesting that legal reform should at least tolerate, if not include, an alternate Christian morality. In addition to enjoying a short stint at Princeton College, Kodama served as an observer in the chambers of Judge George Purnell Fisher of the Supreme Court of the District of Columbia.[98]

---

95. For a critique of the triumphalist narrative of the rise of American democracy, see Keysaar, *The Right to Vote*.

96. In Kodama's resignation letter to Etō Shinpei, he describes his motivation for abandoning Chinese studies, cited in Murakami K., "Kindaiteki daigennin no tōjō," 71.

97. Nakamura F., *Meiji gentō*, 213.

98. An 1871 article in the *Trenton State Gazette*, listed "J. L. Kodama as a Japanese student at Princeton College, but lately arrived in this country"; miscellany in *Trenton State Gazette* 25, no. 116 (16 May 1871): 2.

When the Iwakura Mission arrived in Washington, D.C., Kodama served as a translator and liaison for Japanese dignitaries, particularly Sasaki Takayuki, who was charged with investigating the U.S. judicial system. On April 15, 1872, Kodama was present at a reception held in honor of the mission, attended by Iwakura Tomomi, Itō Hirobumi, Kido Takayoshi, Okubo Toshimichi, and others.[99] Just two weeks later, he was baptized at the Metropolitan M.E. Church "by the Rev. Dr. [John Philip] Newman [and took the name] John Philip."[100] He joined the church "through the teaching and influence of Mrs. [Eliza A.] Fisher," the wife of Judge Fisher.[101] Kodama cultivated proximity to Iwakura, Itō, Kido, and Okubo, who later became Meiji-era greats. Yet he hardly figured in Japanese accounts of the Iwakura trip to Washington, D.C.

Consistent with the sense that civilization and enlightenment included emulation of Europe and the United States in all things, Kodama wrote two memorials to Meiji councilors in Tokyo calling for tolerance of the Christian religion in Japan. An 1872 memorial called for reform in language so obsequious that it was nearly incomprehensible. In that memorial, Kodama described himself as an "unschooled country bumpkin." If one understands early Meiji arguments against religious tolerance as a threat to the nation, then one can find a moment of clarity near the end of Kodama's petition. In it, Kodama wrote, "[I]t is foolish to claim that the teachings of goodness [Christianity] are incompatible with the body politic (*kokutai*)."[102]

The Japan of 1873 to which Kodama returned, the Japan of the "high-collar boom"—a period of great fascination with things foreign—suggested a world of possibility for him. Kodama imagined arrival in Japan followed by a high appointment in the Ministry of Justice. He brought home a rich range of experiences, having lived in a part of the

---

99. "Godey's Armchair: 'Washington Society,'" *Godey's Lady's Book and Magazine* 84, no. 504 (June 1872): 579.

100. "Local Affairs: Metropolitan Church, Baptism of Mr. Kodama," *The Daily National Republican* 12, no. 129 (29 Apr. 1872): 4.

101. "Godey's Arm-Chair: 'Washington Society,'" *Godey's Lady's Book and Magazine* 85, no. 505 (1 Jul. 1872): 91.

102. Letter from Kodama to the councilors, in Murakami K., "Kindaiteki daigennin no tōjō," 70. The letters are held in the Okuma Shigenobu Collection at Waseda University.

world that so many of his countrymen had only heard of, and found so compelling. Having been trained in America at government expense, Kodama anticipated that his skills would garner him a position of authority and influence. Initially, this was not the case. In a bureaucracy with ranks ranging from one, the highest level, to fifteen, the lowest level, Kodama was assigned to the tenth rank. He found this "surprisingly low."[103] It was hardly the "important position in the judiciary" he had anticipated. His situation raises a number of questions. Did Kodama overvalue his experience? Did the Ministry of Justice undervalue it? Had he unwittingly sabotaged his future with the submission of the memorials on Christianity? Was he a poor student of American law? Or was he not yet adept at navigating the world of Japanese officialdom?

Others had faced similar challenges upon returning from study abroad. In terms of finding a job in the nascent bureaucracy, foreign experience or experience working with foreigners in Japan produced mixed results. Not all returnees received official appointments. In addition to those who took government positions, some returnees became private legal advocates. Others received credentials in law through programs offered by foreign instructors at the government law school, the Meihōryō.[104] The centrality of a Meihōryō education to success in the early judicial bureaucracy may explain why Kodama referred to himself as a *Meihōgakushi*—a Meihō scholar—although he had not completed the Meihō course. Toward the end of the 1870s, extraordinary returnees such Hoshi Tōru and Megata Tanetarō translated international experience into entirely new positions with status, and at times pay, commensurate with bureaucrats who trained at home. For example, Hoshi returned to Japan from London in 1877 to receive a plum position in the legal bureaucracy, invented just for him. These arrangements, however, often grew out of previous government experience and personal connections.

Discontented with his appointment, Kodama opted to withdraw from official service in 1873. He alluded to broad legal knowledge in his

---

103. Ibid.
104. Okudaira, *Nihon bengoshishi*, 1363.

letter of resignation. He wrote to the Ministry of Justice that he was learned in Tang, Ming, and Qing legal traditions and then went beyond this to master English and study in the United States. He wrote that with so much knowledge and such a poor assignment he would "never be able to face his peers in the U.S. courts," so he "hoped to resign," knowing that employment as a private legal practitioner was possible. This letter may have been an opening gambit in negotiation for a higher appointment, but the ministry accepted his resignation. He immediately turned to Fukuzawa Yukichi, who became something of a benefactor and patron, setting Kodama up as a temporary instructor at the Keiō School lecturing on the U.S. judiciary. During his time at Keiō, 1873 through early 1874, Kodama completed two parts of a planned ten-part series on family law that drew on Blackstone's *Commentaries on the Laws of England* and James Kent on U.S. law.[105] The work was interrupted by his entry into private practice as a legal advocate.

In 1874, Kodama had his first major case, fashioning himself as an expert in foreign law, an "American legal advocate" (*Beikoku daigenshi*).[106] He represented the Mitani merchant house in a dispute with the Netherlands Trading Society and the Mitsui-affiliated Tokyo Shōsha that intermingled old and new influences. Okudaira Masahiro suggested that Kodama's advocacy in the dispute marked a turning point toward modernity because Kodama submitted Japan's first writ of habeas corpus. The case was also significant as an important commercial dispute involving three companies at the intersection of Japan's past, present, and future. In terms of the past, Kodama represented the long-standing Edo-era merchant house run by Mitani Sankurō. Encounters with foreign companies were very much a marker of the commercial present, in this case, represented by the Netherlands Trading Society. And the future belonged to the Mitsui company. Mitani had defaulted on a $100,000 loan for a commercial venture in rapeseed oil. On February 19, 1874, the Netherlands Trading Society, dissatisfied with a ruling from the Kanagawa

---

105. Kodama, *Ningen kōhō*.
106. Okudaira, *Nihon bengoshishi*, 59–61.

Court, appealed to the Court of the Ministry of Justice.[107] Mitani appeared in court represented by Kodama, Naka Sadakatsu (a *daigennin* associate of Kodama's), and three legal scriveners whose services were required by law. In Okudaira's account, the lead judge, Tamano Seiri, Kodama, and Arnold Willem Pieter Verkerk Pistorius of the Netherlands Trading Society all wore suits. The others in the room wore *haori hakama*, the formal kimono typical of official occasions during the Edo era. On the rail (the bar) between court officials and the parties hung a banner adorned with the imperial seal, the chrysanthemum.[108] With the various parties having staked their sartorial claims, the action began, revealing the contest between different notions of proper legal practice.

In the absence of a commercial or civil code, the proceedings turned to custom and reason (*dōri*) for legal grounds to resolve the dispute. Legal historian Okudaira Masahiro described an exchange between Kodama and Judge Tamano on the legal framework for the proceedings. Kodama and Naka brought into the courtroom a cloth bundle out of which they pulled a number of U.S. law books. Seeing the books, Tamano noted that the trial would follow the French legal model, and not the Anglo-American practices with which Kodama was more familiar. Kodama replied, "[S]hould not matters be adjudicated by a country's own laws? As for proceeding according to the French Civil Code, is it not distasteful in an independent country to apply the laws of another country?" Tamano replied, "This court follows the guidance of French-style legal principles. It is not that we are going to apply the French Civil Code simply as it is."[109] So even before the Great Council of State Decree

---

107. The following draws on the account in Murakami Kazuhiro's "Kindaiteki daigennin no tōjō," which is based on his analysis of digests of trials preserved in Tokyo University's *Meiji shinbun zasshi bunko*. Murakami departs from Okudaira's telling, based on the discovery of a Ministry of Justice trial record. It shows that Tamano was not the presiding judge and the story of the filing of the writ of habeas corpus may have been apocryphal. The trial occurred before the courts opened to the public in 1875; there were no spectators, and although the press was allowed, there were no reporters at the trial.

108. Okudaira, *Nihon bengoshishi*, 63–64.

109. Ibid., 65.

of 1875, the courts had opened "the door for the ingress of foreign law."[110] This was not foreign law in general, but French law. Although Murakami's analysis suggests the improbability of this exchange, the conflict between those with predilections for competing foreign legal models rings true. Okudaira's account depicted tensions among schools of legal thought that were in continual conflict until the completion of the legal codification project. Through the end of the 1890s, interpretive and physical schools formed and fought, each with its own preference for the German, French, or English legal tradition.[111] By the early 1880s, institutional heft compounded the intensity of doctrinal disputes among adherents to laws of other nations.

The more important element of the rapeseed oil dispute for Okudaira than the competing schools was Kodama's supposed filing of a writ of habeas corpus. When the court ordered Mitani to appear in response to one of Kodama's submissions, Kodama protested the order. The court reversed itself, but some days later a different judge ordered Mitani to appear in relation to the same matter. Mitani ignored the order and was arrested and jailed. According to Okudaira, Kodama drafted a writ of habeas corpus that Fukuzawa Yukichi then marked up before it was revised and submitted it to the governor of Tokyo, who subsequently released Mitani. Kodama's supposed drafting of a writ of habeas corpus has suggested to some that Kodama was Japan's first modern lawyer.[112] Yet the documentary support for Okudaira's account is slim. Scholars have found no archival evidence of the filing of the writ and there were no press reports at the trial on which to base either the filing of the writ or the exchange between Seiri and Kodama. No other material supports Okudaira's retelling.

Kodama's fervent Christianity diminished once he was back in Tokyo. State suppression was not the reason. In 1873, under pressure from foreign powers, the authorities had removed statements on public signboards prohibiting adherence to Christianity; even so, the religiosity

---

110. Hozumi, *The New Japanese Civil Code,* 18–19.

111. On adherence to the national legal traditions of differing European countries on the part of bureaucrats, see Yamamuro, *Hōsei kanryō no jidai.*

112. Tezuka, *Meijishi kenkyū zassan,* 81.

Kodama manifested abroad was not on display. What to some observers appeared as flexibility and adaptability represented opportunism to others. Celebration of Kodama was not universal. In 1931, Shirayanagi Shūko wrote that Kodama "had returned to Japan without any legal knowledge whatsoever . . . everything that came out of his mouth was idle quibbling. . . . [H]e was a pettifogger [*sanbyaku daigen*] from the West . . . nothing but a western-haircut, western-clothes wearing, western-book clutching pretentious pettifogger."[113] This claim was part of Shirayanagi's speculation about Kodama's place in clique politics during the transition from Edo to Meiji. The Mitsui house had usurped the merchant house of Mitani, which had for some time been close to Chōshū. In Shirayanagi's telling, the courtroom contest was less a battle between Mitani and the Netherlands Trading Society and more an extension of the personal ties and financial conflicts left over from what Shirayanagi identified as Japan's feudal era. Thus, Kodama's appearance in court was not a harbinger of modernity, but an extension of the social, political, and economic inequalities of feudal Edo reinforced in early Meiji Japan. At the same time as Shirayanagi highlighted the continuities in economic relations, an equally relevant continuity was the primacy of an official appointment as the object of Kodama's career aspirations.

Overall, it was the fluidity of the early 1870s that Kodama and Sono embodied: embrace of cosmopolitanism, remnants of Edo-era economic and political power, and the incipient ascent of the bureaucratic state. Kodama grudgingly came to private legal practice in general, and the Mitani case in particular. He had not become a legal advocate out of enthusiasm but out of frustration with his poor bureaucratic posting. Shortly after filing a number of briefs on behalf of Mitani, Kodama quit private practice in favor of a government post. With both the *Mitani v. Netherlands Trading Society* and the *Mitani v. Tokyo Shōsha* cases still pending, Kodama had taken a job with the Ministry of Justice. The post was at the seventh rank, three ranks higher than the rank he had been offered on his return to Japan from the United States.

---

113. Shirayanagi, *Nihon fugō hasseigaku*, 308–9.

In May 1874, Kodama formally withdrew as Mitani's legal advocate, a month after receiving his official appointment. Later that year, in December 1874, the Ministry of Justice Court issued rulings in disputes arising from the collapsed deal between Mitani, the Mitsui-backed Tokyo Shōsha, and the Netherlands Trading Society: all losses for Mitani. Mitani declared bankruptcy in 1875, an end of business for a major Edo-era merchant family.[114] The following, from an April 1874 bulletin, is instructive:

[A]fter studying law in the United States as an exchange student [Kodama Jun'ichirō] did not take an official appointment; instead, he taught students . . . then became legal advocate to Mitani Sankurō; now he has been appointed to the Ministry of the Right, in the legal system section [*hōseika*], receiving a salary of 70 yen a month.[115]

A merchant house had fallen, yet a former samurai had been granted a central place in narratives of Japan's modern legal practice, displacing Edo-era practitioners and others who practiced during the 1870s, including Sono Tei. In light of his reluctant entry and rapid withdrawal, it is with some irony that Kodama has become Japan's first "modern" legal practitioner.

Even so, as a former samurai practicing law, Kodama brought caché to a kind of work that had previously been imagined as best left to "snakes and scorpions."[116] His final aim, however, was employment in the justice bureaucracy, not private practice. Here, too, Kodama figured in a shared world history of mid-nineteenth-century lawyers and legal practitioners—in this case, a history of ambivalence and even animosity toward private practice.

---

114. The legal wrangling continued. The Mitsui-affiliated creditors seized Mitani's assets, yet the Netherlands Trading Society had less success; thus, in 1880 it sued Mitsui to recover $100,000 "fraudulently obtained" in the rapeseed venture. See, for example, "Law Reports: In the Tokio Joto Saibansho," *Japan Gazette* 26, no. 11 (25 Nov. 1880): 252–53.

115. *Nisshin shinjitsushi* (9 Apr. 1874), cited in Murakami K., "Kindaiteki daigennin no tōjō," 62.

116. Okudaira, *Nihon bengoshishi*, 14.

In 1870s and 1880s Japan, legal advocates faced contempt that lingered from the Edo era.[117] In the face of Meiji reforms that promised "civilization and enlightenment," the presence of former suit solicitors among private legal practitioners smacked of a feudal past.[118] The legitimacy of the Meiji government initially rested on a combination of hearkening back to a past that predated its Tokugawa predecessors while at the same time rushing forward to a European-inflected future. Under the Tokugawa, private legal practitioners faced social derision and outright criminalization of their practice.[119] The advocate of the 1870s faced similar social opprobrium. When Sono and Kodama went to court on behalf of their clients, they fought against prejudices arising from the living Tokugawa tradition. In contrast to their Edo predecessors, their claims to legal authority and the weight of their arguments in court had nothing to do with ownership of an inn lodging parties to disputes. Nor was their authority connected to networks of power vested in family heads, village elders, or guild organizers. In Sono's case, the weight of claims to a legal authority grounded in morality diminished over the 1870s.

Different possibilities opened up for Kodama, tied to his past as a samurai and his future as a bureaucrat trained in the United States. Kodama promoted himself as a former government official who had viewed practice in the States and, as such, was equipped to interpret reason based on what he understood as standard practice abroad. Kodama identified himself as a corrective for the failings of the Tokugawa past. Subsequent analysts have, in turn, recognized him as a pioneer of the private Japanese legal profession. Yet legal practitioners like Kodama emerged alongside the Sono Tels and the suit solicitors who came before the court connecting communitarian ideas of justice with the rule of law. Neither Sono nor Kodama closed the book on the remnants of earlier traditions. Rather, they represent a moment of historical fluidity during which the old litigating public found even easier resolution for

---

117. The Senate (Genrōin) logged at least two petitions calling for the elimination of legal advocacy in the period of its institutionalization from 1875 to 1878. Obinata and Gabe, eds., *Genrōin nisshi*.

118. For an analysis of the Tokugawa/Edo past as a dark age, see Gluck, "The Invention of Edo," 265–66.

119. Okudaira, *Nihon bengoshishi*, 14.

private disputes, along with the increasing possibility of advocates' self-invention in the arena of law. The fluidity of their moment dissipated as former samurai increasingly took up private legal practice. Former samurai began to place their stamp on private legal practice for a number of reasons that, in the end, put law and politics even more powerfully before the public.

CHAPTER 3

High-Minded Legal Associations, Societies, and Journals: Putting Law and Politics Before the Public

The advent of the Meiji regime and the social upheaval that accompanied it created opportunities for such practitioners as Sono and Kodama. Like other private legal practitioners in the 1870s, they grappled with continuities from earlier times, including the lesser-regarded suit solicitors (who had changed their name to legal advocates) practicing in their midst. Former samurai as a group faced different challenges. During the Edo era, the orthodoxy identified the samurai as moral exemplars. Work in the judicial apparatus of the domains or the shogunate was among the tasks a samurai might perform for his lord. The coup of 1868 meant that samurai, although still a status group, lacked the established roles that they had enjoyed under the old regime. Questions emerged about the portability of social status in a new age.

Beginning in 1871, half of the government leadership traveled abroad on the Iwakura Mission seeking revision of the unequal treaties and knowledge of foreign systems of commerce and governance. Those remaining were divided over the possibility of invading Korea as a punishment for supposed insults from the Korean kingdom. Proponents of invasion lost and in the wake of the debate in 1873, former samurai quit positions in government. In their words, they entered the world outside of officialdom, "the field" (*zaiya*). In the meantime, they sought to connect their lives to a greater cause and return to positions of social and political leadership. In a quest for new roles and new opportunities, many former samurai who left positions of power in government in 1873 entered legal practice and established associations of legal advocates. Former samurai increasingly saw that private practice offered them an opportunity to reclaim the mantles of political and moral leadership they had enjoyed during the Edo era.

Through the overthrow of the old regime in 1868, samurai had transformed themselves from models of social rectitude into political actors in new social and political narratives. Yet these new roles were ill defined. Organization by former samurai into associations of legal advocates began as a practical solution to the challenge of establishing positions of economic and social importance in society. The first legal associations dominated by former-samurai legal advocates included the Hokushūsha (北洲舎) of Osaka and the Legal Research Institute in Kōchi. The former focused on profit; the latter emerged out of the aspirations of former samurai to reenter political processes. Before the emergence of these associations in 1874 and 1875, legal advocacy hardly seemed the most efficacious way to achieve renewed political relevance. A former samurai told his younger brother that becoming a legal advocate was akin to becoming a suit solicitor, bringing "shame to those who value truth and justice."[1] Following the 1873 policy split at the top levels of the Meiji government over the proposed invasion of Korea, those who left appointments in officialdom began positioning themselves—in speeches, newspapers, and memorials submitted to the government—as the protectors of the aggrieved in the courts and guardians of the people.

At the same time in other parts of the world, legal advocates were likewise emerging as spokespersons for the public. Sociologist Lucien Karpik has described how, in mid-nineteenth-century France, when the legal advocate spoke, "he claimed to be speaking and acting on behalf of that impersonal figure: the public."[2] In Germany during the 1860s and 1870s, legal theorist Rudolf Gneist promoted the establishment of a free (or independent) legal advocacy (*freie Advokatur*) as a prerequisite for the "realization of the law, of justice" in a unifying Germany.[3] The establishment of new categories of legal practice and reorganization of the courts in 1872 meant the beginning of multiple legal and

---

1. To Shima Manjirō, as quoted in Machida, ed., *Tokyo daigennin retsuden*, 26–27.

2. Karpik, *French Lawyers*, 131.

3. Ledford, *From General Estate to Special Interest*, 54.

political projects. As the oligarchs of the Meiji regime began knitting together a nation-state, former-samurai legal advocates began the process of articulating a public, or general, will. Abstract notions of public moral-ity that had enforced their position at the top of the status hierarchy had long ago stopped serving the lower orders of the samurai status group. The 1870s brought an opportunity to craft a revised moral purpose and con-nect it to meaningful work. Through the framework of legal associations (*daigensha*) founded during the 1870s, former samurai promoted the no-tion of public space, and created within it a lively forum for education, commerce, advocacy, debate, and political activism.

In 1874, the reformist opposition to the Meiji government in Tosa joined a broader process in which commoners and former samurai alike petitioned the new government to reform local and national politics. For-mer samurai, including Shimamoto Nakamichi, who had served in the Meiji justice bureaucracy, and former councilors Itagaki Taisuke and Gotō Shōjirō, worked together to call for a new space that would accommodate what observers identified as "public debate and public opinion."[4] Their petition for the establishment of a national assembly in 1874 argued that it was "through the spread of public debate in the realm . . . that peace be-tween the higher and lower orders and their prosperity" would be achieved.[5] In 1875, commoners and former samurai alike echoed these calls in petitions to the Senate (Genrōin, also translated as Chamber of Elders). Petitioners from Nagasaki to Ibaraki beseeched the government to take action on a range of issues from religious reform to reprimanding Korea. Submissions related to domestic politics included broad requests for reform of the polity, with others focusing on such narrower concerns as the drafting of a civil code, establishment of regional courts, and the public election of local, prefectural, and national representatives.[6] In this moment of growing political engagement, and to gather support for their declaration, Itagaki and others founded associations (including as-sociations of legal advocates) that made public opinion and public de-bate an organizational reality.

---

4. See, for example, Kawahara Masayasu, *Kōgi yoron kōkoku no kibo*, Osaka: Hōbun shoya, 1881.

5. "Minsen giin setsuritsu kenpakusho," in Itagaki, ed., *Jiyūtōshi,* 1:86.

6. Obinata and Gabe, eds., *Genrōin nisshi,* 206–13.

Associations of former-samurai legal advocates, the first of which were the Hokushūsha of Osaka and the Legal Research Institute in Kōchi, began to drive a shift in the social and political meaning of law during the first decades of the Meiji era. As was the case with early legal advocates Sono Tel and Kodama Jun'ichirō, former-samurai legal advocates reconciled new possibilities with existing traditions. To align their new choice of employment in private legal practice with their status, they looked back in time and beyond the borders of Japan. Turning to their own past, former samurai who embraced legal practice as a step toward political change claimed that the politically active legal practitioner of the 1870s emerged out of traditions of samurai as paragons of morality. Looking outward, they noted the coincidence of law and political theory in Europe and the United States that ordained private legal practice as political activism. As the history of former samurai reveals, the establishment of associations by legal advocates pursued a vision of law grounded in the samurai past and associated with a foreign-connected future. While establishing these spaces, former samurai began marking off spaces in which to practice a range of public political activities. Elite commoners eventually joined former samurai in this project, which expanded to include calls for the establishment of a constitutional government. Such activities have been highlighted elsewhere as new kinds of speech; they were also acts of legal activism.

Gradually, the activities of former samurai created a space that had not existed during the Edo era, a space protected by rights within which former samurai and others established an institutional basis for political action. Historian Tetsuo Najita has described how Ueki Emori, a leading theorist of freedom and popular rights, conceptualized this space out of a combination of indigenous and foreign philosophical traditions. Najita described how, in Ueki's view, all people "possessed within themselves an autonomous space that did not owe existence to the government, and allowed individuals, therefore, to criticize the existing regime."[7] As a gift from heaven (*tenpū*), this space was for Ueki a natural right. Ueki's natural-rights thinking combined the Confucian postulation of one's terrestrial presence as a divine gift with international theories of rights. Yet

---

7. Najita, "Civil Society in Japan's Modernity," 103–4.

Ueki's thinking was an abstraction that had not yet emerged on the Meiji ground.[8] It took the activism of legal advocates to render visible a space from which individuals could comment on and even criticize local and national governments. Later, Ueki did seek to ground his activism in practice.[9] In 1884, he studied feverishly for the exam for legal advocacy and was later a central figure in the debates over institution of the civil code.

Legal practice provided a practical and material basis for the movement for constitutional politics in Japan. Through their activities, associations of legal advocates created and subsidized newspapers and journals that explored the legal foundation for society while promoting the aim of establishing constitutional government. This in itself would have been a substantial contribution to the movement, yet associations of private practitioners went even further. Through their educative functions, they laid the intellectual groundwork for social and political activism. Their promotion of legal study later took institutional form as private institutions of higher learning. Public legal and political debates about the role of education and the practice of law occasioned government surveillance and ultimately regulation. Nonetheless, political debate and dissent emerged as powerful alternatives to violent uprisings by other former samurai. Through their activities, legal activists invoked the logic of law and rights to pressure government. The 1870s were years of intense political writing and public speech. Legal advocates and their promotion of legal thought were at the heart of debates over the regulation of association and public assembly and the legal defense of the criminally accused. Legal advocates then connected the issues of the right to assemble and the right to criminal defense back to questions of national strength.

New Work for Former Samurai

Where the Restoration had dissolved social constraints in ways that created opportunities for individuals such as Sono and Kodama, the question of what would become of the samurai as a group remained. Since the

---

8. Julia Adeney Thomas suggests that Ueki's theory of rights did not fully address the individual's relation to the nation because, in a sense, the nation was so ubiquitous. Thomas, *Reconfiguring Modernity*, 154–56.

9. See, for example, Shigematsu, "Jiyushugishatachi to minpōten ronsō."

1600s, the 6 to 8 percent of the population in samurai families embodied a social apex. In the words of Yamaga Sokō, samurai embodied public morality, enabling the lower orders of society to "understand what is fundamental and what is secondary."[10] After 1871, former samurai were "permitted," or forced by circumstances, to engage in agricultural, commercial, or industrial endeavors. In short order, former samurai lost their stipends and swords, and, in turn, lost the economic fruits and the symbols of their status at the top of the social hierarchy. Before 1868, it was possible in rare circumstances for an individual samurai to strike out on his own; however, on the whole, "samurai" referred to a hereditary status group whose members lived within the bounds of status and tradition, tied to domains and domainal lords.[11]

Relations grounded in the old regime created challenges and opportunities for former samurai as individuals and as a group. A central challenge was gainful employment. During Tokugawa times, stipends supported by tax revenues extracted from peasant farmers had put rice in a samurai's bowl. Family ties or connections further benefited those samurai who then worked in the bureaucratized offices of domains and the shogunate. What were samurai to do under the new regime? Iwakura Tomomi noted,

For the past 300 years, the samurai have been the natural leaders in society; they have participated in governmental affairs . . . they alone possess a character that is both noble and individualistic. It is for this reason that the 400,000 samurai of today are the most useful group in society."[12]

Under the rubric of the "rehabilitation of the samurai," utility for the Meiji state meant former samurai participation in and contribution to the market economy. This gave rise to various local and national programs to provide employment, including the reclamation of land in Hokkaido and northern Honshu. Although the hope of government assistance and even a government post may have offered solace to some, it was, in fact, the rare former samurai who was accommodated. There were few formal programs

---

10. Yamaga, "Shidō," 389–90.

11. Samurai could sever ties to their domain (*dappan*) over differing approaches to the *bakufu*, and later drop their support of the Meiji government. Havens, "Scholars and Politics in Nineteenth-Century Japan."

12. In Harootunian, "The Economic Rehabilitation of the Samurai," 433.

and those that existed were often ineffective. By the end of 1873, division within the Meiji regime over invading Korea added another dimension to samurai rehabilitation, putting government-employed samurai out of work, with many harboring resentment against their former employer. Even though samurai had been "domesticated" as functionaries in the employ of domainal and shogunal lords, a martial ethos justified, in part, their position of social superiority. It was in the interest of the new national government for these former samurai to engage themselves in pursuits that were productive and peaceful.

If the samurai were to forego the martial charge of an earlier age, then the end of government stipends created the challenge of finding not just any job, but a job consistent with a centuries-old tradition as "leaders in society." Women such as Sono Tel and former suit solicitors had little to lose in the dramatic revisions of social status tied to work. Things were different for samurai as a status group. Their history served as both an asset and an obstacle. It was an asset in that former samurai enjoyed social capital and connections, with ties to lord, domain, patron, or philosophical school. With the attenuation or dissolution of these ties, work took on new meaning. Itagaki Taisuke recognized this in forming the Risshisha. Established in 1874 to help former samurai help themselves, the Risshisha—often translated as the Self-Help Society—announced itself as an association for the "extension of people's rights; the protection of life; the preservation of autonomy; the achievement of employment; and the proliferation of welfare."[13] The activities of the group encompassed schooling for former-samurai youths, vocational training for adults, and legal training. To support its activities, the Risshisha received a concession from the Meiji state for managing local woodlands.

Yet enterprises did not always succeed by virtue of former samurai involvement as the Risshisha and Itagaki discovered. Personal connections were not as generative as they had been under the Tokugawa, and samurai were not always adept at their new, chosen pursuits. Entrepreneurship was one possibility, but the skills that the samurai had cultivated as administrators under the old regime did not always apply to the new environment. Joint enterprises appeared in which former samurai

---

13. "Risshisha setsuritsu no shuisho," in Itagaki, ed., *Jiyūtōshi*, 1:132.

"would gather together, put up a sign," and engage in pursuits ranging from mining to the mundane.[14] Former Tosa samurai Gotō Shōjirō had quit his government post and had turned to a potentially lucrative business. In 1874, he entered a joint venture with a British enterprise to oversee the Takashima coal mines in Nagasaki through a company called the Hōraisha (蓮莱社). Gotō's management of the Takashima mines, however, was a disaster. The mine project fell apart in litigation with Jardine Matheson, a trading firm and one of the leading foreign firms doing business in Japan. In a failed bid to return former samurai to the land, the Risshisha sent former samurai into villages to cultivate tea.[15] The Risshisha woodlands concession was not successful either, leading the society to negotiate further financing in the form of a government bond for ¥15,000 (which ended up as ¥10,000 when it was finally issued). Failures and frustrations raised the question for former samurai: What form of employment would be most appropriate in a changing society?

Under the Tokugawa, samurai bureaucrats had supervised the resolution of disputes among individuals.[16] The work of the legal advocate emerged as a pursuit that aligned with the former samurai's experience as judicial administrators, more consistent with the samurai ideal than land reclamation, mining, or the cultivation of tea. At the same time, the work of the private legal practitioner had been so reviled throughout society that it seems surprising that former samurai turned to this kind of employment. Suit solicitors of the previous era symbolized conflict and operated only with the reluctant consent of the authorities. Yet, in a few short years, several shifts in the practice and perception of law made legal advocacy an increasingly appealing occupation for former samurai.

One shift was the enthusiastic embrace of law as political theory. In the context of the national project of civilization and enlightenment, opportunities emerged for an intellectual engagement between law and society that had not previously existed. Public intellectuals like Fukuzawa Yukichi and Mori Arinori—educators and translators of foreign legal texts—had begun to reframe Meiji society as a society of laws. In another shift, observers noted how Emile Acollas in France and politicians

---

14. Okudaira, *Nihon bengoshishi*, 80–81.
15. Sotozaki, "Risshisha hōritsu kenkyūjo ni tsuite," 18–19.
16. Wigmore, *Law and Justice in Tokugawa Japan*, 57.

such as Abraham Lincoln in the United States had crafted careers out of private legal practice. The work of the legal advocate (*daigennin*), therefore, opened up possibilities for former samurai to become interpreters and exemplars of a new way of thinking about law and society. What emerged was a revised approach to legal advocacy as an occupation concerned with public morality grounded in law.

In Tosa, the Risshisha established the Legal Research Institute, which focused on law and legal study. The institute served two important purposes for former samurai. First, it provided education in law, which was emerging as a potentially suitable profession, transformed from its lowly suit solicitor origins. Second, it aimed many frustrated former samurai away from the violence of direct action as a response to the loss of their position in society, and toward nonviolent political reorganization and reform. The institute first took form as a "section for legal study" within the Risshisha in 1874 and, later, as the Legal Research Institute in 1879.[17] Programs at the Institute schooled participants in legal practice and sold the legal services of advocates and scriveners. At its peak, the Legal Research Institute was "a 1,200 member organization housed in a brick building in Shinkyōbashi."[18] It is unclear whether or not this endeavor was more successful at placing former samurai in gainful employment than the Risshisha's other endeavors, but it was more attractive to former samurai than other organizations in the prefecture. The closest competitor was an association called the Seikensha that promoted "Chinese studies [Neo-Confucianism]" and provided job referrals to its 800 members from the grounds of the former domainal castle.[19] As the legal arm of the Risshisha, the Legal Research Institute offered former samurai opportunities for employment and an important group affiliation. In this, it filled a social vacuum created by the collapse of the Tokugawa government. Yet the model of a local group—tied to a specific place and

---

17. Sotozaki Mitsuhiro argues that although the conventional wisdom puts the establishment of the Legal Research Institute in 1874, there is better evidence for its establishment in 1879, building on the existence of a "legal research section." Sotozaki, "Risshisha hōritsu kenkyūjo ni tsuite," 13.

18. "Kōchi no seisha," *Tokyo nichi nichi shinbun* (10–11 Aug. 1877), cited in Hirao, ed., *Jiyūminken no keifu*, 37.

19. Ibid. See also the *Chōya shinbun* (26 Jul. 1878), on the societies.

the personalities associated with that place—was soon surpassed by a different model of association that was more flexible, replicable, and open to connecting former samurai and other elites in Meiji society.

In 1874, the same year of the founding of the Risshisha, two legal advocates, a former samurai and an elite commoner, established an association of legal advocates. It was a novel pairing. As a former samurai, Kitada Masatadashi had policed Osaka under Gotō Shōjirō during the early 1870s. Teramura Tomie, a commoner from the domain of Kawagoe, had experience as an administrator of prisons and the courts under the Meiji government.[20] Together they traveled to seek out the advice of mentors and associates on how to establish a new kind of legal services enterprise. In Tokyo, they consulted a serving judge on the form that such an association might take. While there, they also met with Gotō, who had just launched his Takashima coalmine venture in Nagasaki. Gotō's enterprise and the new legal advocacy enterprise, like other former-samurai efforts of the day, had the potential to employ former colleagues and exploit connections.[21] Gotō suggested that Kitada and Teramura subordinate their project to his and locate a bureau of advocates (*daigenkyoku*) within his Tokyo-based company, the Hōraisha. In what was perhaps a prescient act, and with the weight of their connections in Osaka, the two declined Gotō's offer and returned to the Kansai.

After securing a loan of 400 yen, Kitada and Teramura set out to find a location for an office. Eventually they rented a building in the Kitahama area of Osaka, and named their enterprise the Hokushūsha. Kitada and Teramura soon formed a rapport with another former Tosa samurai, Shimamoto Nakamichi. Shimamoto had significant experience in the Meiji legal apparatus. He had worked in Tokyo as prosecutor and chief of police as well as with Etō Shinpei on reform of the prison system.[22] A prominent figure among those who resigned their government posts during the debate over invading Korea, Shimamoto had returned to Tosa in 1873.[23]

---

20. Okudaira, *Nihon bengoshishi*, 102–16.

21. Kobayashi M., "Gotō Shōjirō yori kaishū ikō no Mitsubishi Takashima tankō."

22. Shimamoto figures prominently in dictionaries of Meiji-era historical figures. See, for example, the entry in Tatsuya, *Bakumatsu ishin jinmei jiten*.

23. Kikuyama, "Etō Shinpei no shihō kaikaku," 95.

Shimamoto's interest in connecting political thought and reformist action for the sake of the people intensified over the course of the 1870s, as evidenced by his support for constitutional government, his efforts to build public legal education, and, later, a laudatory book on samurai activist Ōshio Heihachirō. As a mentor to Kitada and Teramura, Shimamoto convinced the two to seek additional funds for an even larger enterprise than they had originally conceived. They followed his advice and approached the Shimada Group, the third-largest financial group in the Kansai after Mitsui and Ono. On the premise that "there would be profit in legal advocacy and the preparation of legal documents," they received a 2,000-yen loan from Shimada.[24] Teramura and Kitada invited Shimamoto to serve as the director of their association of legal advocates.[25] In July 1875, a ward head in Osaka approved the Hokushūsha's request to formalize their venture and establish an "institute for the study of codes" (*ritsugaku kenkyūjo*).[26] The "institute" proposed to "practice legal advocacy[,] . . . . offer the services of scriveners," and train students in law.[27]

The commercial and educative aspects of the group's work were mutually reinforcing. In its charter, the Tokyo branch of the association, which opened in December 1874, stated that it was "completely different from a company such as a commercial company or a publishing company."[28] In Osaka and Tokyo, the association consisted of members and clerks, divided among four sections—advocates, scriveners, administrators, and accountants. The association assigned apprentices the task of copying laws out of government publications, which were on file at the local courts or in its own collection.[29] The Meiji regime was a prodigious producer of legal text. The Ministry of Justice allowed advocates to further reproduce the newly promulgated decrees, circulars, and edicts. Domestic law mixed

---

24. Okudaira, *Nihon bengoshishi*, 105.

25. In a coincidence common to the overlapping personal and business connections of the time, the Shimada Group had also invested in Gotō's Takashima mining venture. Kobayashi, "Gotō Shōjirō yori kaishū ikō no Mitsubishi Takashima tankō."

26. Okudaira, *Nihon bengoshishi*, 105–6.

27. Ibid.

28. Art. 3, "Hōritsu kenkyūkai sōritsu jōrei," cited in Osaka bengoshikia, ed, *Osaka bengoshishi kō*, 1:582.

29. Ibid., 614–15. On copying laws, see Okudaira, *Nihon bengoshishi*, 108.

with international legal and political theory in the legal advocate's list of reading materials.

It was through their encounters with domestic edicts and international works on law and politics that groups such as the Hokushūsha embraced a notion of law that integrated theory and practice. Texts available to legal practitioners during the early 1870s reveal the sources that informed this mix of the theoretical and practical, political and procedural. The Hokushūsha library mirrored the collection of the Ministry of Justice in that it was heavily weighted toward French law, including works on French commercial law, materials on French laws of evidence, and a compilation of constitutions.[30] There were also guides to debit and credit rules, postal regulations, and a copy of the *Shinritsu kōryō* (Principles of the new statutes) among more than fifty titles. The Risshisha's Legal Research Institute had copies of *An Outline of Constitutional Political Forms* (1861), Henry Wheaton's *Elements of International Law* (in Chinese, 1865), *On State Law in the West* (1868), and *Vissering's International Law* (1868).[31] Reading in the law was not limited to apprentice legal advocates. Under the tutelage of the Risshisha, students in Tosa secondary schools also read the Napoleonic Code.[32] Meiji legal reforms had merged with the practitioner's pursuit of a practical and philosophical foundation for his work. These then combined to create a literary culture of reading, copying, and studying legal texts that answered an immediate and practical demand for putting these texts to use in the delivery of legal services.

The prevalence of foreign law texts and the associations that collected and interpreted them shaped the emerging legal discourse in Japan. In the hands of former samurai, this discourse increasingly wove together the

---

30. Osaka bengoshikai, ed., *Osaka bengoshishi kō*, 1:614–15. While the history of the Osaka bar does not include exact bibliographic data, the following are likely the texts in the collection: Uchizawa Izō, *Gofutatsu kisoku shō taishaku hikkei* (Tokyo, 1874); [No author given], *Nihon teikoku yūbin kisoku oyobi bassoku* (Tokyo: Senbunsha, 1875); Ministry of Justice (Meihōryō), ed., *Kenpō ruihen* (Kyoto: Murakami Kanpei, et al., 1873); Ministry of Justice, *Shinritsu kōryō* (Tokyo: Ministry of Justice, 1870); and an anonymous translation of the French Commercial Code of 1838, part of which included a discussion of bankruptcy.

31. Howland, *Translating the West*, 98.

32. Motoyama, "Local Politics and the Development of Secondary Education in the Early Meiji Period," 170.

practicalities of legal practice with law as political theory. In a memoir, Satta Masakuni, a founder of the association of legal advocates that eventually became Hōsei University, described how he followed the Meiji legal transition by devouring legal texts, particularly foreign ones, as they became available to students and practitioners.[33] Satta was a practicing legal advocate during the 1870s. He and his peers learned about law in study groups, through apprenticeship, and through book learning. Satta memorized the preamble of the *Kari keiritsu* (Temporary criminal code), read Mitsukuri Rinshō's translation of the French legal codes, and from time to time participated in a group that translated French commentaries on the codes. Over the course of the 1870s, Satta and other legal practitioners read Rousseau's *Du contrat social* and Montesquieu's *De l'esprit des lois*.

French law and society were not the only models for these advocates. In 1871, Nakamura Masanao [also Keiu] translated Mill's *On Liberty*; from 1873 to 1876, Hoshi Tōru translated Blackstone's *Commentaries on the Laws of England* (*Eikoku hōritsu zensho*).[34] One could also read Mill's *On Representative Government* and the writings of Herbert Spencer in Japanese.[35] Nagamine Hideki translated *On Representative Government* in 1875, Hattori Toku translated the *Social Contract* in 1877, and Ozaki Yukio translated part of Herbert Spencer's *Social Statics* in 1878.[36] As for formal study at the Hokushūsha, beginning in 1877 the association launched regular evening readings of the French civil and criminal codes. Required of all apprentices, attendance was from six to eight in the evening on Mondays and Thursdays. Attendees were expected to do more than simply "read" the laws. They were to compare them with extant Japanese law and debate

---

33. Satta Masakuni, "Hōritsu hensan no hōhō o ronzu" (ca. 1887), cited in Ebashi, "Satta Masakuni," 71.

34. Hoshi, trans., *Eikoku hōritsu zensho*.

35. Osatake, *Nihon kenseishi taikō*, 2:505. For further discussion of reading materials, see Matsuo. "Shihō shiryō."

36. Howland, *Translating the West*, 172–73. The personal stamps on books in the current holdings of university archives reveal other texts that legal advocates had in their collections. Legal advocate Tamura Totsu owned *Furansushi*—an 1878 translation by Oka Senjin and Takashi Jirō of an amalgam of three of Victor Duruy's histories of France: *Petite Histoire de France depuis les temps les plus reculés jusqu'à nos jours* (Paris: 1866); *Histoire des temps modernes depuis 1453 jusqu'à 1789* (Paris: 1869); and *Histoire de France* (Paris: 1870).

them vigorously, while avoiding ad hominem attacks.[37] Theory converged with practicality at the Hokushūsha.

For the commercial side of the association, the combination of theory and practice, education and commerce, was very remunerative. Fees from cases were the property of the association. Charges to clients usually amounted to 10 percent of the amount at stake in a dispute and were adjusted upward or downward based on the projected difficulty of a case. The Hokushūsha adopted a system of members and trainees, with the members, or principals, falling into five ranks, with the trainees or clerks supporting their work in administrative capacities. Members received salaries based on their positions in the five-rank system, with payment corresponding to one's rank. There was no cap on earnings for the first and second ranks. Top personnel received compensation out of the balance after payment to junior personnel. The third rank received 50 yen a month; the fourth, 40 yen; and the fifth, 30 yen. The association employed clerks on a daily and monthly basis. Based on their performance, daily clerks could become monthly clerks and monthly clerks could become members of the Hokushūsha.[38] Monthly clerks were divided into six ranks that received monthly salaries from 6 to 20 yen.

Business boomed. The Hokushūsha had succeeded in developing a socially respectable occupational model that met the needs of an emerging market for legal advocacy. The underground work of suit solicitors during the Edo era now flourished in the open on a new political and economic landscape. The Hokushūsha attracted members with skills in law and finance, including former samurai Iwaki Namio, who left a position in finance to join the group. Iwagami Takashi, who had resigned a post in the Kyoto courts in 1873, also joined.[39] Within months of opening the Osaka location, Shimamoto opened a branch in Tokyo and moved the headquarters of the Hokushūsha there. In December of 1874, with the encouragement of Shimamoto, the management of both entities decided to

---

37. Osaka bengoshikai, ed., *Osaka bengoshishi kō*, 1:617.

38. In the years from 1874 to 1876, the number of monthly and daily clerks ranged from six to sixteen. Compiled from data in Okudaira, *Nihon bengoshishi*, 111–12.

39. Iwagami was Furusawa Shigeru's older brother and later joined Hayashi Yūzō and others in the plot from within the Risshisha to support the Satsuma Rebellion. Shōji, *Kainan aikoku minkenka retsuden*, 114–15.

separate their accounting in the interest of "establishing a long-standing foundation" and "increasing profitability and expanding each enterprise."[40] This was in part in anticipation of Tokyo's ascent as the national center not only for government but also for finance and industry.

An element of prestige was to be had in locating the association's headquarters in Tokyo that signaled the wealth and influence then inhering in the Hokushūsha. Much as government buildings figured as marvels of the new age, the Tokyo office of the Hokushūsha also embodied novelty. Located in the financial district of Nihonbashi, the headquarters building was an impressive tile-roofed, stucco and brick building, featured in a print series on late-nineteenth-century Tokyo.[41] The architecture itself conveyed the openness of the association's activity and its relevance to public space. The building was surrounded by a low wall, with a lantern-lit entryway and, in the representation, was a busy place with *jinrikisha*—the ubiquitous pull carts used for urban transport—parked outside and clients and legal advocates walking in and out. As a further reflection of the profitability of the venture, the management of the Osaka location expressed its appreciation for its clerks' hard work in a July 1876 pleasure cruise on the Yodogawa River. This became a regular event on the calendar, later joined by an October trip to the theater (and bars), and the distribution of "sake money" in November.[42]

In addition to being vibrant centers of commerce, associations of legal advocates also served as intellectual salons, in a sense, where an eminent thinker might stop in after a particularly provocative evening at a debate society. That is what happened on June 1, 1875, when Ueki Emori visited the Tokyo office of the Hokushūsha. He had just attended a meeting of the Meirokusha debate society. He might have been seeking out Shimamoto Nakamichi to further discuss issues about the death penalty raised by Tsuda Mamichi. At the same meeting, Nishimura Shigeki had analyzed the possibilities for overcoming the tension between public and private interests.[43] These kinds of spaces, in which intellectuals and prac-

---

40. Shimamoto Nakamichi, "Tōsai ryosha kuiki no iken," cited in Osaka bengoshi-kai, ed., *Osaka bengoshi shi kō*, 1:591.

41. Shōnandō, ed., *Tokyo seikaku zuroku*.

42. Ibid., 612, 615.

43. Ueki, "Nikki, Part I," 64.

Table 2: Income for the Hokushūsha,
1874–1876 (all income including
gratuities, travel costs, etc.)

Year	Month	Amount
1874	June	0.00
	July	13.00
	August	3105.50
	September	2.00
	October	519.18
	November	355.60
	December	485.39
1875	January	512.27
	February	466.26
	March	104.85
	April	461.81
	May	467.08
	June	160.80
	July	22.88
	August	355.20
	September	463.19
	October	974.14
	November	298.89
	December	846.19
1876	January	530.75
	February	606.29
	March	203.46
	TOTAL	**10,954.73**

SOURCE: Compiled from *Osaka begoshikaishi kō.*

titioners might come together to discuss the concerns of the moment, were not limited to Tokyo. The Hokushūsha opened a third location in Hiroshima in December 1874. In 1875, branches opened in Sakai, Kyoto, and Ōtsu.[44] The association also opened branches in Nagoya, Niigata, Sendai, and Fukushima.[45]

Even as an association of legal advocates like the Hokushūsha brought practitioners and political activists together, entry to legal advocacy at the level of the association and through the licensing exam increasingly

---

44. Okudaira, *Nihon bengoshishi*, 109.
45. Osaka bengoshikai, ed., *Osaka bengoshishi kō*, 1:623.

favored former samurai and, particularly, former samurai affiliated with associations of legal advocates. The membership of the group made a clear distinction with private legal practice's suit inn and suit solicitor past. Former samurai led the ranks of the Hokushūsha's members and clerks. Of the 28 members at the Tokyo headquarters, there were 22 former samurai, 1 member of the aristocracy, and 5 commoners.[46] The Osaka branch had a somewhat more even division between commoners and former samurai. Even so, in 1880, former samurai outnumbered commoners in Osaka, 32 to 25. Despite the long history in both cities of legal practice organized around commoner-run suit inns, former samurai began to re-shape legal practice into a desirable occupation, dominating its upper reaches. In the first licensing exam under regulations for legal advocates in 1876, nearly more than twice as many former samurai passed as did commoners.[47] Also, almost half of those who passed the 1876 exam were affiliated with the Hokushūsha and other associations of legal advocates founded by former samurai.

Former samurai legal advocates defined themselves against what they characterized as the mechanistic practice of law by unlicensed former suit solicitors, who were still practicing due to loose enforcement of licensing requirements by the courts. In creating an intellectual community around emergent issues of politics, law, and society, former samurai differentiated legal thought and practice in the Meiji era from what they identified as an earlier dark age. New ideas of rights and a public governed by laws gained traction in this confluence of the pursuit of prestige, the proliferation of legal texts, and the collective association of new legal advocates. It was also this combination of the practical need for jobs with the social need for preservation of status that inspired a new narrative of the Tokugawa samurai turned modern legal advocate.

One way former samurai distinguished themselves from their Edo predecessors was through assertions of rights. The idea of "extending rights" lay at the core of practice by former samurai. These claims could be political, commercial, educational, or professional; at times the reference was ambiguous, with the ideal of extending rights (*shinken*) appearing as little

---

46. Compiled from data in Okudaira, *Nihon bengoshishi*, 134–35.
47. Compiled from data in ibid., 184–88. See also Murakami K., "Kindai Nihon no zaiya hōsō to sono hyōden," 44.

more than a slogan.[48] The first article of the Hokushūsha's rules for legal advocates and scriveners stated that each would "work without harming bureaucratic authority above while preserving people's rights below."[49] Building on the idea of law as a foundation for protecting rights, the Hokushūsha trained many former samurai as legal advocates who then entered careers in politics. Former samurai Kikuchi Kanji went on to become an Osaka city councilor, prefectural assembly member, Diet member, and prefectural governor. After working as a legal advocate in the Hokushūsha, Kojima Tadasato left in 1876 and became a central figure in the establishment of the Liberal Party.[50]

Hokushūsha alums also pursued careers in the judiciary, commerce, and industry.[51] Revealing the overlapping connections between law, politics, and newspaper publishing during the 1870s and 1880s, Yoshizumi Junzō returned to Tosa to establish a sole legal practice under the name Yūshinkan (誘信館); he then became involved in Liberal Party politics. He was "widely hailed for his speaking" and later founded a newspaper in Hyogo prefecture.[52] Yoshizumi also authored multiple works including a didactic text for women and an 1880 discussion of policies for reforming Japan's finance system.[53] Inoue Tadasoku and Egi Shinobu left the Hokushūsha to become private practitioners as proprietors of the Seirikan (正理館)) and the Kōyōsha (江陽社), respectively. Kōno Togama formed a new practice and was instrumental in drawing Numa Morikazu

---

48. Ōmori, ed., *Daigennin dainin teiyō*, opening pages.

49. "Hōritsu kenkyūkai daisho daigen kisoku," cited in Osaka bengoshikai, ed., *Osaka bengoshishi kō*, 1:583.

50. On Kojima Tadasato, see Mita, *Osaka kumiai daigennin kōhyōroku*, 34–35. Kojima left the Hokushūsha on 21 Dec. 1876, Osaka bengoshikai, ed., *Osaka bengoshishi kō*, 1:616.

51. Shinoda, *Meiji shin risshihen*, 198–99. Former samurai, and associate of Shimamoto, Mawatari (Mato) Shun'yū quit a government post and joined the Hokushūsha. He worked there for two years as a legal advocate in civil suits before returning to the Ministry of Justice, later becoming a judge on the Tokyo Appeals Court.

52. On Yoshizumi's public speaking, see Hanabusa, *Daigennin hyōbanki*, 11. On the Yoshizumi's paper and politics in Hyogo, see Fujii and Fujimoto, "Chihō shinbun ni miru Hyōgo-ken daiikkai sōsenkyo: Kōmin kyōiku kiso shiryō," 127.

53. Yoshizumi, *Nihon zaisei konnan kyūchisaku*, and *Onna kyōkun yomeiri dōgu*. Former Hokushūsha associate Honjō Kazuyuki also became involved in newspapers while editing the proceedings of debates on modern emperors and kings, published in 1878. Honjō, *Kinsei kōchō ron*.

into the emergent political party, the Rikken kaishintō (Constitutional Progressive Party).[54] In a sense, the associations of legal advocates preserved the appurtenances of samurai status in a new social and political order. Additionally, these associations had achieved at least one of their goals: connecting former samurai to meaningful employment.

These groups of legal advocates, in addition to the other organizations such as the Risshisha and the first political parties, connected former samurai and helped them constitute an opposition to the Meiji government. Former samurai and wealthy commoner legal advocates served as leaders and members of the groups so often mentioned in relation to the Meiji-era movement for freedom and popular rights (*jiyū minken undō*), with the campaign for constitutional government at its center. The concentration on rights and public space was not simply a product of political activism by former samurai; it was a product of the activities of associations of legal advocates that sought to expand the ground on which they operated and through which they might shape the future conditions for their practice of law. Even though initially united in the narrow goal of supporting an invasion of Korea, reformists in opposition ultimately rallied around the broader goal of creating a legally constituted state—a constitutional polity. This aim first focused the efforts of former samurai in Tosa and then found other former samurai and elite supporters. The Meiji government recognized the increasing institutionalization of the opposition and noted the links between political parties, schools, and associations of legal advocates. In an 1882 dispatch Yamagata Aritomo warned Itō Hirobumi (during his trip to analyze constitutional governments overseas) that Kōno Hironaka was using an association of legal advocates, the "Shūshinsha, as a base for extending the politics of progressive parties by appealing to legal types."[55] Linking legal practice with political activism reflected, in part, a way of finding new employments appropriate to a former samurai's social and political status. This shift required increasingly formal education of the private legal advocate.

---

54. Davis, *Ono Azusa, A Case Study*, 207.

55. 17 Nov. 1882, correspondence to Itō, in Takii, "Itō Hirobumi taiō kenpō chōsa no kōsatsu," 54.

Educating Legal Advocates

At the same time that former samurai identified their practice of law as protection of rights, they also sought reestablished roles in government. As noted above, the late-nineteenth-century ideal of a legal advocate as public intellectual and politician held great appeal to former samurai. It resonated with their Edo-era status as moral exemplars and their recast identity as defenders against corruption and exploitation. The philosophical groundings of legal advocacy in the first years of the Meiji had added substance and status to the new roles that they had defined for themselves, but there were also new practices and new ways of thinking to master. Legal advocates with a samurai pedigree saw law as both politics and practice. The educational systems that emerged around associations of legal advocates provided a means for becoming proficient in both. Reflecting on the establishment of the Hokushūsha, Shimamoto stated that he had worked to establish the Tokyo branch so that "it could employ legal advocates and scriveners who would study legal principles and put their knowledge to practical use."[56] Over the course of the 1870s, the number of organizations in which samurai might learn about law and politics proliferated. Associations of legal advocates, even informal ones, were natural centers for this: they combined education with employment for advocates or scriveners in training. They were a private sector answer to the government's efforts to train and educate judges and procurators in the Meihōryō and through ad-hoc training sessions with foreign advisers.

In 1875, Bungo domain former samurai Motoda Naoshi established the Association for the Study of Law (Hōritsu gakusha 法律学舎) in Tokyo. Motoda had been educated in his domain's school and, after 1868, studied foreign education systems for the Meiji government. From the early 1870s, he worked in Etō Shinpei's Ministry of Justice along with Mitsukuri Rinshō on the translation of French law. After Etō resigned, Motoda turned his energies to the instruction and practice of law. He and other members of an informal group who met over sake and calligraphy brushes decided to gather some students together and teach them law. The group also sold legal services. His Association for the Study of Law

---

56. Osaka bengoshikai, ed., *Osaka bengoshishi kō*, 623.

attracted all manner of students, some as young as sixteen, requiring that all except bureaucrats have the backing of a guarantor before joining.[57] At the time of its opening, the school boasted the presence of the French legal adviser to the Ministry of Justice, Boissonade, as an occasional lecturer. The monthly schedule, with tutorials nearly every day, was demanding, but also allowed time for client work.

In addition to attending classes, students were required to support the commercial work of the association. This did not sit well with Iizuka Gin'ya, who in 1875 rebelled against the system of apprenticeship. He approached Motoda asking for a revision of the terms governing student participation, including a reduction in the amount of work he and others performed for the association's commercial side. Denied by Motoda, Iizuka and six other students left and, after additional study, formed their own association of legal advocates, the Shinkensha.[58] Their association, located in Tokyo, had some success, with Iizuka arguing multiple cases before the High Court from 1878 to 1880.

Before the 1880s, there was rampant competition and high turnover among the apprenticeship and legal training programs that dominated private instruction in law. With legal knowledge opening the door to new political opportunities and legal practice providing remuneration, associations of legal advocates blossomed. Associations opened one after another in Osaka, Tokyo, and Yokohama, where there was a flourishing market for their services. Without formal certification, licensing, or registration required before 1876, the total number of these early associations is unclear. Associations that combined legal training with the sale of advocacy services opened and closed their doors, or merged with other associations, often after only a year or two. Although at times short-lived, they were ubiquitous in the metropolitan centers and quite common in large and medium-sized regional cities, as revealed in the bar association histories for each prefecture. For example, at the time of the licensing exam of 1876, about 100 people were engaged in the work of legal advocacy in the city of Yokohama. Out of these, only one person—commoner Ueki Okajirō—had passed the licensing exam. Ueki worked for two years in

---

57. Okudaira, *Nihon bengoshishi*, 151–54.
58. Machida, ed., *Tokyo daigennin retsuden*, 42–43.

Table 3. Monthly Schedule at the Association for the Study of Law (*Hōritsu gakusha* 法律学舎)

1	2	3	4	5	6	7
Assembly (1–6pm)	Criminal Law (8am–3pm)	Criminal Law (3–6pm)	Civil Law (3–6pm)	Legal Procedure (3–4pm)		Criminal Law (8am–3pm)
8	9	10	11	12	13	14
Criminal Law (3–6pm)	Civil Law (3–6pm)	Legal Procedure (3–4pm)	Assembly (1–6pm)	Criminal Law (8am–3pm)	Criminal Law (3–6pm)	Civil Law (3–6pm)
15	16	17	18	19	20	21
Legal Procedure (3–4pm)		Criminal Law (8am–3pm)	Criminal Law (3–6pm)	Civil Law (3–6pm)	Legal Procedure (3–4pm)	Assembly (1–6pm)
22	23	24	25	26	27	28
Criminal Law (8am–3pm)	Criminal Law (3–6pm)	Civil Law (3–6pm)	Legal Procedure (3–4pm)		Criminal Law (8–3pm)	Criminal Law (3–6pm)
29	30	31				
Civil Law (3–6pm)	Legal Procedure (3–4pm)	Assembly (1–6pm)				

SOURCE: Compiled from data in Okudaira, *Nihon bengoshishi*, 151–54.

Yokahama before taking his credentials to Tokyo and joining a group established by Ōi Kentarō, the Meihōsha.[59]

By and large, the names of the associations signaled the hybrid nature of morality and law during the 1870s. The associations often incorporated the language of rights or echoed the Confucian tradition in the name of their practice groups. For example, former Hokushūsha legal advocate Tamura Totsu established an Association for the Preservation of Rights (Hokensha 保権舎). The Tokyo areas of Kyōbashi and Nihonbashi saw the establishment of the Law of Received Wisdom Association (Kichi hōsha 貴知法社) and the Association for the Preservation of Peace (Hoansha 保安社). Both were located in areas of Tokyo that had served as centers for Tokugawa-era practitioners of law. An association called the Tōtensha (東天社) formed in Kyōbashi in 1879. Around the same time, associations burgeoned in Tokyo, including a Chūritsusha (中立社), Kenpōsha (研法社), Shinmeisha (審明舎), and Kashinsha (可進社).[60] In Osaka, former student/employees of the Hokushūsha formed the Sanseisha in 1877.

Legal advocates also opened branches of urban associations in the countryside. Independent, locally founded associations of legal advocates emerged as well.[61] In Ibaraki, one could find the Mito Hall for the Study of Law (Mito hōgakkan 水戸法学館) and the Morality Association (Dōgisha 道義舎).[62] In 1876, Numa Morikazu, then a member of the Senate (Genrōin), backed a group of Yokohama legal advocates, the Buntensha (聞天舎).[63] After resigning his government post in 1879 in response to prohibitions on public speaking, Numa became an unlicensed legal advocate himself, founding the Kyūkōsha (九皐舎). He hired licensed legal advocate Kadota Shinpei to administer the association, which, like other associations of legal advocates at the time, combined instruction in law with the sale of legal services.[64]

---

59. Yokohama bengoshikai, ed., *Yokohama bengoshikaishi*, 1:24–32.

60. Okudaira, *Nihon bengoshishi*, 216.

61. Other groups founded during the 1870s included the Shuseisha (守成社, est. 1877), the Deliberation and Law Association (Shinpōsha 審法舎, est. 1878), the Yūgusha (有詡社), the Kyōgisha (協義社), the Kōdan kaisha (講談会社), the Yōyōsha (洋洋社), and the Hokushinsha (北辰社). Ibid.

62. Nakamura Y., "Meiji jūnendai ni okeru daigennin to Meiji hōritsu gakkō," 8.

63. Okudaira, *Nihon bengoshishi*, 200–215.

64. Ibid.

The loose application of licensing norms by the courts and the indifference to licensing among leading legal advocates themselves blurred the boundaries between licensed and unlicensed practitioner. Numa Morikazu represented clients in court without a license; Okudaira noted that "even in an era of licensed advocates, the courts permitted persons such as Ōi Kentarō or Numa to represent clients."[65] A lack of license did not deter Numa, yet he did find it useful to encourage his younger brother, Takanashi Tetsushirō, to sit for the licensing exam (which the latter passed) and to pursue practice as a licensed legal advocate.[66]

The apprentice model of education adopted in the proliferating associations cultivated a large number of former-samurai legal advocates in a short period of time. These newly minted legal advocates became politicized, if they were not already, reading political theory as part of their legal studies. The legal practice that emerged out of these associations involved campaigning for a space for public speech and debate protected by rights. In this new space, legal advocates joined others in discussing the role of law, the efficacy of the state, and the rights of the people. Former samurai within associations of legal advocates learned and taught themselves; they also created openings for non-samurai to apply theory to practice, and political action.

Theory and Practice: Debate Societies, A Party of Patriots, and Law as the New Morality for a New Public

With the post-1868 unraveling of the bonds of samurai duty and responsibility, freedom and liberty emerged as alternatives to domainal fealty. Yet what freedom meant was unclear in the early 1870s. Various influences shaped the potential meanings of "freedom" and "rights" for the former samurai legal practitioner. As former samurai in the regions began rethinking the relationship between state and society, groups of their cosmopolitan, urban counterparts also entered the fray. Public intellectuals such as Fukuzawa Yukichi challenged what they saw as the misguided assumption that freedom simply meant egoism, disorder, or the unbridled

---

65. Ibid.
66. Takanashi later served Numa as a proxy in an ongoing feud with political adversary Hoshi Tōru. Matsuo S., "Shihō shiryō," 53–56.

expression of self-interest. He argued that people misunderstood the foreign concept of "freedom" as "the freedom to starve someone to death, the freedom to commit violent acts of strength, the freedom to commit crimes and escape punishment."[67] In his *Seiyō jijō* (Conditions in the West), Fukuzawa countered the conventional belief that "the greatest freedom in humankind exists in the world of the barbarians."[68] Rather, freedom derived from civility shaped by law. Thus, Fukuzawa argued that freedom emerged out of a society of law. This position found further refinement in Fukuzawa's writing and teaching, and in the actions of private legal practitioners, newspapers, and public lecturers who shaped public understanding of the meaning of "freedom" and "rights" during the last three decades of the nineteenth century.

A reconceptualization of the relationship between the individual and government informed the study of law and politics by former samurai and wealthy farmers and merchants. Even as the government sought to guide and regulate speech on politics during its first decade of rule, talk of law and politics became irrepressible. As Kuga Katsunan put it, the first years of the Meiji period were "a world of free speech."[69] Debate societies and study groups, many with legal-advocate members, formed in Tokyo. With liberty in the foreground, they sought to explore how an engagement with Euro-American ideas of rights might shape the new social and political ethos. Debate societies differed from associations of legal advocates in many ways. Their members joined not for employment but for intellectual exploration and fellowship. Theirs were ultimately theoretical, not practical, endeavors. While many of the members of debate societies worked for the government, they brought together officials and nonofficials alike in fostering discourses on rights, law, and politics. Their exploration of ideas of rights influenced the first political parties and spread into newly emergent public spaces that were available to all who would draw on them and shape them, including legal advocates.

The Meirokusha and the Ōmeisha (the Legal Lecture and Study Group changed its name to Ōmeisha in 1877), founded in 1873 and 1874, respectively, numbered among the first and most prominent debate

---

67. Fukuzawa, *Seiyo jijō*, 33–34.
68. Ibid.
69. Kuga, "Kinjiseironkō," 343.

societies of the 1870s. They have been widely studied as expressions of an urban current of former-samurai political activism.[70] In terms of thinking about former-samurai involvement in legal advocacy, the activity of these groups offers an instructive window into the changing meaning of law in Japan. The Meirokusha placed discussions of law and politics at the center of its activities, despite Mori Arinori's disavowal of discussing "contemporary politics" at meetings.[71] In addition to Mori and Fukuzawa, the group counted among its members Nishi Amane, translator of French law, and Katō Hiroyuki, who had become a scholar of German legal theory (particularly theory of the state influenced by Johann Bluntschli). The Meirokusha promoted a legal approach to society through its debates and through the publication of its journal, the *Meiroku zasshi.* The Meirokusha and the Legal Lecture and Study Group (forerunner of the Ōmeisha) used law as a tool for examining how to reform society and politics. The fluidity of the early years of the Meiji period invited questions such as whether judges should be elected or appointed, whether women should be allowed to participate in politics, and whether adoption should continue as it had in the past. In every instance, these issues appeared couched in the language and logic of legal reform.[72]

There were shortcomings to the Meirokusha's exploration of the foundation for a legal society. Foreshadowing Maruyama Masao's later critiques of official domination of the private sphere, Fukuzawa cautioned in his 1874 inquiry into the work of the scholar, "Gakusha no shokubun o ronzu," that his fellow interpreters of foreign thought were overly concerned with officialdom and poorly versed in private affairs. Fukuzawa argued that officials, many of whom were fellow Meirokusha members, had too much faith in the government's ability to create national strength. Rather, the government should rely on the private sector and let the people take the lead in the various spheres of "law, scholarship, and commerce." Fukuzawa complained that the scholars shaping learning in 1874 "know of officialdom but do not understand the private. They know the art of

---

70. For an overview of the urban intelligentsia and their associations, including the Meirokusha, Ōmeisha, and Kyōzon dōshū, see Kim, *The Age of Visions and Arguments*, 156–63.

71. For the Meirokusha, see Braisted, ed. and trans., *Meiroku zasshi*, 367.

72. On debates at the Ōmeisha, see Maruyama N., ed., *Tōkyō kakusha tōron hikki.*

standing at the top of government but not the ways that exist below government."[73] In other words, many of the members of the Meirokusha were too statist and too elite to truly understand the everyday-life implications of their self-study in political theory. They knew too little about practice. Decades later, historian Suzuki Yasuzō echoed Fukuzawa's criticism of the Meirokusha as elitist and therefore not useful for understanding "the new direction in Japanese politics." The central shortcoming of the Meirokusha for Suzuki was the absence of "the people" (*shomin*) in its proceedings.[74]

Even though the criticisms by Suzuki and Fukuzawa were true in many respects, they overlooked two transformative elements of the work of the metropolitan debate societies. First, the debate societies connected overlapping constituencies to social and political theory, constituencies that included practicing legal advocates. One should think of Ueki Emori visiting the Hokushūsha, for example. Legal advocates consumed and also contributed to the theoretical discourses produced by the debate societies.

Second, even though "the people" may not have directly participated in the Meirokusha itself, the Meirokusha's members and members of other debate societies put legal and political subjects before the people through public debates, journals and newspapers, and speeches. In the process, they instantiated the ideal of a society structured by law and politics. By disseminating the theoretical, high-minded elements of law that concerned public intellectuals and government officials, lecture and study groups ratified the choice that former samurai made in taking up private legal practice. They also gave intellectual heft to legal advocates in their new legal-political role as interpreters of an emerging social and political order. This was particularly true for the Ōmeisha. Its membership reflected social engagement between bureaucrats and nonofficials. It was founded by, among others, Meiji official (and later legal advocate) Numa Morikazu and Kōno Togama before the latter's founding of an association of legal advocates—the Buntensha.[75] Members included such legal advocates as Maruyama Namasa [also Meisei], Tsunoda Shinpei, participants from the Senate (Genrōin), employees of associations of

---

73. Fukuzawa, "Gakusha no shokubun o ronzu," 6.
74. Suzuki, *Jiyūminken*, 59.
75. Fukui, "Ōmeisha to shiritsu hōritsu gakkō," 13–14.

legal advocates, newspaper reporters, teachers, and public intellectuals like Taguchi Ukichi.[76] Numa later went on to become a leader in the Constitutional Progressive Party (Rikken kaishintō, est. 1882).[77]

Although their work in the realm of practice was limited, debate and study societies such as the Meirokusha and the Ōmeisha engaged in the project of sorting out the (legal) grounds on which society should be based. If one thinks of the embrace of freedom and popular rights spreading from urban elites to local activists and then to agriculturalists, connections among metropolitan debate societies and legal advocates were important first steps. In ways unrivalled in previous eras, ideas were communicated between and among former samurai and commoners through public lectures, journals, newspapers, and shared commercial, political, and social endeavors. Associations for public speech and debate created the grounds for intercourse among bureaucrats and a new class of legal activists. These conversations reached beyond official spheres. Communication in public space generated broader debates about the role of law and morality in society, and politics itself. Through their work in associations of legal advocates, as public lecturers on law and politics, and later as heroes in dramatic opposition to the state, former samurai connected private litigation and daily life legal practice to the broader campaign for a constitutional polity.

Though the legal approaches to social change by urban elites gradually spread to the regions, initial efforts to institutionalize spaces from which people could engage in social and political activism remained inchoate and tenuous. Even as private law took on a public dimension, the recognition of a public space from which to promote political change remained problematic. During the Edo period, Ogyū Sorai and Itō Jinsai ruminated on public space, ruminations later identified by Maruyama Masao. Ogyū Sorai wrote of a figurative public in which "people do things together."[78] There were also many literal spaces in which people did things together during the Edo era, from the shogunate-sanctioned guilds of suit inns to the seemingly chaotic markets and stalls that formed at the foot

76. Ibid.
77. Mori, *Meiji jinbutsu itsuwa jiten, jōkan*, 454.
78. Ogyū Sorai, "Benmei I," in Najita, ed., *Tokugawa Political Writings*, 103.

of metropolitan bridges.[79] Yet the ground on which these people operated was not their own. They could not claim the space by right. They
were permitted by the state to engage in activities, often commercial, as
a privilege that the state could, and at times did, revoke. Political activism in public remained problematic through 1868. Thus, although there
may have been a figurative "public sphere" in the first years of the Meiji,
there were no corresponding physical spaces from which to disseminate
legal and political information.

When Shimamoto Nakamichi returned to Kōchi in the company of
Itagaki Taisuke in 1874, he confronted the practical challenge of finding
a site from which to teach his new vision of a legal society. In order to
speak in public about law, he requisitioned an abandoned military bar-
racks. There he gave a lecture on the *Shinritsu kōryō* (Principles of the
new statutes).[80] In doing so, he brought legal information directly to the
local community. Miyatake Gaikotsu noted that the process was a national one, in which "small political speech associations formed in every
region with the name 'something or other association' [meeting to] criticize the government in main halls of temples and borrowed classrooms."[81]
In the years that followed, public spaces for lecture meetings and associations became hallmarks of the age.

Former samurai increasingly concentrated on legal and political activism emerging out of the state's embrace of law. They pressed a number
of changes, all with transformative implications: constitutionalism, reformed legal practice, the idea of a public, and the protection of the political right to assemble and speak freely. Political activists continually
reminded the new state that its power no longer rested simply on the
threat of the use of violence. Under the Tokugawa, independent organization across domainal boundaries had been forbidden; this changed
when the Meiji government established a central, national state. Activism
on behalf of member interests in new political parties and associations of
legal advocates overlapped with activism on behalf of the general interest,
as in the campaign for a constitutional polity. Replacing personal despotism with the rule of law lay at the root of the campaign for constitutional

79. See Jinnai, *Tokyo,* and Sorensen, *The Making of Urban Japan.*
80. Sotozaki, "Risshisha hōritsu kenkyūjo ni tsuite," 13–30.
81. Miyatake, *Meiji enzetsushi,* 17.

government. Petitioning the Chamber of the Left (Sa-in) in their Memorial on the Establishment of a Representative Assembly, former samurai, including Soejima Taneomi, Gotō Shōjirō, Etō Shinpei, and Komuro Nobuo, claimed that the nation's challenges arose from "the want of fixed law in the country, and the fact that the officials proceed according to the bent of their own inclinations."[82] In other words, Soejima and others abhorred personal rule and called for a rule-of-law state. Although there was a dynamic history of legal and associational activity in earlier periods, new methods, new goals, new frames of mind, and new outcomes marked politics under the Meiji.

Informed by legal thought, proponents of a national legislature and legal advocates alike identified a counterpart to the new state, a space they identified as "the public." Yet public political activity had its risks. In a Europe that provided models for the Meiji state, governments and commentators also confronted an emergent public that insisted on having its own interests incorporated into the broader frame of the nation. Defenders of the status quo hearkened back to John Dryden's question about political association, "What right has any . . . association of men . . . to meet . . . in factious clubs to vilify the government?"[83] Factionalism could sink national unity. Attacking factionalism served as the justification for monitoring and suppressing critics of the state. In 1874, Itagaki Taisuke formed what could have been read as a "factious club." To avoid the charge of factionalism, Itagaki established his political group in the name of the "public," calling the group the Aikoku kōtō (Public Party of Patriots). A "public party" was something new—neither a secret, conspiratorial venture nor a private group.[84]

[W]e have given our new party the name "public party [*kōtō*]" to make a clear distinction between it and private parties. Under feudal politics, parties and factions were strictly forbidden, if people joined together in a party, this itself

---

82. Soejima, et al. "Memorial of Soejima Taneomi, etc. on the Establishment of a Representative Assembly," 2:139.

83. Dryden, *The Poems*, vol. 1 (Edinburgh, Scot.: Kincaid, Creech, and Balfour, 1773), 188.

84. Historians of the freedom and popular rights movement correctly note that, in spite of its pretensions as a national party, the Public Party of Patriots was not inclusive, consisting largely of former samurai from Tosa. Suzuki, "Ueki Emori no jinminkenron," 71.

was taken as a sign of insurrection. . . . Thus, in the name of the new party, we have particularly put in the words "public party."[85]

In another innovation, the charter of the group asserted that "the people share fundamental rights" free from state intervention.[86]

Here we can see the political party in Japan originating out of a refined articulation of political rights in public space concurrent with the formation of associations of legal advocates. Other former officials joined Itagaki in his effort to open previously closed spaces and make them public. Many of them had experience in the judicial apparatus of the Meiji government. Gotō Shōjirō, Etō Shinpei, Shimamoto Nakamichi, and Komuro Nobuo all numbered among the founders of the Public Party of Patriots and all had résumés reflecting service in judicial administration.[87] In addition to party activism now coded "public," spaces that were formerly within the bounds of the administrative apparatus of the state also became accessible to society.

Thus, public space expanded. The government opened up courtrooms to journalists in 1872 and to the general public in 1875. Prefectural assemblies established in 1878 became another public space in which the rules governing society were explored, enacted, and debated. By the end of the 1870s, legal journals joined these physical sites as connectors of public political activity. Serial publications and journals pressed further public engagement with matters of law and society. Legal advocate and political activist Ōi Kentarō used the term "public debate and public opinion" (kōgi kōron) to highlight the connection between publicity and the will of the people that intermingled in these spaces.[88]

In addition to the metaphorical public spaces of educative journals, the popular press also provided legal activists with a ubiquitous and con-

---

85. From "Wagakuni kenseishi no yurai," in *Meiji kensei keizaishiron*, cited in Osatake, *Nihon kenseishi taikō*, 2:446.

86. "Aikoku kōtō no honsei (1 Jan. 1874)," in Gikai seijisha henshūbu, ed., *Nihon kenseishi kiso shiryō*, 170–71.

87. Komuro Nobuo also founded an association of legal advocates in Awa called the Self-Help Society (Jijosha自助社). Maeda R., *Hoshi Tōru den*, 131.

88. Ōi, *Jiyū ryakuron*, 4. In terms of chronology, calls for public debate and public opinion fell between late-Tokugawa invocations of public discussion (as *kōron*) and late-Meiji invocations of public opinion (*seron/yoron*). Gluck, *Japan's Modern Myths*, 50.

tinuous space for promoting their aims. By 1875, proponents of constitutional government dominated the leading newspapers. In contrast, backers of gradual political change such as journalist Fukuchi Gen'ichirō lamented the partiality of these endeavors, noting that the political newspapers "merely attack the government, having lost any inclination for independent public discussion."[89] Rather than putting off readers, however, the partisan press framed the early Meiji moment as a great drama. It was in this context that circulation exploded during the late 1870s and early 1880s. As James Huffman has demonstrated, the vernacular press and journals greatly amplified the reach of proponents of freedom and popular rights by "spreading information about the movement's key activities, providing a rationale for its key positions, and agitating directly for wider support."[90] Yet even as it emerged, public space was under attack from the authorities.

Legal advocates merged their calls for a space for political activism with calls for the protection of this space by political rights. Associations founded by former samurai took the lead. In its charter, the Risshisha's Legal Research Institute called for political reform under the rubric of "extend[ing] the rights of the people for the equal welfare of the weak and the strong."[91] This aim echoed the goals of the Public Party of Patriots, which took as its primary purpose the protection of the natural rights of the people.[92] The institute located itself at the forefront of the movement to identify distinctions within the law that would balance power between society and the state. The charter of the institute asserted that the law exists "for the sake of protection of the people's rights."[93] As a seller of legal services, the institute served landowners and financiers who had an interest not only in tax reduction—another plank in the Risshisha platform—but in Weber's idea of contractual protection of property in a new capitalist economy. As the Risshisha articulated a political program,

---

89. Fukuchi Gen'ichirō, in an editorial in the *Tokyo nichi nichi shinbun* (28 Jul. 1876), cited in Huffman, *Creating a Public*, 104.

90. Huffman, *Creating a Public*, 101.

91. Okudaira, *Nihon bengoshishi*, 82–83; Itagaki, ed., *Jiyūtōshi*, 1:138–39.

92. Suzuki, *Jiyūminken*, 71.

93. "Hōritsu kenkyūjo shogen," in Itagaki, ed., *Jiyūtōshi*, 1:138–39. See also Hirao, ed., *Jiyūminken no keifu*, 31–32.

its members opened an institutional space in which they tied the sale of legal services to economic change and political activism.

For legal advocates, associations simultaneously promised political and commercial capital—profit that emerged from a combination of commercial, political, and educative elements in one association. In other words, protection of rights could constitute both a boundary for the space of public debate and a commodity to be sold. The Legal Research Institute, for example, stated that it would "accept requests for the service of advocates and notaries."[94] Much like associations of legal advocates that came to promote the cause of private legal practice as a pillar of early Meiji society, the institute did more than call for a revision of the old order through the promotion of legal thought. It engaged in the day-to-day development of a legal economy in the prefecture. This was a legal economy in two senses: first, the institute itself sold legal services; second, it called for the development of commerce regulated by law. Both ideas of a legal economy came together as the institute promoted its former-samurai employees as adept at private legal advocacy.

A paradox of the early popular rights movement was that as activists called for an expanding "public," they sought to maintain their place of privilege within it. Legal advocates may have sought an extension of rights to the people, yet they did not intend to turn the people-at-large into the holders of these rights. They were not promoting suffrage for commoners (*heimin*) just yet. As Makihara Norio has noted, during the 1870s and 1880s, even the most ardent proponents of inclusion for the ordinary people in the public sphere, such as Ōi Kentarō, saw the people "existing only to be rescued, mobilized, and manipulated."[95] As is common in so many reformist movements, the discussion of rights cordoned off a space for the exercise of public debate and public opinion while also creating a rarefied discourse that legal advocates and intellectuals in general claimed to understand better than others in society.

In language that echoed its claims as a defender against both the outmoded traditions of Chinese thought and contemporary bureaucrats, the institute also identified itself as a defender of the people against a

---

94. Itagaki, ed., *Jiyūtōshi*, 1:138.
95. Makihara, "Ōi Kentarō no shisō kōzō to Osaka jiken no ronri," 96.

different kind of exploitation. In doing so, it invoked political participation as a corrective to the potential excesses of a market economy. It criticized competitors who took up the work of legal advocacy solely for profit, without adhering to a coherent set of ethics. Some legal advocates combined their work with sidelines in high-interest money lending or pawnbroking.[96] Critics charged these legal practitioners with a lack of public morals. The Legal Research Institute argued that advocates who did not promote individual rights and constitutional government had turned away from the vocation of protecting people. There were, in the words of the institute, "many people in this prefecture who hang out the 'shingle' of the notary and the advocate" but who had no interest in promoting legal reform or defending peoples' rights.[97] The institute claimed that these nominal legal advocates exploited "the weak and powerless."[98] This was a dual attack on legal practice solely for profit and the failure of the state to regulate the sale of legal services. These attacks became all the more pressing in the context of the institute's calls for constitutional government. Tosa-based proponents of constitutionalism, such as Itagaki and Gotō, argued that the pursuit of "money-getting . . . tends to fasten [a person's] attention and his interest upon himself alone, making him indifferent to public affairs"; participation in politics meant "his thoughts and feelings would be drawn out of his narrow circle."[99] The gradual expansion of participation in government would allow people to balance their profit-seeking desires with broader social concerns.

For former-samurai legal practitioners, morality remained central, yet it was not the morality of the Neo-Confucian social hierarchy, the five relationships, or familiarity with the Confucian tradition. Rather, this was a rule-based morality that created a social order around individuals who knew and understood law. Though Tosa legalists emphasized rights, they also emphasized responsibilities. They demanded that people act according to the law. Ueki Emori, writing in 1885, reflected on the thinking behind the establishment of the institute back in 1874, the same year in

---

96. Yokohama bengoshikai, ed., *Yokohama bengoshikaishi*, 1:23.
97. Itagaki, ed., *Jiyūtōshi*, 1:138–39.
98. Ibid.
99. Soejima, et al., "Memorial of Soejima Taneomi, etc. on the Establishment of a Representative Assembly," 2:157.

which Kōchi prefecture had sought to restrain the excessive solicitation of lawsuits.[100] Ueki Emori noted that "[a]t the time within the prefecture [common] people with a weak understanding of the law piled lawsuit upon lawsuit. Shimamoto and others within the Society planned to establish a legal research institute . . . in order to rescue them from this sickness."[101] The charter of the Legal Research Institute stated that "the people must know the laws. Those people [who are] ignorant of the law, [who are] unknowing and untouched by it, [will] have brushes with crime, fall into sin, break the law, and disrupt commerce."[102] Here former-samurai activists and the institute identified each individual as a building block for a law-based society. This was the beginning of a radical reinterpretation of the basis of social organization—radical in that it grounded society in the individual and grounded individual responsibility in a society defined by law.

The charter was also radical in its approach to the relationship between responsibility and rule by law. The charter asserted that "responsibility" required that people be more than law abiding, they had to be "law knowing." To this end, legal advocates built on the educative tradition launched by Shimamoto in 1873, the year that he left government employment and began crafting interpretations of government statutes for popular consumption.[103] Legal knowledge became the focus of the cultivation of the moral self and the first step in suppressing criminality. This was a departure from the tenets of Chinese thought—with its focus on cultivation of the self through study of the Confucian classics—as interpreted by Japanese moralists since the seventeenth century. The program of the institute foreshadowed a statement at the Tokyo Association for the Study of Law six years later. At the association's convocation, its director stated that knowledge of law was necessary to become a person in modern society. "If people do not know law, they cannot take one step

---

100. "Kōchi-ken ukagai" (20 Oct. 1874), and "Shihōshō shirei" (24 Mar. 1875), cited in Okudaira, *Nihon bengoshishi*, 50.

101. Ueki Emori, "Risshisha shimatsu kiyo," cited in Sotozaki, "Risshisha hōritsu kenkyūjo ni tsuite," 17.

102. "Hōritsu kenkyūjo shogen," cited in Itagaki, ed., *Jiyūtōshi*, 1:138–39. See also Hirao, *Jiyūminken no keifu*, 31–32.

103. Irokawa Daikichi describes a simplified legal text prepared by an early Meiji advocate. Irokawa, *Rekishika no uso to yume*, 81.

forward; they cannot do a single thing. If one does not know the law, then morally speaking, one cannot be a person. . . . [O]ne must research the law and have some understanding of rights and responsibilities."[104] This was the new blend of law and morality articulated in an organization that within twenty years became part of a consortium that took form as Hōsei University.

Law courts emerged as a central public venue with transformative power. During the Edo era, the adjudication of private disputes had served as sites of moral instruction and discipline, whether it was through the "didactic conciliation" invoked in monetary matters, or the Solomonic authority exercised by the magistrate concealed behind literal and figurative barriers in inquisitorial matters. The appearance of the legal advocate reconfigured the symbolic powers of the court of law. As a newly opened public space, the courtroom attracted its share of attention. In an 1881 digest of Tokyo legal advocates, the editors spoke of the courtroom as a place where, historically, parties to private disputes resolved their misunderstandings under the shadow of "inappropriate violence" (*fushō bōkō*) without proper legal representation.[105] This was how the editors of the digest characterized the Edo-era inquisitorial process led by a magistrate. They argued that a new adversarial process driven by legal advocates would more effectively and humanely reveal the truth in private disputes. Working alone, the judge himself could not interpret the law. It was only through the adversarial process that obscurity would dissipate. To this end, legal advocates "preserve[d] the rights" of their clients, both "the rights of property and the rights inhering in one's life."[106] Through these kinds of claims, legal advocates extended the bounds of their practice. No longer were they mere adjuncts to the state's administration of justice, as envisioned in the Staff Regulations and Operating Rules of 1872. Rather, legal advocates asserted themselves as full participants in the courts— well beyond the practice that emerged during the Edo era.

In the mid-1870s, Itagaki Taisuke's definition of his group as a public party was more a tactic than a grand strategy. His response reflected

---

104. "*Tokyo hōgakusha kaikō no shushi* (Address at the opening of the Tokyo Law School)," *Hōritsu zasshi* (18 Sept. 1880): 4.

105. Machida, ed., *Tokyo daigennin retsuden*, 3.

106. Ibid.

state concerns about factionalism and political action in the private interest. Anxiety that sectoral and even individual interests might tear at the newly emergent unity of the nation-state was not unique to Itagaki and Meiji government officials. Writing about civil society in late-nineteenth-century Europe, Stefan-Ludwig Hoffman noted that, despite their efforts to affirm a separate sphere for their own activities, groups newly engaged in associational activity in Europe "believed that individual interests were by definition narrow and politically destructive."[107] There were those in Japan who also held to this line. Itagaki's repudiation of oppositional politics after returning from travels that included a visit to France reflected this sensibility; in his renunciation of opposition, he came to adhere to the concerns about individual interests that then animated civil society in Europe. By the turn of the twentieth century, a robust Japanese nationalism was emerging around the person of the Emperor. Carol Gluck noted that "in the late [eighteen] eighties and early nineties, talk of morality pervaded public discourse at many levels."[108] Yet before the Meiji nation-state lay claim to discourses of self-cultivation and morality, conflict and contestation about the nature of the polity (*seitai*) or body politic (*kokutai*) was the norm in Japanese society, particularly during the 1870s and 1880s. Associations of legal advocates, debate societies, and the political parties in which they participated or from which they learned strove to embed their ideal of a public morality—derived from law—in social and political relations. The actions of these diverse groups and the challenge that their idea of a contentious and engaged public posed to the state invited government regulation.

The Meiji State Grapples with an Emergent Public

As debate societies, political parties, public meetings, and groups of former-samurai legal advocates organized, they challenged a convention in Japanese politics in which the state, as a matter of course, set the national political agenda. In 1875, the Meiji government began to explore responses to these new political groups. Officials had cause for concern. Although scholars often divide Meiji political activists into camps of

---

107. Hoffman, "Democracy and Associations in the Long Nineteenth Century," 284.
108. Gluck, *Japan's Modern Myths*, 111.

proponents of violence and proponents of speech, there was considerable movement and no clear line between one group and the other. It was a legal reformer who committed the first act of mass former-samurai violence against the Meiji regime. In 1874, ex–minister of justice Etō Shinpei led an uprising in Saga; his interest in law had not precluded the use of arms. This fluidity caused Meiji officials to monitor organizations that, in part, furthered state aims such as the employment of former samurai and legal reform while they also harbored potential threats. Through consultations with legal adviser Boissonade, Inoue Kowashi and others considered how to respond to political speech and assembly.

Particularly worrisome to Meiji officials were horizontal connections across social status and geography. Horizontal associations that transcended economic, political, and even status distinctions were not new to the Meiji period. During the Edo era, many such groups existed, but they usually involved aesthetic or religious pursuits.[109] And even as aesthetic and religious concerns sometimes yielded calls for political change, such calls were seldom societywide or systemic critiques.

The question of how to accommodate public criticism was not unique to Japan. Meiji officials looked abroad in response to their concerns. They explored how European countries regulated assembly and voluntary association. During the mid-1870s, it was at first French law to which Meiji government officials turned. At the Sorbonne, Inoue Kowashi had studied with Gustave Emile Boissonade de Fontarabie; a series of memos from Inoue to Boissonade reveal a particular interest in French regulation of assembly. As an adviser to the Meiji government, Boissonade responded to numerous queries on the subject in his capacity as legal adviser. Doing so was part of his effort to bring the Japanese legal system into alignment with foreign practice; his expertise in natural and private law made him an invaluable resource to his employers.[110] His answers to questions regarding the regulation of association and assembly were methodical and comprehensive.

---

109. Ikegami, *Bonds of Civility*.

110. Boissonade's importance to the legal establishment of the Meiji state has been memorialized in multiple forms, including a 27-floor tower on the campus of Hosei University.

Rather than simply suppressing groups that challenged the regime, the government pursued a flexible approach. Even so, contemporary critics asserted that the new state simply extended feudal despotism. On December 15, 1878, a former samurai from Tosa addressed a group of people on the topic "The Despotism of the Meiji Government" and was jailed.[111] Even so, the manner of regulation of association and assembly marked an extraordinary departure from domestic precedent. One strategy was cooptation of the opposition. Through the Osaka Conference of 1875, Meiji leaders invited political opponents to return to positions of authority. An example of this strategy's success was the temporary return of Itagaki—Tosa activist and founder of the Public Party of Patriots—to the government fold as a councilor. Another element of the government approach was broad acceptance of new groups. Government opponents argued that "patriotism will not be able to develop to its normal degree" without involvement in national affairs that included criticism.[112] The work of Alexis de Tocqueville lent support to their claims. Some decades earlier, the analyst of civil society in the United States had argued that "it is easy to prove that political associations perturb the State . . . but . . . freedom of association in political matters is favorable to the prosperity and tranquility of the community."[113] The Meiji authorities agreed with de Tocqueville that, in principle, association and assembly should be accepted as features of society. This did not mean, however, that groups would enjoy complete freedom. Meiji officials hewed more closely to de Tocqueville's other assertion that "a nation is [not] always at liberty to invest its citizens with an absolute right of association for political purposes."[114] Thus, government approaches to regulation included monitoring and at times dissolving political groups and meetings. In other words, the government endorsed the idea that associations would facilitate social stability in the polity, while simultaneously keeping groups under close surveillance through observation and informers, lest they stray.

---

111. Miyatake, *Meiji enzetsushi*, 33–34.

112. Soejima, et al. "Reply of Soyejima [sic], Gotō, and Itagaki to Kato's Arguments against Representative Government in Japan."

113. de Tocqueville, *Democracy in America*, 127.

114. Ibid., 128.

Inoue brought the issues of association and assembly to Boissonade. He was particularly concerned about keeping elite concerns from arousing popular passions. In an environment of rapidly institutionalizing elite politics, he wanted to keep the volatile—and potentially violent—crowd from undermining new institutions. In this regard, the extracurricular activities of government employees, ranging from the cultural to the political, was of primary concern to the state.[115] As seen in the case of Motoda Naoshi, former Ministry of Justice official turned legal advocate, political organization need not begin with a political agenda. A group that met for the purpose of cultural pursuits, including the practice of calligraphy or the writing of poetry, could morph into something else. In 1875, Boissonade responded to a query from Inoue on the involvement by state employees in clubs or "public associations" (*kōteki na kessha*). Citing French law, Boissonade answered that the French government permitted officials to join private groups whose members numbered fewer than 20, as long as they did not convene in secret. No public official was permitted to be a member of a secret society. As for membership in groups that defied clear classification, such as "epicurean societies," Boissonade argued that the government should be lenient. If the authorities discovered membership in such an association, the participant should simply "receive a warning from their superior."[116]

The state's second concern was public assembly, including meetings of public speakers (*enzetsukai*). There were parallels between approaches by the French and Japanese governments to public assembly that reflected Boissonade's advice. "The right of the citizen to assemble peaceably, without arms," was a guiding principle of French politics since the revolution of 1789, wrote Boissonade.[117] This was a "natural right of the person who exists in society." However, this natural right came with a caveat. "Because the exercise of the right to public assembly could easily lead to a disruption of the public order . . . discussion, on nearly all occasions, of

---

115. For an examination of the overlapping meanings of cultural and political endeavors, see Ikegami, *Bonds of Civility*.

116. The following draws on a 10 Jan. 1876 memo (in French and Japanese) from Boissonade, reprinted in Hosei University (Boissonade), *Note des correspondances avec Monsieur Boissonade*, 64–65.

117. Ibid.

matters of politics, society, or religion were prohibited; however, literature, science, the arts, and good deeds could be discussed."[118] In the subsequent regulation of speech and public assembly in Japan, this emerged as a distinction between political speech (*seidan*) and speech on scholarly or academic matters (*gakujutsu*). This distinction also mapped onto the kinds of matters that could be considered in public and those that could be addressed in private. One could engage in political discussion in private assemblies—debate societies, for example—but not in public speeches designed to inflame public sentiment.

Boissonade also pointed to an overlap in two kinds of activity that required clarification: "assembly" (*shūkai*) referred to a single meeting, or periodic meetings convened in public or private, with "a great number of people, more or less."[119] At such meetings, anyone could participate, without an invitation. When a group met in public, it was subject to Article 291 of the French criminal code. The article, called "Associations and Public Assemblies," was primarily applied to public assemblies, which gave the police the authority to intervene and suspend or disband a meeting. In the case where those convening a public assembly wanted to address matters of politics or religion, they had to collect the names of participants and submit the date, time, and place of the meeting to the head of the prefecture or subprefecture. "The [French] Home Minister had the authority to prohibit a group from meeting at all."[120] In contrast, when an assembly occurred in private, it was not subject to such limits.

Finally, French law further distinguished between public and private assemblies. At a private assembly, every person in attendance had to have been invited, and if the private meeting took place in a public facility, the facility had to be closed to the general public. In such cases, those who were participating in an event that was "neither a 'public assembly' nor a meeting of an 'association' could discuss politics and religion."[121] The exchanges between Meiji government interlocutors and their foreign

---

118. Ibid.

119. Ibid.

120. Ibid., 75, 105. Here, Boissonade cited arts. 291–294 of the French penal code and a special law of 10 Apr. 1834 (Boissonade cites Louis Tripier, *Commentaire de la loi du 24 juillet 1867 sur les societes* [Paris: G. Retaux, 1867]).

121. Ibid.

advisers revealed ongoing anxiety about connecting divisive policy debates to a broadening public.

Absent blanket prohibitions on criticizing the regime, groups of legal advocates, and other political associations of the 1870s flourished in the relatively permissive environment governing such groups. Groups of legal advocates used two primary covers to connect law with politics. First, there was the cover of education, an age-old form of samurai respectability. Many of the early associations, perhaps anticipating the Meiji government's move to regulate association and assembly, identified themselves in their charters as enterprises that combined commercial and educative functions. When the Hokushūsha applied for an occupancy permit in Osaka, it described itself, innocuously, as an "institute for the study of codes" (*ritsugaku kenkyūjo*). The other cover, affirmation of social harmony, was likewise a form of social respectability for former samurai. Names of various associations of legal advocates strategically reflected a degree of conservatism. For example, the Received Wisdom and Law Association (貴知法社) and the Association for the Preservation of Peace (保案社) both evoked the sense of harmony and stability the state sought to uphold. Associations of legal advocates established from the mid-1870s occupied an ambiguous place in the emerging discourse of association and assembly. They were enterprises with multiple functions: they engaged in commerce; members spoke in public on political issues; and they educated and trained students and apprentices.

As it suppressed the press, the government maintained a light hand on public assembly and association through 1877, using direct observation and infiltration to track groups. Suppression picked up after the last mass violence by former samurai in 1877. From 1873 through 1876, former samurai had taken up arms against the state nearly a half-dozen times. In 1874, government forces easily crushed former minister of justice Etō Shinpei's Saga Uprising, but stakes were higher by the time of Saigō Takamori's Satsuma Rebellion in 1877. In Satsuma, private schools provided the bulk of the force marshaled against the Meiji government. Much like associations of legal advocates, these were hybrid institutions that offered a range of instruction. They differed in that the curriculum included martial arts. Again, the porous boundaries between violence and speech as political tactics opened the appeal of the uprising to former samurai beyond Satsuma. Even as violence by former samurai became increasingly outmoded, it remained attractive to some. Morinaga Eizaburō has noted how "Saigō's army attracted the sympathies of disgruntled former samurai in every corner of the country."[122] The Satsuma Rebellion even drew in former samurai of the Risshisha who had dedicated years to constitutional reform and legal processes. Kataoka Kenkichi was an early supporter of Saigō's cause. However, typical of the shifting loyalties of the 1870s, he later changed tack, writing a memorial to the emperor calling for the advancement of "public debate that will be the foundation that sustains the nation." In the memorial, he condemned "uprisings that occur one after the other."[123] Other legal reformist members of Tosa's Risshisha gave more sustained support to the uprising.

Even in their abandonment of oral and written persuasion, the Satsuma Rebellion coconspirators built on the very same personal networks that supported law-abiding associations of legal advocates. The overlapping groups of associations—of legal advocates and nascent political parties—served as fertile ground for exploring the interconnected possibilities of public speech, political organization, protest, and even violence. Even former Tosa samurai pursuing legal reform took up the Satsuma cause. Through Okamoto Kenzaburō, Hayashi Yūzō contacted Takeuchi Tsuna (then supervisor of the Hōraisha's Takashima coal mines operation) to help secure weapons. Takeuchi turned to a Portuguese trader to provide firearms; Shimamoto Nakamichi wrote the contract for the purchase. Meanwhile, the Meiji government was following the machinations of the revolt through an informer, Mizuno Enjirō.[124] On August 8, 1877, police arrested Hayashi Yūzō just before receipt of the shipment of arms. In subsequent months, a flurry of arrests followed: Kataoka, Takeuchi, Okamoto, and Mutsu Munemitsu. In total, 31 people were arrested.[125] An extraordinary tribunal within the Great Court of Cassation heard the matter as a crime against the state, or treason (*kokuji han*). Neither the Principles of the New Statutes nor the Temporary Statutes identified this kind of conspiracy as a crime, but the case went forward anyway. No lawyers or spectators were present.

---

122. Morinaga, *Saiban jiyū minken jidai*, 8.
123. Kataoka, "Risshisha kenpakusho, June 1877," in Itagaki, ed., *Jiyūtōshi*, 1:189.
124. Morinaga, *Saiban jiyū minken jidai*, 11.
125. Ibid., 13.

Even this extraordinary episode of treason reveals the degree to which new legal thought, processes, and practices insinuated themselves into Meiji society, despite the persistence of two old orientations: one toward direct action on the side of disgruntled members of society, and the other toward suppression from a controlling state. Despite Itagaki's protestations about a "public party," swashbuckling former samurai within the Risshisha supported violent political change. Yet they no longer walked in a world of the sword. In securing firearms to support Saigō's army, they drafted a legal document, a contract that defined their relationship with a Portuguese weapons trader. Government surveillance took an official form. The government monitored the activities of renegade former samurai as part of an ongoing criminal investigation. The accused faced the state in a court of law. Although the Great Court of Cassation did create the terms by which the defendants were tried, it did not issue summary justice.

Under the Tokugawa, the conspirators would likely have been made to commit suicide for their misdeeds. Instead, the court handed down sentences that were lenient, considering that the charge was treason. Hayashi received a life sentence reduced to 10 years. Okamoto received a 2-year sentence. Kataoka Kenkichi, who was an original conspirator but then backed out in favor of reform, received a sentence of 100 days. All were dropped from *shizoku* (former samurai) to commoner status.[126] Shimamoto spent 7 months in jail for his involvement.[127] Mutsu, another central figure in the case but a member of the aristocracy, received special treatment. He was sentenced to a 5-year prison sentence and removed from the aristocracy. As for Mizuno, the government informer, he started the conservative newspaper *Akebono shinbun* with Fukuchi Gen'ichirō and became a backer of the government-affiliated political party, the Teiseitō.

In the wake of the Satsuma Rebellion, associations of legal advocates, their members, and "the public" reflected on how they might extend and deepen the links between law and society that would be as transformative as direct action. Some former samurai reacted by promoting the ideal of

---

126. Miyatake, *Bunmei kaika: Saiban hen*, 74–75.
127. Sotozaki, "Risshisha hōritsu kenkyūjo ni tsuite," 22.

spreading rights and responsibilities to all, not just former samurai. Legal advocate Ōoka Ikuzō, who achieved fame as an activist in the freedom and popular rights movement, was a member and director of the Legal Lecture and Study Society (forerunner of the Ōmeisha).[128] According to a biography, in the face of familial criticism, Ōoka rejected the practice of medicine that his father and grandfather had pursued before him.[129] As he moved away from medicine and toward law and politics at the time of the Satsuma Rebellion in 1877, Ōoka brought a suit against Saitama governor Shirane Tasuke on behalf of publicly employed educators in the prefecture.[130] He later explained his shift from medicine to education and, finally, law. Medicine did little more than treat the ills of a single person; in contrast, "if I study politics and law, I will be able to cure the ills of the land."[131] In Ōoka's vision, legal science stood alongside medical science as a practice relying on expertise. Rather than gaining knowledge of human anatomy, the legal advocate had to dissect the social body. Ōoka became a licensed legal advocate in 1879.

If one followed Ōoka's logic, then the social body of a public instantiated by law could become the counterpart to the governing body claimed by the state. An 1881 call for participation in a legal lecture series in Kōchi stated, "Law is the defender of liberty; the preserver of life in a community; the guarantor of property in a community."[132] Here was the *freie Advokatur* at work. As former samurai cured the ills of the land through legal practice, they bridged the gap between local and national, particular and universal. For the state, the danger of associations of legal advocates was that they increasingly operated on, and blurred, the boundaries between the public as it was constituted by the state and competing formulations of public and private interests.

These formulations challenged the historical monopoly on defining public morality claimed by the state. Much as legal advocates had linked individual rights to national power, the state linked abiding by the laws

---

128. The Meiji hōritsu gakkō went on to become another of Japan's leading private universities, Meiji University. Fukui, "Ōmeisha to shiritsu hōritsu gakkō," 15.

129. Kusaka, ed., *Nihon bengoshi kōhyōden*, 34.

130. Shichinohe, "Genkō minpōten wo tsukutta hitobito [16]," 64.

131. Ōoka Ikuzō in Machida, ed., *Tokyo daigennin retsuden*, 1.

132. Ibid.

with national stability. In doing so, the authorities walked a fine line. They wished to see former samurai engaged in productive pursuits, even those somewhat at odds with national goals, as long as they contributed to what the state saw as civilizing social and political change. So although the Great Council of State (Dajōkan) paid close attention to new public spaces from 1874 through 1877, its restraint reflected a dedication to winning over foreign observers and critics while maintaining national stability. It was only after the uprising in Satsuma that the government launched a wide-reaching effort to suppress speech and assembly. In the context of this tension between control and reform, legal journals—in emphatic and even querulous terms—emerged to challenge the logic of new laws suppressing political activism. They focused on questions of central concern to legal advocates, such as public assembly and the possibilities for representing the criminally accused.

Propagating the Public: Law Journals, Public Policy, and Creative Legalism

The 1877 Satsuma Rebellion marked the last expression of large-scale former-samurai violence directed at the new regime. That same year marked the founding of a long-standing and influential publication, the *Law Journal* (Hōritsu zasshi). While Meiji officials spoke to the public through proclamations and decrees, legal advocates began to speak back in legal journals and magazines. In doing so, they joined newspapers and other print media as sites for the contestation of government policy. Law journals differed from newspapers in that they not only targeted an educated audience but also cultivated expert knowledge. Their emergence paralleled the growth of associations of legal advocates and spoke to a growing audience through a nearly national distribution. The *Law Journal* was distributed in Tokyo, Osaka, Kyoto, Saitama, Chiba, Gifu, Ise, Sendai, Echigo, Gōshū, Mito, Kobe, Enshū, Shinshū, Hakone, and Sapporo over the course of two decades—1877 to 1898 (see appendix for a list of journals). The *Law Journal* became the leading publication of its kind and was published by legal advocates and scholars of law. Kanemaru Magane, founder of the Tokyo Association for the Study of Law (Tokyo hōritsu gakusha), a forerunner of Hōsei University, served as one of the *Law Journal*'s first editors. The *Journal*'s readership likely included, at a minimum, people studying law, licensed and nonlicensed legal advocates, and Ministry of Justice officials. Public discourse on all sorts of topics filled the *Law Journal* and legal journals of its kind. In particular, law journals provided a venue for dialogue on the evolving regulation of speech and assembly and legal representation for defendants in criminal matters.[133] In the process, law journals interpreted and shaped debates on legal policy.

In 1875, two years before the *Law Journal* began publication, regulation of print media went into effect, with the goal of suppressing spirited criticism of the regime and its policies. In the *Yūbin hōchi shinbun*, Ueki Emori attacked the Ordinances on Newspapers and a law on defamation as the government's making a "monkey of the people" (*Hito wo saru ni suru seifu*).[134] The press law reflected the range of lessons the Meiji leaders learned from abroad; it was based on a French measure from 1852 in which Napoleon III suppressed the press.[135] Other measures that suppressed political rights instituted between 1874 and 1881 included press controls, controls on submitting memorials to the emperor, prohibitions on political expression by government officials, tightening of earlier laws on newspapers, and laws suppressing public speech and assembly.[136] The press laws did not successfully stifle newspapers: editors were even more virulent in their attacks on government, with some even going to prison (and others hiring dummy editors who went to prison in their stead). The heavy government hand on the mass-circulation newspapers reflected the conclusion that the press could influence public opinion. Notably, however, there are no reports of government suppression of legal journals. The relatively light hand of state regulation on the legal journals may have derived from those journals' self-representation as educative enterprises or limited state capacity of enforcement in the late 1870s.

In any case, if published legal scholarship only affected action in the courtroom or in government ministries, then the light-handed approach

---

133. They also debated the merits of the jury system. Fujita, "Hōkon baishin secchi o ronzu."

134. Suzuki, "Ueki Emori no jinminkenron," 92.

135. Howland, *Translating the West*, 116.

136. Yasumaru and Fukaya, *Minshū undō*, 462. For texts of regulations, see the appendix of Tanaka, *Jiyūminkenka to sono keifu*.

by the government would have been unsurprising. But the impact of articles in legal journals extended beyond scholarship, officialdom, and the court. Debates over policy in law journals manifested a new turn toward the emergence of a public sphere. Links between legal advocacy and public discourse emerged in this sphere. Before 1868, legal pronouncements by the authorities received no public comment. After 1868, a deluge of laws, bureaucratic orders, edicts, and circulars flowed from the government—legal advocates and their journals then made legal interpretation for peers and the public part of their work. A public sphere in which "public opinion can be formed," akin to that described by Jürgen Habermas, emerged out of this encounter between state and society.[137] The Meiji version of this discursive space fell short of Habermas's ideal of a place open to all, where the public could engage in "matters of general interest without being subject to coercion."[138] Yet everywhere, the "public sphere" was an ideal type. The late nineteenth century offers no example of a country where a public sphere existed free of government intervention, open to all. In the United States, women, racial minorities, and laborers faced limited access to spaces where they might "assemble and unite freely, and express and publicize their opinions freely."[139] Throughout Europe, the same groups of persons, particularly laborers, found their ability to assemble constrained. Even though the public sphere was inchoate and uneven from the 1870s on, the public existed as a discursive entity. In Japan, it demanded attention from government officials. Legal advocates emerged as the speakers who called for the existence of such a space, while also acting as the spokespeople within such a space. They criticized the government at public meetings, voicing positions first explored and articulated in legal journals.

Historians know that the Satsuma Rebellion signaled the end of any real internal threat to the stability of the Meiji government from former samurai. Yet this is knowledge gained from hindsight. The event worried the oligarchs and sparked an intensification of surveillance and suppression. Drawing on the advice of Boissonade, the authorities responded with stricter measures on speech and assembly. In July 1878, Great

---

137. Habermas, "The Public Sphere," 398.
138. Ibid.
139. Ibid.

Council of State Decree 29 allowed police to attend meetings and then suspend them "when a speaker inflamed the public and threatened the safety of the nation."[140] On December 4, 1878, the Home Ministry further refined regulation of assembly. It made any criticism of the existing laws, officials, or policies a threat to the nation and stated that police could monitor meetings to determine whether a speech promoted learning or intended harm to the body politic. When the speech was deemed in the interest of education and convened consistent with the laws, then "the [police] shall not obstruct the people's interaction."[141] However, in cases where the contents of a speech "threatened the stability of the nation," the police could then interrupt the meeting and inform higher authorities. The state defined a range of "threats to the safety of the nation" that included "instigating agitation in the people and causing them to despise the nation's laws; looking on government officials with hatred; and show[ing] resentment toward the government."[142] One of the prohibited topics echoed Tokugawa concerns about popular unrest, and prohibited "plotting a forced petition." Another prohibited topic—"conspiring in secret"—reflected state concern about factions and armed actions.[143] Memoranda from Ministry of Home Affairs to the police, following the suppression of the Satsuma Rebellion, reflected an incremental tightening of control on speech and assembly.

State regulation of political activism precipitated sharp reaction from journals published and edited by legal advocates. On December 28, 1878, the *Law Journal* criticized the tightening of curbs on speech and assembly in its column "Hōritsu mondō" (Discourse on law). In this column, a reader or editor raised a legal question, which the *Journal* answered in subsequent issues. Responses drew on legal precedents from abroad to question or criticize policies at home.[144] The *Law Journal*'s subtitle that week was, "Enzetsu rongikai ni tsuki gimon" (Concerns about

---

140. Naimushō, *Tokyo keiri yōran*, 118–22.
141. Ibid.
142. Ibid.
143. Ibid.
144. "Hōritsu mondō: Enzetsu rongikai ni tsuki gimon," *Hōritsu zasshi*, no. 51 (28 Dec. 1878): 7.

speech and debate meetings).[145] It responded to questions about Great Council of State decrees and police bureau circulars that prohibited the opening of public gatherings, attended by "a number of people (*shu*), with the intent to lecture on, or discuss, politics." The regulations of 1878 proscribed, in the most general terms, opening or convening a public meeting. In response to these regulations, the *Law Journal* asked, What did it mean to convene a meeting? How many people constituted "a number" of people? The police circular had suggested that an assembly would be unlawful when it was attended by "a number of people." This term, in the *Journal*'s view, was also ambiguous. The *Journal* continued:

[A]re three or four people "a number of people"? For example, in one family, three siblings all like to study. If they get together with a young boy in the adjacent house is this gathering [illegal]?[146]

The exchange in the *Journal* took the regulations at their word and then showed how their ambiguities rendered them nonsensical. This first volley on the question of political association ended with a statement that fell between exasperation and exhortation: "[W]e must make this wording clear."[147]

Consistent with Boissonade's advice to Inoue Kowashi, a subsequent issue of the *Journal* suggested that the lawfulness of public assembly hinged on intent.[148] With a metaphor from nature common to the nineteenth century and reminiscent of de Tocqueville's theory of groups, the author suggested that, as in nature, where particles come together to form physical bodies, humans, too, must come together to constitute the social bodies necessary for the working of society. Moving from argument by analogy to legal comparison, the *Journal* then examined "the laws of the West." The column traced laws on assembly back to Roman codes, noting that Roman law permitted assembly as long as those assembled harbored no ill will toward the state. In other words, when Roman law looked at assembly, it asked the question, Assembly with what intent? The laws of

---

145. Ibid.
146. Ibid.
147. Ibid.
148. "Hōritsu mondō: Enzetsu rongikai ni tsuki gimon (ni no ichi)," *Hōritsu zasshi*, no. 52 (20 Jan. 1879): 8–9.

the old regime in France permitted assembly, as long as the gathering did not threaten national stability. In fact, the new controls that assigned Home Ministry monitors at public meetings adopted the same standard— that meetings would be suspended if they "threatened the safety of the nation."[149] This was the tack taken by the Meiji government, and the *Law Journal* found this a reasonable standard. It allowed meetings but stopped them when the organizers revealed ill intent by inciting listeners to violence or insurrection.

In light of the dominance of French legal thinking during the 1870s, the laws regarding public assembly in France since the Revolution were of most interest to the author of the "Discourse on Law" in the *Law Journal*. In tracing changes in French laws immediately following the Revolution of 1789, the author likened that event to the Meiji Restoration. The author's reading of French law differed somewhat from Boissonade's in terms of emphasis. The author described how, immediately following the Revolution, French law prohibited all gatherings of soldiers and laborers. Then, only one year later, the law eased blanket prohibitions and moved toward a system of registration. Those seeking to hold political meetings were required to register the time and place of their gatherings with the police. When rallies were not registered, the organizers were fined. The column closed with the statement that "the French are now improving this system so that it will be more open."[150] Japanese observers again looked to Europe to find a replicable model of progressive civilization and enlightenment that could be imported into the Japanese context or used to pressure the Meiji state. What they found, instead, was a somewhat equivocal example of a foreign state suppressing its own population, or at least constraining the ability of that population to enjoy the kinds of freedoms that appeared promised in the texts on theory and constitutions.

There was also the matter of the different contexts in France and Japan, which did not appear in the *Law Journal*'s discussion of regulation of association and assembly. In France, and Europe more broadly, revolutionary labor organizations constituted governments' greatest worry,

---

149. Yasumaru, *Minshū undō*, 462.
150. "Hōritsu mondō: Enzetsu rongikai ni tsuki gimon (ni no ichi)," 8–9.

particularly after 1848. Thus, meetings of groups of laborers occasioned alarm on the part of government observers. In Japan after 1877, revolutionary acts by former samurai constituted the greatest concern. While laborers in Europe were ubiquitous and therefore posed an enormous challenge of state surveillance, in the late 1870s, it was less challenging for the Meiji state to track rabble-rousing former samurai and their allies.

With willful obtuseness, the final *Law Journal* installment on regulation of assembly conflated potential action by political activists with the daily life activities of the general public. It asked, How many people constitute a *shu* or "public" (in "public assembly")? The author noted that the section on "riotous mobs" in the extant criminal code, the Principles of the New Statutes (*Shinritsu kōryō*), "did not define the number of a *shu*. One could liken it to a gang that loots, kills, or steals, certainly not two or three people but maybe more than 7 or 8, maybe 20."[151] The author was unenthusiastic about the idea that if more than 20 people wished to have a meeting about matters of law, learning, or literature, they had to receive permission from the authorities in advance.

For the author of the *Law Journal* column, the absence of advance controls on assembly in favor of on-site monitoring, which prevailed in Japan from the late 1870s, meant that the government of Japan was more flexible than France. This flexibility signaled that Japan "place[d] more value on freedom of assembly" than its European counterpart.[152] This flexibility, however, soon fell away. In a December 9, 1879, proclamation, the police further clarified the procedures for convening a public meeting to discuss politics: the organizers had to notify the authorities three days in advance with the names and addresses of "the organizer and three group members, and . . . the purpose, time, date, and location of the meeting." Meetings not fulfilling these requirements would be summarily disbanded.[153]

As in the case of earlier restrictions on the press, the journals and their readers took up creative readings of government policy in order to evade controls. Law journals and legal advocates used close readings of the law

---

151. Ibid., 4.

152. "Hōritsu mondō: Enzetsu rongikai ni tsuki gimon (ni no ni)," *Hōritsu zasshi*, no. 53 (27 Jan. 1879): 5.

153. "Enzetsukai kaijo tetsuzuki wo shōkai suru ni kotaeru bun," vol. 2, item 27, in Yasui Oshū, *Kisoku yōbun shosoku tōki* (Tokyo: Shōeidō, 1879).

to clarify the legal boundaries of state action, and then those who had legal training pushed the boundaries of the laws or encouraged others to do so. For example, the distinction between political speech and story-telling opened up a loophole that allowed speakers to evade controls on expression and assembly by adhering to the letter of the law. Foreigner Henry Black exploited this approach. At the end of the 1870s and into the early 1880s, Australian-born Black faced suppression for combining the vernacular entertainment form of *rakugo* storytelling at train stations with calls for legal reform and constitutional government. On the advice of legal advocate Numa Morikazu, Black joined a circle of storytellers specializing in warrior epics. Doing so allowed him to evade regulation of public speech that explicitly targeted the regime. All the while, Black continued to call for representative government and criticized laws of conscription in his shows.[154]

While Black blended folk comedic traditions with political messages, others used close readings of laws to open political spaces to the broader public. In 1874, a group of former exchange students to the United States and England established an association called the Kyōzon dōshū to dis-seminate the legal and political ideas that they had encountered abroad. To evade government controls on public meetings, they employed a farci-cal ruse that exploited the rule limiting political discussions to private meetings. In September 1878, the group borrowed a lecture hall and convened a "private" meeting. The event was invitation only. The "invi-tations," however, were printed in major newspapers, including the *Yo-miuri shinbun* and the *Hōchi shinbun*, the day before.[155] Members such as activist Baba Tatsui spoke on the topic "Shakairon" (Theories of society).[156] The meeting attracted an audience of 600.

Having already explored the illogic and inconsistencies of laws on as-sembly, the journals and their legal-advocate interpreters added a legalis-tic inflection to both metropolitan organizations and folk traditions of

---

154. Sasaki and Morioka, "The Blue-Eyed Storyteller," 138–39.

155. Miyatake, *Meiji enzetsushi*, 20–21.

156. Ibid. Ono Azusa, who was on leave from the Ministry of Justice at the time, presented a history of the Kyōzon dōshū. Baba also had a connection with Hoshi Tōru; he studied property and real estate law with Hoshi in England during the 1870s. Ari-izumi, *Hoshi Tōru*, 45. On Ono Azusa and Hoshi, see Teraishi, *Tosa ijinden*, 357.

resistance. Numa Morikazu's own Ōmeisha used a ploy similar to that adopted by the Kyōzon dōshū: at an 1879 meeting, it registered all attendants as members of an association, rendering the public meeting "private"—hence, permitted under the public speech laws.[157] Evasion of government regulation through close reading of the law was not limited to urban centers. Law journals were widely distributed, and the metropolitan activists often had ties to the regions, where public speeches and concomitant evasions of laws on assembly were regular occurrences. In the countryside, legalistic subversion of government control sometimes proceeded with an air of absurdity, as calls for constitutional government intensified. Historian Yasumaru Yoshio has analyzed public assemblies on politics that masqueraded as sporting events, private parties, and funerals. In one mock funeral, the "deceased" was the tongue of a political activist who was forbidden to give speeches under government regulations.[158] Having taken a posthumous name, he was again criticizing the Meiji regime.

A tightening of controls on assembly and public speech continued, culminating in the Assembly Ordinance, promulgated in April 1880. Stricter regulation of assembly reflected increased interest in German models of statecraft.[159] Many of the elements of the 1880 regulations had been foreshadowed piecemeal, including a system of advance notification, notification of the names and addresses of lecturers and speakers, and the site and date of the meeting. After April 1880, prior approval from local officials was required for associations and gatherings on "topics of discussion or debate concerning politics." If the police deemed the lecture topic or the goals of an association "injurious to public peace," then they would "not give their sanction." The ordinance also gave authority to uniformed police to monitor, suspend, and dissolve meetings. In a response to the creative interpretation of earlier rules governing associations, the measure stated, "No political association, intending to lecture or deliberate upon politics, may advertise its lectures or debates,

---

157. Kim, *The Age of Visions and Arguments*, 164.
158. Yasumaru, *Minshū undō*, 467–69.
159. Nakahara, *Meiji keisatsushi ronshū*, 156–64. In English, Lawrence Beer discusses how the Prussian Law of Association of 1850 served as the model for Japanese regulation of association from 1880. Beer, *Freedom of Expression in Japan*, 51

persuade people to enter its ranks by dispatching commissioners or issuing circulars, or combine and communicate with other similar societies." Moreover, the ordinance prohibited "open-air lectures or debates on political subjects."[160] In November 1880, governors received the authority to prohibit persons from speaking for a year if they had been involved in an event that was disbanded. Officials from the police could immediately disband meetings when speakers criticized existing laws or officials, when the contents of speeches strayed from approved topics, and when political speeches were given under the pretext that they were speeches on academic topics. A further revision of the Assembly Ordinance in 1882 strengthened the power of the police to intervene and eliminated the distinction between speeches on political and scholarly topics.

Legalistic readings of the government's regulation of speech and assembly reflected creative expressions of defiance that emerged, in part, from legal advocate and legal journal engagement with Meiji laws. Rather than achieving government control of discourse, suppression of speech often proved the point of activists: that a space for public debate and public opinion was necessary and that legal thinking could open those spaces.

Defending the Nation and the Criminally Accused

The growing engagement between the public and former-samurai private legal practitioners also found expression in the advocacy of legal journals for defense of the criminally accused. Former samurai campaigned for reform of the system of legal defense, again framing themselves as protectors of individuals within the nation. An enlarged role in the criminal justice process would confirm the former samurai's claim to speak for the public and protect individual rights. In subsequent political trials, the most salient of which was the trial in the Fukushima Incident, legal advocates became heroes. Allowing legal defense for the criminally accused, particularly in cases involving foreigners, launched legal advocates on their trajectory toward celebrity status during the early 1880s.

As legal advocates were painfully aware, the countries that had produced the traditions of political rights emulated in Japan were the very

---

160. Ibid.

countries that suppressed Japan through unequal treaties. In terms of domestic governance, within a decade after 1868, a central state had emerged with the capacity to complete a unifying project begun at the turn of the seventeenth century. Still, the unequal treaties and the treaty ports remained a challenge to the sovereignty of the central state. Meiji legal thinkers noted how, in domestic politics, "the world today is already a world of laws, not a world of force."[161] In this, they repudiated violence as a means of political control. At the same time, they recognized that might still made right in international affairs. While the shoring up of the sovereign state lay at the center of the legal reforms proposed by the government, former samurai linked questions of sovereignty to the individual rights of Japanese subjects. In the view of legal advocate activists, overlapping spheres of national sovereignty (*kokken*) and people's rights (*minken*) meant that there could be no Japanese sovereignty in international politics as long as there were no people's rights within Japan.

Analysts linked state sovereignty (*kokken*) and personal rights (*minken*) to four areas of early Meiji contestation: the form of the new state, popular participation in politics, individual rights, and, finally, the place of Japan in international affairs.[162] Activists argued that, as the nation required protection in the international sphere, the subject required protection at home. Even though civil suits between Japanese nationals and foreigners during the 1870s regularly featured private legal representation, the same was not true in criminal cases. Within the bounds of the centralizing state, the fact that foreigners could avail themselves of legal defense in criminal trials and Japanese could not opened up a debate on legal representation for the criminally accused—a debate that ultimately led to reform.

The actions of foreign nationals in Japan who enjoyed extraterritoriality drove home the reciprocal relationship between international inequality and weak protection of individual rights. In May 1876, an incident occurred at this intersection of national and international affairs that exposed the link between the politics of daily life and the international quest for respect. It also revealed the vulnerability of Japanese at home

---

161. "Tokyo hōgakusha kaikō no shushi" (Address at the opening of the Tokyo Law School), *Hōritsu zasshi* (18 Sept. 1880): 4.

162. Howland, *Translating the West*, 130.

in ways that projected this logic back into domestic politics while inten-
sifying the debate over legal representation for the accused in criminal
trials.[163] An American woman managing a hotel in a foreign community
in Tokyo went out to buy some vegetables. She picked out goods from a
local greengrocer but refused to pay the asking price. When the
greengrocers—both husband and wife—demanded payment, other foreigners attacked them. In the fight that followed, the female greengrocer's ribs and nose were broken and she was near death. In subsequent
days, the Americans involved in the incident hired legal representation
and pushed for action against the greengrocers in a Japanese court. Because this was a criminal matter, the greengrocers were not allowed a
legal representative.[164] The greengrocers argued their innocence, but it was
clear that if the government did not ease the prohibition on legal representation for criminal defendants, the greengrocers would lose their case.
In response, the Ministry of Justice issued a circular on May 25, 1876,
stating, "Although it has been the natural custom not to allow [legal]
advocates in criminal matters . . . [in cases involving foreigners] there is
no other way to protect the people of the nation."[165] The decree opened
the way for legal representation in criminal cases involving foreigners by
allowing petitions for legal representation in such cases; the courts seldom refused.

Legal journals contributed to the debate over how to handle the fall-
out from the fight and highlighted the interconnection between individual rights and national sovereignty. They amplified claims from the late
1870s made—as noted by Douglas Howland—by people's rights "advocates such as Ueki [Emori] and Fukumoto [Nichinan] . . . asserting a
causal relationship between the expansion of the people's right(s) and national stability, strength, and reputation."[166] Promotion of legal defense
for the criminally accused was among the first matters taken up by the
Journal in 1877.[167] The *Journal* unambiguously urged the Meiji government to allow the criminally accused access to legal representation in *all*

---

163. The story below appeared in Osatake, *Meiji keisatsu saiban shi*, 193–94.
164. Hattori, "The Legal Profession in Japan," 119.
165. Osatake, *Meiji keisatsu saiban shi*, 194–95.
166. Howland, *Translating the West*, 135.
167. Colophon for the *Hōritsu zasshi*, no. 51 (28 Dec. 1878).

cases.[168] The *Journal* argued that, as in civil cases where legal representation "extended a person's rights" and "was of benefit to society," legal representation should be allowed in criminal cases.[169] Societies and journals called on the government to expand the right of representation to criminal trials. The call for legal defense for the criminally accused galvanized diverse proponents of reform, who demanded criminal defense as a legal right. Supporters included private legal advocates and government officials trained in the Ministry of Justice's institute for legal training. In June 1879, Ministry of Justice official Isobe Jirō submitted a proposal arguing for legal representation for the criminally accused.[170] Isobe pointed to the illogic of limiting legal representation to criminal cases involving foreigners. He argued that representation must be extended to all criminal cases, because in contrast to civil cases, "[t]his is about more than gaining or losing money, it is about imprisonment."[171]

The nearly universal support for reform can be credited to the inequities that arose from criminal cases involving foreigners. Since the mid-1870s, legal advocates and law experts had issued wide-ranging calls for action that strengthened the pressure for access to legal defense. At the same time, the calls for reform were part and parcel of the new idea of a society of laws and legally informed individuals protected by rights. The 1880 Code of Criminal Instruction (also translated as Code of Criminal Procedure) went into effect in 1882. It allowed legal representation in all criminal cases and required it in the most serious cases.[172] Legal advocates and theorists of popular rights had successfully linked the promotion of individual rights at home to national sovereignty, or the "nation's rights" abroad.

The publication of long-running legal journals opened up an interpretive world of legal scholarship and political activism to legal advocates and a growing number of domestic legal scholars. Editorials and

---

168. "Daigen bengo no keiji ni kakubekarazaru o ronzu," *Hōritsu zasshi*, no. 4 (11 Sept. 1877): 42–43.

169. Ibid.

170. Originally in *Yuehōgaku hakushi Isobe Jirō*, cited by Osatake, *Meiji keisatsu saiban shi*, 197.

171. Osatake, *Meiji keisatsu saiban shi*, 197–98.

172. The Code of Criminal Instruction, Great Council of State Decree No. 37, art. 381, sect., I 1880.

research articles alike created a forum in which texts and readers engaged questions of governance, politics, and power. As the column "Discourse on Law" and expressions in other legal journals showed, legal texts were not "final words" but instead opening statements in debates that ranged back in time to ancient Rome and forward in time to a vision of a more progressive Japan (or France). A vision of the transformative power of law suggested that advocates could create a better society not simply by transforming the self through the strengthening of individual morality, but that the ills of all of society could be cured by the ministrations of the legalist.[173] Increasingly, former samurai claimed that they were particularly well suited to this task. In part, they ratified this claim by linking it to an invented tradition of samurai activism on behalf of commoners during the Edo era.

Ōshio Heihachirō's Uprising: A Useable Past for a Political Future

Legal practice came to occupy a central place in the former samurai political activism of the 1870s as former samurai cast themselves as champions of the people. The story of samurai as protectors of the powerless was a narrative concoction that mixed actual practice with invented history. In practice, Edo-era samurai had administered justice in both the domains and the commissions of the shogunate. Kataoka Kenkichi noted their history as arbiters of conflict in an 1877 Memorial to the

---

173. The most celebrated case of involvement of a legal journal in a policy debate came in the controversy over the adoption of the civil code in the late 1880s and early 1890s. Proponents of the institution of a French-based civil code (largely advocates trained in the French tradition) quarreled with those who sought to delay the adoption of the code, particularly advocates trained in England and, to a lesser extent, those partial to German law. In 1891, the law journal *Hōgaku shinpō*, the successor to *Hōri seika*, carried an influential article in which legal scholar Hozumi Yatsuka claimed that the adoption of the French-based civil code, as it was then drafted, would "end filialty and loyalty" to the emperor (*minpō idete chūkō horobu*). The campaign for a delay succeeded. The compromise position introduced principles of other European codes into the draft. (A similar contest unfolded over the institution of the commercial code, with various partisans squaring off and appealing for public support through the medium of print.) After revision, a "new" civil code came into force in 1898. There are numerous accounts of this debate over the code. For a focus on legal journals in the debate, see Chūō daigaku shichi jūnenshi hensanjo, ed., *Chūō daigaku shichi jūnenshi*, 37.

Emperor. "[S]amurai have always taken part in the administrative affairs of their various han [domains] . . . their minds have thus been familiarized with political matters, and they are not content to be deprived of all their prerogatives."[174]

As for invented history, there were very few instances where Edo-era samurai had acted as champions of the people in the sense defined by their Meiji successors. A vivid illustration of a constructed narrative that cast samurai as champions of the people came in the renewed interest in the career of a former inspector in the office of the Osaka city magistrate—Ōshio Heihachirō.[175] A principled stand against the government by Ōshio informed Shimamoto Nakamichi's thoughts on the political pursuit of legal practice. In 1887, Shimamoto completed a biography of Ōshio that elevated the profile of one of the few samurai who publicly questioned the corrupt practices of the Tokugawa shogunate. In the process, Shimamoto laid broader and deeper historical roots for political activism grounded in law than former samurai really had.

Shimamoto, since his early emergence as a leading figure among legal advocates, had had a long-abiding interest in Ōshio, an Edo-era justice official. Shimamoto himself was a former samurai and a former police official in the Meiji Ministry of Justice. Having advised Kitada Masatadashi and Teramura Tomie on the founding of the Hokushūsha, he drew upon the past as a way of articulating a coherent future for a legal activism that emerged out of the samurai tradition of concern for the common good. In 1890, Shimamoto paid homage to Ōshio in his book *Seiten hekireki* (Thunderbolt from the blue). During the famine of 1837, Ōshio and a band of followers attacked merchant warehouses and government offices in Osaka in response to private greed and failed public policies that caused farmer suffering. Shimamoto described the context that gave rise to Edo-era corruption and self-interest:

In its waning years, the shogunate had lost its legitimacy. Edicts were largely in disarray. Bribery abounded. Even among lower officials—particularly those in positions such as procurator [*machiyoriki*] and public examiner [*ginmiyaku*]—if there was profit in it and to extend their power, they might call a deer a horse. . . .

---

174. Kataoka, "Memorial Presented to the Emperor by the Risshisha," 2:204.
175. Morris, *The Nobility of Failure*, 8.

[Officials] often slid into bribery, committing acts of corruption, without the least bit of a spirit of love for the people.[176]

In Shimamoto's account, Ōshio was no renegade. Rather, by the Confucian logic of governance, Ōshio's uprising was permissible and even required. Shogunal rulers were no longer wise and just: they had strayed from what was right and had corrupted knowledge itself through their distortions. They invited retribution.

Shimamoto's retelling of Ōshio's story was more than a simple Confucian condemnation of corruption. He recast it as an allegory for himself and his time: Shimamoto and other former-samurai legal practitioners challenged the state during the 1870s and 1880s in the interest of establishing a constitutional polity and "extending rights." Just as Ōshio had held fellow samurai to a higher standard of justice than that of contemporary practice, so too did Shimamoto. In the face of opposition, Ōshio pushed reform of the Osaka public examiner's office; Shimamoto had also worked on controversial reforms under Etō Shinpei at the Ministry of Justice. Just as Ōshio left his government position to save the people, so too had Shimamoto left government service to become a pioneer in the establishment of associations of private legal practitioners. Shimamoto also drew upon Ōshio's story in a way that legitimized rights in terms of the samurai tradition and Confucian ideals. Here one saw former samurai extracting a "useable past" from the Edo period. Instead of the discredited Neo-Confucian orthodoxy that supported the Tokugawa state, Shimamoto intermingled a rereading of Ōshio as a popular hero with the morality of Ōyōmeigaku (Wang Yang Ming thought— the unity of thought and action, or "intuitionism"). Shimamoto affirmed a revised raison d'être and justification for the former-samurai legal advocate. This reason-for-being departed from the domestic legal tradition of the suit solicitor (who was seen as craven, if mentioned at all) and the foreign legal practitioner, and located rights advocacy in a deeper, recuperated Edo past.

As Ōshio had joined thought with action to rescue the people, Shimamoto did likewise; his study of rights drove his involvement in the movement promoting constitutional government. Shimamoto cast Ōshio

---

176. Shimamoto, *Seiten hekireki*, 4.

as an enforcer of legal standards to which the government itself was accountable; Ōshio was a protagonist in a world governed by law, fighting for the correct execution of laws that were just, but "in disarray." The problem was not necessarily the legal system but those charged with enforcement. Late-shogunate and mid-Meiji officials alike had distorted the truth to serve themselves, following in the footsteps of a villain from Chinese history, the Qin-era eunuch Zhao Gao, who forced those around him to face death if they did not "call a deer a horse." Under the shogunate, conditions had deteriorated so much that Ōshio was an outlaw in his own time, if a hero in retrospect. By drawing on the remarkable story of Ōshio, Shimamoto effectively displaced the history of private legal practice by lowly Edo-era suit solicitors who, at times, helped commoners "call a deer" a deer. In their stead, Shimamoto focused on a publicly oriented, high-minded samurai: a convergence of correct thought and dramatic action. It did not matter that Ōshio was a state official. His quest for justice began with his departure from office and emerged out of a critique of the state grounded in a familiarity with law.

During his tenure as an Osaka judicial official, Ōshio had prosecuted bribery in his own office. At the same time, he became increasingly frustrated with the failure of government policies to mitigate suffering from the famines during the Tempō era. Shimamoto Nakamichi's reinterpretation of Ōshio's story amplified Ōshio's "feelings of love for the people."[177] The action that Shimamoto promoted, though, was not necessarily a frontal assault on the state but rather a celebration of a samurai who used acts of speech to transform his world. In addition to a description of Ōshio Heihachirō's life story, *Seiten hekireki* also reproduced Ōshio's tracts. For Shimamoto, Ōshio's central mode of expression was speech, not violence. A few decades after Ōshio's uprising, Shimamoto and fellow former-samurai legal advocates claimed rhetorical skills that, combined with their knowledge of the law, equipped them to engage in public acts on behalf of others. Shimamoto invoked a narrative of political change led by a samurai, while decentering the violent and revolutionary nature of the act itself. By statute, the work of the legal advocate consisted of acts of speech, the act of "speaking to others" (*daiben*) and

---

177. Ibid.

"speaking on behalf of others" (*daigen*). For Shimamoto, the tale of Ōshio's Osaka uprising justified opposition to Edo/Tokyo despotism while furthering both legal activism and verbal and written expressions of political ideas.

Samurai and their former-samurai successors shared a capacity to directly challenge the orthodoxy on its own terms, a privilege enjoyed by few in Edo and early Meiji societies. After 1868, former samurai exploited their position of social privilege to question their peers in government. Even as they stepped out of positions in the state and entered society ("the field," or *zaiya,* as they called it), they preserved their prerogative to interpret the good and the right. In Shimamoto's telling, even as outlaws, Ōshio and his successors in the freedom and popular rights movement were not radicals. Rather, they were proponents of a just order governed by law. The dramatic title of *Seiten hekireki* signaled the novelty of Shimamoto's reading of Ōshio's uprising: he offered a new reading for his time by placing heterodox Confucian political and social thought in the context of a society ruled by law. Thus, the story connected expectations for the early decades of Meiji rule with Ōshio's expectations of legal consistency in an earlier age. As viewed by Shimamoto, former samurai who performed the work of private legal advocacy inherited a historic function as moral exemplars and administrators of justice.

An element of alchemy shades Shimamoto's retelling of Ōshio's 1837 revolt. History remembered Ōshio because he was extraordinary. He was a thunderbolt from the blue, the righteous bureaucrat who first turned the law on his peers. When his actions did not yield relief for the people, he turned on the governing system itself with cannon fire. Yet from the perspective of law in the service of the people, the context was more complex, both in 1837 and in the early decades of the Meiji era. At both ends of the nineteenth century, farmers asserted themselves through the legal processes of lawsuits and petitions, and extra-legally through uprisings and other measures such as mass flight from their villages. Shimamoto's celebration of Ōshio served as an intervention during a Meiji moment when righteous farmers were also coming to the fore as models of political activism.

Just a few years before the publication of *Seiten hekireki*, Komuro Shinsuke's 1884 publication, *Tōyō gijin hyakkaden* (100 martyrs of the

Orient), memorialized the vanquished leaders of farmer uprisings. In Komuro's retelling of the past, complete with *furigana* for easy reading of complex Chinese characters, peasants seized their own destiny. The opening tale about agriculturalist Totani Shin'emon tells how Totani submitted a direct petition to the shogunate asking for debt relief, which the shogunate accepted and acted upon. But because Totani had pursued justice outside of prescribed channels, he was punished. Much as Shimamoto had recast Ōshio as a forefather of the movement for freedom and popular rights, Komuro retold the Totani episode as a quest for freedom. Foreshadowing farmer uprisings in the early 1880s, Totani was not seeking relief from his samurai betters as an inferior supplicant but had instead "sacrificed his life for liberty."[178] Komuro scoured the Edo-period past for farmer activists with pedigrees akin to that of Totani and Sakura Sōgorō. He then serialized their stories in newspapers, thereby making the people the protagonists in their own liberation and connecting them to the movement for liberty and rights. At the same time, the farmer-hero called into question the notion that former-samurai elites were the only legitimate occupants in the vanguard of legal and political change.

The hagiographies penned by Komuro and Shimamoto featured Edo-era heroes but wrote suit solicitors and suit inns out of the picture. This was in some ways a puzzling omission, in that suit inns and suit solicitors exercised considerable influence on the Edo-era judicial landscape and at times worked in the interest of the people themselves. Well before Ōshio, legal practitioners operating on the edge of respectability had cultivated knowledge of Tokugawa and domainal law. They deployed their knowledge in the service of clients who used legal processes to achieve their own aims: for example, as drafters of documents that helped petitioners bring private disputes before magistrates or ease tax burdens in a bad crop year. Yet the inclusion of suit solicitors in either tale would have muddied the waters (or clouded the sky). The heroism of the failed samurai or farmer uprising derived from the protagonist's moral purity. Totani (and other martyrs) in Komuro and Ōshio in Shimamoto abandoned self-interest for the greater good. These heroic narratives of samurai and

---

178. Komuro, *Toyo gijin hyakkaden*, 15.

farmers shared a world in which politics consisted of ideals and abstractions. Shimamoto's and Komuro's concocted worlds minimized the power of profit and the concerns of the market. Theirs was not the world of the suit solicitor and suit inn.

Self-interest was anathema to many of the movement idealists of the 1870s and 1880s. Beyond a celebration of Ōshio, *Seiten hekireki* was also an attack on greedy, corrupt, amoral officials, a characterization that many former-samurai legal advocates mapped onto the new political leaders whom they accused of selling land for personal profit and other acts of corruption.[179] Even though the Meiji coup had overturned Tokugawa rule, former samurai suggested that the new despotism of the regime echoed that of the old. The foundation for this narrative was a description of the evils of the Edo era, particularly its arbitrary exercise of power. Though the Meiji state of the 1890s established a civil bureaucracy that hired on the basis of merit, the 1870s were years of state ineffectiveness and even caprice. This reminded former samurai and legal advocate Shima Manjirō of the bad old days, when "adjudicative power was wielded by little more than one person"—the magistrate.[180] Narratives by legal advocates not only identified the Meiji state as the villain but also disseminated that criticism in a broad and public way. One example appeared in a biography of Nakajima Matagorō. In the mid-1870s, Nakajima received an offer from a fellow former samurai to take a position in the Ministry of Foreign Affairs; Nakajima responded that he preferred legal advocacy to "becoming a slave to bureaucratic authority."[181] He went on to work in an association of legal advocates established by Hoshi Tōru and was later a member of the Liberal Party.

If the new authorities had the power to enslave former samurai, how might they exploit farmers—through a widely condemned, unfair tax burden on agriculture or the establishment of conscription in 1872? Successive farmer uprisings suggested that Japanese subjects saw the officials of the new Meiji regime as more akin to the bad-guy daimyo Hotta Masanobu of the Sakura Sōgorō story than the fair and just shogunal mag-

---

179. Shimamoto, *Seiten hekireki*, 67–72.

180. Maruyama N., ed., *Tokyo kakusha tōron hikki*, 2.

181. Nakajima Matagorō was born a samurai in Echizen in 1852. Machida, ed., *Tokyo daigennin retsuden*, 40.

istrate Ōoka Echizen. What was new during the 1870s was that reform of the legal system not only created ways in which people could legally express their discontent but also a new way of thinking about law as the frame for that expression. Before 1868, legal practitioners operated on the periphery; after 1872, legal advocates came to the fore, with Sono, Kodama, and former suit solicitors helping clients navigate the new judiciary. At the same time, a new kind of legal advocate emerged from the tribulations of former samurai. This advocate studied, read, and practiced law in an association, thereby creating an unprecedented vehicle for public discourse and debate. Out of this discourse arose definitions of a just and an unjust state and the role of law in protecting people's rights. Former samurai then turned to moral ideas that had legitimated earlier challenges to state authority, using these to justify the new practice of legal advocacy and legal interpretation. As former samurai and legal advocate Shima Manjirō put it, advocates must "extend the power of the law to the people in general."[182] In Shima's formulation, rights were something that the legal advocate claimed and mobilized on behalf of others. Yet doing so required spreading knowledge and connecting that knowledge to a broader public.

By the end of the 1870s, questions of rights and responsibilities—what they were, who could claim them, and in what ways they were consistent or inconsistent with Japanese traditions—had become the leading questions of Japanese politics. Legal advocates drove such questions to the fore through their political activism. Not all former samurai became legal advocates, nor were all legal advocates politically involved; yet the overlap between associations of legal advocates, political associations, newspapers, law schools, law journals, apprenticeships within the associations, and the emerging political parties shaped the process of carving out a space for public debate and public opinion during the 1870s and early 1880s. Associations of legal advocates and political associations (*seisha*) shared memberships, meeting spaces, and approaches to political change. Advocates were united in their calls for the establishment of representative government and their repudiation of armed force, which other disgruntled former samurai embraced. Former-samurai legal

---

182. Maruyama N., ed., *Tokyo kakusha tōron hikki*, 2.

advocates added new tactics to a political activism that had previously been limited to violence. No longer did the opposition need to rely on the use of arms—as former-samurai activists had done when they drew their swords to make a point during the Saga Uprising of 1874 and the Satsuma Rebellion of 1877. Nor did protesting farmers need to appeal to the arbitrary justice of social betters, as they did when they pleaded with Edo-era local officials for tax or debt relief. Instead, much like parties to private disputes who turned to the courts to resolve conflicts, political activists could appeal to legal norms to promote political change and resolve conflicts.

Former samurai joined together with other elites and created associations that simultaneously interpreted and then disseminated legal thought, while at the same time embedding it in practices with deep indigenous roots, including the litigated resolution of private disputes and folk opposition to state suppression. Out of legal practice, former samurai and elite commoners then applied their new knowledge and frames to the movement for a constitutional polity in Japan. This was a revised approach to legal practice, in which organized legal practice became political in the interest of a broader public. What remained unclear was to what extent, and at what levels, the evolving political and legal systems would respond to the activism of legal practitioners.

CHAPTER 4

The Possibilities and Limits of Politics: Legal Advocates and the Formation of Political Parties

As Japan moved into the 1880s, the social and political fluidity of the 1870s waned. The 1870s had been a decade of dynamic eclecticism in which legal advocates and the state gradually worked through the meaning and form of a society grounded in law. In 1880, the Ministry of Justice refined the regulations for private legal practice that had been set forth in 1876. Increasingly, legal advocates such as Sono Tel, who had operated under a more flexible regime, found practice full of obstacles. Yet for former samurai who had used legal advocacy as an entrée into politics, the 1880s suggested promise. During the decade of the 1870s, interpretations of the Meiji Emperor's Charter Oath of 1868 as a call for constitutional government in Japan had hardened. Activist Ozaki Yukio recalled how the Charter Oath "meant more . . . than having a million allies. A clear national policy had been set. Devoting our energies to the cause of constitutional government was to obey the Imperial will and serve the empire."[1] Thus, the 1881 Imperial Edict pledging that a constitution would be drafted by decade's end signaled the possibility of a constitutional and representative government consistent with the oath. Increasingly, constitutional politics meant the consideration of individual and occupational concerns. An 1881 digest of legal advocates articulated an approach to politics that was new to the Meiji period, stating, "[R]ights

---

1. Ozaki, *The Autobiography of Ozaki Yukio*, 6–7.

emerge out of the relationship between authority and interests."[2] Others held the idea that politics was only possible through the triumph of law, which could mediate the interests of government on one side and groups in society on the other. Thus, when the legal advocate—acting as a protector of rights—engaged in legal speech, it was nearly synonymous with political speech. Whether oriented toward material interests or abstractions, training in law was training in politics.

The career of Hoshi Tōru, a legal advocate and politician, exemplified the social and political transformation in legal advocacy, as well as the application of legal education to a political career. Though he was a commoner, Hoshi was selected by the Meiji regime to study abroad in 1874. He parlayed his legal training as Japan's first British barrister into an exalted position in government service and, eventually, into the funding and promotion of political party activism. Hoshi's remarkable career is indicative of broader shifts in how law was practiced, regulated, and viewed as an occupation in Japan during the 1870s and 1880s. Hoshi, along with many other legal advocates, shaped the political landscape of the 1880s through his promotion of public discourse and party activism. This new class of advocates also experienced limits.

As party organization and activity developed, political speech and action found new outlets. This did not escape notice of the state. Intensified political action by legal advocates and their affiliated political parties invited increased government surveillance and suppression. After initiating public assembly regulations in 1878, the government tightened those regulations in 1880 and revised them again two years later. The more stringent restrictions came in response to the flourishing associations that promoted political change at public assemblies. The controls gave a stronger hand to the prefectural governors, allowing the authorities throughout Japan to suspend a speaker for up to a year for violating the laws on speech. Also, government tolerance for the practice of calling public assemblies "private parties" or "funerals" (in which attendants mourned the death of a tongue now prohibited from speaking) had waned. Despite tightened governmental controls, with the establishment of a representative assembly on the horizon, legal advocates and their associated political parties redirected

---

2. Machida, ed., *Tokyo daigennin retsuden*, 1.

their energies. In addition to speeches criticizing officials, they intensified activities aimed at winning seats in the promised governing body.

Legal advocates like Hoshi Tōru offered themselves as leaders of public opinion while serving political parties. In the course of Hoshi's career he leveled sometimes-ostentatious affronts to incompetent public officials, evaded limits on joint practice with fellow legal advocates, competed with other legal practitioners (such as notaries), debated interpretations of law, backed a newspaper, and supported a political party. Many advocates engaged in law and politics broadly, but few careers so thoroughly touched the transformation of legal and political culture. Hoshi was a commoner who straddled the domestic and the international worlds while developing a successful career as a politically involved legal advocate. He was such an extraordinary figure that he became a legend in his lifetime; stories about him turned his experiences as an advocate into allegories for all Meiji legal practitioners and their relationship with the courts. They also popularized the practice of legal advocacy.

Hoshi's career spanned group and factional affiliations. At times, he joined cause with radical opponents of the Meiji regime, including legal advocate and activist Ōi Kentarō. At other times he worked with legal-advocate reformists who, like Hatoyama Kazuo, promoted "cooperation" through parliamentary politics as a feature that separated "civilized" from "uncivilized" nations.[3] Also, like many who taught law as much as they practiced it, Hoshi was something of a mentor to many legal apprentices. Hoshi's career combined bureaucratic service, commercial legal practice, support of party politics, promotion of himself as a politician, and elevation of ethical and training standards for legal practitioners. In this, he set an example for lawyer-politicians into the twentieth century, such as Takagi Masutarō and Saitō Takao.

Hoshi Tōru and the Possibilities of Politics

Hoshi's story highlights the possibilities and problems of meritocratic advance under the Meiji regime. Born a commoner in 1850, Hoshi took

---

3. In 1882, Hatoyama compiled a collection of parliamentary rules of order: Hatoyama, *Kaigi hō, kan*, 1–3. Hatoyama had studied law in the United States at Columbia and Yale Universities. See Toyoda, *Hatoyama Ichirō*.

advantage of the shifting social landscape in the 1870s to elevate his own position. He became a dominant, if polarizing, figure in the fields of both law and party politics.[4] Along with many political activists in his day, Hoshi began his career as a government official. Yet, once he left the comfort of his government post, he became a champion of the litigating public and those who spoke on its behalf.

Like many other legal advocates who rose to prominence in the late nineteenth century, Hoshi's education included foreign language study. He gained a reputation for his skill with English and, in 1872, the governor of Kanagawa prefecture, Mutsu Munemitsu, enlisted Hoshi to teach English at the Shumonkan (修文館).[5] Working in the former site of the military training academy of the Tokugawa shogunate placed Hoshi in the port city of Yokohama. By appointment of the Great Council of State, Hoshi took a position as tax and tariff inspector for the Ministry of Finance. His time in Yokohama, however, was clouded by a contretemps with the British foreign service. In correspondence, Hoshi referred to the sovereign of England as "Her Majesty, the Queen," while referring to the Japanese sovereign as "Emperor."[6] Britain's minister plenipotentiary to Japan, Harry Parkes, objected: he argued that the queen, too, should be referred to as an emperor (*kōtei heika*). Hoshi would not back down, arguing that the British themselves referred to their sovereign as "Her Majesty, the Queen." Complaints about Hoshi's own imperiousness did not help his position.

Yet Hoshi's personal ties and fluency in the English language salvaged his career. Ironically, the solution in September 1874 was to dispatch Hoshi to England for formal study of law.[7] Hoshi moved to London, where he was inducted into the Middle Temple on January 25, 1875. While there, he

4. In the year of his death, biographies of Hoshi ranged from the hagiographic by Fujii Chikukan (*Hoshi Tōru seikai meishi*) to the scathing by Natsuyama Shigeki (*Hoshi Tōru*). Others were more measured including Masaoka, *Jidai shisō no gonge*. More recent accounts include Kawasaki, *Hoshi Tōru to sono jidai*.

5. American Samuel Robbins Brown was an instructor at the school. Students included Ono Azusa and Nakahama Tōichi. Okudaira, "Hoshi Tōru den," 50.

6. Okudaira, *Nihon bengoshishi*, 228–29. See also Kobayashi S., *Watakushi no atta Meiji no meihōsō monogatari*.

7. There were nearly 100 other Japanese students in London at the time that Hoshi was there. Ariizumi, *Hoshi Tōru*, 34–35.

studied the leading legal thought of the time, including John Austin's *The Philosophy of Positive Law* and the writings of Sir William Blackstone.[8] Hoshi lodged in a flat at Adelphi Terrace, London. His accommodation itself was an education in professionalism and the public sphere. The Adelphi, an eighteenth-century monument to classicism, served as offices and lodging for lawyers, doctors, and architects. While he was a resident, it also housed clubs, societies, and institutes, including the Green Room Club, which provided accommodations for actors and writers such as Richard D'Oyly Carte and George Bernard Shaw. From the Adelphi, Hoshi commuted to the Middle Temple in the judicial quarter. By the end of his time in London, he had become the first person from Japan to be become a barrister. The pomp, circumstance, and wax seals of Victorian England certified his mastery of English law. On June 13, 1877, London's Honourable Society of the Middle Temple announced in the "Dining Hall of the said Society" that Hoshi Tōru "hath paid all duties which were owing by him to the Society and the officers." Thus, the society called Hoshi to the "Degree of the Utter Bar."[9] Hoshi returned to Tokyo in 1877, a barrister of the Middle Temple.[10] When he arrived in Tokyo, he confronted a challenge similar to that of Kodama Jun'ichirō coming back from his studies. Hoshi's training meant that his skills far exceeded those required in his old posting in the tariff office. As a qualified barrister, he was better suited to work as a private legal advocate; yet, at the time, there was very little prestige in the private practice of legal advocacy.

---

8. In addition to John Austin's importance as a theorist of positive law, his approach to sovereign power was also influential in Japan during the late nineteenth century. See Minear, *Japanese Tradition and Western Law*, 18–19.

9. Kokkai toshokan (National Diet Library), Hoshi Tōru monjo, Kensei shiryōshitsu, Document #313, The Honourable Society of the Middle Temple.

10. The Council of State ordered Hoshi to England to study law on 29 September, 1874. Hoshi engineered this development with the assistance of his patron, Mutsu Munemitsu. Okudaira, "Hoshi Tōru den," 53. The Ministry of Finance ordered Hoshi to return in Jan. 1877, in the wake of administrative reform. Hoshi delayed his return so that he could receive accreditation as a barrister at law before heading to Japan via the United States in Oct. Okudaira, "Hoshi Tōru den," 54. See also Ariizumi, *Hoshi Tōru den*, 44–45.

In 1877, when former samurai revolted against the Meiji regime in the Satsuma Rebellion, Hoshi had not publicly committed his loyalties to either side. The community of legal advocates to which he returned was focused on questions of rights and legal theory. Practicing law in an atmosphere electric with armed rebellion and assertions about freedom and popular rights meant that Hoshi had to choose his allies carefully lest he be relegated to the oppositional fringe and thus slip from the circles of bureaucratic power in Tokyo that seemed so accessible while he studied in London.[11] By eschewing the work of the "legal advocate in political opposition," at least initially, Hoshi endeavored to disentangle himself from the persistent social bias against legal practice and create something new.

Unlike those who called themselves legal advocates, yet had no training, experience, or license, Hoshi had the distinction of being a barrister. Hoshi emulated the legal and cultural practices of Europe, hoping to transcend the boundaries of status and position that shaped the conflict between legal advocates and representatives of the state in Japan. He wore the clothes of a British barrister and presented himself, as a London barrister would, as the equal of his government counterparts. When Hoshi mounted a *jinrikisha* for court, he did not wear a kimono in which to stash one of the widely available guides for private legal advocates. When headed for court, he favored suits tailored in London. This gesture signaled that Hoshi sought to achieve parity with the bureaucrats in the Japanese courtrooms of the late 1870s and early 1880s. Though Hoshi wore European dress in the courtroom, his enactment of Anglo-professionalism was not the dandyism that former samurai found so risible. Jason Karlin notes that Hoshi had a "reputation as a skilled fighter" and was known for his "passionate masculinity."[12] He was a living repudiation of the Edo-era suit solicitor who had worked in the shadows. By acting the part, he created a new role.

Hoshi's pugilism won notoriety in the courtroom. His approach to the law occasioned collisions between the government's French-influenced notion of the courts as a site of the expression of state power and a British-

---

11. Matsuo S., "Shihō shiryō," 41–54.
12. On clothing and masculinity in Meiji, see Karlin, "The Gender of Nationalism."

influenced notion of the elite barrister as an equal to the other officers of the court. Hoshi's personal contest for respect reflected the larger contest over social status for legal advocates as incipient professionals. One of Hoshi's eulogists recalled, "Hoshi must have had the sense that he was the first [legal practitioner] worthy of respect in Japan."[13] True or not, he was the champion of all of those who did not have a rejoinder to humiliations visited upon them by the bureaucratic state.

In that moment of social and political fluidity characteristic of Japan upon Hoshi's return in 1877, he transformed himself from a local tax inspector into an elite advocate with a government sinecure. He convinced the minister of finance, Ōkuma Shigenobu, to support the establishment of a new state counselor position in Japan, similar to that of the Queen's Counsel in England. Hoshi argued that his pedigree as an English barrister made him superior to Japanese legal advocates, particularly those who had once worked as suit solicitors. Itō Hirobumi and Minister of Justice Ōki Takatō agreed, and the position of Ministry of Justice Counsel-Designate (*fuzoku daigennin*) was established under the authority of Sanjō Sanetomi in December 1877.[14] This assignment, given to Hoshi, included a monthly salary of ¥100, equivalent to a full-time bureaucrat of the seventh rank. The position required Hoshi to handle legal matters affecting the government and to promote the extension of civil law under the Meiji regime.[15] The post also allowed him to take private clients. Two more advocates followed in his footsteps. In 1879, both Megata Tanetarō, who had studied law at Harvard College, and Sōma Nagatane, who had studied law at Columbia and Yale Colleges, joined Hoshi as counsel-designates, but without salary.[16] They also applied to the United States consul general to receive permission to practice law in the consular courts of the United States.[17] They both received permission in 1880.

---

13. Kobayashi S., *Watakushi no atta Meiji no meihōsō monogatari*, 5.

14. Okudaira, "Hoshi Tōru den," 55. See also Okudaira, *Nihon bengoshishi*, 232–33.

15. Okudaira, "Hoshi Tōru den," 55.

16. Murakami K., "Kindai Nihon no zaiya hōsō to sono hyōden," 72. Also see Okudaira, *Nihon bengoshishi*, 293–95.

17. Sōma Nagatane wrote books on Anglo-American law, including *Beikoku soshōhō* [Civil procedure in America], published in 1884 (Tokyo: Bungakusha), and *Eibei baibai hō* [Anglo-American transactional law] published in 1881 (Tokyo: Kongōkaku). Megata was one of the founders of a private law school that eventually became Senshū University.

The Ministry of Justice charged the counsel-designate with acting as the advocate for officials in "suits related to the ministries" and also for poor persons "without resources."[18] The counsel-designate also had to keep hours at the Ministry of Justice. However, there were very few government cases for Hoshi, and he was notoriously averse to taking on indigent defendants.[19] Meanwhile, his for-profit private practice flourished. He hired legal advocates to work for him in an association called the Yūisha (有為社), and his fame grew based on his courtroom success, bringing further demand for his services.[20] De jure, the counsel-designate received the same treatment in the courtroom as other advocates. Yet there were differences. The counsel could practice without submitting to the normal licensing procedures for advocates and enjoyed the deferential treatment reserved for state officials. After a time, and in the absence of government cases, Hoshi increasingly ignored the requirement that he frequent his office at the Ministry of Justice. Instead, he focused on his private clients.

Financial success and status among litigators ranged widely, from struggling unlicensed legal advocates to the wealthy Hoshi. On the whole, however, legal advocates had not achieved the exalted position of the esteemed barristers in England whom Hoshi emulated. And, despite the entry of former samurai into the legal field during the 1870s and 1880s, legal advocates continued to work under a cloud of contempt that lingered from the Edo era. In the face of Meiji legal reforms that promised "civilization and enlightenment," the service relationships between suit inns and commissions embodied backwardness. Suit solicitors had faced social derision and conducted their work in conditions that were, at best, uncertain and insecure. The tendency for critics to identify the shortcomings of legal advocacy with the discredited practices of an "old regime" was not unique to late-nineteenth-century Japan. At the turn of

---

On the consular courts, see Chang, *The Justice of the Western Consular Courts in Nineteenth-Century Japan*.

18. "Fuzoku daigennin o mōke kitei o sadamuru gi ni tsuki ukagai," in Okudaira, *Nihon bengoshishi*, 232.

19. Matsuo S., "Shihō shiryō," 54. Matsuo wrote of how, some years later, Hoshi deliberately antagonized a public procurator in order to be dismissed from serving as a court-appointed legal advocate for an indigent defendant.

20. Nakamura, *Meijiteki ningenzō*, 46.

the nineteenth century, France's post-revolutionaries entertained the failed dream of making legal advocates "unnecessary."[21] However, by the 1870s, advocates there had achieved elite status and privilege.[22] In Japan, by contrast, the legal practitioner of the Edo era was considered complicit in an administrative tradition of corruption, not revolution. The shadow of the Edo-era legacy might explain, in part, why the biographies of the leading figures of the movement for constitutional politics in Japan tended to omit or downplay the practice of legal advocacy in the accounts of their careers.

In the interest of improving the status of legal practitioners, Hoshi joined the minister of justice and the chief justice of the high court in promoting new regulations for legal advocates that went into effect in June 1880.[23] Having transcended his own status as commoner, he worked to elevate the status of an entire occupation and create a profession. Advocates had been ridiculed as inferior to judges and procurators because they were not required to pass uniform, nationally recognized examinations. One of the new laws promoted by Hoshi rectified this. The Ministry of Justice wrote a national exam and sent it directly to local procurators under its aegis, rather than allowing local officials to write and proctor exams as they wished, as had been the practice since 1876.[24] As noted in chapter 2, exams used for licensing from 1876 to 1880 were a poor measure of the test taker's understanding of the law. The questions often reflected, at best, the idiosyncratic interests of the examiners, and, at worst, their unsteady grasp of national law.[25] After 1880, the exams became more formalized. Central administration made test standards clearer and the tests became more selective. From 1876 to 1880, the government licensed advocates at an average of 217 persons a year. After 1880, it became more difficult to become a licensed legal advocate; the pass rate dropped from 44 percent in 1876 to 16 percent in

21. Merryman, *The Civil Law Tradition*, 28–29.

22. Bell, *Lawyers and Citizens*, 210–15.

23. Maeda R., *Hoshi Tōru den*, 126–27.

24. Under the 1876 regulations on licensed advocates, the Ministry of Justice restricted practice to the regional court where an advocate was registered.

25. On the challenges faced by local officials in comprehending national laws, see Kasumi, "Criminal Trials in the Early Meiji Era," 34–49.

1880 and 8 percent in 1881. In the four years following the revision, the average number of licenses that the government granted per year fell to 126, this in spite of a dramatic increase in applicants over the same period (see chapter 2, table 1).

In addition to the more rigorous exam instituted in 1880, the ministry issued codes of conduct for a more ethical practice of legal advocacy. The new regulations demanded that licensed advocates practice with honor, sincerity toward the client, legal knowledge, alacrity, and fair pricing. Legal advocates who used the courtroom as a site in which to ridicule existing laws or disrespect officials would be penalized. The regulations also prohibited acts outside of the courtroom such as barratry—instigating unfounded suits—and extortion. People who were categorically excluded from serving as legal advocates included women, minors, persons with outstanding obligations as a result of a bankruptcy or indemnity, persons convicted of theft or fraud, persons having served a criminal sentence of more than a year, and officials and quasi-officials (*junkanri*).

The 1880 revisions on licensing established government-regulated bar associations affiliated with the regional courts. Existing associations of advocates were instructed to disband. The Office of the Procurator supervised processes in which all legal advocates had to join the bar association in their jurisdiction, paying an annual licensing fee. These bar associations, under the supervision of the Office of the Procurator, drafted charters and democratically elected chairs and vice chairs. Again, this was a state measure that was uneven in its application. De jure, all manner of legal associations, except for the mandatory bar associations tied to the courts, were prohibited. De facto, other associations continued to operate under false pretexts or in the open. Despite the unevenness, Hoshi and others saw state-sanctioned bar associations and selective licensing of advocates as a way of elevating the status of legal advocacy, distinguishing it from the more transactional duties fulfilled by notaries and scriveners. Hoshi held that by formalizing associations and linking the bar to the courts, the 1880 regulations put advocates on the same plane as judges and procurators. In a retrospective on legal practice, Hoshi recalled somewhat hyperbolically how advocates before 1876 "processed papers and legal interpretation was just a dream," but with the advent of the 1880 regulations, "advocates earned more respect in society."[26] At first, Hoshi's position among private legal practitioners flourished under the new regime, as he took leadership of the Tokyo Bar Association.

Beyond Hoshi, the overall effect of the 1880 regulations was to drive the energies of legal advocates toward specialization. The regulations did this by prohibiting the formation of the hybrid associations of legal advocates typical of the previous decade. These regulations instead mandated participation in bar associations tied to regional courts monitored by procurators. Article 22 stated that "outside of the bar associations, legal advocates could not join into associations, take on a name, and conduct business . . . doing so would be a punishable offense." In response, groups of legal advocates focused on a range of pursuits: legal publishing, public speech, political party activism, legal education, or the sale of legal services. Overlap remained, and associations flouted the rules, yet the regulations did have an effect. The regulations drove legal advocates to focus. Severed from their hybrid associations and looking to the promise of the establishment of a constitutional monarchy, politically minded legal advocates supported political parties more directly. Education-minded legal advocates focused on legal instruction. They responded to a market for legal services related to test-directed education, ranging from training in private law schools to test-preparation books and pamphlets. Aspring legal advocates turned to the private law schools that were founded in the early 1880s increasingly shorn of apprenticeship obligations. Profit-minded legal advocates focused on commercial legal practice.

The new licensing requirements also meant that in order to continue to operate a joint practice, advocates had to break the law. Doing so was not difficult. Even though the regulations mandated an abrupt end to associations of legal advocates, the regulations were loosely enforced. Some prominent associations disbanded; other equally prominent groups reorganized and continued their activities. The Tokyo branch of the Hokushūsha continued to practice under the same company name written with different Chinese characters.[27] In May 1880, the Osaka Hokushūsha disbanded and then reconstituted itself, in the same location,

---

26. Hoshi Tōru, "Bengoshi hōan ni kansuru iken," *Kōko shinbun* (9 Dec. 1890): 1.
27. Okudaira, *Nihon bengoshishi*, 460–62.

under the management of Teramura Tomie.[28] The personnel and office remained the same. Teramura maintained the group in the building formerly operated by the Hokushūsha and contracted with the previous management to take over its clients. To observe the letter of the law, other legal advocates organized lawsuit-oversight companies (*shishō kanteisha*) that then "introduced" clients to advocates. By positing that legal advocates were operating independently, the companies maintained the fiction that they were complying with laws against joint practice even though associated legal advocates remained company principals or employees.

Hoshi himself also ignored the rules, evidence of his increasing disdain for legal procedure during the early 1880s. At the same time, he focused on bolstering the reputation of qualified legal advocates while ridiculing substandard practices by procurators and judges.[29] Accounts of the early 1880s describe a boldly insubordinate Hoshi. In a criminal case in which Hoshi served as the court-appointed advocate, he needled the procurator. After the procurator had held forth for over an hour, Hoshi said, "That was extremely long winded."[30] The procurator became angry and replied that explaining facts and drawing conclusions was not "long winded" and that saying so constituted defamation of a public official, a criminal act. Hoshi replied, "If you write out the characters for 'long winded' they simply mean, talk that has gone on for some time. How does that amount to defaming an official?" The judge looked on in surprise.

The exchange, which began in the morning, lasted into the afternoon. By the end of it, Hoshi had been removed from the case by the court and was relieved of his responsibility for representing an indigent criminal defendant. He escaped a reprimand, which was attributed to his ability to negotiate with the court.[31] The person recalling this inci-

---

28. Other associations that disbanded included the Association for the Preservation of Rights (Hokensha 保権舎), the Law of Received Wisdom Association (Kichi hōsha 貴知法社), the Buntensha (聞天舎), and the Association for the Study of Law (Hōritsu gakusha 法律学舎). Ibid., 310–11.

29. Kadota, "Nihon bengoshishi daigennin jidai izen," 34–35.

30. This took place around the time of the trial in the Fukushima Incident (a critical moment in Hoshi's career and in law in general); Matsuo S., "Shihō shiryō," 54.

31. Ibid.

dent thought that Hoshi's goal all along had been to get out of his appointed service on the case.

This and other stories reveal that Hoshi was a proponent of new regulations, yet he believed he could interpret them to his benefit. Even as the government sought to criminalize criticism in every venue, including through regulation of public assembly and innovative applications of the revised Criminal Code of 1880 (instituted in 1882), it could not contain the legal and political maneuvers of Hoshi. Here was someone who both championed the rule of law and, at the same time, bent the law to his own will. Meiji reforms had created new opportunities for commoners, such as Hoshi. Evident was a gradual falling away of rigid status distinctions—a circumstance that pointed toward possibilities in politics. Hoshi's reputation for outspoken commentary on officials' competence—including officials of the court and those who stood before it—reflected his tirelessness in exploiting his own experience, experience that gained him a foothold in the upper reaches of Japanese society. Further expanding this foothold, he capitalized on his participation in the political opposition by integrating an oppositional pose into his courtroom persona. In the process, he turned the Meiji idea of bureaucratic contempt for the people on its head.

Before 1880, associations of legal advocates had formed voluntarily, reflecting the sensibilities and biases of the members of each group. After 1880, the advent of more stringent regulations meant that bar associations attached to the regional courts formed under state mandate. These new, mandatory bar associations brought legal advocates together, regardless of personal or ideological predispositions. The bar associations combined both friends and enemies. This mix of strange bedfellows drove legal advocates to look elsewhere for ideological and political camaraderie. The new political organizations that formed out of, and in addition to, the hybrid law associations operated in an environment of uncertainty that paralleled the challenges facing Hoshi.

At the same time, legal advocates contested, among themselves, the leadership of the bar associations. In the Tokyo Bar, Hoshi's cavalier approach to human relations began to catch up with him. Some legal advocates resented his privileged place within the Ministry of Justice and the special consideration and remuneration he received as a counsel-designate. Others found his strong-arm tactics as head of the Tokyo Bar

Association disquieting. Hoshi's position at the ministry was soon imperiled. As happened before, Hoshi would use politics to find his way, but a fall came first.

In 1881, shortly after the ministry's imposition of new regulations and ethical standards, the *Tokyo nichi nichi shinbun* ran editorials critical of litigiousness and new legal practices. The *Nichi nichi* was not just any newspaper. Fukuchi Gen'ichirō, government-official-turned-journalist, backed a gradualist approach to constitutionalism and was often at odds with former samurai from Tosa who sought immediate reform. A March 14 editorial attributed to Fukuchi targeted legal advocates in particular. It claimed that they drummed up business, filed false suits, and stole from clients.[32] In intemperate language that likened legal practice to "leprosy," the editorial suggested that civil litigation was anathema to Japanese tradition.[33] With powerful encouragement from Hoshi, the Tokyo Bar Association demanded an apology. Fukuchi ran another equally acerbic editorial. The bar responded with a civil suit claiming defamation. After a contentious meeting on the question, the membership of the Tokyo Bar agreed to enter the suit in toto, with the entire membership listed as plaintiffs.

On this issue, Numa Morikazu, a leading member of the Ōmeisha and an unlicensed legal advocate, emerged as a powerful rival. Despite a history of personal animosity with Fukuchi, Numa persuaded his younger brother Takanashi Tetsushirō to act as legal defense for the *Nichi nichi*.[34] When the *Nichi nichi* countersued, Takanashi's involvement caused an immediate uproar. Takanashi was a member of the Tokyo Bar Association; could a plaintiff in a case also act as the legal representative for the opposing party? The suit worked its way through the courts, ending up at the Tokyo High Court on appeal. In the meantime, Shimamoto Nakamichi of Hokushūsha fame led a three-person group that mediated a resolution, which was possible because "there [had] been no injury or

---

32. For full coverage of the dispute, the trial, and the mediated settlement, see the series of articles in the *Hōritsu zasshi*, beginning with no. 190 (June 1881). Also, Okudaira summarizes the dispute and the case in *Nihon bengoshishi*, 342–47.

33. Huffman, *Politics of the Meiji Press*, 132.

34. Matsuo S., "Shihō shiryō," 53–56.

death" as a result of the conflict.[35] The negotiated settlement left a number of legal issues unresolved. To name a few: Could a group, or collection of groups (such as the bar associations nationwide), bring a legal action as if they were an individual? Who was the rightful defendant in a case against a newspaper, the owner or the editor? In a case involving defamation, can a party demand a public apology? Can a party to a suit be both a plaintiff and legal counsel for the defendant?[36]

Much as the negotiated settlement of the case left legal questions unresolved, it also amplified ill will toward Hoshi. The dispute paralleled growing factionalism within the Tokyo bar. In 1880, Hoshi's critics initiated a successful movement to eliminate Japan's "Queen's Counsel" system, which was abandoned in 1881, only three years after its launch.[37] The three existing counsel-designates had a choice: public or private practice. Sōma and Megata became judges in the service of the state and later turned to legal education. Hoshi shifted to the private sector, focusing on work as a legal advocate. The personal animosity growing between Numa and Hoshi as a result of these events persisted long after the dispute, even coloring their later political endeavors.

Without government affiliation, Hoshi still garnered respect and considerable earnings, but less of both. He was now even further removed from the wax-sealed civility of the Middle Temple. Practicing outside of any official role, Hoshi was subjected to the disregard that came with the "reverence for officials and contempt for the people" (*kanson minpi*) that he had delighted in inverting. At least, that is how Hoshi and his peers depicted the judicial administration with which they contended; "Hoshi made no allowances for bureaucrats who slighted him."[38] One observer

---

35. "Tokyo daigennin yori Nippōsha ni kakaru soshō no wakai," *Hōritsu zasshi*, no. 193 (28 Aug. 1881): 3.

36. In a series of articles, the *Law Journal* endeavored to answer these questions. To focus on one, the *Journal* gave its view on who should be the rightful defendant by analyzing the Newspaper Regulations of 1875, which identified the party responsible for the content of a newspaper. Reasoning from a statute targeting criminal liability, the *Journal* wrote that the editor bore responsibility for the content of a newspaper and should be a named defendant in the suit. Ibid., 1.

37. "Shihōshō fuzoku daigennin o haishi suru no ken ukagai," cited in Okudaira, *Nihon bengoshishi*, 333–34.

38. Kobayashi S., *Watakushi no atta Meiji no meihōsō monogatari*, 5.

recalled that, to Hoshi, "the officials who made up the courts were little more than a crash-course legal circle."[39] This was a reference to the abbreviated training program that the Ministry of Justice established to increase the number of judges during the 1870s. The struggle over status determined by affiliation with private practice or state service continued to color political activism by legal advocates. There was not yet a sense that the state and the private practitioner might come together on a neutral ground identified with "the public" or "public interest."

Driven from his position as counsel-designate in 1881 and rejecting a bureaucratic post, Hoshi turned to private practice—and politics—with relish. In a way that would have been inconceivable for a suit solicitor of the previous era, Hoshi parlayed his legal knowledge into profits and prestige for himself and for his clients. When he represented Gotō Shōjirō in a commercial dispute, Hoshi deployed a strategy that improved both his business and his political career. In an 1880 matter involving Gotō and Jardine Matheson over the Takashima coal mine's default on a loan from Matheson, Gotō hired Hoshi to protect his assets from foreign creditors. Hoshi negotiated a settlement, profiting handsomely.[40] The case became Hoshi's entrée into politics. The move had appeal for him: he could mingle in the ranks of former samurai and pursue legal and political activism on another level. He joined the Liberal Party, with the backing of Gotō, in 1882. When Gotō recommended that Hoshi be invited to join the Liberal Party (Jiyūtō), party president Itagaki Taisuke reportedly asked, "Isn't he all about money?"[41] The concern was that Hoshi's interest was financial gain, not the party's causes of tax reform and promotion of a constitutional polity.

Eventually, Ōi, Hoshi's colleague in the Tokyo Bar Association, formally invited Hoshi to join the Liberal Party.[42] As it turned out, Hoshi was indeed all about money: he was both wealthy and a dedicated fund-

---

39. Ibid.

40. Maeda R., *Hoshi Tōru den*, 139.

41. Ibid., 138. In contrast, Baba Tatsui is often cited as an activist who entered the Liberal Party (Jiyūtō) solely for reasons of ideological sympathies. See, for example, Nishida Chōju, "Baba Tatsui," in Meiji shiryō kenkyū renrakukai, ed., *Minken kara nashionarizumu e*.

42. Maeda R., *Hoshi Tōru den*, 143.

raiser. Due to his monthly salary from the Ministry of Justice (from 1878 to 1881) and fees from Gotō and other private clients, Hoshi was one of the wealthiest advocates in Japan by the beginning of the 1880s.[43] Among legal advocates, Hoshi was not alone in his success at profiting from private practice and political activity. When he tapped popular-rights sympathizers for a 1,000-yen contribution to a fund for the Liberal Party newspaper (a considerable sum), seven out of ten donors were legal advocates. Unsurprisingly, wealth mattered in Meiji politics, particularly for commoners. Or, as Kyu-Hyun Kim has put it, "Wealth was one of the key prerequisites for allowing one to become politically active in the parliamentarian movement."[44] After he joined the Liberal Party, Hoshi focused on the party's finances and outreach. His first measures included identifying the sources of funds in the party and making clear distinctions between personal and party monies. In radical moves for his time, Hoshi publicly disclosed the identities of contributors and rationalized the Liberal Party's bookkeeping. This was consistent with Itagaki's earlier emphasis on transparency before the public.

Hoshi also supported the party's newspaper, the *Jiyū shinbun*, with his own funds and solicited contributions from other legal advocates as well.[45] His fund-raising drive to resuscitate the Liberal Party's flagging newspaper took him to local lecture societies and associations of advocates around the country.[46] The Liberal Party appealed for support from local notables by emphasizing the party's tax reduction policy; in addition, Hoshi used the *Jiyū shinbun* to press for the long-standing goal of constitutional government and expanded political participation. In these ways, Hoshi wove together the strengths of legal advocacy, particularly the financial resources it generated, with the promise of politics. From the 1880s, the revised regulations on legal advocates that the state imagined might divide these two elements actually renewed legal-advocate dedication and interest in political activism. In Hoshi's case, the factionalism within the democratized Tokyo Bar Association brought to a head resentment over the special privileges he enjoyed in the Ministry of Justice

---

43. Ibid., 138.
44. Kim, *The Age of Visions and Arguments*, 194–95.
45. Ariizumi, *Hoshi Tōru*, 65–67. See also Maeda R., *Hoshi Tōru den*, 148.
46. Itagaki, ed., *Jiyūtōshi*, 1:721–24; Ariizumi, *Hoshi Tōru*, 75–85.

and drove him into the private sector. Legal advocates such as Hoshi and like-minded reformers in the Ministry of Justice devised new regulations, with the intention of professionalizing legal advocacy. Even though the state might have hoped that the reform regulations of 1880 would domesticate legal advocates, bringing them into a tighter orbit with the courts, in the short term, the regulations had the opposite effect. The move to eliminate associations of legal advocates, which was loosely enforced, allowed many groups to continue operating and focused legal advocates on political activism at the national level.

Legal Advocates and the Political Parties

Hoshi may have been in the vanguard in studying law abroad and earning entry into the ranks of British barristers, but he was a follower with regard to the entry of legal advocates into the ranks of Japanese party politics. The Tosa-based legal advocates and others who launched what would in 1881 become the national Liberal Party celebrated revolutionary change on the French model and recruited adherents to their vision of politically active legal practice through loosely affiliated networks of political parties, legal advocacy, law schools, legal journals, and newspapers. State supervision of bar associations tied to regional courts and the prohibition of associations of legal advocates spurred legal advocates and their associations to focus their energies.

The regulation of legal advocacy reflected a trend toward the disambiguation of legal and political organizations manifest in other countries during the late nineteenth century as well. In the 1870s, for example, the French government effectively held the political activities of *avocats* (advocates) in check by requiring that they forego "a particular [political] program in exchange for the exercise of autonomy in professional matters."[47] Ironically, Meiji government policies produced the opposite outcome. Despite Meiji government attempts to concentrate advocates in state-sanctioned, semi-autonomous bar associations, grievances concerning the court system and political restrictions outside of the courts drove legal advocates toward other ends. Many redirected their energies toward political activism. Before the regulations of 1880, advocates selected the legal

---

47. Bell, *Lawyers and Citizens*, 210–15.

associations that reflected their political and legal orientations. After 1880, the politically minded turned their energies to participation in the emergent national political parties, the Liberal Party and the Constitutional Progressive Party. Legal-advocate leadership and involvement in party politics was a nationwide phenomenon. In addition to founding political party branches and sponsoring public speeches and newspapers, associations of advocates also supported political parties by defending political activists in court.

The political transformations of the period and the publicly oriented debates by legal advocates stoked activism. Advocates remained passionate about the extension of rights that had animated them during the 1870s; in fact, they became even more engaged in the wake of the state's 1881 promise to establish a constitutional polity. That same year, legal advocate Shima Manjirō used the journal of the Ōmeisha to call on his fellow advocates to do more to influence politics in the coming constitutional order. He urged associations to abandon aimless dialogue and instead focus on the political struggles at hand. Political parties were central to the movement for rights and liberty.[48] First, advocates needed to join with like-minded individuals and "make donations to strengthen the foundation of people's rights." Second, they needed to "establish schools to cultivate politicians." And third, they needed to "form associations of the local leaders of each region and make their strength one."[49] The article concluded that there were enough schools but there was not enough work being done to form federations of associations, particularly "among the people of influence today . . . the sophisticated gentlemen . . . the legal advocates."[50] Shima considered existing associations, particularly local political associations, to be underfunded and "too vague" about their goals.[51] Shima's call was an extension of the former samurai's long quest to return to influential positions in government and an opportunity for elite commoners to gain entry to political processes. Legal advocates—former samurai and commoner alike—responded. Throughout the country during the early 1880s, legal advocates formed political

48. Obinata, *Jiyū minken undō to Rikken kaishintō.*
49. Shima, "Shinbun kisha oyobi daigennin shoshi ni tsugu," 20–21.
50. Ibid., 23.
51. Ibid., 21.

associations and pledged their allegiance to two political parties, the Liberal Party and the Constitutional Progressive Party (Rikken kaishintō).

Associations of legal advocates of the mid-1870s, such as the Hokushūsha, were already very much embedded in dense local networks of personal loyalties. It was only by the end of the 1870s that, through new systems of accounting and management, associations reorganized their business practices in ways that allowed them to operate in multiple settings so that they were less reliant on local ties. As for the political parties, shortly after their founding in the early 1880s, they underwent a similar process. With the formation of the Liberal Party in 1881, a political party had, for the first time, expanded beyond geography and personal loyalty to include participation from across the archipelago.

The Liberal Party took up several issues that garnered broad appeal from former samurai and wealthy farmers. It argued for tax reduction; the end of the unequal treaties that had reduced the ability of Japanese companies to compete with foreign ones; and the establishment of an elected assembly, which would expand participation in political affairs. The Liberal Party charter outlined the party's political objectives around the idea of a society of individuals united by law; the charter focused on rights, constitutionalism, and national unity: "(1) Our party will extend freedom, preserve rights, increase prosperity, and reform society; (2) Our party will endeavor, with all its strength, to establish a beneficent constitutional polity; and (3) Our party will cooperate in unity with those in the Japanese nation who share our goals."[52] In response to calls for membership in late 1881 and early 1882, 32 local political associations responded. These groups were a mixed bag of political associations (*seisha*), remnants of associations of legal advocates (*daigensha*), and debate and study societies. Their leadership from across the country sent letters expressing their interest in affiliating with the new national party.

Many of the local activists who submitted letters to the Liberal Party requesting affiliation were legal advocates. The readers of the letters at the party's national headquarters were likely also legal advocates. Shi-

---

52. Itagaki, ed., *Jiyūtōshi*, 2:416.

mamoto Nakamichi, the proprietor of the Tokyo Hokushūsha, occupied a position in the party's leadership. At a level below him were advocates Maejima Toyotarō and Ōi Kentarō, and, below them, advocate Nakajima Matagorō.[53] The competing political party, the Constitutional Progressive Party, counted among its leaders practicing legal advocates Hatoyama Kazuo, Ōoka Yūzō, and Kadota Shinpei.[54]

Work as a legal advocate occupied many of the leading participants in the tightly overlapping local circles of debate and study societies, political groups, newspapers, nascent local political party branches, and law schools. Although the legal work of the participants in the movement for constitutional government and the founders of the early political parties was hardly a secret, it has not been sufficiently salient in histories of the late nineteenth century. Figures receive mention not as legal advocates but, as in the case of Shimamoto Nakamichi—as Etō Shinpei's right-hand man or a Liberal Party leader. Histories of Numa Morikazu focus on his work as a government official, his role in the Ōmeisha, or his newspaper activities; yet, like Shimamoto, Numa worked as a private legal advocate and both founded and was instrumental in founding associations of legal advocates. Though historians have begun collecting data and analyzing the number of political activists engaged in private legal work during the late 1870s and early 1880s comprehensive, data has yet to be compiled. Even so, a close reading of the careers of many of these figures reveals a stint, a sideline, or a first or second career as a private legal advocate.

In the case of the Liberal Party, Hoshi worked to link the party's appeal to the concerns of the broader public through public speeches and newspapers that drew on the efforts of regional legal advocates. The broader effort included institutional reform of the party itself. At a March 1883 general assembly, Hoshi promoted rules that centralized power in party headquarters. The new rules expanded membership on the party's central committee from 10 to 30 members and required new members to have two or more sponsors to join the party. To shore up its finances, the

---

53. Except where otherwise noted, the following on the regional branches of the Liberal Party draws on Terasaki, "Jiyūtō no seiritsu."

54. Morinaga, *Nihon bengoshi retsuden*, 242.

party instituted 25-*sen* annual dues.[55] Even as Hoshi worked to expand support for the Liberal Party through a process of rationalization and transparency, he himself began to draw on the strength of the party to challenge his critics and competitors.

Into his promotion of the party, Hoshi wove elevation of the work of the private legal advocate together with the work of the party politician. In the process, the legal advocate took a position that overlapped and converged with the party activist: both authored critiques of the Meiji state grounded in legal and political theory, defended those accused of political crimes, and promoted law as a key to joining the "comity of nations" and, in turn, the foundation for national strength. Hoshi turned his energies to undermining the competing Constitutional Progressive Party, the party of his rival from the *Nichi nichi* case, Numa Morikazu. Hoshi denounced that party's members as rejects of the government's clique politics, even calling for physical attacks on Numa while criticizing the party's backers, including the Mitsubishi Company. In vigorous challenges to his political opponents, Hoshi blurred the line between the broader goals of the party, the "public interest," and his professional and private interests. Schisms in legal circles and party politics translated into action in the streets. By 1887, tensions between Hoshi and Numa ran so high that former-samurai ruffians affiliated with Hoshi and Numa provoked street fights with each other.[56]

In the end, Hoshi did not realize his goal of rationalizing administration of the Liberal Party. Private and public interest percolated together, leaching one into the other as personal, professional, and political conflicts worked themselves out among the political parties. Despite his stated efforts, Hoshi's own personal relationships and private rivalries remained animating factors in membership and party policy. Yet even as personal allegiances and struggles marked the emergence of parties in politics, broader appeals—particularly appeals to a shared interest in the establishment of a constitutional polity, a country governed by law—drew together the various regions from the bottom up.

---

55. Ariizumi, *Hoshi Tōru*, 72–73.

56. On a fight between Numa and Hoshi and their followers, see Ozaki, *The Autobiography of Ozaki Yukio*, 92–93. On this incident and ruffians in politics during the Meiji period in general, see Siniawer, *Ruffians, Yakuza, Nationalists*, 47–48.

Legal Advocates and the Building of Local Party Branches

Whether the practitioner was a former suit solicitor or a former samurai, legal advocacy was a local endeavor for most of the 1870s. By the early 1880s, things had changed. Legal advocates throughout Japan began to connect their activities to the national movement for freedom and popular rights, working through regional newspapers and national political parties. Drawing on newspaper accounts and local histories, Terasaki Osamu has shown that, in contrast to earlier political associations, which always fell short of their national aspirations, the Liberal Party was truly a national political party. The lists of members of local branches of the Liberal Party, which Terasaki uncovered in his study, show that legal advocates drove much of the local party activity in the early 1880s.[57]

At the end of the 1870s, licensed legal advocacy was an overwhelmingly urban pursuit, as was political party organization. In light of the deep connections between the Risshisha, the Hokushūsha, and party leaders such as Itagaki Taisuke and Gotō Shōjirō and their efforts to link law and politics, it is unsurprising that legal advocates constituted the majority of the leadership of the political party branches, in general, and the Tokyo branch of the Liberal Party, in particular. A half year after the establishment of the Tokyo branch in late 1881, Shimamoto Nakamichi was elected its chair. There were five other legal advocates in the branch's leadership, including Ōi Kentarō, often remembered for his involvement in a plot to meddle in domestic Korean politics. The initial urbanism of the party suggested that it was only focused on politics as theory, or elite concerns. Yet the party showed early signs of pursuing a broad base of popular support. In June 1882, rumors revealed that the party leadership was brokering an interassociational alliance with "a famous boss among the fire-fighting groups."[58] The potential merger of a political organization dominated by former-samurai legal advocates with a firefighting group was reminiscent of the strange bedfellows typical of the Edo urban scene. A newspaper reported that the boss would bring 2,000 associates—an

---

57. Terasaki, "Jiyūtō no seiritsu," 109–91.

58. On firefighters, see Kelly, "Incendiary Action: Fires and Firefighting in the Shogun's Capital," 327.

unprecedented (and somewhat unbelievable) number of members—with him in his promise to cooperate with the Liberal Party.[59] Not only would this have been an enormous influx of supporters, it would have also extended the reach of the party faithful beyond its core of wealthy farmers and former samurai elites. The public was expanding.

From 1881 to 1882, Liberal Party branches sprang up throughout the country, mostly led by legal advocates. At the branch level, associations of legal advocates that formed in defiance of the 1880 regulations served as centers for party activists. For example, on the outskirts of Tokyo, an association called the Kōtokukan (広徳館) served as the Liberal Party headquarters in the area and also sold legal services. Its charter, discovered by historian Irokawa Daikichi, included provisions on the supervision of legal cases, introductions to legal practitioners, mediation of disputes, and preparation of legal documents. Like so many other hybrid associations of the late 1870s and early 1880s, the Kōtokukan served as a material base for political activism.

Other examples illustrate how legal advocates directly contributed to the rise of political parties and political action. From the distant reaches of northern Japan, a politically active advocate sent a letter to the Tokyo headquarters of the Liberal Party announcing the formation of a Hakodate branch in December 1881. The *Chōya shinbun* reported that the legal advocate pledged to engage in party activities in Hokkaido. The following June, he joined a fellow northerner in participating in a national meeting of the party.

In Iwate, the Morioka branch of the Liberal Party had its roots in an association that opened in 1873 as a reading room for youths. In 1878, the activities of the study group and reading room took on a distinctly political cast. Four years later, the Morioka branch emerged—with legal advocate Fuse Naganari as a prominent member who presented public lectures for the group.[60] Fuse had already been elected to the prefectural assembly. His public speaking on behalf of the party, in addition to his legal practice, was emblematic of the hybrid advocate-activist career to

---

59. It is unclear how many members there were in the Tokyo branch of the Liberal Party. In 1882, the Ibaraki branch aimed to attract around 1,400 members. Terasaki, "Jiyūtō no seiritsu," 132.

60. Ibid., 113–14.

which the legal advocates of the 1870s and early 1880s aspired. A February 1881 issue of a regional newspaper described how "Prefectural Assembly Member Fuse Naganari, licensed advocate . . . was elected in a by-election and, if in the morning the assembly met, he went to court in the afternoon. If the assembly met in the afternoon, he went to court in the morning. Other assembly members accommodated his schedule, wondering which half of the combination of political advocacy (*daigi*) or legal advocacy (*daigen*) would wear him out!"[61] Fuse had realized the vision of the advocate as a voice for the hopes of the people in multiple, overlapping venues: through argument in the courtroom, through speeches in public, and through representation in electoral politics.

At the heart of the spread of political activities among advocates was the kind of horizontal organization considered anathema to Japanese politics. In addition to connecting to the national Liberal Party, local political groups created regional ties while their members also reflected the overlapping kinds of advocacy embodied in Fuse's career. As legal advocates formed the Mito branch of the Liberal Party, they were also launching local leaders onto the national political stage. In 1881, 28-year-old Seki Shinnosuke (who applied for a license as an advocate in 1882) and Aoyanagi Kyūhei (licensed as an advocate since 1876) joined seven other residents of Mito and surrounding communities to form the Ibaraki branch of the Liberal Party. In December 1881, the group selected Seki, Aoyanagi, and a third person who was not a legal advocate to serve as directors of the branch. In its charter, drafted in December 1881 or early 1882 under Seki and Aoyanagi as the legal experts in the group, the branch pledged to "protect liberty and expand the sphere of rights."[62] In 1885, Seki became the president of the government-sanctioned Mito Bar Association. He was later elected municipal representative to the Mito City Assembly and in 1890 was elected to the prefectural assembly.[63] Of the 28 legal advocates licensed in Ibaraki from 1876 to 1893, one went on to become a prefectural assembly member (Nishigaki

---

61. Osatake, *Meiji keisatsu saiban shi*, 206.

62. Terasaki, "Jiyūtō no seiritsu," 130.

63. In 1892, Seki took a seat in the Lower House of the Diet and was elected ten times in a row (until 1912). During these terms, he was affiliated with the Rikken Seiyūkai. Mito bengoshikai hensan iinkai, ed., *Mito bengoshikaishi*, 41.

Masayoshi) and others went on to become members of the Lower House of the Diet.

In Shizuoka, Maejima Toyotarō's early career illustrated a dynamic blend of legal and political activism. Before he became a leader in the Liberal Party and while he was studying for his advocacy license, Maejima organized political lectures in Shizuoka City that began in 1879 and continued into the early 1880s.[64] He funded a newspaper and in 1881, invited Itagaki and others to come to Shizuoka and discuss the establishment of a political party in the prefecture.[65] Maejima was also the founder of the political association Gakunan Seiryōsha. Later, with Murakami Magoichirō (a licensed advocate since 1878) and nonadvocate Kobayashi Kisaku, he formed a speech association, the Kakuminsha.[66] Among other activities, the group sponsored lectures that criticized the shortcomings of clique politics. The talks generated a crowd: even at 3 *sen* a head, they often attracted more than 200 listeners. The events were more popular than the moralistic lectures on self-cultivation that were presented for free by members of social reform movements during the same period. Maejima temporarily halted his political speeches following the assembly ordinance of 1880, but resurrected them later that year. In their new incarnation, the speeches were so popular that listeners overflowed halls, standing outside.[67] On temple grounds and in lecture halls, legal-advocate activists organized speeches that connected their political concerns to those of a listening public. Through encounters in these spaces with people ranging from *jinrikisha* pullers to local politicians, legal advocates made political issues matters of general interest.[68] The speech meetings emerged out of Maejima's group, the Gakunan Seiryōsha, and laid the basis for the establishment of the Gakunan Liberal Party in Shizuoka in early 1882.

Eventual legal advocate Suzuki (born Yamaoka) Ototaka joined the Gakunan Liberal Party that same year. Suzuki's employment at the time

---

64. Bengoshi Unno Shinkichi Kankō iinkai, ed., *Bengoshi Unno Shinkichi*, 9.
65. Terasaki, "Jiyūtō no seiritsu," 147.
66. Bengoshi Unno Shinkichi Kankō iinkai, ed., *Bengoshi Unno Shinkichi*, 9.
67. Ibid, 15.
68. On the demographics of audiences at speeches by political activists, see Yasumaru, *Minshū undō*.

he joined the party is unclear, but he sat for and passed the licensing exam for advocates in the latter half of 1885.[69] Of 1,468 candidates, he was one of the 44 (3 percent pass rate) who passed the exam.[70] He participated in one of the more democratic processes of Liberal Party establishment, at least in comparison to the practices of other party branches for which records remain. In the typical branch, a group of local elites convened and adopted a charter. That charter then served as the rules governing subsequent general meetings of the branch. In contrast, the Shizuoka branch announced a meeting open to the general public. At that meeting, the attendees adopted resolutions that became the rules governing the party. The first resolution stated that the party sought to "reform the state"; the second, that the party sought to establish a "constitutional polity in which debate was sacrosanct"; and the third, that the branch accepted Itagaki Taisuke as the party president—"[i]f one agreed with these three principles, then one was allowed to join the party without argument."[71] Other regional activists responded. A branch emerged in Gumma in 1879, when protagonists in the Yūgensha (有言社), a speech association that tied itself to the Liberal Party, became the Jōmō Yūshikai (上毛有志会) in 1880. The Jōmō Yūshikai became the center of the region's movement to establish a national parliament.[72]

The state responded to these political party activities with suppression. In 1882, Maejima faced a charge of lèse-majesté (injury of the emperor) for talking about society as reaching "from the Emperor above to the hungry below who live beneath bridges."[73] At the trial stemming from the incident, he received a three-year sentence and a fine of 200 yen. The advocate in the case, Arakawa Takatoshi, was particularly passionate in Maejima's defense. Arakawa was also charged with lèse-majesté for remarks he made during the trial; he received a sentence of three years and

---

69. Okudaira, *Nihon bengoshishi*, 1395.

70. Ibid., 1371. For a biography of Suzuki, see Terasaki, "Shizuoka no jiyū minkenka," 63–64. In the United States, "[i]n the period between 1870 and 1890, admission to the bar tightened noticeably": Stevens, *Law School*, 25–26.

71. Terasaki, "Jiyūtō no seiritsu," 148.

72. Hōsei daigaku daigakushi shiryōka iinkai, ed., *Hōritsu gaku no yoake to Hōsei daigaku*, 166–84.

73. Maeda R., *Hoshi Tōru den*, 169.

a fine of 90 yen.[74] Regulation and punishment of public speakers may have blocked one branch of the Liberal Party in Shizuoka; however, they failed to stifle a broader enthusiasm for the consumption of political speech.

In Hamamatsu, at the other end of Shizuoka, an alternate branch of the Liberal Party sprang up in 1882. Newspaper reports of the time indicate that legal advocate Sawada Ichirō was a leading participant in party activities and a driving force in its leadership.[75] When the Meiji government passed laws suppressing branch affiliation with a national political party, the group recharacterized its relationship with the national Liberal Party; then ended its activities in 1884.

Legal advocates drove the formation of political parties further southwest as well.[76] In Okayama, at least three advocates—Sawada Shōzō (licensed advocate from 1876), Ishiguro Hakoichirō (licensed in 1876), and Nakayama Ken joined other local leaders to establish the San'yō branch of the Liberal Party. The branch had a resounding start in 1882, with a public lecture that the *Chōya shinbun* reported as being attended by 3,500 people or more. In addition to holding regular meetings and sponsoring public speeches, the group resolved to "publish a newspaper in order to foster the principles of the party."[77] However, the San'yō branch encountered difficulties later that year when the local authorities suppressed the branch's newspaper, the *San'yō shinpō*. An internal debate followed, presumably over what course the branch should take in response to government suppression, and in the meantime, the government prosecuted members of the branch. Members were fined between 10 and 12 yen.[78] How the branch resolved these troubles is unclear. Yet, clearly, legal advocacy was a rich pool from which the Liberal Party, as well as

---

74. Ibid.

75. Terasaki, "Jiyūtō no seiritsu," 149–51. Kim, *Age of Visions and Arguments*, lists Nakano Jirozaburo, Sawada Yasushi, and Aoike Kotaro as party branch founders, 394.

76. Terasaki, "Jiyūtō no seiritsu," 162.

77. Ibid.

78. The involvement of advocates in party politics occurred elsewhere in the southwest, too. Advocate Noguchi Keiten (licensed 1877) was the vice chairman of the party branch in Shimane. Andō Tadashi (licensed 1876) was one of four directors of the branch of the Liberal Party in Kagawa. Fujino Masataka (licensed 1877) represented the Ehime branch of the Liberal Party at the national party's general meeting in 1882.

the Constitutional Progressive Party, drew local leaders and expanded political networks.

The Constitutional Progressive Party numbered legal advocates as stalwarts in its local branches as well. Legal advocate Numa Morikazu, who had established an association of advocates, the Buntensha, and stoked the *Tokyo nichi nichi* newspaper's attacks on Hoshi, played an important role in the founding of the Constitutional Progressive Party. The Ōmeisha, a Tokyo debate society with seven legal advocates in its membership, also dissolved into the party. Much like those whose associational activities overlapped with party politics in the Liberal Party, the members of the Constitutional Progressive Party exploited the complementary aspects of legal advocacy and party participation. Takanashi Tetsushirō and Matsuo Seijirō, both members of the Ōmeisha, formed an association of advocates in the early 1880s. Matsuo went on to a position of influence in the Constitutional Progressive Party and was elected chair of the state-sanctioned Tokyo Bar Association in 1886.[79] Takanashi later enjoyed a career as an illustrious orator in the Lower House of the Diet.

Membership in the Constitutional Progressive Party was less widespread than the Liberal Party, but still had a broad reach. The kind of federation building called for by Shima connected national and local legal advocates within this party as well. Maruyama Namasa, a legal advocate, party activist, and journal editor, went to Tochigi to speak to a group organized by political activist Tanaka Shōzō, in 1883.[80] Tanaka began his career with the 1878 establishment of the *Tochigi shinbun*—"one of Japan's earliest regional newspapers and a consistent advocate of popular rights"—and was also elected to the prefectural assembly.[81] When Tanaka introduced Maruyama to the audience, he described the latter as a member of the Constitutional Progressive Party, a member of the Ōmeisha, and a journalist. At the same time, he was a person interested

---

Founder of the Self-Help Society's legal research institute, Shimamoto Nakamichi, took the lead of the Liberal Party's branch in Kochi. Ibid., 167–75.

79. Matsuo S., "Shihō shiryō," 48.

80. Fukui, "Ōmeisha to shiritsu hōritsu gakkō," 26–29. Maruyama Namasa was a member of the Mito Law Hall.

81. George, "Tanaka Shōzō's Vision," 95.

in the "research and spread of knowledge about politics and law as a member" of an association called the Chūsetsusha (中節社). The Chūsetsusha combined the sale of legal services with political activism for a national assembly. Maruyama simultaneously wrote editorials for the *Tochigi shinbun* and oversaw civil and criminal cases for the Chūsetsusha.[82] Tanaka's introduction of Maruyama highlighted the various overlapping and emerging constituencies in the 1880s for newspapers, party politics, and legal services.

These constituencies came together to hear Maruyama give public speeches in late 1882 and early 1883 on what electoral politics might bring. These speeches, such as "Seijika no mirai" (The politician's future) and "Naikaku kōsenron" (Public election of the cabinet), located the politically active legal advocate at the center of party politics.[83] Writing in 1981, historian Nakamura Yūjirō repeated the claim often made by advocates themselves that, during the late 1870s and early 1880s, "one must think of law as nearly equaling politics."[84] Another historian, Fukuchi Shigetaka, has placed private legal practitioners at the vanguard of rights consciousness in Japan: "[L]egal advocates taught the people of the nation to assert their rights, and with political activists making speeches here and there the political consciousness of the people, and their ideas of rights, developed dramatically."[85] Yet such conclusions were not unanimous. Irokawa Daikichi dismissed the contributions of legal advocates to the movement for constitutional government, even as he documented the activities of politically active legal advocates.[86] This seeming contradiction emerged from Irokawa's normative reading of history, particularly the processes of law and social change. Worrisome to Irokawa was the general absence of rights claims on the part of the people as they sought to achieve political change.

Irokawa argued that the absence of law as a departure point for activism reflected competing understandings of the meaning of "law." The

---

82. Ibid.

83. Ibid.

84. Nakamura Y., "Meiji jūnendai ni okeru daigennin to Meiji hōritsu gakkō," 18.

85. Fukuchi, *Meiji shakaishi*, 42. On the advocate as part of the "enlightenment movement" in the Meiji period, see Irokawa, *Rekishika no uso to yume*, 49.

86. For Irokawa Daikichi, see Irokawa, *Jiyūminken* and *Rekishika no uso to yume*.

people had one interpretation, the state another. As Irokawa would have it, the popular understanding of law reflected a weak consciousness of legal rights as an instrument of political or social change. In the place of assertions of rights, people appealed to community norms. On the other side of the equation, the state's use of law revealed little concern with individual rights. Both characterizations reflected elements of state and society during the 1880s yet overlook important parts of the picture. Beyond Irokawa's analysis, legal advocates promoted political rights even as the nineteenth-century nation-state increased in its power and ability to ignore those rights. Yet without private legal advocates, particularly those who were politically engaged, there would not have been the widespread drafting of the people's constitutions that Irokawa studied.

The drafter of the Itsukaichi constitution, Chiba Takusaburō, could not have crafted his constitutionalism alone. His approach to government during the 1880s benefited from the translation work of legal advocates during the 1870s and emerged out of an indigenous history of domestic legal engagement. Though it is unclear whether Chiba ever worked as a legal advocate, on one occasion he did style himself a "Distinguished Professor of Japanese Law," the kind of title often used by unlicensed legal advocates to attract clients.[87] Legal advocates and their Tokugawa forebears were instrumental in putting the state's interpretation and understanding of the law before the people, not only as a process for resolving private conflict but also as a framework through which to pursue a broad agenda of change. As demonstrated, legal advocates promoted constitutionalism—law as a framework for a new kind of polity and as a basis for rights claims.

Irokawa's diminution of the importance of the role of legal advocates reflected his emphasis on the people as political amateurs in the movement for constitutional government. Irokawa's thinking was also consistent with a more general obfuscation of the centrality of legal advocates in shaping political culture in late-nineteenth-century Japan. Legal advocates complicated the Meiji state's narrative of itself as the sole force for top-down change after 1868. Private legal advocacy was incompatible with the narrative typical of early-twentieth-century histories, which

---

87. Irokawa, *The Culture of the Meiji Period*, 106–8.

focused on law as the province of elite jurists and legal scholars who trained abroad in the tradition of corresponding heroes of the European Enlightenment. Former-samurai legal advocates also fit poorly into later Marxist histories of class struggles or narratives of the people against the state. At the time, the Meiji government's political party had no need for private legal practitioners; Morinaga Eizaburō states unequivocally that "in the party of government patronage, the Teiseitō, there was not a single legal advocate."[88]

Legal advocates in opposition to the regime used political party activism to protect and extend people's rights. As legal advocates organized around rights, they also devised new social and political functions as critics of the state. The government was compelled to respond to this new tack. The 1880 revision of the criminal code that took effect in 1882 brought the legal advocate into criminal trials. With the revision, legal-advocate protagonists in the freedom and popular rights movement increasingly took positions front and center in a public legal arena: the courtroom. In February 1882, Hoshi Tōru established the Rich with Virtue Hall (Kōtokukan 厚徳官), an association of legal advocates that operated in defiance of the 1880 regulations limiting legal practitioners to sole practice. Ōi Kentarō joined Hoshi in defending members of the movement for freedom and popular rights charged with criminal offenses.[89] Hokushūsha founder Kitada Masatadashi also joined the group, which took as its aims the "cultivation of legal thought in the youth of the Liberal Party" and defense of "men of purpose and others without means who have brushes with the law."[90] The courtroom became a new venue for political theater animated by political parties. The first national performance featuring the Kōtokukan was the trial in the Fukushima Incident. Consistent with dominant narratives about the interplay between the Meiji state and society, it included an arch villain—governor Mishima Michitsune [also, Tsūyō]—and heroes—the defendants and their legal advocates.

---

88. Morinaga, *Nihon bengoshi retsuden*, 242.

89. Kokuritsu kokkai toshokan (National Diet Library), Kensei shiryōshitsu, Hoshi Tōru monjo, *Hoshi Tōru denki kōhon*, 76–3, 132–35.

90. Ibid. See also Okudaira, *Nihon bengoshishi*, 445.

The Trial in the Fukushima Incident

Legal advocates used the law to turn the tables on the government and increasingly parlayed their legal expertise into building cases against suppression of political activity. In 1883, the Liberal Party weighed the possibilities of a courtroom fight over the governor's attempts to put down the local branch of the party in Fukushima. Private legal advocates like Hoshi sought to make the court a site in which the government, rather than the political activist, was on trial. Other party leaders questioned whether legal advocates could turn the trial, as a political event, to the party's advantage. With members of the local branch in jail, should the party rally around a polarizing figure like Hoshi and vigorously combat the charges in court, or should it appeal to the government through a petition for clemency?[91] Proponents of courtroom action won out; the pursuit of a litigated solution reflected legal advocates' pull within the party.[92] The trial hinged on a central question: Did calls for overthrow of the regime in the charter of the local branch of the Liberal Party represent simply a rallying cry for government opponents or a treasonous conspiracy? The question reflected tensions between local interests and national government prerogatives.

In 1882, the centrally appointed governor of Fukushima, Mishima Michitsune, had been looking for grounds on which to suppress the local Liberal Party. In the autumn of that year, the party supplied them when it opposed the governor and his proposal to build a local road.[93] The prefectural assembly, led by Kōno Hironaka, had voted down the proposal, but Mishima advanced the plan with support from Tokyo. Opposition to the construction project intensified. In October, failing to secure an injunction from the Wakamatsu Court, opponents of road construction appealed to the Miyagi Appeals Court. When road opponents joined in a public rally, Mishima had the leaders of the rally arrested. On November 28, 1882, with opponents to construction jailed in the Fukushima

---

91. Hoshi Tōru, Ōi Kentarō, Hayashi Kazuichi, and others pushed for a courtroom battle over the incident. Ide, et al., eds., *Jiyū minken kimitsu tantei shiryōshū*, 170.

92. Ibid.

93. Standard histories of the event include Kitakōji, *Fukushima jiken monogatari* and Takahashi, *Fukushima jiyūminken undōshi*.

Kitakata police station, Liberal Party adherents joined a mob of thousands that attacked the station. The governor used the riot as further justification for acting against the local party branch. Mass arrests followed.

In December 1882, police burst into the local Liberal Party headquarters at the Hall with No Name (Mumeikan) and arrested party leaders. Those arrested included founder and chair Kōno Hironaka and branch leaders Hirashima Matsuo, Tamono Hideaki, Aizawa Yasukata, Hanaka Kyōjiro, and Sawada Seinosuke. Government informers had infiltrated the group and told the police of a charter calling for overthrow of the regime and a membership oath sealed with promises of death for those who betrayed the group's cause.[94] The defendants were charged with "a crime against the state"—treason—and tried by the Court Extraordinary in Tokyo for plotting a rebellion. The maximum penalty for the offense was death. During the trial, argument hinged on whether the defendants had committed treason by including in the charter of the party the word "overthrow" (*tenpuku*), as in calling for the "overthrow of despotic government." Also in question was the nature of this branch of the Liberal Party: Was it a secret society? Did its activities amount to a conspiracy against the Meiji state? The last article of its membership oath stated that those who revealed group secrets should take their lives by the sword. The legal defense team in the trial included Ōi Kentarō and Hoshi Tōru, backed by their group, the Kōtokukan, with Hoshi defending Kōno, Kitada Masatadashi defending Aizawa, and Ōi Kentarō defending Tamono.[95]

The trial received national media attention.[96] During the proceedings, the defendants and the defense vigorously attacked government policies and the symbol of those policies in Fukushima, the appointed governor Mishima. The press, particularly the *Jiyū* and *Chōya shinbun*, widely reported antigovernment criticism and published serialized accounts of the trial.

---

94. For reports of government informants on the Fukushima Liberal Party, see Ide, et al., eds., *Jiyū minken kimitsu tantei shiryōshū*.

95. "Oath (of the Liberal Party in Fukushima)" cited in Shimizu K., *Fukushima jiken kōtō hōin saiban iiwatashi sho*, 2–3.

96. This account of the Fukushima Incident draws on Wagatsuma, et al., *Nihon seiji saiban shiroku, Meiji*, 15–30.

The defense team sought to avoid the death penalty and presented its case over three days. It challenged the strength of the government charge in light of the paucity of physical evidence, including the absence of the original charter, which served as the basis for the claim of treason. Testimony by government informers and statements made by the defendants while in police custody enabled the court to piece together a draft of the charter consisting of five articles. Even so, the court did not have an actual copy of the charter. The first article stated that the Liberal Party sought to establish a politics of public expression and to "overthrow despotic government," the public enemy of freedom.

In arguments for the defense, Hoshi pointed out that there were many ways of achieving a change in government, and that there was no evidence that the defendants were proposing violent means to do so. Hoshi cited French law, the inspiration for Japan's Criminal Code, and argued that rebellion meant calling up soldiers and deploying troops. The defense argued that there was little indication, aside from the testimony of government informants, that the group was actually planning to overthrow the Meiji government. Indeed, Kōno and the other defendants had not made concrete plans to achieve their aims. They had not raised funds nor had they collected arms or stores in preparation for a rebellion.[97]

During the trial, Hanaka testified that earlier statements that the defendants had made about the charter under interrogation did not reflect the fullness of thought behind the document. He and other defendants further argued that what the courts had pieced together was a draft. There had been discussions of replacing the word "overthrow" with "reform" (*kairyō*), but because the party simply meant to "turn a new leaf," they left the language as it was.[98] From the stand, defendants claimed that their group "opposed despotic government worldwide"; they were not specifically plotting to overthrow the Meiji government. The defense argued that the government was pursuing the wrong charge: the defendants had not committed treason. Yes, they conceded, the defendants had clearly overstepped the laws regulating speech, but they were not traitors. Instead, they had broken laws on expression.

---

97. Nakamura K., *Hoshi Tōru*, 51–54.
98. Shimizu K., *Fukushima jiken kōtō hōin saiban iiwatashi sho*, 13.

The court was not persuaded. In his ruling, Judge Tamano Seiri found the group's calls for the "overthrow of government" treasonous. "They conspired with rebellion as their goal."[99] Tamano pointed to the evidence of the charter and the many times throughout the trial that the defense, both during the defendant's testimony and in the mouths of the legal defense team, had called for the overthrow of despotic government. Throughout interrogations the defendants stated quite clearly that they believed that the government of Japan was despotic. He also noted how the defendants had stated—under interrogation at police stations and in court—that they appealed to other members to join the party and its pledge. Hence, the court found that the aim of the party was not simply to attack "world despotism and if it was, Japan was included."[100]

The ruling found much evidence contrary to the claim made by "Hironaka and others that this was solely an instance of words without deeds."[101] Moreover, if the group simply meant to "turn a new leaf," why did members take a secret blood oath sealed with the threat of death?[102] Through careful reasoning based on the evidence of the informants, the defendants themselves, and testimony during the proceeding, the court found the plotters guilty of a conspiracy to "overthrow the state" according to Article 121 of the Criminal Code, along with other crimes, including conspiracy. A range of punishments was available to the court, including capital punishment and life imprisonment. However, without explanation, the court forewent the application of the death penalty and set Kōno's sentence at seven years in prison. The other five defendants received sentences of six years each and later received a reduction in their sentences.

Although the trial did not end in an acquittal, the courtroom proceedings stemming from the Fukushima Incident ended in a partial victory for the defendants, their defense team, and the Liberal Party. The defendants had avoided death and had abundantly criticized the state during the trial. The defense teams could rightly take credit for this outcome. And the movement for freedom and popular rights received a

---

99. Ibid., 2–3.
100. Ibid., 7.
101. Ibid., 5.
102. Ibid., 15.

boost from the attention the proceedings garnered. Accounts of the trial popularized the Liberal Party program while also centering attention on newspaper coverage of politics, valorizing the work of the legal advocate, and putting legal arguments and processes before the broader public through legal and political speech as entertainment.

The press disseminated, through newspaper reports and broadsides, the critique of power that legal advocates and their clients promoted during the trial. These newspapers and journals were often funded by the legal advocates themselves and widely circulated their ideas about rights, freedom of speech, and opposition to oppression as it had been expressed during the trial.[103] Youths, in particular, enthusiastically followed press coverage of the arguments in court.[104] Young readers eagerly awaited the *Jiyū shinbun*, greeting group recitations from its pages with "cheer[s] and applause."[105] Tokutomi Kenjirō [also Roka], fourteen at the time of the incident, recalled in his memoir, "During the outcry over the Fukushima Incident, we fought each other for the papers to read the court proceedings."[106] Lawyers who came to prominence in the early twentieth century, such as Fuse Tatsuji, wrote of how inspirational they found the generation of legal advocates active at the time of the Fukushima Incident. The newspapers had made heroes of the defendants and their legal advocates.

Neither illiteracy nor government suppression of the press effectively blocked popular interest in these avowedly political trials. Even applying the press laws of 1875, the Council of State could not keep the political arguments that advocates made in court from reaching the eyes and ears of the public. In a bid to circumvent government controls on assembly and speech, Liberal Party activist Okunomiya Kenshi performed the court proceedings from the Fukushima trial in the *kōdan* style.[107] Traditionally used for religious exegesis, the *kōdan* had evolved into a form of

103. On the centrality of the *Jiyū shinbun* to Liberal Party activism, see Matsuoka, *Jiyū shinbun o yomu.*
104. Nakamura Y., "Meiji jūnendai ni okeru daigennin to Meiji hōritsu gakkō," 4. See also Irokawa, *Rekishika no uso to yume,* 50–51.
105. Ueda, *Concealment of Politics,* 66–67.
106. Ibid., 77.
107. Ibid., 80.

popular, if at times didactic, entertainment and gave the speakers cover from government regulation. The Fukushima Incident marked a turning point toward the intensification and spread of the movement for popular rights. The press and public performance turned what began as a fight over parochial issues dominated by former samurai into a drama that highlighted national tensions.

Along with newspapers, legal advocacy had found its footing as an institutional alternative to employment within an ascendant state. It took practical form with schools, canonical texts, standardized tests, and accreditation. At the same time, it embraced high ideals of defense of rights and constitutional government. From the time of the Fukushima trial, increasingly large numbers of persons sat for the license in legal advocacy.[108] The number of advocate-hopefuls increased from 439 in 1876 to more than 1,500 in 1881 and 1882. In 1883 and 1884, over 2,000 candidates sat for the licensing exam (see chapter 2, table 1). Legal practice was no longer a disrespected pursuit operating from the shadows, but had become a force shaping the nature of politics. The appeal of advocacy—including the high ideals that legal advocates embodied in their political activism—was a feature of the early and mid-1880s, evident in the increased numbers of candidates who took the licensing exam.

Beyond the instructive elements in the contest between political party and state, the general public found the drama invigorating. This new political energy found expression in what historians later identified as the "violent incidents," episodes in which commoners, loosely affiliated with local or national political parties, reacted violently to the economic effects of government policies. With the outburst of violent, direct action in the early 1880s, the government response was increasingly severe. The Ministry of Justice learned that popularization of the opposition was an unintended consequence of the Fukushima Incident trial. The ministry came to understand that by casting the episode as a serious threat to national security, it had inadvertently drawn interest to the activists and

---

108. Veterans of the courts, such as clerks and procurators, also left government to establish associations of advocates. For example, Shibukawa Nakajirō, with Ōi Kentarō, formed the Clear Law Hall (Meihōkan 明法館) in 1883. Shibukawa quit his post as a clerk of the court and established an association in conjunction with a former procurator. Okudaira, *Nihon bengoshishi*, 462.

their trial. In the subsequent Kabasan and Chichibu Incidents of 1884, in which farmers violently protested government suppression, the ministry handled things differently. To reduce attention from the press, the state tried these later defendants on other charges, such as theft and attempted murder (rather than as traitors), and conducted the proceedings in regional criminal courts rather than in the Court Extraordinary.[109] This approach yielded more severe sentences; following the Kabasan Incident of 1884, Tominaga Masayasu and others were sentenced to death.

In response to government suppression, the conclusions that the two leading legal advocates for the defense—Hoshi and Ōi—drew from the verdict in the Fukushima trial varied dramatically. Since March of 1882, Hoshi and Ōi had shared the vice-chairmanship of the government-sanctioned Tokyo Bar Association under Chairman Hatoyama Kazuo.[110] However, they ended the Fukushima trial at odds about the efficacy of the courtroom as a site for contesting politics. The dissolution of their alliance came to represent the two main opposing views within the Liberal Party on how to advance the party project.

Hoshi came out of the trial affirmed in his conviction that persuasion and public appeals could succeed. Increasingly powerful in the party due to the use of his own finances, Hoshi remained invested in sustaining the group through advocacy in the courts and on the stump. In May 1884, he launched a newspaper, the illustrated *Jiyū no tomoshibi* (Lantern of Liberty).[111] On the masthead was a print of the British House of Parliament on the Thames. Historians have described the paper as an expression of Hoshi's interest in reconciling "wisdom with force" or "harmonizing legalism with revolutionary democracy."[112] Competing currents flowed through its pages, reflecting an eclectic editorial course. Indulging samurai nostalgia, the front page serialized political fiction by authors including Komuro Shinsuke. The paper also served as a platform for promoting gender equality. From May to June of 1884, the paper serialized *Dōhō shimai ni tsugu* (To my sisters), an essay on women's rights by activist

---

109. Tezuka, *Meijishi kenkyū zassan*, 114.
110. Maeda R., *Hoshi Tōru den*, 128.
111. Ariizumi, *Hoshi Toru*, 88.
112. From Gotō Yasu, "Meiji jūnananen no gekka shōjiken ni tsuite," cited in Ariizumi, *Hoshi Tōru*, 88.

Kishida Toshiko.[113] By 1885, the newspaper had become the third-largest daily, with a circulation of nearly 14,000—nearly half of the circulation of the leading Osaka *Asahi shinbun* and just short of the 15,000 claimed by the second-place *Yomiuri shinbun*.[114] As Hoshi shored up the Liberal Party's center, he also reached out to the general public through the *Lantern of Liberty*.

The light that seemed to shine on Hoshi did not extend to Ōi, whose client in the Fukushima trial, Tamono Hideaki, died in prison. Ōi's interest shifted away from speech, persuasion, and the slow work of political institution building. After the trial, his relationship with Hoshi began to unravel. As Hoshi focused on his publishing enterprise, Ōi began to consider violent opposition as a more effective path to political change than negotiated reform. Frustrated with the slow pace of legal processes, Ōi began to move toward the event for which he became most notorious, the 1885 plot to spark a revolution in Korea. Meanwhile, Hoshi continued to promote his vision of a polity organized around public debate and public opinion through the activities of the bar association, speeches, and engagement with national and local branches of the Liberal Party.

Hoshi Tōru and "The Limits of Politics"

In advance of a trip abroad, Itagaki, having overcome his initial suspicion of Hoshi, designated him as acting president of the party. During Itagaki's absence, Hoshi remained a relentless campaigner for financial support for the party. From September 1883 to September 1884, he traveled to Shizuoka, Saitama, Gumma, Tochigi, Chiba, Ibaraki, Osaka, and Niigata campaigning for contributions.[115] In Shizuoka, in response to calls for violent action against the government from a crowd of listeners, Hoshi urged restraint. He stated, "[T]here are two methods of political reform, peaceful and violent . . . reform by peaceful means is the most

---

113. Anderson, *A Place in Public,* 107–8. There is also a translation of the essay in Sievers, *Flowers in Salt,* 37.

114. Huffman, *Creating a Public,* 142.

115. Kokuritsu kokkai toshokan (National Diet Library), Kensei shiryōshitsu, Hoshi Tōru monjo, *Jiyū shinbun* (17 Sept. 1884) cited in *Hoshi Tōru denki kōhon,* 76–4, sect. 34.

pressing business facing our country."[116] On September 21, 1884, Hoshi gave a speech on the limits of politics, "Seiji no genkai." The speech argued that to guarantee liberalism, "the functions of the government must be restricted."[117] More than 1,000 people attended, including 34 police.[118] Most broadly, the speech was a reaction to ongoing government suppression of public speech.

Rather than attack the Meiji government directly, Hoshi discussed domestic politics by way of allegory. When he meant to say that Japan needed a parliament immediately, not simply the promise of a parliament or the establishment of a parliament without any real power, Hoshi said, "[E]ven though there is a Diet in Germany, it is only a Diet on paper."[119] And the promises to establish a duma in Russia were no less encouraging for proponents of constitutional politics than were the promises of a parliament in Japan. Hoshi was less ambiguous in his criticism of government intervention in the economy: "There are those who say it is necessary for government to promote agriculture, commerce, and industry. This view is sorely mistaken. Leave the practice of commerce to merchants; it is absolutely not something for official intervention. Official intervention yields great harm and few benefits. The same in agriculture."[120] Hoshi went on in this vein until a plainclothes policeman and uniformed patrolmen interrupted him.[121] The authorities expelled all of the listeners from the hall at around ten o'clock in the evening.

Police called Hoshi in for interrogation, but he refused on the grounds that he had an official rank. The police urged that Hoshi be arrested and tried, but the Office of the Procurator favored administrative sanction. The following morning, Hoshi sent someone in his stead to hear the decision of the authorities while he left for his next speaking engagement.

---

116. Ibid.

117. Maeda R., *Hoshi Tōru den*, 171.

118. Estimates of attendance vary. Nakamura Kikuo (*Meijiteki ningenzō*, 60) describes 1,800 in attendance; Maeda R. describes thousands (*Hoshi Tōru den*, 171).

119. The complete text of Hoshi's speech, "The Limits of Politics," appears in Maeda R., *Hoshi Tōru den*, 171–74. It is also included in Itagaki, ed., *Jiyūtōshi*, 3:725–27, and in Okudaira, *Nihon bengoshishi*, 476–79. All of these accounts draw on police records.

120. Maeda R., *Hoshi Tōru den*, 173.

121. Accounts of Hoshi's arrest include Terasaki, "Meiji 17nen"; Maeda R., *Hoshi Tōru den*, 167–89; and Okudaira, *Nihon bengoshishi*, 477–82.

The police took this as flight, caught Hoshi in a nearby town, and on the evening of September 22, 1884, arrested him for defaming a public official. On October 16, proceedings began; on December 18, the court found Hoshi guilty. The ruling read:

The defendant . . . in a political speech entitled the "Limits of Politics," in which he claimed that our politics, like the politics of Russia and Germany, is harmful and without benefit . . . went on to say that the responsibility for this lies with current officials; in other words, he defamed Sanjō, the great minister of state, and the Home, Army, Navy, Education, Agriculture, Commerce, and Industry ministers. . . . Article 141 of the Penal Code states that those who, in word or deed, defame an official are liable to more than one month or less than a year of prison and from 5- to 50-yen fines. . . . Moreover, taking into consideration Ministry of Justice circular No. 1 of 1880, Article 22, Heading 10 of the Regulations for Advocates, and Article 14, Heading 2, and Article 23, Article 24, and Article 25, the defendant shall be expelled from the registry of legal advocates. . . . Procurator Hayashi Hisa.[122]

Hoshi was sentenced to six months in prison, fined 40 yen, was disbarred, and lost the official court rank that he had been granted upon his return from England. This was for defaming, among others, Sanjō, one of the ministers responsible for his appointment as a Ministry of Justice counsel only six years earlier.

In the meantime, without Hoshi at the helm, the Liberal Party foundered in the face of challenges from above and below. While Hoshi was fighting to keep his freedom, the leadership fought over the party's future. Failure to reach its financial goals in the mid-1880s compounded intraparty differences. Dissent intensified further after Itagaki's 1883 return from travels in Europe and America. Revelations that the trip was funded by the Mitsui Company with support from the government called Itagaki's loyalties into question. In a sweeping shift, Itagaki abandoned contestation with the government in favor of cultural and economic reform that would achieve parity with Europe and the United States. He urged all political parties to support the government and to focus on "cultivating the energy" necessary to catch up with "Western civilization."[123] By

---

122. Maeda R., *Hoshi Tōru den*, 179–81.
123. Itagaki, ed., *Jiyūtōshi*, 3:654.

making this shift, Itagaki slighted the efforts made by Liberal Party stalwarts in his absence, including Hoshi. As a result, Itagaki faced criticism from within the party for "abandoning politics in favor of social reform."[124] At the same time, the intensification of popular outbreaks against the Meiji government in the name of the Liberal Party created its own challenges. The excitement of public speeches and fiery rhetoric in person and print had animated enthusiasm for reform. There was little popular interest in returning to the didacticism of self-cultivation and the focus on high culture suggested by Itagaki's civilizational turn.

While Itagaki was calling for a social and cultural transformation, the violent incidents of the early to mid-1880s called into question the future direction of the movement to extend popular rights in advance of the establishment of a constitutional polity. Direct action at Gumma, Kabasan, and Chichibu, in which farmers took up the mantle of rights activism for themselves, challenged the vision of the public entertained by legal advocates in which former samurai and their elite allies interpreted the public good. In contrast, farmer activists advanced a vision of what Andrew Barshay identified as a "communitarian public" that threatened both the government's definition of a public coterminous with the state and the former samurai's assertion of public interest as the sum of private (material) interests as proxy for the greater good.[125] In October 1884, squeezed between government and popular pressure, and against the wishes of Hoshi, the party disbanded.[126] Meanwhile, Hoshi appealed the ruling that he had defamed public officials. He lost. After settling his household affairs, he entered Niigata Prison in April 1885.

With leading Liberal Party activists in jail, including Hoshi Tōru and Maejima Toyotarō, and others (such as Itagaki) having withdrawn from politics in the face of the violent incidents, the mid-1880s was a period of transition. A new wave of violent former-samurai activism was cresting with Ōi Kentarō in the lead. While Hoshi was in jail, his former colleague and fellow legal advocate Ōi plotted an armed conspiracy to back revolutionaries on the Korean peninsula, contrary to government policy. Arrests and charges in the plot came late in 1885.

---

124. Maeda R., *Hoshi Tōru den*, 164–65.
125. Barshay, *State and Intellectual in Imperial Japan*, 7.
126. Maeda R., *Hoshi Tōru den*, 189.

Hoshi turned his time in prison into a period of reflection on his place in politics and, more broadly, the legal and political reforms that would revise Japan's place among the great powers. Hoshi's notion of the world outside Japan differed from Ōi's adventurist view or the resonant moralism that Sono and Kodama had cultivated during the 1870s. At an earlier time, "international" might have meant "opportunity" for Hoshi. Even when he came up against the inequality of the international treaties in Yokohama of the early 1870s, he had turned things around, rising to positions of power and influence in state and society. Hoshi returned to the question of the international in the mid-1880s, from the inside of his prison cell. In 1886, just ten years after his return from England and his translation of Blackstone's commentaries on English law, "international" for Hoshi meant something dramatically different. The international arena was now an almost Darwinian contest among competing nations, with survival determined by the coherence of a nation's legal and political system. European and American imperialism ran amok in Asia, Africa, and the Pacific. Hoshi's systematic study of the politics of constitutional government during his prison term reveals a shift in his thinking. Through an examination of world systems of representative government he noted that Europe and the United states were not as progressive as they proposed to be and that Japan was not as regressive as foreign narratives suggested. The book-length result of his study of theory and practice was his *Kakkoku kokkai yōran* (Overview of the national assemblies of various countries). Published in 1886, it opened with an inquiry into the theoretical basis for national assemblies. It explored the strengths and weaknesses of bicameralism; the legitimacy of the constitutional monarch; the responsibilities of a cabinet; the power of the purse; limits on the electorate; candidacy, election, terms, and salaries of parliamentarians; and proportional representation.

In its discussion of the legal structures of foreign polities, it was not an unusual work. What made the text unusual was its comprehensive and critical treatment of the practice of representative government the world over. It offered the reader a country-by-country analysis of every part of the globe. A critique of Japan's domestic politics was implicit in an encyclopedic tour of representative governments insofar as Japan, and the rest of Asia, were glaring absences: every other world region had polities that in some way reflected the public will.

In this project, what one could call Hoshi's "prison papers," he grappled with his career and his world. What the project yielded for Hoshi personally was not only an analysis of domestic politics in international context but also a sense that his earlier high esteem of the Middle Temple may have been misguided—the status hierarchy of England had seduced him. He never completely repudiated that chapter of his career, preserving the wax seal that he had received from the Temple until his death, but he began to view international and domestic politics with a more jaundiced eye.

One of the first elements in Hoshi's critical analysis of Great Britain was the right of the House of Lords to punish its own members.[127] In Great Britain, the legal system condoned preferential treatment for lords on the basis of social and political status. Differential legal treatment based on social status was an ongoing issue in a Meiji Japan that had recently invented an aristocracy, gentry, and commoners. Uniform treatment before the law was a position embraced by Hoshi's *Lantern of Liberty*.[128] As a commoner who sought social equality and personal power, this issue was dear to Hoshi. During the 1870s, members of Japan's aristocracy (*kazoku*) suspected of a crime could only be investigated after the emperor had reviewed the charges against them. They could only be punished if the emperor approved the sanctions.[129] Successive revisions of the Criminal Code eliminated preferential treatment for former samurai and aristocrats by the end of the nineteenth century.[130] By contrast, in England, members of the House of Lords accused of felonies could demand trial by their fellow lords through 1925. It was only in that year that public outrage over the acquittal of a lord who killed a person while driving drunk ended this kind of preferential treatment.[131] For Hoshi, well aware of the practice of national comparison so popular at the time, and resident in a country where unequal treaties still prevailed, Japan was ahead of its European counterparts in some areas, but behind in others.

---

127. Hoshi Tōru, *Kakkoku kokkai yōran*, 51–52.

128. Ariizumi, *Hoshi Tōru*, 89–90.

129. *Shinritsu kōryō*, sect. 1, art. 2.

130. Yet even as it was eliminated, it was extended, in some cases, to bureaucrats. Nakamura K. *The Formation of Modern Japan*, 58.

131. See Cantor, *Imagining the Law*, 105.

As Japanese legal practitioners deepened their understanding of the international context for law and political change, a monolithic "West" became less and less a model of enlightenment or an object of unquestioning emulation. An increasingly informed approach to foreign systems highlighted the inapplicability of the idea of "civilization and enlightenment," a slogan that had once animated legal advocates such as Hoshi. In his book on electoral systems, Hoshi used descriptions of parliamentary practices of other nations to simultaneously highlight Japanese progress in certain areas while critiquing the absence of constitutional government overall. By doing so, he avoided the trap of other government critics who simply advocated copying from what they imagined was a more advanced and progressive West. Hoshi's book revealed that progress, in both the East and the West, was an uneven prospect.

Out of this realization, Hoshi emerged as a more pragmatic politician. Always aware of comparative measures of status and engaged with issues of finance and strategic advantage, he became increasingly oriented toward power politics. On the eve of the establishment of the Diet, the champion of the extension of rights to the public began to shift toward a focus on the mechanisms of political power. Beginning as early as 1886 and taking full form from 1887 to 1889, Hoshi Tōru and Gotō Shōjirō organized a unity movement (*daidō danketsu undō*) that would coordinate the political associations, clubs, and parties then opposed to the government. Although the establishment of a constitutional government was imminent, three major issues remained: the lingering problem of unequal treaties, freedom of assembly and expression, and land tax reduction. Increasingly, the unity movement took strength from the idea that politics should reflect the interests of those in society—particularly their economic interests—and not simply assert the theoretical ideals of liberty and freedom.

In an earlier editorial, Shima Manjirō had argued for just the course that Hoshi and Gotō were taking. That legal advocates (and journalists) were particularly well suited to serve a reconfiguration of the "public interest" (*kōeki*).[132] For Shima, the "public interest" was the sum of the material interests of different parts of the private sector. The legal advo-

---

132. Shima, "Shinbun kisha oyobi daigennin shoshi ni tsugu," 16–23.

cates who had prepared for constitutional politics, and had even been government officials themselves, could best represent these interests. They could speak to the government on behalf of private interests in the government's own language. Since rule by law was the organizing principle of the new regime, legal advocates were the natural agents of the public interest. In fact, each segment of society should organize to promote its own interests. The agriculture and commerce sectors would promote their causes; meanwhile, the newspaper reporter and the advocate would work for the "public interest and the public good" (*kōri-kōeki*).[133] A new focus on interests did not mean rights discourses disappeared. A preface to an 1883 review of advocates, the *Daigennin hyōbanki*, articulated a vision of the profession's place in a constitutional polity: "A member of parliament works to realize the rights and freedoms of the people [as a collectivity]; the legal advocate works to protect the rights and freedoms of the individual."[134] The advocate-politician could do both. Finding the common ground between overlapping sectarian interests and the greater good was the challenge for those seeking a unified front from which to shape government policy.

In this context, Hoshi turned to a new strategy to fracture the Meiji oligarchs' grip on the political agenda. In its reworked form, public interest emerged as the sum of private, material interest and was the realm of the legal advocate, the newspaper reporter, and the politician. The charge of the bureaucrat lay elsewhere: in advancing the national interest in the international sphere. In the late 1880s, Hoshi targeted the Meiji leadership for weakness in this area. The government had not revised the unequal treaties and, thus, had failed to defend the national interest. His instrument was an anonymous memorial to the emperor on the question of treaty revision. To appease foreign critics of Japanese justice, a faction within the government, led by Inoue Kaoru, had proposed the inclusion of foreigners as judges in Japanese courts. Hoshi saw this as an opening for embarrassing the government, yet it appeared he might not have an opportunity to exploit it. On December 25, 1887, under the Peace Preservation Ordinance of that year, he was banned from Tokyo and its

133. Ibid., 17.
134. Adachi J., *Daigennin hyōbanki*, preface.

environs for a period of three years for his leadership of the unity movement. At some remove from the political center, and using the anonymous memorial as his genre of choice, Hoshi leaked some of the treaty revision proposals under consideration, including the proposals to include foreign judges on Japanese courts and to give favorable treatment to foreign capital in the sale of mining and other rights. The memorial used strong language to condemn even the government's consideration of allowing foreigners to sit on Japanese courts.[135] In order to expand the document's political appeal, Hoshi and fellow drafter Ozaki Yukio also included tax relief and freedom of expression and assembly as targets for reform. Hoshi achieved the desired effect; the memorial became something of a cause célèbre.

The storm of reaction was furious. Opponents to the inclusion of foreign judges in Japanese courts ranged from conservative Tani Kanjō, who objected on nationalist grounds, to foreign legal adviser Boissonade, who thought the revisions were less favorable than the terms of the extant treaties. Strong objections came from legal advocates and their bar associations. The Tokyo bar joined the unity movement in opposition to the proposal. The movement argued that the employment of foreign judges would amount to the surrender of Japanese sovereignty. In a season of social events intended to convince foreign diplomats of Japanese civility, the Tokyo bar censured the Meiji regime for avoiding hard choices on legal reform in favor of "danc[ing] its way into the hearts of foreigners with fancy balls."[136] The potency of the memorial was evident in the government's subsequent efforts to suppress it. When the drafters circulated copies among colleagues, the government convicted the drafters on charges of "secret publishing." Even well after the proposal was no longer being considered, the government tried to prosecute students at Waseda University for circulating copies of the memorial.[137]

Government officials backed down from the proposal to include foreign judges in Japanese tribunals. Hoshi's role in the revelations was discovered, and on July 3, 1888, he was sentenced to a year and ten months

---

135. Irokawa, Gabe, Makihara, et al., *Meiji kenpakusho shūsei.*
136. Matsuo S., "Shihō shiryō," 50–51.
137. Ibid.

in jail for revealing state secrets.[138] In a general amnesty on February 11, 1889, the anniversary of the mythic first crowning of a Japanese emperor, Hoshi was released from prison and received a pardon for his earlier conviction for slandering an official. In March 1889, he was restored to good standing at the Tokyo bar. Yet during his absence, the movement for unity had collapsed; it had become rudderless with the entry of its leader, Gotō Shōjirō, into government as minister of communications. Among members, a division emerged over whether the movement should identify itself as a political or nonpolitical organization. Also, events had dampened enthusiasm for one of the causes uniting its members across the political spectrum: an attempt on Foreign Minister Okuma Shigenobu's life suspended negotiations for treaty revision, removing that issue from focus. Hoshi subsequently embarked on a trip to Europe and the United States and, upon his return, initiated a renewed program of political-party building.

As Hoshi spent his time on the eve of the establishment of a constitutional polity exploring representative government in practice and rebuilding political coalitions, Ōi Kentarō was engaged in an even more spirited return to the roots of the liberal tradition. Earlier in his career—in 1876 under the supervision of Mitsukuri Rinshō—Ōi had translated the laws governing the French parliament and prefectural assemblies for the Ministry of Education. In a sense, he had already completed his own study of the structures of parliamentarianism. In Ōi's writings of the late 1880s, one sees a return to the first principles of the freedom and popular rights movement; in particular, the quest for liberty. As Hoshi increasingly became an adept acolyte of the place of material interests in the pursuit of political power, Ōi reaffirmed the pursuit of liberty as a key element in the métier of the legal advocate. In his 1889 *Jiyū ryakuron* (Short treatise on liberty), one can see Ōi merge the strains of the professional interest of the legal advocate with an interested political public seeking "public debate and public opinion."[139] Ōi insisted that Japan must institute "rule by both the Prince and the People—in other words, free

---

138. While he was in prison, Hoshi's wife brought him books from his library, at times ordering additional books from a vendor in the United States. Nakamura K., *Hoshi Tōru*, 76–77.

139. Ōi, *Jiyū ryakuron*, 4.

politics."[140] A primary characteristic of free politics was that laws would apply to all people uniformly, a "normalized" law for "every person of every kind throughout the entire nation."[141] For Ōi, the idea of the political public and the rule of law were integrally linked. He demanded that the state fulfill its promise of equality before the law, a promise that was frequently undermined by actual practice and status distinctions.

Ōi's call for an inclusive politics diverged from the organization of elites pursued by Gotō and Hoshi in the unity movement. Ōi demanded that the government "listen to the opinions and assertions of the people—in other words, persons of every kind and every region."[142] These were strong words in 1889, on the eve of the first session of the Diet, in which voting laws limited the electorate to approximately 1 percent (all male) of the population, primarily through requirements of minimum tax payments. Ōi called for a political space where the people would decide laws through debate, "a public opinion polity (*kōron seitai*), a representative polity (*daigi seitai*), and a free polity (*jiyū seitai*)."[143] Establishment of a genuine "constitutional polity" (*rikken seitai*) offered the most promise for the opening of this kind of space. As Hoshi increasingly turned toward a politics grounded in material interests, Ōi emphasized a different tack. Even with markedly different visions of politics, their careers and political activism emerged out of the rich history of their legal advocacy.

Political activists who also worked as legal advocates are not new to narratives of the freedom and popular rights movement. Yet, they have figured minimally in scholarship that has clearly identified the government as the "superego" of Meiji politics, and its "id" as the people and their practices of folk festivals and reenactments of peasant uprisings.[144] Advocates and their associations positioned themselves as the mediating

---

140. Ibid. Historians have identified Ōi, variously, as a creature of the radical wing of the freedom and popular rights movement, a proponent of populist politics, a nationalist, and a militarist (see Hirano, *Ōi Kentarō*, 1–7). One must add to this, Ōi the parliamentarian. Ōi, *Furansu shūhō shūkai sanji shūchō*.

141. Ōi, *Jiyū ryakuron*, 5.

142. Ibid.

143. Ibid.

144. The terminology here is mine. For a historiography, see Gluck, "The People in History."

force in the politics of the period, operating in the interstices of the protest-and-suppression dialectic from 1874 to the mid-1880s. They decried both "despotic government" and traditions of violent protest, suggesting instead that government officials and the people come together in a space of public debate governed by rationality. This was a self-serving move on their part: they offered themselves as the agenda setters and mediators of this space. At the same time, the leaders of the political parties increasingly identified with moneyed interests over the course of the 1880s and into the 1890s.

Hoshi spoke of the limits on politics during the 1880s; these were more than just limits borne of government suppression of speech and assembly. Limits on politics also stemmed from significant absences and presences during the 1880s. Absent was a parliament in which a national politician could legitimately ply his trade, although the government had promised to convene such an assembly at the end of the decade. Present were three political parties that were not just competitors but mutually hostile enemies (the Imperial Rule Party, the Constitutional Progressive Party, and the Liberal Party). Without a state-sanctioned national space within which to debate issues, and with fierce battles over who might dominate the ballot in 1890, the parties were in a state of constant conflict. With Itagaki on sabbatical and Hoshi Tōru tied down, the people, unwilling to remain spectators, pushed their way into the ring.

Broad political engagement across the entire archipelago was new to the Meiji period. Audiences at public speech meetings, members of new political parties, readers of legal journals, spectators in trials, apprentices in associations of legal advocates, readers of newspapers, and members of political associations, just to name a few, came together to engage in the common cause of public speech and public opinion. At its root, the cause consisted of two aspects: it was an assertion of the legitimacy of the act of freely coming together, and it was also a demand that the state sanction such acts (and the spaces in which they were committed), both at the local level and in a nationally elected assembly. At the intersection of politics and the public, legal advocates and their associations campaigned for public debate and public opinion while also combining professional concerns with appeals to general and narrow interests. At the same time, through associations of advocates, and then the transformation of these associations into political party branches and private schools of law, advocates identified new "publics." As self-appointed interpreters of public interests, associations of legal advocates directly challenged government dominance in political action on matters both public and private. Political activism over the course of the late 1870s and 1880s—activism that was often led by legal advocates or those whom they had trained—made this challenge possible.

CHAPTER 5

Working Within the State: Institutionalization of Interest and the Making of a Profession

From the 1890s, legal-advocate politicians turned their attention to the work of winning power in the representative government established by the Meiji Constitution. During the previous decade and a half, they had derived political leverage from opposition to the regime in power, a primary source of their self-identification. Legal advocates increasingly paired the term "in the field" (*zaiya*)—a reference to their position outside government or official circles—with the term "legal circles" (*hōsō*). There was irony in this linguistic move, a move aimed at strengthening the distinction between legal advocates and judges and procurators. In fact, legal–advocate politicians began to shed their outsider status and move into official positions of power and influence. In the process, they distinguished themselves in their new positions by dismissing and criticizing other legal practitioners, including notaries and legal scriveners on the side of private practice, as well as judges and procurators serving the state. Rights language remained important, yet the focus increasingly shifted to shoring up the power of the profession. By 1890, legal advocates worked to gain seats in an elected assembly, which would make them part of the constitutional system for which they had campaigned since 1874. Heading into the first Diet election, legal-advocate candidates claimed that they were best equipped to make national policy. After the election, legal-advocate politicians used their disproportionate strength in the Diet to pass a lawyer's law in 1893 that changed the name of their profession but had little effect on the nature of its practice. In 1897, lawyers established a national association, the Japan Lawyers' Association (Nihon bengoshi kyōkai).

These were triumphs from the perspective of the profession. The creation of a new occupation through Diet legislation marked the first time that any occupational group had driven the legislative process in the Diet for its own ends. Yet this was not a Whiggish history. Ultimately, the legal advocates' instrumental approach to law signaled a gradual shift toward accommodation with the state. The end of the nineteenth century meant the end of unified activism on what, for a time, had been progressive causes. The establishment of a constitutional polity, legal defense for the criminally accused, dissemination of legal knowledge, the right to assembly, the right to free speech—all of these had been achieved to a degree that satisfied many former samurai and elite commoner activists. An original rationale for the movement identified extending rights to the people in the interest of strengthening the nation. By the end of the century, Japan's international strength was evident in its 1895 victory in the Sino-Japanese War, suggesting that if people's rights contributed to national strength, then perhaps the correct balance had already been achieved. Even so, there emerged legal advocates such as Yamazaki Kesaya and Fuse Tatsuji who sustained the more progressive ideals of the freedom and popular rights project well into the twentieth century.

During the 1870s, overlapping pursuits had come together in associations of legal advocates that combined educative, commercial, and political functions. However, the 1880 regulations on legal advocacy drove legal advocates to specialize; similar institutionalization occurred in other fields at the same time. As print media commercialized and industrialized, the fluid movement of legal advocates working for or financing newspapers and journals while also dabbling in private practice diminished. Many newspapers and journals opened (and closed) during the three decades after 1868, some after runs of only a month or two. The same was true for associations of legal advocates providing legal education. After years of intense competition among associations of legal advocates that combined educative and commercial functions during the 1870s and early 1880s, some associations focused on education and converted into freestanding, private law schools. During the 1880s, the law schools reorganized or merged with other institutions and, from the 1890s, became private colleges and universities. Kodama's shift from bar to bench during the 1870s was an indicator of the fluidity with which advocates moved between roles in law at that time. By the 1890s, training in the law faculty at the Imperial University meant that the Ministry of Justice drew few judges from the ranks of private legal practitioners.

Among legal-advocate associations that had disbanded as a result of the 1880 regulations on advocates, some redirected their energies to political party activism and the press, and others focused on an educative mission. Private law schools were a new form of organization; many emerged out of associations of legal advocates that had previously combined political, commercial, and educational functions—a differentiation of function that coincided with domestic and international trends. The training of legal advocates shifted from apprenticeship to full-time, formal schooling. This was roughly contemporaneous with a similar process in the United States, in which legal training became increasingly institutionalized.[1] In Japan, private legal practitioners were instrumental in the establishment of schools of law and in educating an emergent generation in legal and political thought.

During the early 1880s, a vibrant market in legal education meant that schools competed with one another to attract students. Amano Ikuo has described how "for those able and ambitious young people from families of low status or income . . . [the legal advocate's] licensing exam offered a shortcut to success."[2] The time in formal schooling was shorter than the normal course, which allowed the student to pay his way through apprenticeship. Under the revised regulations of 1880, political party adherents opened formal schools somewhat severed from private practice but still sympathetic to party aims. Even though "success" increasingly meant financial stability, schools remained concerned with political party affiliation through the first years of the 1880s. Schools also divided along lines of affinity with foreign practice traditions. Proponents of French practices included three former students of Boissonade who founded the Meiji Law School: Kishimoto Tatsuo, Yashiro Misao, and Miyagi Kōzō.[3]

---

1. Stevens, *Law School*, 21–22.
2. Amano, *Education and Examination in Modern Japan*, 108.
3. Politicians who attended the Meiji Law School (later Meiji University) included: a prefectural assembly member and Diet representative from Tochigi; a prefectural assembly member and Diet representative from Nagano; a Nara City assemblyman; a Tokyo city assemblyman; a Tokyo city and prefectural assemblyman; and a Tokyo city assemblyman and Diet representative. Yui, "Meiji hōritsugakkō sotsugyōsei no chōsa,"

An Anglo-American group consisting of those who had studied in the United States, led by Sōma Nagatane, Tajiri Inajirō, and Megata Tanetarō, founded the Senshū School in 1880. Competing private law schools began consolidating and, by 1885, the leading private schools came to be known as the "big five" law schools: Senshū, Meiji, Tokyo Senmon School (est. 1880), Tokyo Law School (est. 1881), and the English Law School (est. 1885). Senshū later became Senshū University; Meiji became Meiji University; and Tokyo Senmon School became Waseda University. Ōoka Ikuzō, who went on to become the Speaker of the lower house of the Diet, was involved with associations of legal advocates that first became the Tokyo Law School and then emerged as Hōsei University. Chūō University had its roots in the English Law School (Igirisu hōritsu gakkō).[4] Some students at these schools sought to become legal advocates, others aimed to win appointment in the civil bureaucracy or become entrepreneurs. At the time, the founders of these schools could not have known that they would become mainstays of private higher education during the twentieth century; when first established, law schools struggled in a competitive environment to maintain their existence.

Law emerged from the nineteenth century at the heart of higher education: an unexpected consequence of the Meiji legal reforms was the transformation of law into a new way of organizing knowledge. The activism of legal advocates had deepened and accelerated this process with their establishment of law schools in the private sector. The Ministry of Justice raced to keep pace. Following the French model, it established schools serving the Education and Justice ministries to train bureaucrats for each ministry. Ministry of Education officials argued that there were "schools for the army, schools for the navy . . . a school to train judges within the Ministry of Justice," thus, there should also be a school for the other branches of government.[5] In 1886, the Law Faculty of the Imperial University (Teikoku daigaku) was created out of the various ministerial programs with the express purpose of training a broad range of civil

---

4. Masumi, *Nihon seitōshi ron*, 2:49–54.

5. Civil servants were divided into those who were "appointed by memorial (. . . on recommendation of the highest minister or the ministers as a group, *sōnin*)" and those who were "appointed by seal (. . . by a minister holding delegated authority, *hannin*)." Spaulding, *Imperial Japan's Higher Civil Service Examinations*, 19.

servants.[6] The graduates of this new program had an advantage over others pursuing work in the expanding bureaucracy. Where usual practice required that the candidate for appointment as a higher bureaucrat (*sōnin*) take an exam and then perform work during a probationary period, graduates of the Imperial University were exempt from the exam requirement. Education at the new university increasingly served as a key to plum bureaucratic posts and a guarantee of a secure and prestigious career.

In 1885, the Ministry of Education, interested in expanding its brief, made private law schools an offer. If they submitted to regulation of their curriculum, their students would receive treatment similar to that enjoyed by graduates of the Imperial University.[7] The five leading private law schools accepted. They reduced control over their curriculum in exchange for special treatment of their graduates in the application process for judicial and regular bureaucratic appointments. For their students, these law schools had gained privileged access to bureaucratic careers available to the graduates of public schools; for themselves, they had gained a competitive edge over other private schools. These schools then attracted the top-ranked students, who sought the status and smoothed career path that came with the government's seal of approval. This advantage allowed the private law schools to solidify their financial base.

By sacrificing a degree of control over their curriculum to the ministry, hybrid institutions that had operated out of corner buildings selling legal services and training legal apprentices ended the churning process that had closed the doors of so many law schools and law associations during the 1870s and early 1880s. Over time, the law schools that cooperated with the state became full-fledged private universities. How was one to read the apparent readiness to surrender a kind of academic freedom for access to the bureaucracy? Was this an economic imperative or a Herbert Spencerian effort to help students succeed in the world (*risshin shusse*)? Masumi Junnosuke has answered that "schools that had once trained legal advocates, newspaper reporters, and local elites were now integrated into the state bureaucracy."[8] At the same time that the major law schools were working to gain preferential treatment for their graduates in civil service

---

6. The following draws on Masumi, *Nihon seitōshi ron*, 2:49–54.
7. Ibid.
8. Ibid., 50.

exams, public intellectuals were campaigning for a stronger distinction between scholarship and politics. In 1883, Fukuzawa Yukichi argued that "politics must be separate from learning."[9] When the work of partisan politics or the bureaucracy impinged on private education, this was to the detriment of all. Because academics in publicly controlled schools had to answer to state authorities, they could not challenge state positions or policies. Because the cultivation of knowledge benefited the nation, any threat to independent intellectual inquiry threatened both the academic endeavor and the nation itself. For Fukuzawa, the pursuit of truth was hampered by government intervention and by party politics. He criticized the politicization of learning in the hands of the state while at the same time complaining that political party affiliation disrupted independent inquiry: yes, people should learn about politics, but not every person need become a politician.

The rapprochement between the schools and the state that Fukuzawa lamented rendered ambiguous a space of learning that had previously been a bastion of opposition to state prerogatives. During the 1870s and the early 1880s, for former samurai seeking a way back into politics, law was political theory in the service of criticism of the state. By the middle of the 1880s, legal education was reoriented toward preprofessionalism and support for state-centered bureaucratic structures.

Where associations of legal advocates had filled multiple functions at the same time, the formalization of legal education after 1880 made the leading private schools increasingly attentive to competition among their graduates. Previously, associations of legal advocates had recruited apprentices, connected them to political activism, and drawn on collateral commercial activity to support political activism by the Liberal Party and the Constitutional Progressive Party and their associated newspapers. The law schools of the late 1880s and early 1890s, however, increasingly focused on student success on exams. In contrast to hybrid associations of legal advocates that served as a platform for criticism of the early Meiji state, private school administrators exercised self-restraint on matters of academic freedom and government criticism.

---

9. The essay "Gakumon to seiji o bunri subeshi" (Politics Must Be Separate from Learning) was serialized in the *Jiji shinpō* from 20 Jan. to 5 Feb. 1883. The essay appeared as "Gakumon no dokuritsu," in Fukuzawa, *Fukuzawa zenshū*.

Ironically, faculty at the public universities were less reticent. They were more likely to profess ideas that were anathema to the emergent, imperial orthodoxy of the early twentieth century. The most notorious conflicts over suppression of academic freedom had their roots at public universities such as Tokyo Imperial University, an institution under the direct supervision of the Ministry of Education. At the turn of the century, Minobe Tatsukichi began lecturing on his version of the separation of powers (the organ theory) at the Imperial University.[10] This was a philosophy that later outraged imperial nationalists. Meanwhile, the quest for occupational advance had quieted other students and scholars of law. Where private legal education had before stood outside of the state apparatus, by the middle to late 1880s, it had reoriented itself toward careerism and a concentration on testing that came to typify Japanese higher education.

A Broader Platform for a Narrower Politics

On the eve of the opening of the Diet, legal advocates continued to build on the roles in which they had cast themselves: protectors of rights and spokesmen for public opinion. In addition, they increasingly identified themselves as policy makers. Legal advocates remained a force in the political parties as they entered the era of constitutional politics. And it was the state-sanctioned "public" space of the Diet in which they continued their battles with the Meiji oligarchs over issues of speech and questions of legal reform, including a proposed revision of the criminal code. With the advent of the national Diet, the notion of "the public" had changed again—the putative purpose of the new national body was to identify and serve something called the "public interest." How long would people acquiesce to the notion that an electorate consisting of a narrow sliver of the population should speak for everyone else? "The public" remained a site of ongoing contestation. With a few exceptions, the legal advocates who had historically focused on "extending rights" increasingly turned their attention to achieving power in the emergent framework of constitutional government.

---

10. Miller, *Minobe Tatsukichi*.

Within the electorate, voters were persuaded that those who identi-fied "law" as their primary occupation could be effective political repre-sentatives. In the first parliamentary election, legal advocates won seats in numbers disproportionate to the licensed legal advocates' numbers among candidates. In the 1890 election, 22 practitioners of the law tied with local bureaucrats for the third position in the new body, after large landowners and manufacturer/merchants. In the Diet election of 1892, legal advocates also took their place among large landowners, manufac-turer/merchants, and local politicians.[11] Landowners and entrepreneurs may have outnumbered legal advocates, both in society and in the Diet, yet legal advocates capitalized on their claims of familiarity with parlia-mentary bodies to achieve electoral and policy success. Many of the advocates who had themselves campaigned for the establishment of a national assembly prevailed in the parliamentary elections. Hayashi Ka-zuichi was one such politician who trumpeted his legal qualifications while campaigning for a seat.[12] A former chair of the Tokyo Bar Associa-tion, he ran in Tokyo in the election of 1892. Licensed as a legal advocate in 1879, Hayashi had aided Itagaki Taisuke in the organization and promotion of the Liberal Party. He then switched to the Constitutional Progressive Party and won the endorsement of party leaders, including legal advocate Hatoyama Kazuo. The *Kaishin shinbun* promoted Hayashi, citing his qualifications as both a legal advocate who "champions rights and washes away false charges" and a "proponent of a constitutional polity and an opponent of the evils of clique politics."[13] And though "the rural gentry class" and "commercial and professional middle class" dominated the occupational groups represented in the 300-member Diet, private

---

11. The source also notes that "there are those who have multiple occupations; for example, a commercial farmer who is also a company employee, or a lawyer who is also an assemblyman in a prefectural or municipal assembly. In these cases, the primary oc-cupation is listed." "Shinsenkyo shūgiin giin zokuseki oyobi shokugyō betsu," *Hōritsu zasshi*, no. 934 (10 Mar. 1894): 1044–45.

12. Kusaka, ed., *Nihon bengoshi kōhyōden*.

13. Hayashi Kazuichi suisensha (Hatoyama Kazuo, Tsunoda Shinpei, Tokyo-fu Daijū ku senkyonin Yūshisha Ichidō), "Hayashi Kazuichikun no ryaku rireki," *Kaishin shinbun, furoku*, no. 2696 (9 Feb. 1892): 3. Hatoyama Kazuo was a lawyer-politician in the Constitutional Progressive Party, as was Tsunoda Shinpei, who was formerly a member of the House of Representatives. See Terasaki, "Jiyūtō no seiritsu," 140.

legal practitioners enjoyed disproportionate influence.[14] Hoshi Tōru became Speaker of the House in 1891 and was followed in this position by other legal advocates/lawyers, including Hatoyama Kazuo, who was elected to the Diet in 1894 and took the Speaker's chair in 1896, and Ōoka Ikuzō, elected in 1890 (Speaker from December 1911 to March 1914).

By the end of the 1880s, the draw of electoral politics and the increasingly formal processes of registration and mandatory association in regional bar associations reduced the possibilities for self-invention that had characterized the early years of legal advocacy. During the transition from Edo to Meiji in the 1870s and early 1880s, legal advocates practiced in an environment of remarkable fluidity. In the early 1870s, women could practice law and an inexperienced former samurai could gain prominence litigating a major private dispute. All of this became less and less possible. Gone was the fluidity that Sono Tel experienced when, in the early 1870s, she embarked on her legal career. The push for licensing and certification had foreclosed possibilities for female legal advocates. By the 1890s, a woman practicing private law had become unthinkable; in 1893, Sono was back in Japan receiving support and encomiums from foreign travelers for a planned girls' school.[15] Her project had "enlisted the sympathy of the nobility." Accounts describe an opening ceremony for her school attended by financier and industrialist Shibusawa Eiichi. The project of educating and cultivating good wives and wise mothers in support of state goals corresponded to Sono's subsequent educative efforts. Moreover, the social conservatism of her Confucian-Christian piety readily reconciled with the resurgent Confucian conservatism of the 1890s.

As systems for employing those trained at home and abroad were first developing, male legal practitioners, particularly those with a samurai pedigree, faced few barriers to moving from private practice into the highest ranks of officialdom. Out of private practice since 1874, Kodama had risen within the courts. He took a seat on Japan's high court, the Great Court of Cassation (Daishinin), in October 1890. From there, he sat in judgment of his former partner Naka Sadakatsu, from his days of private legal practice in the Mitani case. Naka, now a judge, came

---

14. Mason, *Japan's First General Election,* 197.
15. Gordon, E., *"Clear Round!,"* 197–98.

before Kodama's court on charges of bribery. Kodama did not recuse himself from the Naka proceedings and was instrumental in Naka's 1894 acquittal. Immediately thereafter, Kodama resigned from the high court citing debilitating illness. The illness could not have been too debilitating. Immediately following his resignation, and despite his professed infirmity, an imperial appointment to the House of Peers returned him to state service until his death in 1916 at 71 years of age. From humble beginnings in private practice, Kodama had reached the pinnacles of officialdom in the judicial branch and was then appointed to the representative branch of the Meiji government.

By the 1890s, private legal practice had largely distanced itself from Edo-era ignominy, and practitioners had set similarly high goals. For former samurai, it was less necessary to justify taking up the occupation of legal advocacy. This shift can be credited, in part, to Shimamoto Nakamichi, a pioneer in improving the acceptability and relevance of legal advocacy. In 1892, as the Diet debated the reform of rules governing legal practice and political activism, Shimamoto died. He had been a fervent promoter of the extension of rights in a samurai tradition of moral stature and leadership, serving as an editor of the *Jiyū shinbun* and remaining active in Liberal Party activism until his death at the age of 65. In the process of elevating the status of private legal practice, Shimamoto and other former-samurai practitioners had made the terms for entry into the occupation increasingly rigid. Gone were the days when a commoner could receive funds for study abroad, become a barrister at government expense, and then receive a tailor-made government sinecure upon his return, as Hoshi had. The final stages of the careers of Sono, Shimamoto, Kodama, and Hoshi revealed the differing possibilities for private legal practitioners as they entered the 1890s.

These divergent figures succeeded in the new social and political hierarchies because, with the exception of Sono, they had a hand in creating them. In the case of Sono, her femininity and her enthusiasm for public leadership eventually found reconciliation in the realm of education. Sono, who had benefited from the liberalization of legal practice in the early 1870s, returned to Japan to found a school that would reinforce the very social hierarchies from which she had fled. As noted earlier, Sono's school complemented the national project of cultivating good wives and wise mothers, and her shift to education reflected her ambivalence about private legal practice. As she put it, profiting from conflict among others was wrong.

Kodama, who had grudgingly entered private legal practice when denied the bureaucratic posting he desired, had become a stalwart of the new order as a judge and then a peer. Shimamoto had become an establishment figure in the Liberal Party. Hoshi was an ambassador. Each climbed the rungs of incipient professional hierarchies and enjoyed the rewards of long service. Each had abandoned the oppositional posture typical of their earlier careers. These career shifts were not simply born of age. They were, with a few exceptions, typical of the broader contours of the profession as it emerged during the 1890s.

Even as they eased their oppositional posture, legal advocates continued their campaign to convince the public that private practitioners were best suited to elective office and that other legal practitioners, such as legal notaries and scriveners, were not. They focused particularly on fellow voters who met the 15-yen annual tax and residence requirements. In this, legal advocates sought to extend Shimamoto's work by promoting the legal advocate as a moral exemplar fit for representative office. Private practice had come a long way since the time of the shadowy work of the Edo-era suit solicitor. Still, legal advocates running for election faced the challenge of association with the old and discredited Tokugawa tradition of suit solicitors and suit inns.

In order to make distinctions between themselves and other personnel active in the courts who had little training, advocates used speeches, newspaper editorials, and policy proposals. They denigrated both judges and procurators on one side and scriveners, conveyancers, and lay practitioners on the other. Yet things had been changing dramatically since the 1870s, when holdovers from the earlier era with little training were numerically dominant. By 1890, the legal sphere was crowded with more established institutions and agents. In an 1890 article in the *Legal Journal*, legal advocate Shōbashi Isshō wrote that the number of people who claimed expert knowledge of the law rivaled the "stars in the sky."[16] Both public and private law schools figured prominently in the major cities. Bar

---

16. Shōbashi Isshō, "Kōsei shōsho sanbyaku dainin no riki to narazaru koto o nozomu," *Hōritsu zasshi*, no. 794 (18 Feb. 1890): 3.

associations brought together legal advocates in every prefecture. Despite regulations prohibiting joint practice, licensed (and unlicensed) legal advocates operated out of law offices nearly everywhere. Legal journals enjoyed national distribution. All of these new agents and institutions claimed a hand in legal reform and, often, electoral politics.

Consolidation of gains that associations of advocates had made in the 1870s and 1880s—including the establishment of a uniform national test, adoption of codes of ethics in the bar associations, and seats won in electoral bodies—elevated the social status of legal advocates generally. These gains by legal advocates also generated competition with other private legal practitioners. In contrast to the rights claims and high ideals that dominated during the mid-1870s, the politics of the nascent profession increasingly focused on inequalities with judges and procurators that arose in the course of the advocate's work, the kind of inequalities that Hoshi Tōru had confronted in his attempt to improve advocates' stature before the licensing reforms of 1876 and 1880. These inequalities were redressed, in part, through negotiations between regional bar associations and the courts over "special treatment" for legal advocates. In response to long-standing complaints about the scheduling of court appearances, the Tokyo Bar Association successfully requested that the High Court and the Tokyo Court of Appeals "give a legal advocate at least five days notice before calling him to court" and that any summons distinguish between morning and afternoon sessions.[17] The bar also requested that space be set aside for their members' *jinrikisha* on the grounds of courthouses and that the system of submitting one's name card to enter and exit the courts be abolished. Response to these requests varied, but for the most part they were granted. By 1887, advocates were permitted to ride within the gates of many courts in *jinrikisha*, although the High Court rejected the Tokyo Bar Association's request for parking, due to a lack of space.[18] Whereas these kinds of petty grievances had also been a feature of previous activism on the part of associations of legal advocates, they increasingly occupied the center of concerns that focused more on status than rights or legal standing.

---

17. Art. 1 and 2 of 28 May 1886, "Seigan dōnen rokugatsu tsuitachi Daishinin shirei," in Okudaira, *Nihon bengoshishi*, 492–96.

18. Ibid., 494.

Legal advocates also had complaints stemming from their sense of disrespect at the hands of the judicial administration. A revision of the courtroom layout had equalized the physical position of parties to adversarial disputes, placing the advocate alongside the parties represented. In criminal cases, legal advocates had found it to their disadvantage to face both judges and public prosecutors from below—a spatial relationship typical of courtrooms in civil law countries, but one that they felt indicated low regard reminiscent of the Edo era. This sense of low regard extended to other areas as well. Under the Courts Organization Law of 1890, those who had served as judges or procurators could receive licenses as legal advocates without an examination. Meanwhile, a person who had worked solely as a legal advocate but had ceased practicing, even for a day, would immediately lose his privilege to practice and be required to retake the licensing exam. At the time, the *Law Journal* called this an expression of "partial respect, partial contempt for legal advocates."[19] On the one hand, the law was favorable in that it removed from the bench judges whom legal advocates viewed as unqualified and ill-disposed toward progressive legal regimes. These were often judges who took their positions when qualifications for judicial appointments were less stringent and when private legal practitioners were treated more arbitrarily. Legal advocates argued that many of these judges were not up to the task of administering justice in the new court system. On the other hand, legal advocates noted how "weeding out" (*tōta*) the judiciary might transplant poorly qualified and conservative judges into their own ranks. Also, those who cherished the days of a politically active legal advocacy worried that judges-turned-advocates would further diminish enthusiasm among private legal practitioners for political activism. Personal and policy differences may have divided political parties backed by legal advocates, but legal advocates were united in opposition to government suppression of their engagement with politics. The objections came to nothing. Under the Itō Hirobumi cabinet in 1893, fiscal austerity measures consolidated the bench. Judges and procurators resigned and entered the ranks of private law practice rather than face unemployment.[20]

---

19. "Daigennin shiken shikaku no seigen," *Hōritsu zasshi*, no. 797 (3 Mar. 1890): 23.
20. "Hanji-kenji no tōta," *Hōritsu zasshi*, no. 922 (10 Sept. 1893): 535–36.

Even though judges and procurators could easily become legal advocates, the reverse was not true. In 1890, a proposal for correcting this inequality appeared in the *Law Journal*. The proposal suggested that the state first give graduates of certified law schools a new status: *daigenshi*, or "gentlemen" who plead on behalf of others, as opposed to the *daigennin*, or "people" who plead on behalf of others. Second, it proposed that the Ministry of Justice should select judges and procurators from the ranks of the *daigenshi*.[21] One part of the measure would have been redundant. Advocates had already taken to calling themselves "gentleman advocates" (*daigenshi* 代言士) or "scholar advocates" (*daigenshi* 代言師) to distinguish themselves from unlicensed lay-practitioners masquerading as licensed legal advocates (*menkyo daigennin*).[22] The Ministry of Justice was cold to the idea and rejected it. By the end of the 1890s, the newly formed national association of lawyers reacted by calling for an increase in hiring judges from among the ranks of legal advocates in order to unify the bench and the bar (*hōsō ichigen*), an unfulfilled item on the agenda into the twenty-first century.

Legal advocates struggled to change the terms of "partial respect, partial contempt" they faced in their interactions with the Ministry of Justice. In criticizing conveyancers (later, notaries), legal advocates commented that the "notary perform[ed] administrative functions under the supervision of the public officials," while legal advocates operated independently.[23] Government officials could not intrude into the "private practice" of the legal advocate in the way that officials supervised the notary, who was "a so-called public functionary and as such, a quasi-bureaucrat [*junkanri*]."[24] Where during the 1870s and 1880s the political efforts of the legal advocate had focused on a broad notion of the public sphere, the politics of the profession had gradually narrowed his focus. With this narrowing came new attention to the private side of the public-private divide. Legal practitioners began to yield the "public" to the government, associating the term with officialdom and administrative

---

21. "Kiji: Daigenshiken," *Hōritsu zasshi,* no. 793 (13 Feb. 1890): 27–28.

22. Yokohama bengoshikai, ed., *Yokohama bengoshikaishi,* 1:23.

23. Hōma Koji, "Kōshōnin no shikaku ni tsuite no mondō ni kotau," *Hōritsu zasshi,* no. 747 (18 June 1889): 595–96.

24. Ibid.

control. The incipient profession increasingly focused on the task of client advocacy in and out of the courtroom.

Separating Gold from Gravel

From 1890 to 1893, legal advocates campaigned in the newly established Diet for a law that would regulate their practice and change the name of "legal advocacy" itself. In the decades since 1872, the term "legal advocate" (*daigennin*) had become colored by association with unlicensed practitioners who engaged in unethical legal practices (*sanbyaku daigennin*). Advocates abandoned efforts to recast their occupation out of the old system and instead began campaigning for a new name for their occupation. The term "lawyer" (*bengoshi*) had appeal, being completely untainted by the unsavory elements tied to the *daigennin* tradition. This marked a shift toward the emergence of the lawyer in Japanese history, as legal advocates began to rally around increasing professionalization, including the adoption of a new name for private legal practice. Law schools also backed legislation that would require more training to amplify the distinction between licensed legal advocates or lawyers and unlicensed pettifoggers. As one observer noted in an 1890 discussion of the five leading law schools, highly trained legal advocates among private legal practitioners at large were simply "gold mixed in with the gravel."[25]

Professionalization implied the creation of a fiefdom in which legal advocate/lawyers would govern themselves. Harsh criticism of notaries and lay practitioners was part of the legal advocate's strategy to discount competitors in the eyes of judges and clients. It was also part of the argument for why legal advocates were worthy of autonomy and others were not. In an article penned by a legal advocate entitled "Notarized Documents as a Tool of Pettifoggers," the author sardonically wrote that he had "a deep trust in all of the notaries across the nation."[26] Unlicensed practitioners, he argued, posed a threat to the unknowing consumer of legal services. Such practitioners "manipulated the notaries and, having won their trust, rode unlearned and ignorant little

---

25. Shōbashi Isshō, "Godai hōritsu gakkō no seigan," *Hōritsu zasshi*, no. 799 (13 Mar. 1890): 4.
26. Shōbashi, "Kōsei shōsho sanbyaku dainin no riki," 3.

people" to court.[27] Once in court, lay practitioners made false claims, sometimes with documents validated by notaries. During the transformation from legal advocate to lawyer in 1893, proponents of the new status singled out the unethical and unlicensed legal advocates in their ranks for misconduct and greed. Such claims echoed criticisms of the early 1880s about legal advocates who "fired up the plaintiff with groundless claims . . . and then lost" cases and "submitted complete lies as legal briefs."[28] There was also a concern that, even if the profession changed its name from "advocate to lawyer," exploitative practices would continue.[29] The answer was an invocation of ethics that would elevate lawyers above other practitioners; hence, the call from among supporters that a lawyers law would "wash clean the bad practices of the society of legal advocates."[30] The question of establishing an ethical occupation continued to dog private practitioners. An improved code of ethics would justify an extension of greater powers of self-regulation and control to the prefectural bar associations; this was another iteration in ongoing calls for reform of legal advocates in the interest of improving status.

Another, even more radical, proposal surfaced during the Diet's debate over a lawyers law—the proposal would have led to the elimination of notaries and scriveners.[31] Critics argued that the documents certified by "law's little helpers" received little weight in the courts because of weak oversight; thus, the notarial occupation should be scrapped and transferred to public officials.[32] In response to frequent claims of fraud, and the fact that judges could "freely dismiss the authenticity of notarized documents," one proposal suggested locating the notaries in the municipal offices of local government. Analysts urged closer supervision or an outright government takeover of the work of the notary.

Similar criticisms plagued legal scriveners. Speaking at an anniversary meeting of the successors to legal scriveners, High Court Judge

---

27. Ibid.

28. "Bengoshi no taigū," *Hōritsu zasshi*, no. 923 (25 Sept. 1893): 569–70.

29. Ibid.

30. "Kiji: Daigenshiken," 26.

31. "Shasetsu: Kōshōnin hitsuyō no teido," *Hōritsu zasshi*, no. 911 (25 Mar. 1893): 121–25.

32. Shōbashi, "Kōsei shosho sanbyaku dainin no riki," 4.

(and, later, legal historian) Osatake Takeki wrote that of the three private legal occupations—legal advocates, notaries, and scriveners—the scriveners had "fallen behind" in comparison to legal advocates.[33] In the eyes of their legal-advocate critics, legal scriveners had not developed ethical, licensing, and training appurtenances necessary for forward progress. He went on to say that "the relationship between the [legal advocate] and the scrivener is like that between the doctor and the pharmacist. . . . Like doctors, [the legal advocate] can make a diagnosis, but leave the adjustment of the medicine to the pharmacist—the scrivener is like the pharmacist."[34] And, as in the medical analogy, the doctor—like the lawyer or legal advocate—had come to occupy a position superior to the pharmacist by the end of the nineteenth century. Local regulations reflected anxiety about scriveners that echoed anxieties about the suit solicitors of the Edo era.[35] Kōchi prefecture required that scriveners register with the local police in order to exclude scriveners who "posed a potential threat to public peace and morals."[36] There were also stipulations prohibiting scriveners from "intervening in any aspect of legal suits including solicitation of representation, barratry, supervision, mediation, and introduction" of legal business.[37] Nor could the scrivener allow the use of his address or place of business as an office for legal advocacy.[38] The scrivener was to certify documents at fixed prices that were clearly indicated within his place of business and to identify himself as the preparer of the documents that he produced.[39] In the legal advocate's telling, notaries and scriveners were the true inheritors of the ills of the suit solicitor, not legal advocates.

---

33. Osatake, "Shihōshoshihō kaisei jicchi, sanshūnen kinengō," cited in *Nihon shihōshoshishi*, 2.

34. Ibid., 8.

35. A 1904 ordinance in Toyama Prefecture constrained scriveners who sought to open multiple branches by requiring that they receive permission from the local police bureau for each office that they proposed to open. Toyama kenrei dai 82 gō, Article 2, cited in Nihon shihōshoshikai rengōkai, ed., *Nihon shihōshoshishi*, 268.

36. Kōchi kenrei dai 51 gō, art. 4, sect. 2, cited in Nihon shihōshoshikai rengōkai, ed., *Nihon shihōshoshishi*, 272.

37. Art. 5 in ibid.

38. Art. 7 in ibid.

39. Arts. 10, 11, and 13 in ibid.

Scriveners, in a practice that echoed the Edo era, operated out of tea-houses known as "registry teahouses."[40] Because of the length of time necessary to prepare documents for a trial, the client would arrive early in the morning and, over the course of the day, purchase food from the proprietor. These enterprises profited from the rental of seat cushions as well.[41] Lawyers argued that in these earthen-floored establishments, "the evil of private conspiracies found roots, close to the dirt."[42] Here, the image evoked was one of the scrivener and the client, huddled on a dirt floor, conspiring to defraud someone in a civil suit.

By the 1890s, the image of the scrivener in the dirt contrasted sharply with the legal advocate's self-presentation as the hero of the people. As part of the ongoing project of regulating legal practice, legal scholars and others backed the Ministry of Justice in the submission of a new law for legal advocacy. Diet debates began December 1890. On December 4, Minister of Justice Yamada Akiyoshi proposed to the House of Peers a new law governing legal practice.[43] His statement revealed that advocates had successfully linked private practice with the defense of people's rights: "It is not within the ability of the judge in the court alone to protect the body, and the rights, of the people of the nation."[44] The ministry had come to agree with Machida Iwajirō's earlier contention that the adversarial process and defense of rights by private legal practitioners would yield truth and justice. In its proposal for a new law, the government envisioned a highly differentiated legal profession in which licensing fees and bonds would qualify practitioners to argue court cases at different levels within the judiciary.[45] In addition, a lawyer would register with the bar association and pay a bond to argue in the High Court and lower courts. The bond would be forfeit if, in the eyes of the court, the lawyer acted unethically or failed to follow court procedure. The amounts were 250 yen, 150 yen, and 100 yen.[46] The government proposal elicited immediate criti-

---

40. Nihon shihōshoshikai rengōkai, ed., *Nihon shihōshoshishi*, 255–56.
41. Ibid.
42. Shōbashi, "Kōsei shōsho sanbyaku dainin no riki," 4.
43. Nihon daigaku, ed., *Yamada Akiyoshiden*.
44. From the records of the House of Peers, cited in Okudaira, *Nihon bengoshishi*, 591–92.
45. Art. 8, "Bengoshi hōan," cited in Okudaira, *Nihon bengoshishi*, 595.
46. Art. 10 in ibid.

cism from bar associations, particularly those in Tokyo and Osaka.[47] Fierce opposition to the bonds and fees from lawyer-politicians doomed the initial proposal, which was resubmitted to the Diet in 1891. Again, it provoked condemnation from state-sanctioned bar associations, particularly the Tokyo bar, and again foundered in the face of opposition from lawyer-politicians.[48]

In February 1892, the government submitted a revised version of the law to the House of Representatives. At the time, the Speaker of the House was Hoshi Tōru. He appointed a special committee to consider the bill, one that included such leading legal-advocate politicians as Hatoyama Kazuo, Motoda Hajime, and Ōoka Ikuzō.[49] Draft legislation from this committee eliminated the high licensing fees and bonds. However, issues remained that held up the proposal in conference between the two houses. These issues included whether lawyers should be required to post a bond at all and how to define the boundaries of a lawyer's practice. Another point of contention was whether or not a lawyer's work should be limited to the courtroom.[50] Standing up in court was prestigious, yet transactional work was profitable, too.

There were also calls—couched in terms of "culling legal advocates"— for reevaluating the qualifications of advocates who had been licensed under the 1876 and 1880 regulations.[51] Even with prestigious legal advocates as sponsors, the torrent of other legislation accompanying the opening of the session delayed passage of the measure. The Diet passed the Lawyers Law on February 25, 1893.[52]

The Lawyers Law and accompanying regulations promulgated by the Ministry of Justice were primarily a superficial change. They did not dramatically alter the power relationship between legal practitioners and

---

47. Tōkyō bengoshikai hyakunenshi hensan kankō tokubetsu iinkai, ed., *Tokyo bengoshikai hyakunenshi*, 111–16.

48. Okudaira, *Nihon bengoshishi*, 604–6.

49. Ibid., 606.

50. "Bengoshi hōan, shōhō ichibu shikō hōan, saibansho koseihō kaiseian no zenjutsu ikan," *Hōritsu zasshi*, no. 909 (25 Feb. 1893): 411–13.

51. Ibid., 412.

52. Art. 60, "Hōritsu dai7gō, Bengoshi hō, Fusoku." "If, within 60 days of the implementation of this law, current advocates request registration as lawyers, they will become lawyers without need for examination." In Okudaira, *Nihon bengoshishi*, 616.

their counterparts in the Ministry of Justice except in the area of lawyer discipline. The law further codified the existing practice, that a lawyer must be "an adult male Japanese subject" who had passed an examination administered according to the regulations of the Ministry of Justice.[53] The law also included provisions for "those with status as judges and procurators" to become lawyers, as well as graduates of the imperial universities and the earlier legal-training institutes of the Ministry of Justice.[54] There was also a measure that precluded lawyers who had been registered for fewer than three years from arguing before the Great Court of Cassation (a limitation overturned in 1900, following intense lobbying from the Japan Lawyers' Association). Lawyers enthusiastically welcomed one positive departure from past practices: a provision for due process in cases where lawyers were disciplined.[55] At the time of the promulgation of the law, the Ministry of Justice issued a circular requiring that lawyers and other legal practitioners appearing in court wear a uniform. For lawyers, the uniform included a black moiré hat with black brocade and a black smock with a white arabesque around the neck and shoulders.[56] The Lawyers Law changed the name of legal advocates and required that they wear a uniform; for historians, the law marked another turning point toward the modern lawyer, free from some of the ambiguities of earlier periods.

Increasingly, the lawyer spoke less and less for an inchoate public and more and more for a client's specific interests. In contrast to path breakers such as Shimamoto and Hoshi, who sought to transcend or transform social bonds and change the polity through legal practice, former bureaucrats came to the fore within the emergent private legal profession. After graduating from the Imperial University in 1890, Hara Yoshimichi worked in the Department of Mines in the Agriculture and Commerce Ministry and, after the passage of the Lawyers Law, became a lawyer in

---

53. "Hōritsu dai7gō, Bengoshi hō," in Okudaira, *Nihon bengoshishi*, 610–16.
54. Ibid.
55. Ibid., art. 32: "In matters where a lawyer is to be sanctioned, a Court of Sanction must be opened in the court of appeals that has jurisdiction."
56. Judges wore the same smock, with the arabesque in purple thread, red for the procurators. The court reporter wore a plain smock with a green arabesque on the collar. "Bengoshi no shokufuku," *Hōritsu zasshi,* no. 912 (Apr. 1893): 185. See also Okudaira, *Nihon bengoshishi*, 616–19.

1893. Hara went on to become a founding member of the Japan Lawyers' Association and the Imperial Lawyers' Association. Drawing on connections and expertise that he had developed in government service, he later cultivated such clients as the Mitsui Company, Mitsubishi Bank, and other leading corporations.[57] By the end of the 1890s, the fluidity that allowed legal practice to offer gender, career, or status mobility to oneself (Sono, Kodama, Hoshi) or political mobility to others (Shimamoto) had dissipated. Although professionalism did not preclude political activism, the ambiguities of legal practice under the Tokugawa, the open opportunities of the 1870s, and then the intense activism of the 1880s yielded to increasing accommodation to the prerogatives of the state and the nation.

The Profession and Rapprochement with the State

In terms of professional politics, 1890 marked the beginning of a period of intense organization. Following the establishment of the Diet, there was a turn-of-the-century boom in the formation of new professional associations.[58] These groups formed in the welter of the "political fever" then gripping Japan.[59] Much like lawyers, medical doctors sought to turn education and specialization into professional and commercial advantage by making distinctions between licensed and unlicensed practitioners.[60] And just as associations of lawyers had influenced the draft Lawyers Law, the turn-of-the-century Greater Japan Doctors' Association responded to state efforts to regulate their occupation. The doctors aimed to block government control of the practice of medicine proposed as a "doctors association law," which would have established government-dominated associations of doctors in each prefecture. Doctors organized

---

57. Hara, *Bengoshi seikatsu no kaikō*, 4–5. Hara recalled that "working in the Commerce and Industry Bureau of the Ministry of Agriculture and Commerce benefited me greatly." Ibid., 7. See ibid., 313–18 on how Mitsui became one of Hara's clients.

58. The boom began in the mid-1890s and continued into the 1910s. See Muramatsu, et al. *Sengo Nihon no atsuryoku dantai*, 56–68. For an exploration of the structural challenges to interest representation that emerged in Japan at the end of the nineteenth century, see Pekkanen, *Japan's Dual Civil Society*.

59. On political fevers, see Gluck, *Japan's Modern Myths*, 22–23.

60. Masuda, *Oisharon*.

a group called the Anti–Doctors' Association League in 1898.[61] As for voluntary associations in other branches of legal practice, judges and procurators organized the Association of Legal Circles (Hōsō kyōkai 法曹協会) in 1891. In 1908, the group incorporated. It was not until 1927 that legal scriveners organized a voluntary, national association, the Japan Federation of Scriveners.[62]

In 1897, the Japan Lawyers' Association (Nihon bengoshi kyōkai) institutionalized the interests of lawyers in a national professional association. Lawyer Hanai Takuzō complained that even after the passage of the Lawyers Law of 1893, lawyers still ranked below judges and procurators in legal circles. Specifically, he claimed that in "many of the other civilized nations," lawyers had won positions of influence as political leaders and that in Japan, "they must not tolerate being at the bottom of the legal system."[63] Instead, they must "look to legislation, look to politics, look to interaction with others, and look to the practical arts" to advance within legal circles.[64] Accordingly, in June 1896, lawyer Hatoyama Kazuo convened an organizational meeting in Tokyo of nearly 100 lawyers and called for the establishment of a national association that would promote the interests of private legal practitioners. A subsequent meeting in February 1897 attracted more than 200 lawyers. The association was established in June 1897.[65] The leadership was a who's who of the Tokyo legal profession. It included the leading legal lights of the past, present, and future (with the notable exclusion of Hoshi Tōru, who had alienated his fellow lawyers with his brashness). There were political activists of the late nineteenth century, including lawyer Nakajima Matagorō and jurist-turned-lawyer and founder of Meiji Law School, Kishimoto Tatsuo. Then there were those who would come to prominence in the twentieth century, including lawyer-advocates for the establishment of a jury system, Hara Yoshimichi and Egi Chū [also Makoto]. The charter of the association promoted ethics and offered to reform the legal system: in particular, the civil and commercial codes. In this new, national associa-

---

61. Iwanami, ed., *Ishikai hōan hantai shimatsu.*
62. Nihon shihōshoshikai rengōkai, ed., *Nihon shihōshoshishi,* 440.
63. Hanai, "Bengoshi no seiryoku, chii, taigū," 54–61.
64. Ibid.
65. Ibid.

tion, lawyers came together to advance a range of issues that they had promoted both individually and through association with political parties, debate societies, and law associations since the first years of Meiji rule. Noteworthy, too, was the sense that associations in society formed a foundation of national strength that had emerged out of adherence to legal reform. The Japan Lawyers' Association pledged to help Japan "hold its own against the countries of the world and to realize the glory of the rule of law."[66] In this statement, one sees the leaders of the profession at the end of the 1890s hearkening back to the 1870s and the powerful sense of Japan's subordinate place among the great powers at that time, a position that remained salient in the face of the unequal treaties that still prevailed.

So, too, remained the tenuousness of the spaces out of which groups in society might form in opposition to the state. During the 1870s and 1880s, speech, association, and legal advocacy lacked guarantees of a site in which to operate without intervention by the Meiji government. The state extended its oversight of organizations in the public sphere with the 1898 Civil Code's terms governing the regulation of "corporate persons in the public interest" (*kōeki hōjin*).[67] Considering the government's predilection for setting the terms for the "public good" (*kōeki*) in other areas, it is no surprise that it also did so with regard to the regulation of incorporated voluntary associations. Article 34 of the civil code identified two kinds of "corporate persons in the public interest": "incorporated associations" (*shadan hōjin*) and "incorporated foundations" (*zaidan hōjin*). In theory, incorporated associations were designated as membership organizations, the activities of which focused on member activities. Incorporated foundations acted in the public interest through a high level of capitalization. The code defined the public good as "the objective of worship, religion, charity, education, arts and crafts, and other activities for public interest, and not for profit." Associations received status as a "corporate person" upon receiving permission from the "relevant [government] agency."

---

66. "Nihon bengoshi kyōkai no ninmu," *Nihon bengoshi kyōkai rokuji* 1, no. 1 (1897): 30–31.
67. Matsuo H., *Minpō no taikei: Shiminhō no kiso*. For the laws in practice, see Moriizumi, *Kōeki hōjin hanrei kenkyū*.

The Japan Lawyers' Association formed a year before the promulgation of the civil code but did not seek state imprimatur for its activities. Even when it became an option, the Japan Lawyers' Association forewent incorporating in the public interest (*kōeki hōjin*); instead, it remained outside the purview of a "relevant ministry," which, in its case, would have been the Ministry of Justice. Incorporation, and thereby submission to oversight by the ministry, would have opened the association to meddlesome intervention by bureaucrats. Instead, lawyers promoted self-regulation through the groups that were monitored by the ministry, the prefectural bar associations. Just a decade or two before, activists had focused on "rights" as protections for an incipient public sphere. In the newly institutionalized political realm at the turn of the twentieth century, in which voluntary associations representing commercial and professional interests proliferated, a new term reflected the concerns of these groups: self-rule, or autonomy (*jichi*).[68] The shift in language did not signal that the contest over the right to expression and assembly had been won. Rather, the mainstream of private legal activism had changed course.

Private legal practitioners now operated within an increasingly diverse public sphere. No longer under attack from the state, voluntary associations worked within a new frame of constitutional politics to promote their aims. To do so effectively, the Japan Lawyers' Association wove together its national leadership with its local membership. Annual meetings and the publication of an association journal tied the metropolitan lawyers of Tokyo to their counterparts in the rest of the country. The monthly journal of the association, entitled *Nihon bengoshi kyōkai rokuji*, examined legal issues and disseminated resolutions of the association as part of a broader engagement in policy making. In addition to articles on legal policy, the journal published feature articles on the activities of regional bar associations, poetry contributed by members, and accounts of member trips abroad. Much like the *Law Journal* and other legal journals of the 1870s, the journal also addressed controversial issues such as the forced resignation of a Japanese judge from an imperial court in

---

68. For an examination of the legal profession and the issue of autonomy, see Daini Tokyo bengoshikai, ed., *Bengoshi jichi no kenkyū*. For a rumination on autonomy (*jichi*) in it broadest sense(s), see Ishida, *Jichi*.

Taiwan.[69] Thus, the association remained active as a commentator on issues like the judge's forced resignation, yet it did not marshal the kind of nationwide activism that had connected legal advocates to the people in earlier decades. Instead, it had defined autonomy as the regulation of the profession's administrative affairs. The profession should be allowed to examine, license, and disbar its members—according to the association— based on an independent system of professional ethics. This marked a shift away from the political activism of the 1870s and 1880s that had focused on the idea of personal autonomy or the autonomy of a voluntary association that could be exercised freely. Increasingly, the association's activism played out on the pages of its journal, in the halls of the Diet, and on committees of relevant ministries, not in the streets, in public lecture halls, or in the pages of the popular press.

The establishment of the Diet was central to this shift. The Diet had emerged as the premier venue for contesting legal and political questions. Through its journal and resolutions, the Japan Lawyers' Association backed the call for lawyer leadership of parliamentary politics that continued the project launched by legal advocates. Commenting on the Diet, the association stated that it had the power to "affect the rights and responsibilities of the subjects of the empire."[70] Yet, "[l]ooking at the 300 members of our parliament, many have not yet experienced the study of law, thus legislators blindly oppose or support much of the legislation that is proposed."[71] Therefore, it "welcomed" the efforts of the more than 40 lawyers among its members, including Hatoyama Kazuo, Motoda Hajime, and Hanai Takuzō, who were elected to the national Diet in 1899.

In addition to becoming a force in electoral politics disproportionate to their numbers in society, lawyers took positions as heads of ministries and other political appointments. In the administration of 1898, lawyers occupied the positions of vice minister in the Home Ministry, the

---

69. At a time of increasing ideological tension during the 1930s, the question of autonomy took on crisis tones that echoed earlier calls for the protection of rights. In a 1930 work, socialist lawyer Fuse Tatsuji called for an examination of "every issue, first of all, from the perspective of autonomy (*jichi*) including morality, politics, law, and economics." Fuse, *Jichi kenkyū kōwa*, 2.

70. "Bengoshi to daigishi," *Nihon bengoshi kyōkai rokuji* 2, no. 6 (1898): 84.

71. Ibid., 77, 84.

Ministry of Justice, and the Ministry of Foreign Affairs. A lawyer also held the governorship of Osaka, and lawyers occupied other leading bureaucratic positions.[72] This was a marked change from the 1870s, when Nakajima Matagorō repudiated a fellow former samurai who offered him work in the Ministry of Foreign Affairs, stating that he would not become "a slave to bureaucratic authority."[73] This same Nakajima took the post of vice minister of foreign affairs in 1898. Hoshi also received a high appointment in 1896, as ambassador to the United States. While serving in that post, he called in vain for the Japanese government to authorize naval obstruction of the U.S. annexation of Hawai'i in 1898. His observation of the U.S. seizure of an independent kingdom furthered his education in international power politics, an education begun in the Yokohama tariff bureau and refined in his critical analysis of representative governments in his writing in 1886. The annexation of Hawai'i, a kingdom that had once been a signatory to unequal treaties with Japan, signaled a dramatic turn in the balance of power in the Pacific. The kinds of questions that had occupied Hoshi since the 1860s again came to the fore. As ambassador, he directly confronted the international conditions that had lent urgency to the Meiji state's legal reforms. Although on the verge of abrogation when he was ambassador, the unequal treaties were in the background as the United States expanded its presence in the Pacific. At the same time, Hoshi confronted these geopolitical changes from a new position of influence at home, which he had achieved by dint of his own labor.

Other private practitioners joined Hoshi in moving from the opposition to positions within new structures of power and authority. Lawyers entered the good graces of the state as they worked on behalf of Japan's large corporations and participated in the Diet. At the same time, bureaucrats left government posts and joined the ranks of lawyers. Criminal convictions arising from political crimes were not obstacles to coming in from the "field." Activists who had been convicted in the 1877 Risshisha plot to back Saigō's army, legal advocates among them, became cabinet ministers; Kataoka, Ōe, and Takeuchi enjoyed careers in the Diet.[74] These changes signaled that the fledgling profession was mov-

72. Okudaira, *Nihon bengoshishi*, 774.
73. Machida, ed., *Tokyo daigennin retsuden*, 40.
74. Morinaga, *Saiban jiyū minken jidai*.

ing away from its predisposition to check and critique government, and had moved toward a rapprochement. Members (and founders) of the Japan Lawyers' Association made accommodations that enabled them to work with the Ministry of Justice. Instead of a focus on the political practices of opposition, the association pursued compromise to navigate the ambiguous space between its own political and professional ideals and state power. The constitutional politics of the 1890s was no longer a politics of embattled heroes staring down Meiji officials. Instead, the opposition was increasingly diversified and no longer looking in from the outside.

This new context favored a new kind of lawyer-activist. Many of these emerged from the ranks of the Japan Lawyers' Association, including Egi Chū, Hara Yoshimichi, and Hanai Takuzō. All three figured largely in the history of early-twentieth-century politics, particularly Hara, a successful proponent of the jury (instituted in 1928), a minister of justice (1927–29), and chair of the Privy Council (1940–44). Lawyers remained connected to the mainstream political parties, the Kenseitō, and the Seiyūkai. Through relationships with parties at the local and national levels, lawyers promoted an agenda of legal reform. Yet, even as they did so, they contended with the other institutions of imperial politics. The Ministry of Justice bureaucracy, the Privy Council, and the House of Peers emerged as the leading foils of the Japan Lawyers' Association.

In its first decades, battles with the Ministry of Justice often frustrated the association; despite this, conflict with the ministry taught leading lawyers how to mobilize allies and how to negotiate positions on policy among members of the national association. Revision of the criminal code, an issue the association took up shortly after its founding, reflected the tenor of the times. Proposals for revision included the suggestion of a return to the Chinese-influenced temporary codes that had been in effect during the first years of Meiji rule. In its journal, the association called this "the greatest problem facing the people of the nation today."[75] Once again, rights language came to the fore: "The problem of human rights of the people remained, particularly infringements of human rights

---

75. Nagashima, "Keihō kaisei to jinken mondai," 39.

(*jinken*) related to liberty."[76] The debate was still a lively one. Despite efforts in the lower house to undo controls on speech and assembly, a member of the House of Peers labeled them a "necessity." According to the association's journal, however, there had been calls "on a number of occasions, by members of the House of Representatives, to abolish laws of control, ranging from newspaper ordinances suppressing freedom of expression to ordinances that controlled freedom of assembly. As had been the case during earlier periods, the "public" that the author suggested defending was not the democratic masses but, rather, persons "of status, [persons] of position."[77]

In its campaign to obstruct a regressive revision of the criminal code, the association mobilized the local bar associations and lawyer-politicians in the Diet. In an emergency resolution, the association called on the Ministry of Justice to grant it prior review of proposed revisions to the criminal code and the right to submit its opinions on the law to the Imperial Diet as "government proposals." This would have been an unprecedented concession from the government. Unsurprisingly, the proposal was denied. Even so, the campaign achieved its primary purpose: blocking some of the more repugnant reform proposals, such as the return to the Chinese codes that included liberal application of the death penalty. It was not until 1907 that the government promulgated a revised criminal code, a document shaped by input from the association. Lawyers had attained a goal of former-samurai legal advocates: they were now integrated in the policy process as participants in deliberative councils, as politicians, and as advisers to the government. Where, previously, legal advocates had shaped political outcomes through legal and political activism from the outside, now lawyers were operating within networks of state power.

There were exceptions to this story, some of them quite celebrated. From the turn of the century, Yamazaki Kesaya used the courts to challenge economic inequality. Similarly, Fuse Tatsuji emerged as a lawyer who represented the interests of tenant farmers and laborers. Yet their activism did not hold back the trends of the times: in the course of pro-

76. Ibid.
77. Ibid., 42.

fessionalization, the leadership of the profession had transformed. The private practice of law had accommodated itself to the workings of the national state.

The story of nineteenth-century private legal practice is a story of continuous negotiation among clients, the state, practitioners, their associations, and activists. During the decades after 1872, legal advocates and their associations helped to change society in dramatic ways. They contributed to the emergence of legal thought as a means of interpreting the social and political order. They helped to place lawyers in a position of privilege as interpreters of the law inside and outside the courts. As participants in ongoing debates on policy, the Japan Lawyers' Association had a stake in the success of government legal reforms. The shift to constitutional politics allowed lawyers to capitalize on their position within a politics that they and their predecessors had, in part, created. The nineteenth century left a legacy of legal and political activism, increasingly understood at the time under the rubric of human rights. Lawyers came to relish their role as the courtroom defenders of the accused, even as the scope and the depth of mainstream legal practitioner activism decreased from the 1870s to the 1890s. Its leadership provided legal teams to defendants in all of the high-profile political cases of the early twentieth century, including the trial of anarchists in the Kōtoku Shusui Incident and many lower-profile cases as well. To further human rights protections, the Japan Lawyers' Association drove the passage of a jury law in the late 1910s and early 1920s. Even as the profession splintered ideologically during the 1910s and 1920s, lawyers of different stripes continued to promote the preservation of individual rights.

The Last of Hoshi Tōru and the Question of Modernity

By 1900, Hoshi Tōru had been humbled. His imperiousness had alienated fellow lawyers in the Tokyo bar; a no-confidence vote had removed him from the House leadership. No longer a politician in the national Diet, he was elected to a seat in the Tokyo Municipal Assembly. If he still held a torch for liberty, he had taken it to a dark place. In light of overwhelming evidence, he was close to facing charges of involvement in a corruption scandal related to sewage treatment.

From the time of Mr. Hoshi Toru's ascendancy . . . a creed prevailed that political influence was a valuable asset which its possessor might turn to his own profit provided that public loss did not evidently ensue. This dangerous doctrine soon exercised a widely demoralising influence. Nearly every service came to be considered purchasable, and in many instances the reservation as to public interest received no respect whatever.[78]

Evidence suggests that Hoshi had allowed the pursuit of personal power and material interest to overtake an earlier dedication to the greater good. This was not the vision of parliamentary politics that had stirred advocates and activists during the 1870s and 1880s.

Hoshi's alleged betrayal offended the public trust at multiple levels. Selling influence was a betrayal by a political representative entrusted with acting for the benefit of all. Influence peddling also contradicted the evolving myth of Japan's modernity: that the nation worked as one in the interest of the emperor. For those who imagined a politics of pure principle, any kind of horse trading or compromise was a wayward act. Where Hoshi had once been the incarnation of the legal advocate in opposition to government despotism, he had come to embody its opposite. Or so his assassin, Iba Sōtarō, wrote in a statement of purpose that he sent to the Municipal Assembly, the newspapers, and the two houses of the Diet on June 21, 1901. He then rushed into the municipal council chamber and stabbed Hoshi with a short sword, shouting, "Traitor Hoshi."[79] A leader in the formation of Meiji legal advocacy died.

Yet, the contest over protecting rights, a public sphere, and autonomy for organized interests persisted. These were the continuing challenges for democratic politics—challenges not unique to Japan: how to formulate the public interest, how to identify the public good, and how to balance the ideal of the greater good with the material interests of individuals, groups, and corporations. Hoshi clearly understood the theory and practice of electoral politics and demonstrated that the first decades of

---

78. Brinkley, *Japan and China*, 4:251–52.

79. The scene is recounted in the various biographies of Hoshi, including Ariizumi, *Hoshi Tōru*; Wagatsuma, *Nihon seiji saiban shiroku (Meiji)*, 336; and Kobayashi S., *Watakushi no atta Meiji no meihōsō monogatari*. A partial English translation of Iba's statement appeared in "Survey of the World: The Assassination of Hoshi Toru," *Independent* [New York] 53, no. 2749 (8 Aug. 1901): 1832.

the Meiji era could not be measured against an idealized, progressive West. Such has been the tack of scholars such as Maruyama Masao, who wrote that Japan lacked both "the genuinely idealistic politician who remains steadfastly faithful to truth and justice . . . [and the] politician who is prepared fearlessly to trample underfoot all accepted standards of morality. . . . [W]e find neither the humble, inward looking approach nor the naked lust for power."[80] The history of political activism by private legal practitioners reveals something else. Some activists, such as Ōi Kentarō, charted a path of "truth and justice." Meanwhile, Hoshi ended his career trampling on "accepted standards of morality." At the turn of the century, foreign observers wryly noted that Hoshi had mastered Walpolian—or Tammany Hall—politics. In other words, he cultivated the politics of patronage. His legal and political career had entered uncharted waters where idealism gave way to an acute awareness of systems of power. A political movement in the interest of rights and liberty was no longer his polestar.

Did the legal transitions of Japan's nineteenth century end with a finality corresponding to Hoshi's clear end? Hoshi's death did not open the way for the rise of an ideal state that balanced law and morality. Rather, the legal history of the nineteenth century marked continued conflict around several processes: contests over the public sphere; expanding and contracting freedoms in relationship to assembly, suffrage, and speech; and the evolving issue of legal representation. In Japan, as in the rest of the world, vibrant contestation over the legitimate boundaries of state power within a nation had a genesis in the nineteenth century. Whether motivated by profit or politics, justice or education, Japan's nineteenth-century private legal practitioners tied their practice to concerns that were public and private. Their practice straddled old ideas of public morality and folk justice, mixing these with emergent ideas of rational law, morality, legal codes, political rights, and social roles. By 1890, proponents of legal rationalism, public speech, and persuasion had achieved their goal of establishing a national assembly. Yet this was not a full realization of the potential of their initial activism. They had not created a public sphere open to every voice in society, as envisioned in the idealism

---

80. Maruyama M., *Thought and Behavior in Modern Japanese Politics*, 11.

of Ōi Kentarō. Laborers, tenant farmers, women, communists, and new religionists, among others, faced suppression.

The cancers of militarism and ultranationalism that began to predominate at the turn of the twentieth century fed on social and economic inequalities. As scholars of the legal profession in Germany have noted, specialist knowledge and the privileges that came with it did little to cure the new ills of the twentieth-century nation, and often reinforced them.[81] Throughout the modern world, nationalism, backed by mythologized historical and political narratives, strengthened itself. Japan was no exception. Yet analysis of the legal practice of the nineteenth century reveals a different kind of Japanese past. The history of legal practice points away from a national narrative grounded in elemental cycles of violence. Instead, it reveals a history of engagement with the challenge of reconciling politics to law: a process of modernity continuing and unfolding.

---

81. Ledford, *From General Estate to Special Interest.* An even more damning account of the history of German private and public practitioners can be found in Müller, *Hitler's Justice.*

Appendix
Meiji Law Periodicals[a]

OFFICIAL NOTICES

Journal Title		First Pub.	Last Pub.
Gaimushō nisshi	外務省日誌	1868	1877
Kyōbushō nisshi	教部省日誌	1868	1877
Naimushō nisshi	内務省日誌	1868	1877
Monbushō nisshi	文部省日誌	1868	1877
Kōbuntsūshi	公文通誌	1872	1874
Niigataken chihōchi	新潟県治報知	1873	1878
Kana tsuke ofuregaki	かなつけおふれがき	1873	1875
Shinreiben	新令弁	1873	-na-[b]
Kanpō gojūnisshi	官報五十日誌	1875	1877
Kōfu no utsuri	公布之寫	1875	1881
Kanrei shinshi	官令新誌	1875	1883
Kanrei zenshi	官令全誌	1875	1876
Fukoku zenpō	布告全報	1875	1879
Kanrei zenpō	官令全報	1876	1885
Kōfu nippō	公布日報	1877	1881
Sakai ken kōfu ruishi	堺県公布類誌	1877	1877
Futatsu kaishaku	布達解釈	1877	1878

COLLECTIONS OF COURT RULINGS AND PRECEDENTS

Journal Title		First Pub.	Last Pub.
Shihōshō nisshi	司法省日誌	1873	-na-
Kōbunshi dankei roku	公文誌断刑録	1875	1875
Daishinin hanketsu roku	大審院判決録	1875	1876
Daishinin minji hanketsu roku	大審院民事判決録	1876	(cont)

(continued)

COLLECTIONS OF COURT RULINGS AND PRECEDENTS (continued)

Journal Title		First Pub.	Last Pub.
Daishinin keiji hanketsu roku	大審院刑事判決録	1876	(cont)
Tōkyō jōtō saibansho bōchō roku	東京上等裁判所傍聴録	1875	1876
Tōkyō jōtō saibansho hanketsu roku	東京上等裁判所判決録	1876	1877
Jōtō saibansho minji hanketsu roku	上等裁判所民事判決録	1880	1880
Tōkyō saibansho hanketsu roku	東京裁判所判決録	1880	1880
Tōkyō chūzai saibansho hanketsu roku	東京重罪裁判所判決録	1882	-na-
Saiban saishi	裁判粋誌	1888	(cont)

LAW AND LEGAL THEORY

Journal Title		First Pub.	Last Pub.
Hōri zasshi	法理雑誌	1874	1875
Hōritsu zasshi	法律雑誌	1877	1894
Genkō hōritsu mondō	現行法律問答	1879	1880
Hōritsu shisō	法律志叢	1880	1886
Kōhō zasshi	講法雑誌	1881	1881
Meihō shirin [c]	明法志林	1881	(cont)
Hōritsu sōdan	法律叢談	1881	1883
Hōritsu shinbun	法律新聞	1881	1882
Hōmon zasshi	法門雑誌	1882	1882
Naigai hōritsu shinpō	内外法律新報	1882	1883
Hōritsu mondō shinshi	法律問答新誌	1882	1883
Fukuoka hōritsu zasshi	福岡法律雑誌	1882	1882
Hōgaku kyōkai zasshi	法学協会雑誌	1884	(cont)
Hōgaku kōgi hikki	法学講義筆記	1884	-na-
Hōgaku mondō zasshi (Kyōto)	法学問答雑誌(京都)	1884	-na-
Meihō zasshi	明法雑誌	1885	-na-
Hōritsu gakujutsu mondō zasshi	法律学術問答雑誌	1885	1886
Chūō hōgakkai zasshi	中央法学会雑誌	1885	1885
Hōgaku ronshi	法学論誌	1885	1886
Nihon hōritsu zasshi	日本法律雑誌	1886	1888
Hōritsu ōyō zasshi	法律応用雑誌	1886	(cont)
Chūgai hōgaku shinpō	中外法学新報	1886	1886
Tōkyō hōgaku zasshi	東京法学雑誌	1886	1886
Hōritsu keizai shinpō	法律経済新報	1886	1886
Hōsei shisō	法政志叢	1886	1892
Tōkyō hōritsu shinbun	東京法律新聞	1887	1887

(continued)

Journal Title		First Pub.	Last Pub.
Bankoku hōritsu shūhō	万国法律週報	1887	1887
Tōyō hōgaku sōshi	東洋法学叢誌	1887	(cont)
Hōritsu senmon zasshi	法律専門雑誌	1887	-na-
Hōgaku sokusei zasshi	法学速成雑誌	1887	1889
Bankoku hōritsu shūran	万国法律集覧	1887	-na-
Tōkyō hōgakkō zasshi	東京法学校雑誌	1888	1888
Nihon no hōritsu	日本之法律	1888	1894
Saiban igaku zasshi	裁判医学雑誌	1888	1888
Hōsō	法叢	1889	1889
Hōgaku shūshi	法学集誌	1889	-na-
Hōri seika[d]	法理精華	1889	(cont)
Hōgaku zasshi	法学雑誌	1889	1889
Kensei shinshi	憲政新誌	1889	1889
Kenpō zasshi	憲法雑誌	1889	1890
Chūgai hōritsu shūshi	中外法律集誌	1889	-na-
Kenpō gyōsei gaku	憲法行政学	1889	1889
Hōgaku shirin	法学志林	1889	1890
Zeihō zasshi	税法雑誌	1889	1890

[a] Compiled from "Zappō," *Hōgaku kyōkai zasshi* 50, no. 6 (1932): 187–89.

[b] The list was compiled by an anonymous author from government records and the collection at the Meiji shinbun zasshi bunkō; "-na-" refers to journals about which there was insufficient information, and "(cont)" refers to those journals that were in press in 1932.

[c] Not formally affiliated with *Igirisu Hōritsu Gakkō* but, from 1885, its editor was Takahashi Isshō and its manager was Hatoyama Kazuo; from 1886, Masujima was the manager. Mainichi shinbunsha, *Daigaku shirīzu: Chūō daigaku.*

[d] Chūō daigaku shichi jūnenshi hensanjo, ed., *Chūō daigaku shichi jūnenshi*, 13.

Works Cited

Archival Collections

First Tokyo Bar Association Archive
Second Tokyo Bar Association Archive
National Diet Library, Kensei shiryōshitsu
University of Tokyo, Law Faculty Archive
Ministry of Justice Library Archive

Periodicals

Hōgaku kyōkai zasshi
Hōgaku ronsō
Hōritsu ronsō
Hōritsu shinbun
Hōritsu shinpō
Hōritsu zasshi
Hōseishi kenkyū
Hōsōkai zasshi
Japan Gazette
Jiyū to seigi
Kōko shinbun
Meihō shisō
Meiji daigaku kiyō
Nihon bengoshi kyōkai rokuji; title changed to *Hōsō kōron* after 1925
Ōmei zasshi
Seigi
Shihō kenkyū

Articles and Monographs

Abbott, Andrew. *The System of Professions: An Essay on the Division of Expert Labor*. Chicago, IL: University of Chicago Press, 1988.

Adachi Gennosuke [also Motonosuke], ed. *Tōkyō bengoshikaishi*. Tokyo: Tōkyō bengoshikai jimusho, 1935.

Adachi Jūkichi. *Daigennin hyōbanki*. Tokyo: Chitsuzandō, 1883.

Amano Ikuo (William Cummings and Fumiko Cummings, trans.). *Education and Examination in Modern Japan*. Tokyo: University of Tokyo Press, 1990.

Anderson, Marnie S. *A Place in Public: Women's Rights in Meiji Japan*. Cambridge, MA: Harvard University Asia Center, 2010.

Aoki Michio. "Kinsei minshū no seikatsu to teikō." In *Seikatsu, bunka, shisō: Ikki*, vol. 4, ed. Aoki Michio, et al. Tokyo: Tōkyō daigaku shuppankai, 1981, 167–226.

Ariizumi Sadao. *Hoshi Tōru*. Tokyo: Asahi shinbunsha, 1983.

Arnold, Matthew. "Report on the Systems of Popular Education in France, Holland, and the Canton's of Switzerland." *Reports of the Assistant Commissioners, Parliamentary Papers*, vol. 21, pt. 4. London: Education Commission, 1861.

Austin, John. *The Province of Jurisprudence Determined*. New York: Cambridge University Press, 1995.

Barshay, Andrew. *State and Intellectual in Imperial Japan: The Public Man in Crisis*. Berkeley, CA: University of California Press, 1988.

Beer, Lawrence. *Freedom of Expression in Japan: A Study in Comparative Law, Politics, and Society*. Tokyo: Kodansha International, 1984.

Beerens, Anna. "Interview with a Bakumatsu Official: A Translation from 'Kyūji Shimonroku' (2)." *Monumenta Nipponica* 57, no. 2 (Summer 2002): 173–206.

Bell, David. *Lawyers and Citizens: The Making of a Political Elite in Old Regime France*. Oxford: Oxford University Press, 1994.

Bengoshi Unno Shinkichi kankō iinkai, ed. *Bengoshi Unno Shinkichi*. Tokyo: Bengoshi Unno Shinkichi iinkai, 1972.

Berry, Mary Elizabeth. "Conventional Knowledge in Early Modern Japan." In *Public Spheres, Private Lives in Modern Japan, 1600–1950: Essays in Honor of Albert Craig*, ed. Gail Lee Bernstein, Andrew Gordon, and Kate Wildman Nakai. Cambridge, MA: Harvard University Asia Center, 2005, 19–52.

———. *Japan in Print: Information and Nation in the Early Modern Period*. Berkeley, CA: University of California Press, 2006.

Blackstone, Sir William (Hoshi Tōru, trans.). *Eikoku hōritsu zensho*, 3 vols. Tokyo: Higashinari Kamejirō, 1873–1876. Original title: *Commentaries on the Laws of England*.

Blankenburg, Erhard, and Ulrike Schultz. "German Advocates—A Highly Regulated Profession." In *Lawyers in Society: The Civil Law World*, ed. Richard Abel, et al. Berkeley, CA: University of California Press, 1988, 124–59.

Botsman, Daniel. *Punishment and Power in the Making of Modern Japan*. Princeton, NJ: Princeton University Press, 2005.

Bousquet, Georges. *Le Japon de nos jours*, vol. 2. Paris: Hachette, 1877.

Bouwsma, William. "Lawyers and Early Modern Culture." *American Historical Review* 78, no. 2 (1973): 303–27.

Bowen, Roger. *Rebellion and Democracy in Meiji Japan: A Study of Commoners in the Popular Rights Movement*. Berkeley, CA: University of California Press, 1980.

Braisted, William R., ed. and trans. *Meiroku Zasshi: Journal of the Japanese Enlightenment*. Cambridge, MA: Harvard University Press, 1976.

Brinkley, Frank. *Japan and China: Their History, Arts and Literature*, vol. 4. London: Jack, 1904.

Brooks, C. W. *Pettyfoggers and Vipers of the Commonwealth: The "Lower Branch" of the Legal Profession in Early Modern England*. New York: Cambridge University Press, 1986.

Brown, Philip C. *Central Authority and Local Autonomy in the Formation of Early Modern Japan: The Case of Kaga Domain*. Stanford, CA: Stanford University Press, 1993.

Burrage, Michael. "Revolution and the Collective Action of the French, American, and English Legal Professions." *Law and Social Inquiry* 13, no. 2 (1988): 225–77.

Buyō Inshi. "Seji kenmonroku." In *Nihon shomin seikatsu shiryō shūsei*, vol. 8. Miyamoto Tsuneichi, et al. comp. Tokyo: San'ichi shobō, 1968, 641–766.

Cahn, Edmond. "Goethe's View of Law—With a Gloss out of Plato." *Columbia Law Review* 49, no. 7 (Nov. 1949): 904–20.

Cantor, Norman. *Imagining the Law: Common Law and the Foundations of the American Legal System*. New York: Harper Collins, 1997.

Carr-Saunders, Alexander Morriss, and Paul Alexander Wilson. *The Professions*. Oxford: The Clarendon Press, 1933.

Chang, Richard. *The Justice of the Western Consular Courts in Nineteenth-Century Japan*. Westport, CT: Greenwood Press, 1984.

Ch'en, Paul Heng-chao. *The Formation of the Early Meiji Legal Order: The Japanese Code of 1871 and its Chinese Foundation*. London: Oxford University Press, 1981.

Chūō daigaku shichi jūnenshi hensanjo, ed. *Chūō daigaku shichi jūnenshi*. Tokyo: Chūō daigaku, 1955.

Confucius (Burton Watson, trans.). *The Analects of Confucius*. New York: Columbia University Press, 2007.

Daini Tōkyō bengoshikai, ed. *Bengoshi jichi no kenkyū*. Tokyo: Nihon hyōronsha, 1976.

Davis, Sandra. *Intellectual Change and Political Development in Early Modern Japan: Ono Azusa, A Case Study*. Rutherford, NJ: Fairleigh Dickinson University Press, 1980.

Dawson, John. *Oracles of the Law*. Ann Arbor: University of Michigan Law School, 1968.

de Tocqueville, Alexis (Henry Reeve, trans.). *Democracy in America*, vol. 2. New York: Henry Langley, 1845.

Dore, Ronald. *Education in Tokugawa Japan*. Berkeley, CA: University of California Press, 1965.

Ebashi Takashi. "Satta Masakuni: taitoru naki hōgakusha no unmei." In *Hōritsu gaku no yoake to Hōsei daigaku*. Hōsei daigaku daigakushi shiryō iinkai, ed. Tokyo: Hōsei daigaku, 1992, 68–82.

Epp, Robert. "The Challenge from Tradition: Attempts to Compile a Civil Code in Japan, 1866–78." *Monumenta Nipponica* 22, no. 1/2 (1967): 15–48.

Friedman, Lawrence. *A History of American Law*. New York: Simon & Schuster, 1985.

Fuess, Harald. *Divorce in Japan: Family, Gender, and the State, 1600–2000*. Stanford, CA: Stanford University Press, 2004.

Fujii Chikukan. *Hoshi Tōru seikai meishi*. Osaka: Matama seikadō, 1901.

Fujii Jintarō. *Outline of Japanese History in the Meiji Era*, vol. 7. Tokyo: Ōbunsha, 1958.

Fujii Noriyuki and Fujimoto Hyakuo. "Chihō shinbun ni miru Hyōgoken daiikkai sōsenkyo: kōmin kyōiku kiso shiryō." *Gakkō kyōikugaku kenkyū* 6 (1994): 125–40.

Fujita Michiyo. "Hōkon baishin secchi o ronzu." *Hōritsu zasshi*, nos. 60–61 (8 and 15 Mar. 1879).

Fukuchi Shigetaka. *Meiji shakaishi: Nihon rekishi shiriizu*, vol. 4. Tokyo: Kōbundō, 1955.

Fukui Jun. "Ōmeisha to shiritsu hōritsu gakkō." *Meiji daigaku kiyō*, no. 4 (Mar. 1984): 12–37.

Fukuzawa Yukichi. *Fukuzawa zenshū*. Tokyo: Jiji shinpōsha, 1898.

———. "Gakusha no shokubun o ronzu." In *Gakumon no susume*, vol. 4. Jan. 1874.

———. *Seiyo jijō, Gaihen*, vol. 1. Tokyo: Shōkodō, 1867.

Fuse Tatsuji. *Jichi kenkyū kōwa*. Tokyo: Shimada shoten, 1930.

George, Timothy S. "Tanaka Shōzō's Vision of an Alternate Constitutional Modernity for Japan." In *Public Spheres, Private Lives in Modern Japan, 1600–1950*, ed. Gail Lee Bernstein, Andrew Gordon, and Kate Wildman Nakai. Cambridge, MA: Harvard University Press, 2005, 89–116.

Gikai seijisha henshūbu, ed., *Nihon kenseishi kiso shiryō*. Tokyo: Gikai seijisha, 1939.

Gluck, Carol. "The Invention of Edo." In *Mirror of Modernity: Invented Traditions of Japan*, ed. Stephen Vlastos. Berkeley, CA: University of California Press, 1998, 262–84.

———. *Japan's Modern Myths: Ideology in the Late Meij Period*. Princeton, NJ: Princeton University Press, 1985.

———. "The People in History." *Journal of Asian Studies* 38, no. 1 (Nov. 1978): 25–50.

Gordon, Andrew. *Labor and Imperial Democracy in Prewar Japan*. Berkeley, CA: University of California Press, 1992.

Gordon, Elisabeth Anna. *"Clear Round!" or, Seeds of Story from Other Countries: Being a Chronicle of Links and Rivets in This World's Girdle*. London: Low, Marston & Company, 1893.

Griffis, William Elliot. *The Mikado's Empire*. New York: Harper & Brothers, 1906.

Habermas, Jürgen. "The Public Sphere." In *Rethinking Popular Culture: Contemporary Perspectives in Cultural Studies*, ed. Chandra Mukerji and Michael Schudson. Berkeley, CA: University of California Press, 1991, 398–404.

Haley, John O. *Authority without Power: Law and the Japanese Paradox*. New York: Oxford University Press, 1991.

Hall, John Carey, trans. "The Tokugawa Legislation, Part II" *Transactions of the Asiatic Society of Japan* 38, no. 4 (1911): 286–319.

———. trans. "The Tokugawa Legislation, Part IV," *Transactions of the Asiatic Society of Japan* 41 (1913): 696–803.

Hanabusa Seijirō. *Daigennin hyōbanki*. Osaka: Hanabusa Seijirō, 1886.

Hanai Takuzō. "Bengoshi no seiryoku, chii, taigū." *Nihon bengoshi kyōkai rokuji* 2, no. 7 (1898): 54–61.

Hara Yoshimichi. *Bengoshi seikatsu no kaikō*. Tokyo: Hōritsu shinpōsha, 1935.

Hardacre, Helen, and Adam Kern, eds., *New Directions in the Study of Meiji Japan*. Leiden: Brill, 1997.

Harootunian, Harry. "The Economic Rehabilitation of the Samurai in the Early Meiji Period." *Journal of Asian Studies* 19, no. 4 (Aug. 1960): 433–44.

———. "Late Tokugawa Culture and Thought." In *The Cambridge History of Japan: The Nineteenth Century*, ed. John W. Hall, Marius Jansen, et al. New York: Cambridge University Press, 1989, 158–268.

Haruhara Gentarō. "Kinsei Ōsaka no senso, koso, dōjitsunegai." *Hoseishi kenkyū* 6 (1955): 164–76.

———. "Kujiyado no senden bira." *Jiyū to seigi* 15, no. 1 (1965): 39–40.

———. *Ōsaka no machibugyōsho to saiban.* Tokyo: Fuzanbō, 1962.

———, comp. *Senryū to hōritsu.* Osaka: Haruhara Gentarō, 1940.

Hatoyama Kazuo. *Kaigi hō, kan.* Tokyo: Ogasawara shobō, 1882.

Hattori Takaaki (assisted by Richard Rabinowitz). "The Legal Profession in Japan: Its Historical Development and Present State." In *Law in Japan: The Legal Order in a Changing Society,* ed. Arthur Taylor von Mehren. Cambridge, MA: Harvard University Press, 1963, 111–51.

Hauser, William B. *Economic Institutional Change in Tokugawa Japan: Osaka and the Kinai Cotton Trade.* New York: Cambridge University Press, 1974.

Havens, Thomas. "Scholars and Politics in Nineteenth-Century Japan: The Case of Nishi Amane." *Modern Asian Studies* 2, no. 4 (1968): 315–24.

Hayashi Tadasu. *For His People, Being the True Story of Sogoro's Sacrifice, Entitled in the Original Japanese Version "The Cherry Blossoms of a Spring Morn."* New York: Harper, 1903.

Hayashiya Reiji, Ishii Shiro, Aoyama Yoshimitsu, et al. *Zusetsu hanketsu genpon no isan.* Tokyo: Shinzansha, 1998.

Henderson, Dan Fenno. *Conciliation and Japanese Law: Tokugawa and Modern,* 2 vols. Seattle, WA: University of Washington Press, 1965.

———. "'Contracts' in Tokugawa Villages." *Journal of Japanese Studies* 1, no. 1 (1974): 51–90.

———. "Promulgation of Tokugawa Statutes." In *Traditional and Modern Legal Institutions in Asia and Africa,* ed. David C. Buxbaum. Leiden: Brill, 1967, 9–25.

Hiramatsu Yoshirō (Dan Fenno Henderson, trans.). "Tokugawa Law." *Law in Japan* 14, no. 1 (1981): 1–48.

Hirano Yoshitarō. *Ōi Kentarō.* Tokyo: Yoshikawa kōbunkan, 1965.

Hirao Michio. *Jiyūminken no keifu: Tosaha no baai.* Kōchi: Kōchi shimin toshokan, 1970.

Hoffman, Stefan-Ludwig. "Democracy and Associations in the Long Nineteenth Century: Toward a Transnational Perspective." *Journal of Modern History* 75, no. 2 (June 2003): 269–299.

Holmes, Oliver Wendell. "The Path of Law." *Harvard Law Review* 10 (1897): 457–78.

Honjō Kazuyuki. *Kinsei kōchō ron.* Osaka: Bunkaidō, 1878.

Hōsei daigaku daigakushi shiryō iinkai, ed. *Hōritsugaku no yoake to Hōsei daigaku.* Tokyo: Hōsei daigaku, 1992.

Hōsei University (Gustave Boissonade). *Note des correspondances avec Monsieur Boissonade: premier cahier pour les questions.* Tokyo: Hōsei University, 1978.

Hoshi Tōru, trans. *Eikoku hōritsu zensho,* 3 vols. Tokyo: Higashinari Kamejirō, 1873–1876. Original title: *Commentaries on the Laws of England* (Blackstone, Sir William).

———. *Kakkoku kokkai yōran.* Tokyo: Reitakukan, 1886.

Howell, David. *Capitalism from Within: Economy, Society, and the State in a Japanese Fishery.* Berkeley, CA: University of California Press, 1995.

Howland, Douglas. *Translating the West: Language and Political Reason in Nineteenth-Century Japan.* Honolulu, HI: University of Hawai'i Press, 2001.

Hozumi Nobushige. *The New Japanese Civil Code, As Material for the Study of Comparative Jurisprudence.* Tokyo: Tokyo Printing Company, 1904.

Huffman, James. *Creating a Public: People and Press in Meiji Japan.* Honolulu, HI: University of Hawai'i Press, 1997.

———. *Politics of the Meiji Press: The Life of Fukuchi Gen'ichirō.* Honolulu, HI: University of Hawai'i Press, 1980.

Ide Magoroku, et al., eds. *Jiyū minken kimitsu tantei shiryōshū: kokuritsu kōbunshokan zō.* Tokyo: San'ichi shobō, 1981.

Ihara Saikaku. *Honchō ōin hiji.* Translated by Thomas Kondo and Alfred Marks as *Tales of Japanese Justice.* Honolulu, HI: University of Hawai'i Press, 1980.

Ikegami Eiko. *Bonds of Civility: Aesthetic Networks and the Political Origins of Japanese Culture.* New York: Cambridge University Press, 2005.

———. *The Taming of the Samurai: Honorific Individualism and the Making of Modern Japan.* Cambridge, MA: Harvard University Press, 1995.

Inoue Kowashi. *Fukkoku shihō sanshoku kō.* Tokyo: Isandō, 1878.

Irokawa Daikichi (Marius Jansen, trans.) *The Culture of the Meiji Period.* Princeton, NJ: Princeton University Press, 1985.

———. *Jiyūminken.* Tokyo: Iwanami shoten, 1981.

———. *Rekishika no uso to yume.* Tokyo: Asahi shinbunsha, 1974.

Irokawa Daikichi, Gabe Masao, Makihara Norio, et al. *Meiji kenpakusho shūsei,* vol. 8. Tokyo: Chikuma shobō, 1999.

Ishida Takeshi. *Jichi.* Tokyo: Sanseidō, 1998.

Itagaki Taisuke, ed. *Jiyūtōshi,* vols. 1–4. Tokyo: Aoki shoten, 1955.

Ives, E. W. "The Common Lawyers of Pre-Reformation England." *Transactions of the Royal Historical Society,* vol. 18 (1968): 145–173.

———. *The Common Lawyers of Pre-Reformation England: Thomas Kebell, a Case Study*. New York: Cambridge University Press, 2008.

Iwanami Bien, ed. *Ishikai hō hantai shimatsu*. Tokyo: Kōshinsha, 1899.

Iwatani Jurō. "Kindai Nihon hōseishi kenkyū ni okeru 'gakushiki' hanji to no sōgū." In *Nihon hōsōkai jinbutsu jiten: bekkan kaisetsu*, ed. Murakami Kazuhiro. Tokyo: Yumani shobō, 1996, 1–22.

———. "Meiji shoki minshū no soshō seikatsu: shiryō no naka ni miru Nihon hō no kindai." *Sanshokuki* (Oct. 1994): 6–12.

Jinnai Hidenobu. *Tokyo: A Spatial Anthropology*. Berkeley, CA: University of California Press, 1995.

Jones, Robert. *A History of the French Bar: Ancient and Modern*. Philadelphia, PA: T. & J. W. Johnson, 1856.

Kadota Kōkichi. "Nihon bengoshishi daigennin jidai izen." In *Bengoshishi*, ed. Tōkyō bengoshikai. Tokyo: Tōkyō bengoshikai, 1939.

Kagan, Richard. *Lawsuits and Litigants in Castile, 1500–1700*. Chapel Hill, NC: University of North Carolina Press, 1981.

Karlin, Jason. "The Gender of Nationalism: Competing Masculinities in Meiji Japan." *Journal of Japanese Studies* 28, no. 1 (Winter 2002): 41–77.

Karpik, Lucien (Nora Scott, trans.). *French Lawyers: A Study in Collective Action, 1274–1994*. Oxford: Clarendon Press, 1999.

———. "Lawyers and Politics in France, 1814–1950: The State, the Market, and the Public." *Law and Social Inquiry* 13, no. 4 (Autumn 1988): 707–36.

Kasumi Nobuhiko. "Criminal Trials in the Early Meij Era, with Particular Reference to the Ukagai/Shirei System." In *Law in Japan: A Turning Point*, ed. Daniel H. Foote. Seattle, WA: University of Washington Press, 2007, 34–49.

Kataoka Kenkichi. "Memorial Presented to the Emperor by the Risshisha, Advocating the Establishment of a Representative Assembly, June 1877." In *Meiji Japan through Contemporary Sources*, vol. 2, ed. Centre for East Asian Cultural Studies. Tokyo: Centre for East Asian Cultural Studies, 1970, 184–211.

Katsu Kokichi (Teruko Craig, trans.). *Musui's Story: The Autobiography of a Tokugawa Samurai*. Tucson, AZ: The University of Arizona Press, 1995.

Kawasaki Masaru. *Hoshi Tōru to sono jidai*, 2 vols. Tokyo: Heibonsha, 1984.

Kelly, William. *Deference and Defiance in Nineteenth Century Japan*. Princeton, NJ: Princeton University Press, 1985.

———. "Incendiary Action: Fires and Firefighting in the Shogun's Capital." In *Edo and Paris: Urban Life and the State in the Early Modern Era*, James

McClain John Merriman, Ugawa Kaoru, eds. Ithaca, NY: Cornell University Press, 1994, 310–31.

Keysaar, Alexander. *The Right to Vote: The Contested History of Democracy in the United States*. New York: Basic Books, 2001.

Kikuyama Masaaki. "Etō Shinpei no shihō kaikaku." *Hōseishi Kenkyū* 39 (1989): 91–120.

———. *Meiji kokka no keisei to shihōseido*. Tokyo: Ochanomizu shobō, 1993.

Kim, Kyu-Hyun. *The Age of Visions and Arguments: Parliamentarianism and the National Public Sphere in Early Meiji Japan*. Cambridge, MA: Harvard University Asia Center, 2006.

Kitakōji Ken. *Fukushima jiken monogatari: Jiyū e no sakebi*. Tokyo: Kokusho kankōkai, 1974.

Kobayakawa Kingo. "Kinsei minji saiban tetsuzuki ni okeru 'kuji'—toku ni honkuji ni tsuite." *Hōgaku ronsō* 47, nos. 2–3 (1942): 176–206, 343–81.

———. *Kinsei minji soshō seido no kenkyū*. Tokyo: Yūhikaku, 1957.

Kobayashi Masaaki. "Gotō Shōjirō yori kaishū ikō no Mitsubishi Takashima tankō." *Kanto gakuin daigaku keizaikei*, no. 215 (Apr. 2003): 71–87.

Kobayashi Shunzō. *Watakushi no atta Meiji no meihōsō monogatari*. Tokyo: Nihon hyōronsha, 1973.

Kodama Jun'ichirō. *Ningen kōhō*. Tokyo: Yōjo shunsha, 1873.

Koizumi Terusaburō. *Meiji reimeiki no hanzai to keibatsu*. Tokyo: Hihyōsha, 2000.

Komuro Shinsuke. *Tōyō gijin hyakkaden*, vol. 1. Tokyo: Angaidō shuppan, 1884.

Kornicki, Peter. *The Book in Japan: A Cultural History from the Beginnings to the Nineteenth Century*. Leiden: Brill, 1998.

Krause, Elliott. *Death of the Guilds: Professions, States, and the Advance of Capitalism, 1930 to the Present*. New Haven, CT: Yale University Press, 1996.

Kriegel, Blandine (Marc LePain and Jeffrey Cohen, trans.). *The State and the Rule of Law*. Princeton, NJ: Princeton University Press, 1995.

Kuga Katsunan (Barbara Teters, trans.). "Kinjiseironkō: Thoughts on Recent Political Discourse." *Monumenta Nipponica* 26, no. 3/4 (1971): 319–93.

Kukita Kazuko. "Naisai to kujiyado." In *Saiban to kihan, Nihon no shakaishi*, vol. 5, ed. Yamaguchi Keiji, et al. Tokyo: Iwanami shoten, 1987, 318–49.

Kusaka Nanzanshi, ed. *Nihon bengoshi kōhyōden*. Tokyo: Seikyōdō, 1891.

Larson, Magali. *The Rise of Professionalism: A Sociological Analysis*. Berkeley, CA: University of California Press, 1977.

Ledford, Kenneth. *From General Estate to Special Interest: German Lawyers 1878–1933*. Cambridge, UK: Cambridge University Press, 1996.

Machida Iwajirō, ed. *Tōkyō daigennin retsuden.* Tokyo: Senshindō, 1881.

Maeda Masaharu. "An Introduction to the History of Japanese Popular Association Law." *Kwansei Gakuin University Annual Studies* 8 (Oct. 1959): 139–56.

Maeda Renzan. *Hoshi Tōru den.* Tokyo: Takayama shoin, 1948.

Mainichi shinbunsha. *Daigaku shirīzu: Chūō daigaku.* Tokyo: Mainichi shinbunsha, 1971.

Maki Hidemasa and Fujiwara Akihisa, eds. *Nihon hōseishi.* Tokyo: Aoki shoin, 1993.

Makihara Norio. "Ōi Kentarō no shisō kōzō to Ōsaka jiken no ronri." In *Ōsaka jiken no kenkyū,* ed. Ōsaka jiken kenkyūkai. Tokyo: Kashiwa shobō, 1982, 30–107.

Maruyama Masao. *Thought and Behavior in Modern Japanese Politics.* New York: Oxford University Press, 1969.

Maruyama Namasa, ed. *Tōkyō kakusha tōron hikki,* vol 1, no. 1 Tokyo: Chitsuzandō shuppan, 1881.

Masaoka Geiyō. *Jidai shisō no gonge: Hoshi Tōru to shakai.* Tokyo: Shinseisha, 1901.

Mason, R. H. P. *Japan's First General Election, 1890.* Cambridge, UK: Cambridge University Press, 1969.

Masuda Kyūichi. *Oisharon.* Tokyo: Tōadō shobō, 1911.

Masumi Junnosuke. *Nihon seitōshi ron,* vol. 2. Tokyo: Tōkyō daigaku shuppankai, 1966.

Matsuo Hiroshi. *Minpō no taikei: Shiminhō no kiso.* Tokyo: Keiō gijuku daigaku shuppankai, 1997.

Matsuo Seijirō. "Shihō shiryō: hōsō konjaku banashi." *Nihon bengoshi kyōkai rokuji* 22 (Feb. 1918): 41–54.

Matsuoka Kiichi. *Jiyū shinbun o yomu: Jiyūtō ni totte no jiyū minken undō.* Nagoya: Yunite, 1992.

McClain, James and Wakita Osamu, eds., *Osaka: The Merchant's Capital of Early Modern Japan.* Ithaca, NY: Cornell University Press, 1999.

Meiji shiryō kenkyū renrakukai, ed. *Minkenron kara nashionarizumu e.* Tokyo: Ochanomizu shobō, 1957.

Merryman, John. *The Civil Law Tradition: An Introduction to the Legal Systems of Western Europe and Latin America.* Stanford, CA: Stanford University Press, 1985.

Mezur, Katherine. *Beautiful Boys/Outlaw Bodies: Devising Kabuki Female Likeness.* New York: Palgrave Macmillan, 2005.

Miller, Frank. *Minobe Tatsukichi: Interpreter of Constitutionalism in Japan.* Berkeley, CA: University of California Press, 1965.

Minami Kazuo. *Bakumatsu toshi shakai no kenkyū.* Tokyo: Hanawa shobō, 1999.

———. "Edo no kujiyado." *Kokugakuin zasshi* 68, nos. 1–2 (1967): 68–83.

Minear, Richard. *Japanese Tradition and Western Law: Emperor, State, and Law in the Thought of Hozumi Yatsuka.* Cambridge, MA: Harvard University Press, 1970.

Mita Rokutarō. *Ōsaka kumiai daigennin kōhyōroku.* Osaka: Tanketsudō, 1887.

Mito bengoshikai hensan iinkai, ed. *Mito bengoshikaishi.* Mito: Mito bengoshikai, 1992.

Miyamoto Tsuneichi, et al., comp. *Nihon shomin seikatsu shiryō shūsei,* vol. 8. Tokyo: San'ichi shobō, 1968.

Miyatake Gaikotsu. *Bunmei kaika: saiban hen.* Tokyo: Hankyōdō, 1926.

———. *Meiji enzetsushi.* Tokyo: Yūgensha, 1926.

Mori Senzō. *Meiji jinbutsu itsuwa jiten, jōkan.* Tokyo: Tōkyōdō shuppan, 1965.

Moriizumi Akira. *Kōeki hōjin hanrei kenkyū.* Tokyo: Yūhikaku, 1996.

Morinaga Eizaburō. *Nihon bengoshi retsuden.* Tokyo: Shakai shisōsha, 1984.

———. *Saiban jiyū minken jidai.* Tokyo: Nihon hyōronsha, 1979.

Morris, Ivan. *The Nobility of Failure: Tragic Heroes in the History of Japan.* New York: Noonday Press, Farrar Straus Giroux, 1988.

Motoyama Yukihiko. "Local Politics and the Development of Secondary Education in the Early Meiji Period: The Case of Kōchi Prefecture." In *Proliferating Talent: Essays on Politics, Thought, and Education in the Meiji Era,* ed. Yukihiko Motoyama, Richard Rubinger, and J. S. A. Elisonas, and trans. Albert Craig. Honolulu, HI: University of Hawai'i Press, 1997, 148–94.

Müller, Ingo (Deborah Schneider, trans.). *Hitler's Justice: The Courts of the Third Reich.* Cambridge, MA: Harvard University Press, 1991.

Murakami Kazuhiro. "Kindai Nihon no zaiya hōsō to sono hyōden." In *Nihon hōsōkai jinbutsu jiten: bekkan kaisetsu,* ed. Murakami Kazuihiro. Tokyo: Yumani shobō, 1996, 44–72.

———. "Kindaiteki daigennin no tōjō: Kodama Junichirō to Naka Sadakatsu." *Hōritsu ronsō* 70, nos. 2–3 (Nov. 1997): 43–93.

———. *Meiji rikon saiban shiron.* Tokyo: Hōritsu bunkasha, 1994.

———, ed. *Nihon hōsōkai jinbutsu jiten.* Tokyo: Yumani shobō, 1996.

Muramatsu Michio, et al. *Sengo Nihon no atsuryoku dantai.* Tokyo: Tōyō keizai shinpōsha, 1986.

Murray, James, et al., eds. *Oxford English Dictionary: Being a Corrected Reissue,* vol. 7. Oxford: Clarendon Press, 1970.

Nagashima Jūtarō. "Keihō kaisei to jinken mondai." *Nihon bengoshi kyōkai rokuji* 2, no. 10 (1898): 38–47.

Naimushō Keishikyoku. *Tōkyō keiri yōran.* Tokyo: Keishikyoku, 1879.

Najita, Tetsuo. "Civil Society in Japan's Modernity: An Interpretive Overview." In *Civil Society, Religion, and the Nation: Modernization in Intercultural Context—Russia, Japan, Turkey*, ed. Gerrit Steunebrink and Evert van der Zweerde. Amsterdam: Rodopi, 2004, 101–16.

———. *Tokugawa Political Writings*. Cambridge, UK: Cambridge University Press, 1998.

Nakada Kaoru. *Hōseishi ronshū*, vol. 3, part 2. Tokyo: Iwanami shoten, 1946.

Nakahara Hidenori, *Meiji keisatsushi ronshū*. Tokyo: Ryōsho fukyūkai, 1980.

Nakamura Fumiya. *Meiji gentō: kaikaki hōritsusho monogatari*. Tokyo: Bunka shuppan kyoku, 1976.

Nakamura Kichisaburō. *The Formation of Modern Japan as Viewed from Legal History*. Honolulu, HI: East-West Center Press, 1962.

Nakamura Kikuo. *Hoshi Tōru*. Tokyo: Yoshikawa kōbunkan, 1963.

———. *Meijiteki ningenzō: Hoshi Tōru to kindai Nihon seiji*. Tokyo: Keiō tsūshin, 1957.

Nakamura Yūjirō. "Meiji jūnendai ni okeru daigennin to Meiji hōritsu gakkō." *Meiji daigakushi kiyō* 1 (1981): 2–18.

Nakamura Yukihiko, ed. *Kinsei chōnin shisō, Nihon shisō taikei*, vol. 59. Tokyo: Iwanami shoten, 1975.

Natsuyama Shigeki. *Hoshi Tōru*. Tokyo: Bunseisha, 1901.

Negishi Kinjū, ed. *Soshō hikkei*. Tokyo: Negishi Kinjū, 1874.

Nihon bengoshi rengōkai, ed. *Nihon bengoshi enkakushi*. Tokyo: Nihon bengoshi rengōkai, 1959.

Nihon daigaku, ed. *Yamada Akiyoshi den*. Tokyo: Nihon daigaku, 1963.

Nihon shihōshoshikai rengōkai shihōshoshishi hensan iinkai, ed. *Nihon shihōshoshishi (Meiji-Taishō-Shōwa senzen hen)*. Tokyo: Gyōsei, 1981.

Nihon shiseki kyōkai, ed. *Hōan ikō* (*Zoku Nihon shiseki sōsho*), vol. 4. Tokyo: Tōkyō daigaku shuppankai, 1975.

O'Brien, Suzanne. "Splitting Hairs: History and the Politics of Daily Life in Nineteenth-Century Japan." *Journal of Asian Studies* 67 (2008): 1309–39.

Obinata Sumio. *Jiyū minken undō to Rikken kaishintō*. Tokyo: Waseda daigaku shuppanbu, 1991.

Obinata Sumio and Gabe Masao, eds. *Genrōin nisshi*, vol. 2. Tokyo: San'ichi shobō, 1981–1982.

Ogyū Sorai. "Benmei I." In *Tokugawa Political Writings*, ed. Tetsuo Najita. Cambridge, UK: Cambridge University Press, 1998, 35–113.

Ōhira Yūichi. "Kinsei Nihon no sojō: sogan tetsuzuki no kōsatsu ni mukete." *Ritsumeikan hōgaku*, vols. 3–4, nos. 271–272 (2000): 826–53.

Ōi Kentarō (with Mitsukuri Rinshō), trans. *Furansu shūhō shūkai sanji shūchō*. Tokyo: Ministry of Justice, Tokyo, 1876.

———. *Jiyū ryakuron*. Osaka: Shōbidō, 1889.

Ōishi Shinzaburō and Hayashi Reiko, eds. *Ōoka Echizen no Kami Tadasuke no nikki*, 3 vols. Tokyo: San'ichi shobō, 1972–75.

Ōishi Shinzaburō and Nakane Chie (Conrad Totman, ed. and trans.). *Tokugawa Japan: The Social and Economic Antecedents of Modern Japan*. Tokyo: University of Tokyo Press, 1990.

Okazaki Tetsuji. *Edo no shijō keizai: rekishi seido bunseki kara mita kabunakama*. Tokyo: Kōdansha, 1999.

Okudaira Masahiro. "Hoshi Tōru den," *Nihon bengoshi kyōkai rokuji* (Feb. 1917).

———. *Nihon bengoshishi*. Tokyo: Gannandō shoten, 1971.

Ōmori Takayuki, ed. *Daigennin dainin teiyō*. Tokyo: Ōmori Takayuki, 1878.

Ōno Masao. "Shokugyōshi toshite no bengoshi oyobi bengoshi dantai no rekishi." In *Kōza: Gendai no bengoshi 2—bengoshi no dantai*, ed. Ōno Masao. Tokyo: Nihon hyōronsha, 1970, 1–123.

Ooms, Herman. *Tokugawa Ideology: Early Constructs, 1570–1680*. Princeton, NJ: Princeton University Press, 1985.

———. *Tokugawa Village Practice: Class, Status, Power, Law*. Berkeley, CA: University of California Press, 1996.

Osaka bengoshikai, ed. *Osaka bengoshikaishi kō*, vol 1. Osaka: Ōsaka bengoshikai, 1937.

Osatake Takeki. "Daishonin to iu koto." *Hōsōkai zasshi* 2, no. 9 (1931): 109–23.

———. *Meiji keisatsu saiban shi*. Tokyo: Hōkōdo shoten, 1926.

———. *Nihon kenseishi ronshū*. Tokyo: Ikuseisha, 1937.

———. *Nihon kenseishi taikō*, 2 vols. Tokyo: Nihon hyōronsha, 1938–1939.

———. "Shihōshoshihō kaisei jicchi, sanshūnen kinengō." In *Nihon shihōshoshishi (Meiji-Taishō-Shōwa senzen-hen)*, ed. Shihōshoshishi hensan iinkai. Tokyo: Nihon shihōshoshikai rengōkai, 1981.

Ozaki Yukio (Fujiko Hara, trans.). *The Autobiography of Ozaki Yukio: The Struggle for Constitutional Government in Japan*. Princeton, NJ: Princeton University Press, 2001.

Pekkanen, Robert. *Japan's Dual Civil Society: Members without Advocates*. Stanford, CA: Stanford University Press, 2006.

Provine, Doris. "Courts in the Political Process in France." In *Courts, Law, and Politics in Comparative Perspective*, ed. Herbert Jacob, et al. New Haven, CT: Yale University Press, 1996, 177–247.

Rabinowitz, Richard. "The Historical Development of the Japanese Bar." *Harvard Law Review* 70 (Nov. 1956): 61–81.

Ravina, Mark. *Land and Lordship in Early Modern Japan.* Stanford, CA: Standford University Press, 1999.

Redesdale, Algernon. *Tales of Old Japan.* Rutland, VT: Tuttle, 1966.

Reitan, Richard. *Making a Moral Society: Ethics and the State in Meiji Japan.* Honolulu, HI: University of Hawai'i Press, 2010.

Riles, Annelise, ed. *Rethinking the Masters of Comparative Law.* Portland, OR: Hart Publishing, 2001.

Roberts, Luke. "The Petition Box in Eighteenth-Century Tosa." *Journal of Japanese Studies* 20, no. 2 (Summer 1994): 423–58.

Rueschemeyer, Dietrich. "Comparing Legal Professions Cross-Nationally: From a Professions-Centered to a State-Centered Approach." *American Bar Foundation Research Journal* 11, no. 3 (Summer 1986): 415–46.

Sasaki Miyoko and Heinz Morioka. "The Blue-Eyed Storyteller: Henry Black and His Rakugo Career." *Monumenta Nipponica* 38, no. 2 (Summer 1983): 133–62.

———. "Rakugo: Popular Narrative Art of the Grotesque." *Harvard Journal of Asian Studies* 41, no. 2 (Dec. 1981): 417–79.

Schaede, Ulrike. "Forwards and Futures in Tokugawa-Period Japan: A New Perspective on the Dojima Rice Market." *Journal of Banking and Finance* 13 (1989): 487–513.

Shichinohe Katsuhiko. "Genkō minpōten wo tsukutta hitobito [16]." *Hōgaku seminaa* 55, no. 668 (2010): 64–67.

Shigematsu Yu. "Jiyushugishatachi to minpōten ronsō." *The Waseda Review of Socio-science* 11 (2005): 175–90.

Shima Manjirō. "Shinbun kisha oyobi daigennin shoshi ni tsugu." *Ōmei zasshi*, no. 32 (25 Oct. 1881): 16–23.

Shimamoto Nakamichi. *Seiten hekireki.* Tokyo: Hakubunsha, 1887.

Shimizu Kahei, *Fukushima jiken kōtō hōin saiban iiwatashi sho.* Tokyo: Seihodō, 1883.

Shinoda Shōsaku. *Meiji shin risshihen.* Osaka: Shobidō, 1891.

Shirayanagi Shūko. *Nihon fugō hasseigaku: kashi kaikyū kakumei no kan.* Tokyo: Chikura shobō, 1931.

Shklar, Judith. *Legalism: Law, Morals, and Political Trials.* Cambridge, MA: Harvard University Press, 1964.

Shōji Shintarō, *Kainan aikoku minkenka retsuden.* Osaka: Maekawa bun'eikaku, 1880.

Shōnandō Shoten, ed. *Tōkyo seikaku zuroku.* Tokyo: Shōnandō shoten, 1987.

Sievers, Sharon. *Flowers in Salt: The Beginning of Feminist Consciousness in Modern Japan.* Stanford, CA: Stanford University Press, 1983.

Silberman, Bernard S. *Cages of Reason: The Rise of the Rational State in France, Japan, the United States, and Great Britain.* Chicago, IL: University of Chicago Press, 1993.

Silver, Mark. *Purloined Letters: Cultural Borrowing and Japanese Crime Literature, 1868–1937.* Honolulu, HI: University of Hawai'i Press, 2008.

Siniawer, Eiko Maruko. *Ruffians, Yakuza, Nationalists: The Violent Politics of Modern Japan, 1860–1960.* Ithaca, NY: Cornell University Press, 2008.

Smith, Adam. *The Wealth of Nations.* New York: Collier and Son, 1902.

Soejima Taneomi, et al. "Memorial of Soejima Taneomi, etc., on the Establishment of a Representative Assembly, January 17, 1874." In *Meiji Japan through Contemporary Sources*, vol. 2, ed. Centre for East Asian Cultural Studies. Tokyo: Centre for East Asian Cultural Studies, 1970, 134–41.

———. "Reply of Soyejima, Gotō, and Itagaki to Kato's Arguments against Representative Government in Japan, 20 February 1874." *Transactions of the Asiatic Society of Japan* 42, pt. 1 (1914): 440–48.

Sōgō Masaaki and Hida Yoshifumi, eds. *Meiji no kotoba.* Tokyo: Tōkyōdō shuppan, 1986.

Sone Hiromi. "Kyōhōki no soshō saibanken to uttae." In *Kōza: Nihon kinseishi, genroku kyōhōki no seiji to shakai*, vol. 4, ed. Yamada Tadao. Tokyo: Yūhikaku, 1980.

Sono Tel. *The Japanese Reformer: An Autobiography.* New York: Hunt and Eaton, 1892.

Sonoo Takashi. *Minji soshō, shikkō, hasan no kin-gendaishi.* Tokyo: Kōbundō, 2009.

Sorensen, Andre. *The Making of Urban Japan: Cities and Planning From Edo to the Twenty-first Century.* London: Routledge, 2002.

Sotozaki Mitsuhiro. "Risshisha hōritsu kenkyūjo ni tsuite 'shibenren kaishi' no hihan ni kotaeru." *Kōchi tanki daigaku kenkyū hōkoku: shakai kagaku ronshū* 33 (Mar. 1977): 13–37.

Spaulding, Robert. *Imperial Japan's Higher Civil Service Examinations.* Princeton, NJ: Princeton University Press, 1967.

Steenstrup, Carl. *A History of Law in Japan until 1868.* Leiden: Brill, 1991.

Stevens, Robert. *Law School: Legal Education in America from the 1850s to the 1980s.* Chapel Hill, NC: University of North Carolina Press, 1983.

Suleiman, Ezra. *Private Power and Centralization in France: The Notaires and the State.* Princeton, NJ: Princeton University Press, 1987.

Suzuki Yasuzō. *Jiyūminken.* Tokyo: Hakuyōsha, 1948.

———. "Ueki Emori no jinminshukenron: jiyūminken undō no rironteki shidōsha." In *Minkenron kara nashonarizumu e*, ed. Meiji shiryō kenkyū renrakukai. Tokyo: Ochanomizu shobō, 1957, 84–113.

Takahashi Satoshi. *Edo no soshō: Mishuku mura ikken tenmatsu.* Tokyo: Iwanami shoten, 1996.

Takahashi Tetsuo. *Fukushima jiyūminken undōshi: sono tōsa to kenkyū.* Tokyo: Rironsha, 1963.

Takayanagi Kenzō (assisted by Thomas Blakemore). "A Century of Innovation: The Development of Japanese Law, 1868–1961." In *Law in Japan: The Legal Order in a Changing Society,* ed. Arthur Taylor von Mehren. Cambridge, MA: Harvard University Press, 1963, 5–40.

Takayanagi Shinzō and Ishii Ryōsuke, eds. *Ofuregaki kanpō shūsei.* Tokyo: Iwanami shoten, 1934.

Takesue Hiromi. *Nikkō no shihō: oshioki to kujiyado.* Tokyo: Zuisōsha, 2001.

Takeuchi Makoto. "Festivals and Fights: The Law of the People of Edo." In *Edo and Paris: Urban Life and the State in the Early Modern Era,* ed. James McClain, et al. Ithaca, NY: Cornell University Press, 1994, 384–406.

Takii Kazuhiro. "Itō Hirobumi taiō kenpō chōsa no kōsatsu." *Jinbun gakuhō* 80 (March 1997): 33–77.

Takikawa Eiichi. "Meiji shoki no hikiainin: Maebashi shishin saibansho hanketsu rei kara." *Hōseishi kenkyū* 19 (1994): 1–41.

Takikawa Masajirō. "Edo shoki ni okeru kujishi kin'atsu." *Jiyū to seigi* 2, no. 4 (1951): 19–32.

———. *Hasegawa Heizō: sono shōgai to ninsoku yoseba.* Tokyo: Asahi Shinbunsha, 1982.

———. *Kujishi kujiyado no kenkyū.* Tokyo: Akasaka shoin, 1984.

———. "Kujishi Makoshi Kyōhei Okina no kotodomo." *Jiyū to seigi* 2, no. 9 (1951): 49–52.

———. "Nihon bengoshishi sobyō." *Jiyū to seigi* 2, no. 9 (1951): 16–26.

———. "Nihon bengoshishi zenshi kujiyado no kenkyū: kujiyado henjutsu 'hikkae' no shōkai." *Waseda daigaku hikaku hō kenkyūjo kiyō* no. 8 (1959).

Tanaka Sōgorō. *Jiyūminkenka to sono keifu.* Tokyo: Kokudōsha, 1949.

Tatsuya Naramoto. *Bakumatsu ishin jinmei jiten.* Tokyo: Gakugei shorin, 1978.

Taylor, Thomas Wardlaw, Jr. "On the Conception of Morality in Jurisprudence." *The Philosophical Review* 5, no. 1 (1896): 36–50.

Teraishi Masamichi. *Tosa ijinden.* Tokyo: Rekishi tōshosha, 1976.

Terasaki Osamu. "Jiyūtō no seiritsu (Meiji 14nen) to Jiyūtō chihōbu." In *Kindai Nihonshi no shin kenkyū,* vol. 3, ed. Tezuka Yutaka. Tokyo: Hokuju shuppan, 1981, 109–91.

———. "Meiji 17nen: Hoshi Tōru kanri bujoku jiken no ichi kōsatsu." *Komazawa daigaku hōgakubu seijigaku ronshū,* no. 16 (20 Sept. 1982): 27–75.

———. "Shizuoka no jiyū minkenka, Suzuki Ototaka shōden." In *Kindai Nihonshi no shin kenkyū*, vol. 2, ed. Tezuka Yutaka. Tokyo: Hokuju shuppan, 1981, 57–111.

Tezuka Yutaka. *Meijishi kenkyū zassan.* Tokyo: Keiō tsūshin, 1994.

———, ed. *Kindai Nihonshi no shin kenkyū,* 9 vols. Tokyo: Hokuju shuppan, 1981–1991.

Thomas, Julia Adeney. *Reconfiguring Modernity: Concepts of Nature in Japanese Political Ideology.* Berkeley, CA: University of California Press, 2001.

Toby, Ronald P. "Both a Borrower and a Lender Be: From Village Moneylender to Rural Banker in the Tempō Era." *Monumenta Nipponica* 46, no. 4 (Winter 1991): 483–512.

Tōkyō bengoshikai hyakunenshi hensan kankō tokubetsu iinkai, ed. *Tokyo bengoshikai hyakunenshi.* Tokyo: Tōkyō bengoshikai, 1980.

Tōkyō daigaku shiryō hensanjo, ed. *Dai Nihon kinsei shiryō: shichū torishimari ruishū.* Tokyo: Tōkyō daigaku shuppankai, 1959.

Totman, Conrad. *The Green Archipelago: Forestry in Preindustrial Japan.* Berkeley, CA: University of California Press, 1989.

Toyoda Minoru. *Hatoyama Ichirō: eisai no kakei.* Tokyo: Kōdansha, 1989.

Tsukada Takashi. "Danzaemon shihai to shinchō yado." *Shigaku zasshi* 92, no. 7 (1983): 47–90.

Ueda, Atsuko. *Concealment of Politics, Politics of Concealment: The Production of "Literature" in Meiji Japan.* Stanford, CA: Stanford University Press, 2007.

Ueki Emori. "Nikki, Part I." In *Ueki Emori shū*, vol. 7, ed. Ienaga Saburō, Sotozaki Mitsuhiro, et al. Tokyo: Iwanami shoten, 1990.

Umemori Naoyuki. "Spatial Configuration and Subject Formation: The Establishment of the Modern Penitentiary System in Meiji Japan." In *New Directions in the Study of Meiji Japan*, ed. Helen Hardacre and Adam Kern. Leiden: Brill, 1997, 734–67.

Upham, Frank. "Weak Legal Consciousness as Invented Tradition." In *Mirror of Modernity: Invented Traditions of Modern Japan*, ed. Stephen Vlastos. Berkeley, CA: University of California Press, 1998, 48–66.

Usami Hideki. "Kinsei Kyōto no aitai sumashirei." In *Kyōto chiikishi no kenkyū*, ed. Akiyama Kunizō. Tokyo: Kokusho kankōkai, 1979.

Ushiomi Toshitaka, ed. *Nihon no bengoshi.* Tokyo: Nihon hyōronsha, 1972.

Vlastos, Stephen. "Opposition Movements in Early Meiji." In *Cambridge History of Japan*, vol. 5, ed. Marius Jansen. Cambridge, UK: Cambridge University Press, 1989, 367–431.

Wagatsuma Sakae. *Shin hōritsugaku jiten.* Tokyo: Yūhikaku, 1952.

Wagatsuma Sakae, et al. *Nihon seiji saiban shiroku (Meiji)*, vol 2. Tokyo: Daiichi hōki shuppan, 1969.

Walthall, Anne. "Japanese Gimin: Peasant Martyrs in Popular Memory." *American Historical Review* 91, no. 5 (Dec. 1986): 1076–1102.

———. *Peasant Uprisings in Japan: A Critical Anthology of Peasant Histories.* Chicago, IL: University of Chicago Press, 1991.

———. "Village Networks: Sodai and the Sale of Edo Nightsoil." *Monumenta Nipponica* 43 (1988): 279–304.

Weber, Max. (H. H. Gerth and C. Wright Mills, trans.). *From Max Weber: Essays in Sociology.* New York: Oxford University Press, 1973.

———. *Max Weber on Law in Economy and Society.* Cambridge, MA: Harvard University Press, 1954.

White, James. *Ikki: Social Conflict and Political Protest in Early Modern Japan.* Ithaca, NY: Cornell University Press, 1995.

Wigen, Kären. *The Making of a Japanese Periphery, 1750–1920.* Berkeley, CA: University of California Press, 1995.

Wigmore, John H. *Law and Justice in Tokugawa Japan,* vol. 1. Tokyo: Kokusai bunka shinkōkai, 1969.

———. *A Panorama of the World's Legal Systems.* Washington, DC: Washington Law Book Company, 1936.

Wittfogel, Karl. *Oriental Despotism.* New Haven, CT: Yale University Press, 1957.

Witz, Anne. *Professions and Patriarchy.* London: Routledge, 1992.

Yamaga Sokō. "Shidō." In *Sources of Japanese Tradition*, ed. Ryusaku Tsunoda, William Theodore de Bary, and Donald Keene. New York: Columbia University Press, 1958, 389–90.

Yamamuro Shin'ichi. *Hōsei kanryō no jidai: kokka no sekkei to chi no rekitei.* Tokyo: Bokutakusha, 1984.

Yamanouchi Katsuro, ed. *Minji soshō meyasu gaihyō.* Tokyo: Shūeidō, 1876.

Yasumaru Yoshio and Fukaya Katsumi. *Minshū undō: Nihon kindai shisō taikei,* vol. 21. Tokyo: Iwanami shoten, 1989.

Yasutake, Rumi. *Transnational Women's Activism: The United States, Japan, and Japanese Immigrant Communities in California, 1859–1920.* New York: New York University Press, 2004.

Yokohama bengoshikai kaishi hensan iinkai, ed. *Yokohama bengoshikaishi,* 2 vols. Yokohama: Yokohama bengoshikai, 1980.

Yoshida Yutaka, ed. *Shōka no kakun.* Tokyo: Tokuma shoten, 1973.

Yoshimoto Shinji, ed. *Kyūji shimonroku: Edo bakufu yakunin no shōgen,* vol. 1. Tokyo: Iwanami shoten, 1986.

Yoshizumi Junzō. *Nihon zaisei konnan kyūchisaku: ichimei, shiheiron.* Osaka: Kinjakudō, 1880.

————. *Onna kyōkun yomeiri dōgu*. Osaka: Satō Nobuyoshi, 1880.

Yui Tsunehiko. "Meiji hōritsugakkō sotsugyōsei no chōsa." *Meiji daigakushi kiyō*, no. 3 (31 Mar. 1983): 1–21.

Zollman, Carl. "The Constitutional and Legal Status of Religion in Public Education." *Journal of Religion* 2, no. 3 (May 1922): 236–44.

Index

Abbott, Andrew, 14n23, 110
Acollas, Emile, 139
Adams, Herbert Baxter, 85
Aikoku kōtō. *See* Public Party of
    Patriots
aitai sumashi (mutual settlement),
    46, 52
Aizawa Yasukata, 232
Akebono shinbun, 175
Amano Ikuo, 253
Amended (Criminal) Code (*Kaitei
    ritsurei*), 93
Amida Buddha, 40
Analects, The, 19, 31
Andō Tadashi, 226n78
Anti-Doctors' Association League,
    272
Aoki Michio, 75
Aoyanagi Kyūhei, 223
apprenticeship, 17, 104, 155, 209; in
    daigensha, 104, 142, 144, 152, 249,
    253; in suit inns, 64, 103
Arakawa Takatoshi, 225
Asahi shinbun, 238
Asakusa, 55, 60, 70, 114
Assembly Ordinance, 185–86

Association for the Preservation of
    Peace (Hoansha), 154, 173
Association for the Preservation of
    Rights (Hokensha), 154, 210n28
Association for the Study of Law
    (Hōritsu gakusha), 151–52, 210n28
Association of Legal Circles (Hōsō
    kyōkai), 272
associations, 15, 22, 133–34, 143, 164,
    171, 173, 198; as "corporate person,"
    273; early incarnations of, 16, 135;
    monitoring of, 170, 200; and
    political activism, 136, 163. *See also*
    associations of legal advocates
    (*daigensha*)
associations of legal advocates
    (*daigensha*), 5, 141, 151, 164, 168,
    174–75, 197, 218, 248, 252, 256,
    262, 279; and apprentice model of
    education, 155; blossoming of, 152;
    disbanding of, 208–9, 216; as
    intellectual salons, 146; and
    lawsuit-oversight companies, 210;
    licensing exams, 148; and manda-
    tory bar associations, 208–9, 211;
    and morphing into law schools, 6,

Harvard East Asian Monographs
(*out-of-print)

Harvard East Asian Monographs

325. Micah S. Muscolino, *Fishing Wars and Environmental Change in Late Imperial and Modern China*
326. Robert I. Hellyer, *Defining Engagement: Japan and Global Contexts, 1750–1868*
327. Robert Ashmore, *The Transport of Reading: Text and Understanding in the World of Tao Qian (365–427)*
328. Mark A. Jones, *Children as Treasures: Childhood and the Middle Class in Early Twentieth Century Japan*
329. Miryam Sas, *Experimental Arts in Postwar Japan: Moments of Encounter, Engagement, and Imagined Return*
330. H. Mack Horton, *Traversing the Frontier: The* Man'yōshū *Account of a Japanese Mission to Silla in 736–737*
331. Dennis J. Frost, *Seeing Stars: Sports Celebrity, Identity, and Body Culture in Modern Japan*
332. Marnie S. Anderson, *A Place in Public: Women's Rights in Meiji Japan*
333. Peter Mauch, *Sailor Diplomat: Nomura Kichisaburō and the Japanese-American War*
334. Ethan Isaac Segal, *Coins, Trade, and the State: Economic Growth in Early Medieval Japan*
335. David B. Lurie, *Realms of Literacy: Early Japan and the History of Writing*
336. Lillian Lan-ying Tseng, *Picturing Heaven in Early China*
337. Jun Uchida, *Brokers of Empire: Japanese Settler Colonialism in Korea, 1876–1945*
338. Patricia L. Maclachlan, *The People's Post Office: The History and Politics of the Japanese Postal System, 1871–2010*
339. Michael Schiltz, *The Money Doctors from Japan: Finance, Imperialism, and the Building of the Yen Bloc, 1895–1937*
340. Daqing Yang, Jie Liu, Hiroshi Mitani, and Andrew Gordon, eds., *Toward a History Beyond Borders: Contentious Issues in Sino-Japanese Relations*
341. Sonia Ryang, *Reading North Korea: An Ethnological Inquiry*
342. Susan Huang, *Picturing the True Form: Daoist Visual Culture in Traditional China*
343. Barbara Mittler, *A Continuous Revolution: Making Sense of Cultural Revolution Culture*
344. Hwansoo Ilmee Kim, *Empire of the Dharma: Korean and Japanese Buddhism, 1877–1912*
345. Satoru Saito, *Detective Fiction and the Rise of the Japanese Novel, 1880–1930*
346. Jung-Sun N. Han, *An Imperial Path to Modernity: Yoshino Sakuzō and a New Liberal Order in East Asia, 1905–1937*
347. Atsuko Hirai, *Government by Mourning: Death and Political Integration in Japan, 1603–1912*
348. Darryl E. Flaherty, *Public Law, Private Practice: Politics, Profit, and the Legal Profession in Nineteenth-Century Japan*